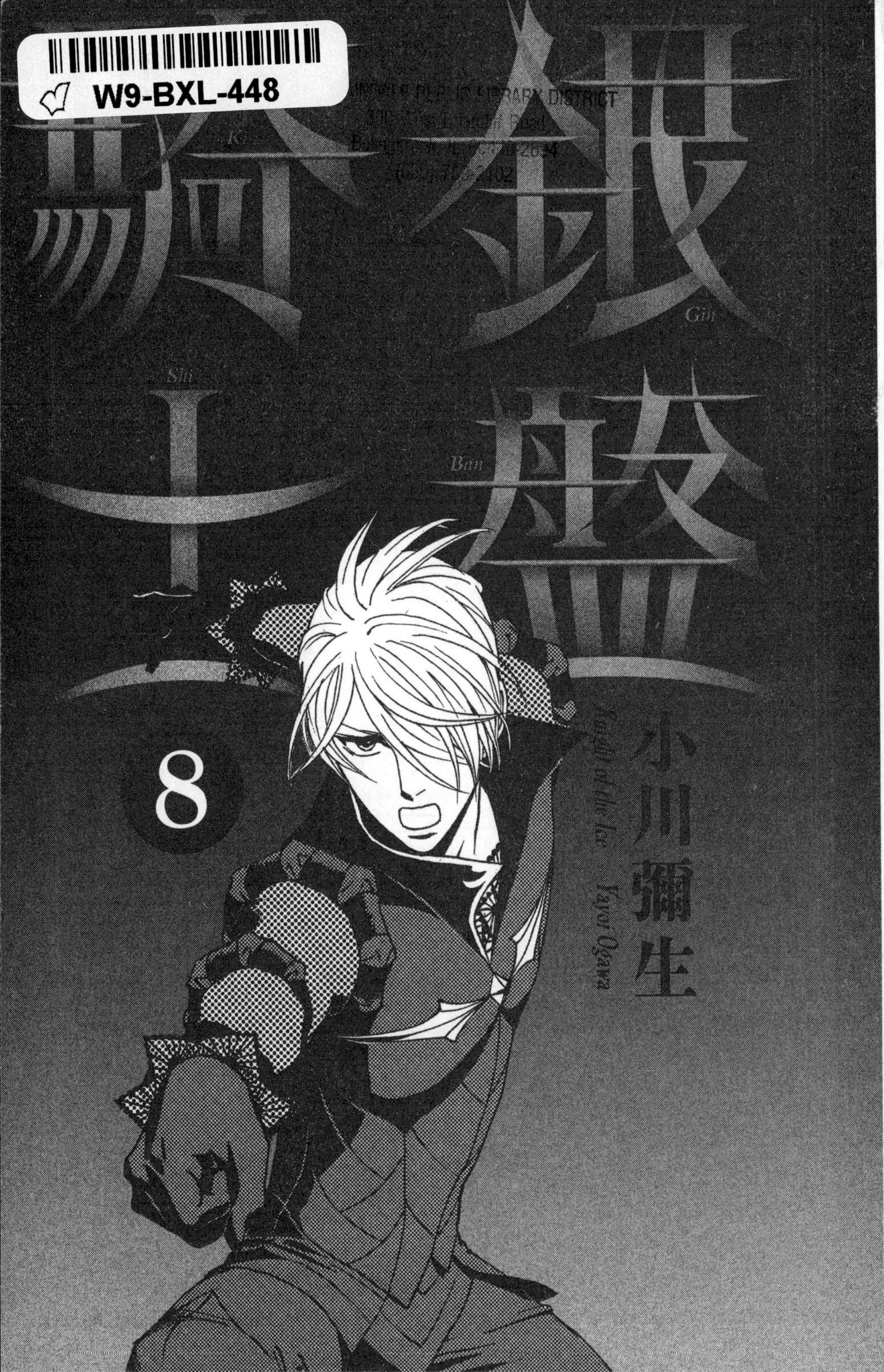

銀盤騎士
Gin Ban Ki Shi
8
小川彌生
Knight of the Ice
Yayoi Ogawa

Characters

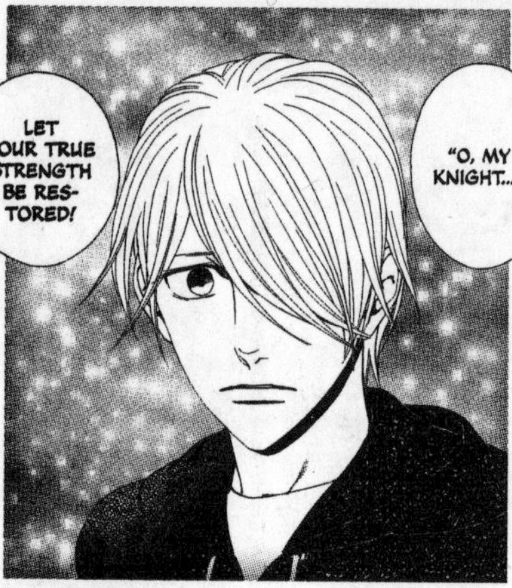
LET YOUR TRUE STRENGTH BE RES-TORED!
"O, MY KNIGHT..."

Kokoro Kijinami

Japan's top men's figure skater. One of his greatest strengths is the beauty his height lends to his quadruple jumps. He cracks easily under pressure, but he's gotten more consistent since Chitose started reciting their magic spell for him. He and Chitose have been friends since childhood, and he was two years behind her in school.

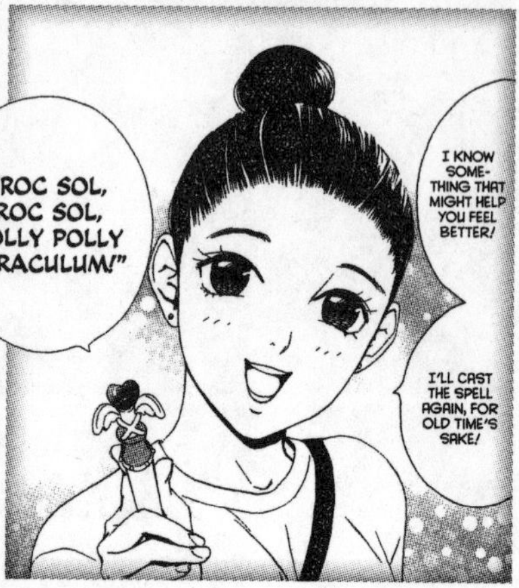
I KNOW SOME-THING THAT MIGHT HELP YOU FEEL BETTER!
"ROC SOL, ROC SOL, POLLY POLLY MIRACULUM!"
I'LL CAST THE SPELL AGAIN, FOR OLD TIME'S SAKE!

Chitose Igari

An editor for the health-and-lifestyle magazine *SASSO.* She's so short that she often gets mistaken for an elementary schooler. She also accompanies Kokoro to competitions and pretends to be his personal trainer. It was Moriyama's idea. She's been having heart problems.

Magical Princess Lady Lala is a magical girl anime that used to air on TV. Chitose and Kokoro loved it, and they often played pretend as the characters.

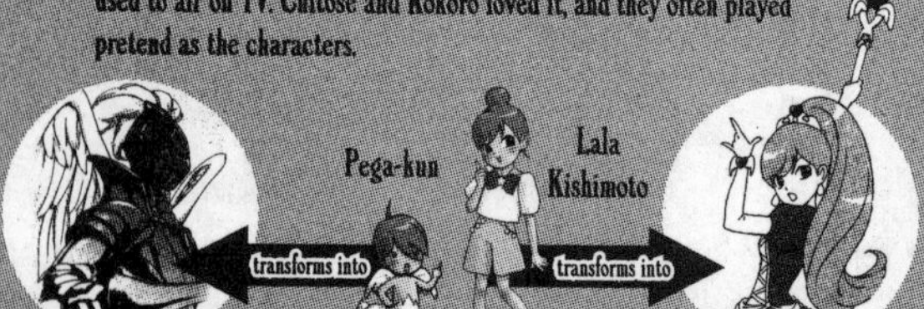
Pega-kun
Lala Kishimoto
transforms into
transforms into
Pegasus Knight
Lady Lala

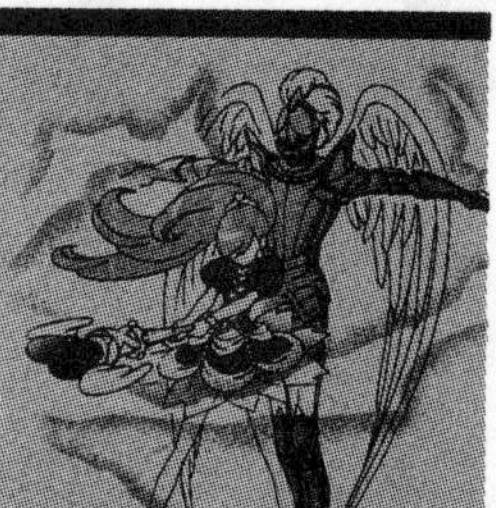

Kokoro's Father

President of the Kijinami Group, a company that runs a number of boutique ryokan.

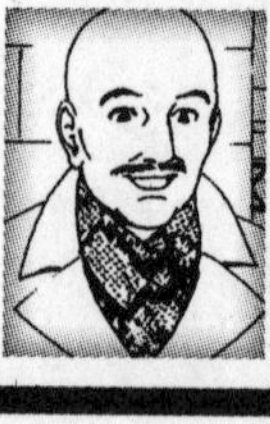

Yayoi Ogata

A manga artist. She went to the same college as Chitose and knows about her relationship with Kokoro.

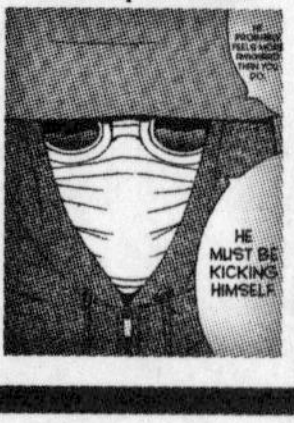
HE MUST BE KICKING HIMSELF

Reiko Yano

An employee in Kodan Publishing's PR department. She's married, but she's having an affair with Sawada.

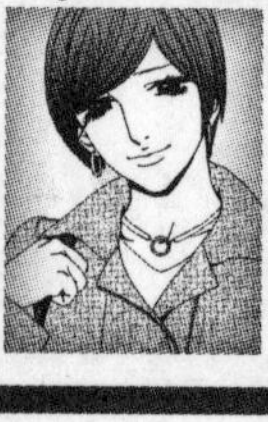

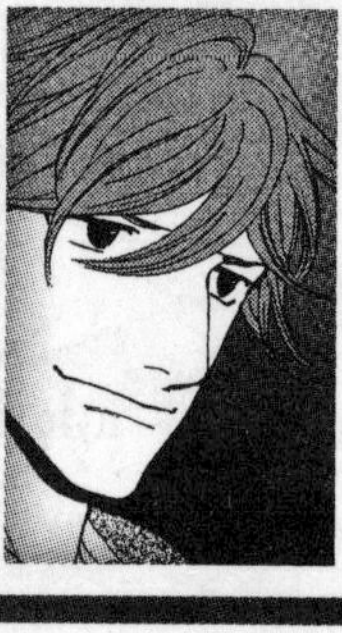

Koichi Sawada

The head of the editorial department for Kodan Publishing's magazine *SASSO.* He's good at his job, but can be somewhat lacking in delicacy...

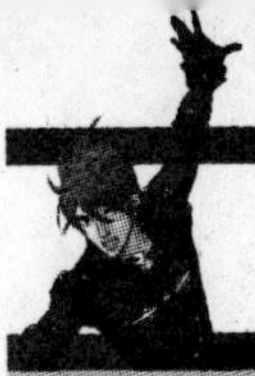

Knight of the Ice

Kokoro's Staff

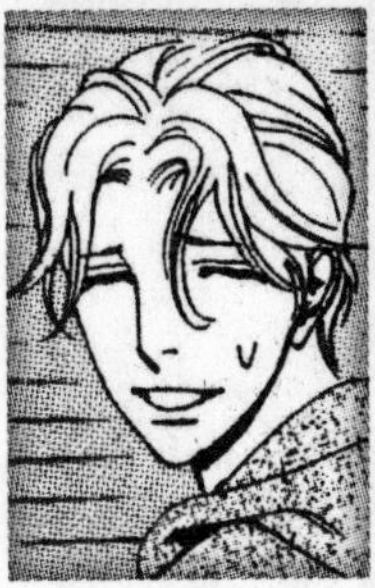

Kenzo Dominic Takiguchi

Kokoro's personal trainer.

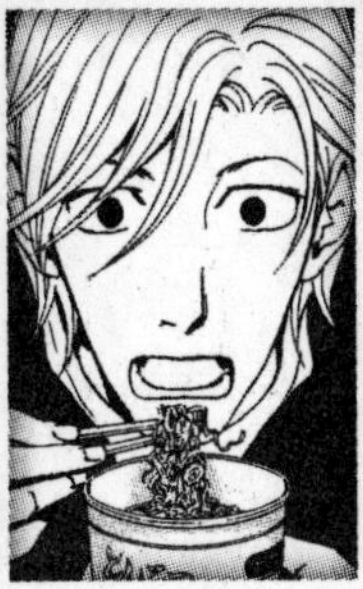

Hikaru Yomota

Kokoro's assistant coach and a former ice dancer.

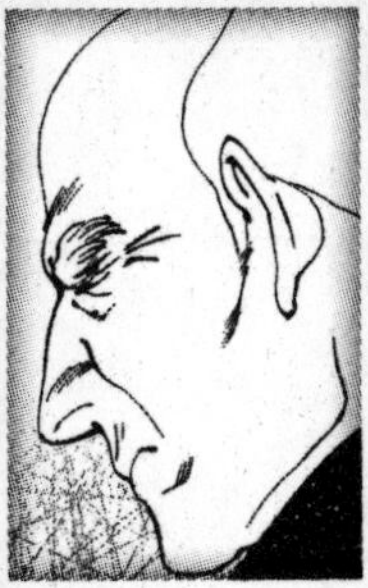

Takejiro Honda

Kokoro's coach and longtime rival of Raito Tamura's grandfather and coach, Masato Tamura.

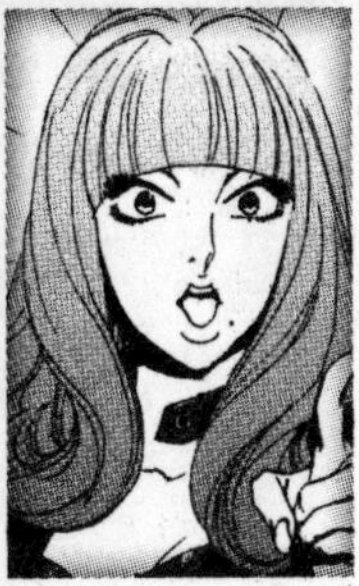

Moriyama

Kokoro's manager. She's not afraid to get a little pushy if that's what it takes to get results.

Kokoro's Rivals

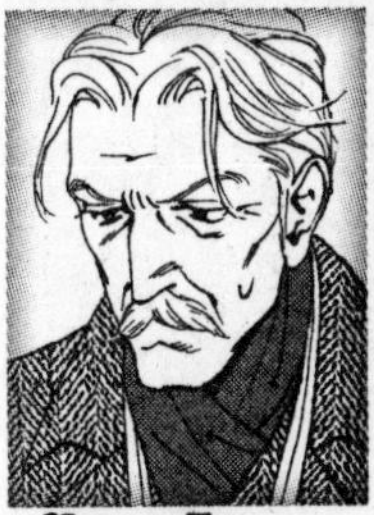

Masato Tamura

Raito Tamura's grandfather and coach.

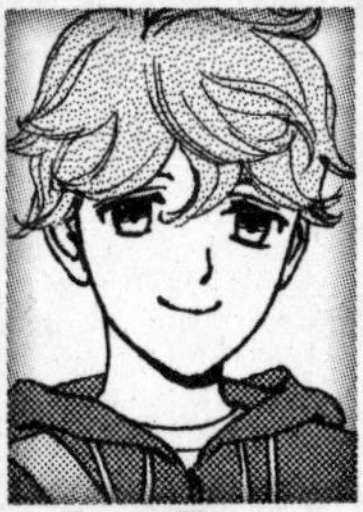

Fuuta Kumano

He can always rely on his speed and his devilish cuteness.

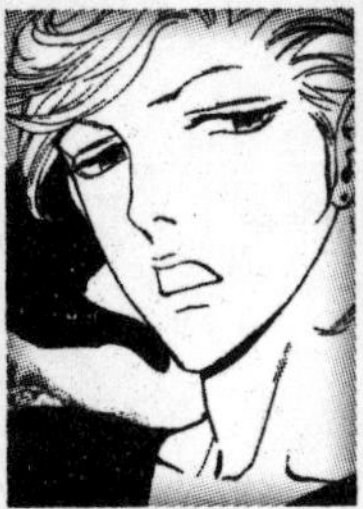

Raito Tamura

He dazzles the crowd with his passion and expressiveness.

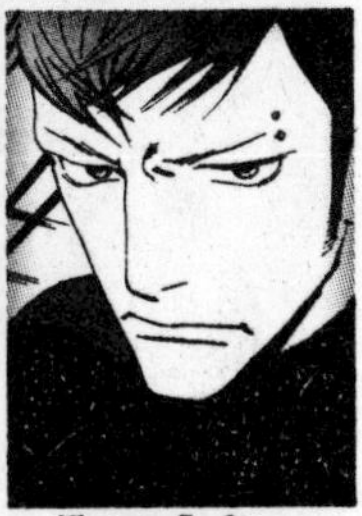

Taiga Aoki

His greatest strength is his ability to land two different quad jumps.

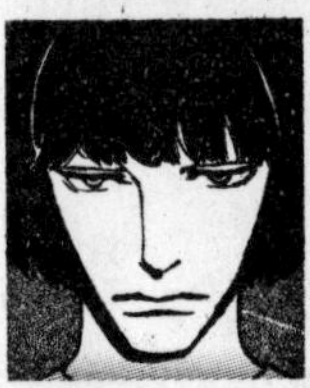

Ilia Sokurov

Russia's young top skater. He's an extreme klutz.

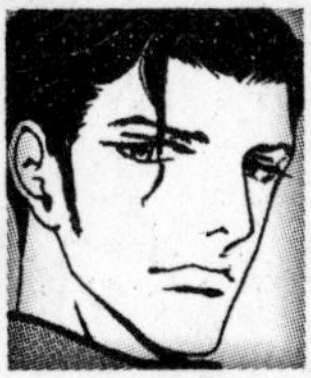

Kyle Miller

An American skater. He and Louis are known together as "KyLou."

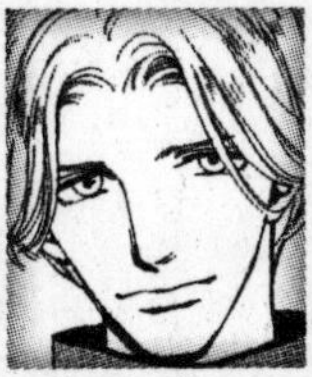

Louis Claire

A Canadian skater. He's a year younger than Kokoro and is the reigning World Champion.

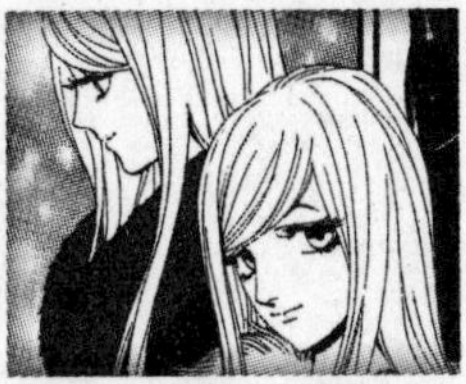

Maria & Anna Kijinami

Kokoro's younger twin sisters. Maria is in a relationship with Taiga.

Contents

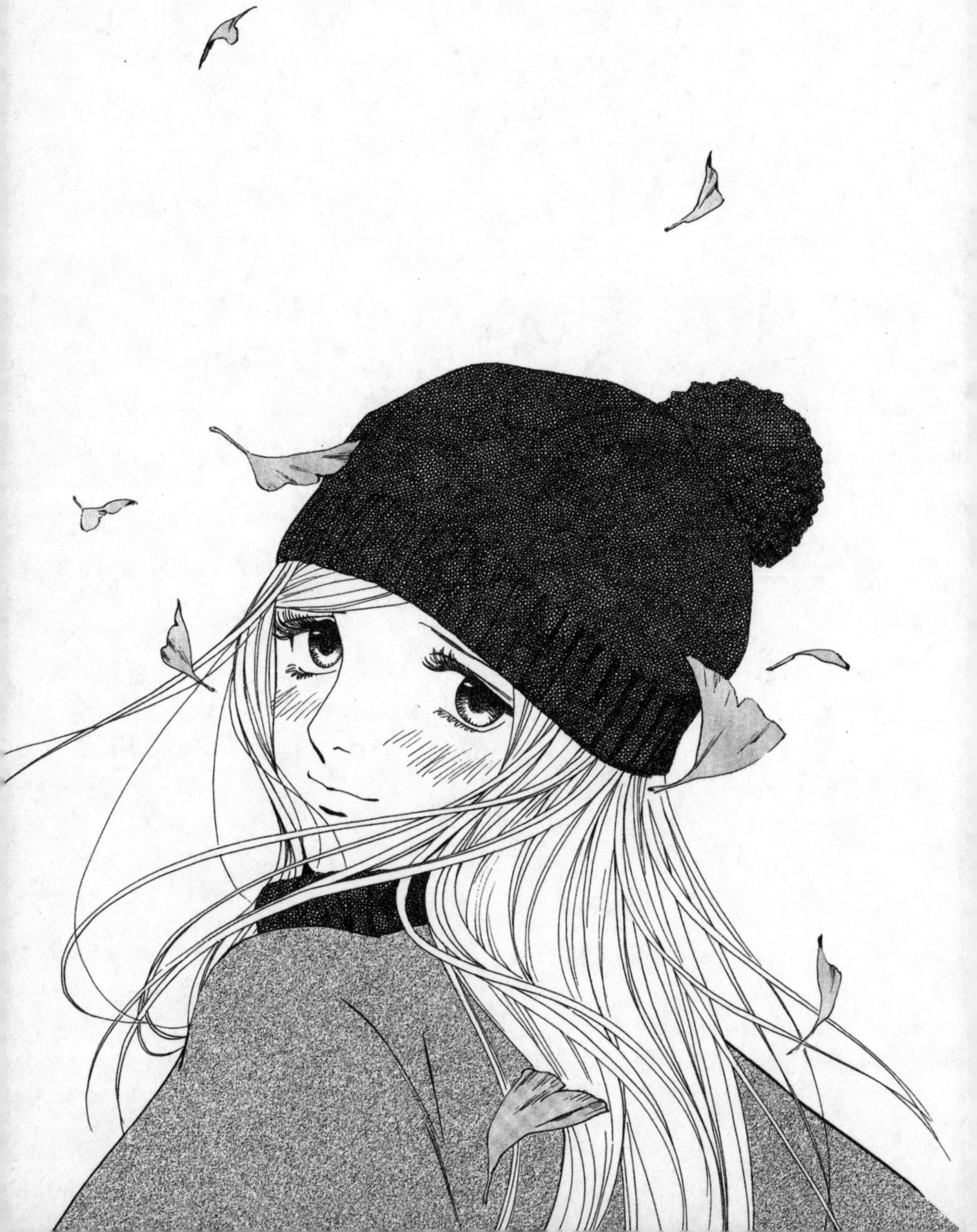

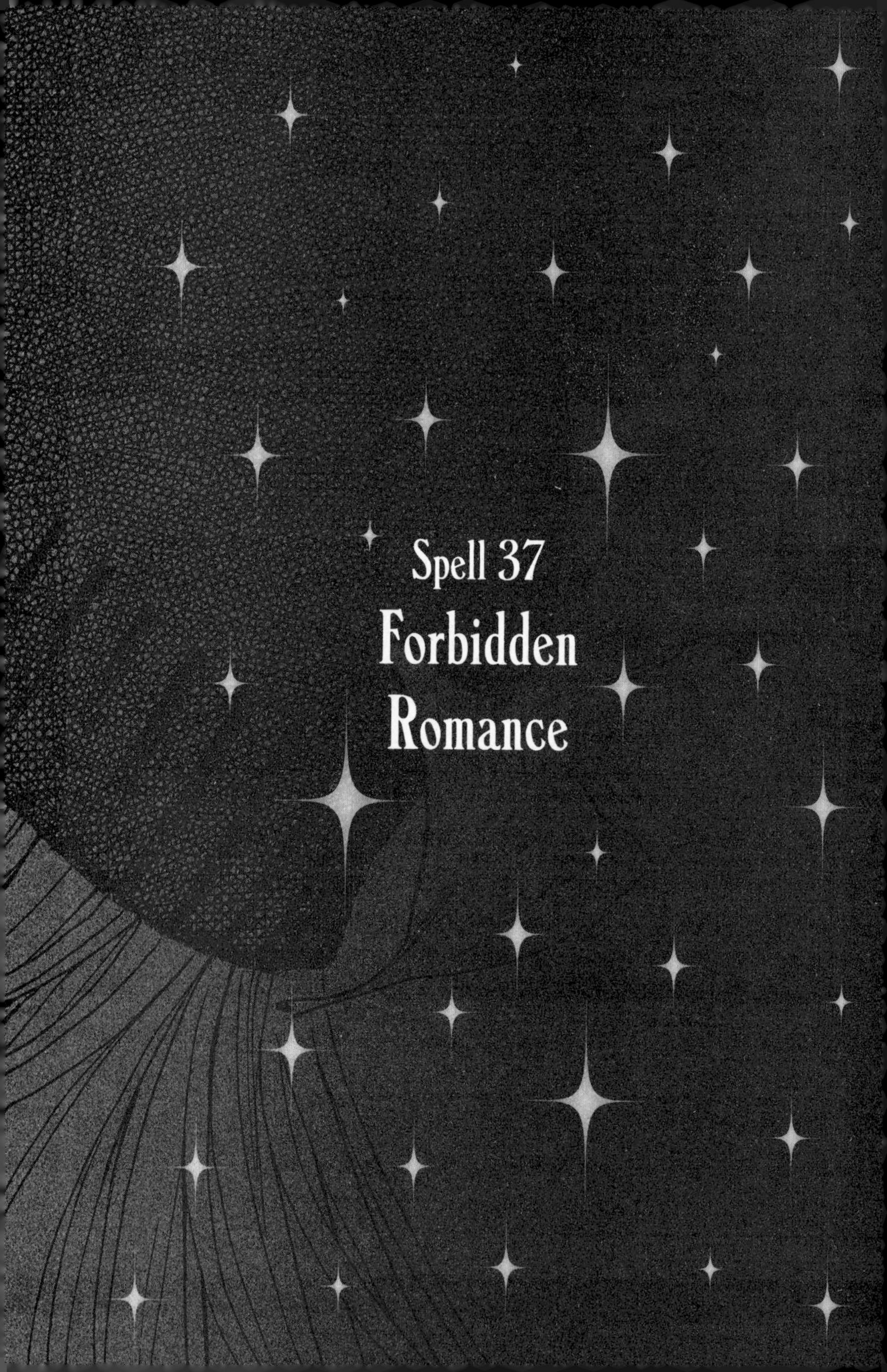
Spell 37
Forbidden
Romance

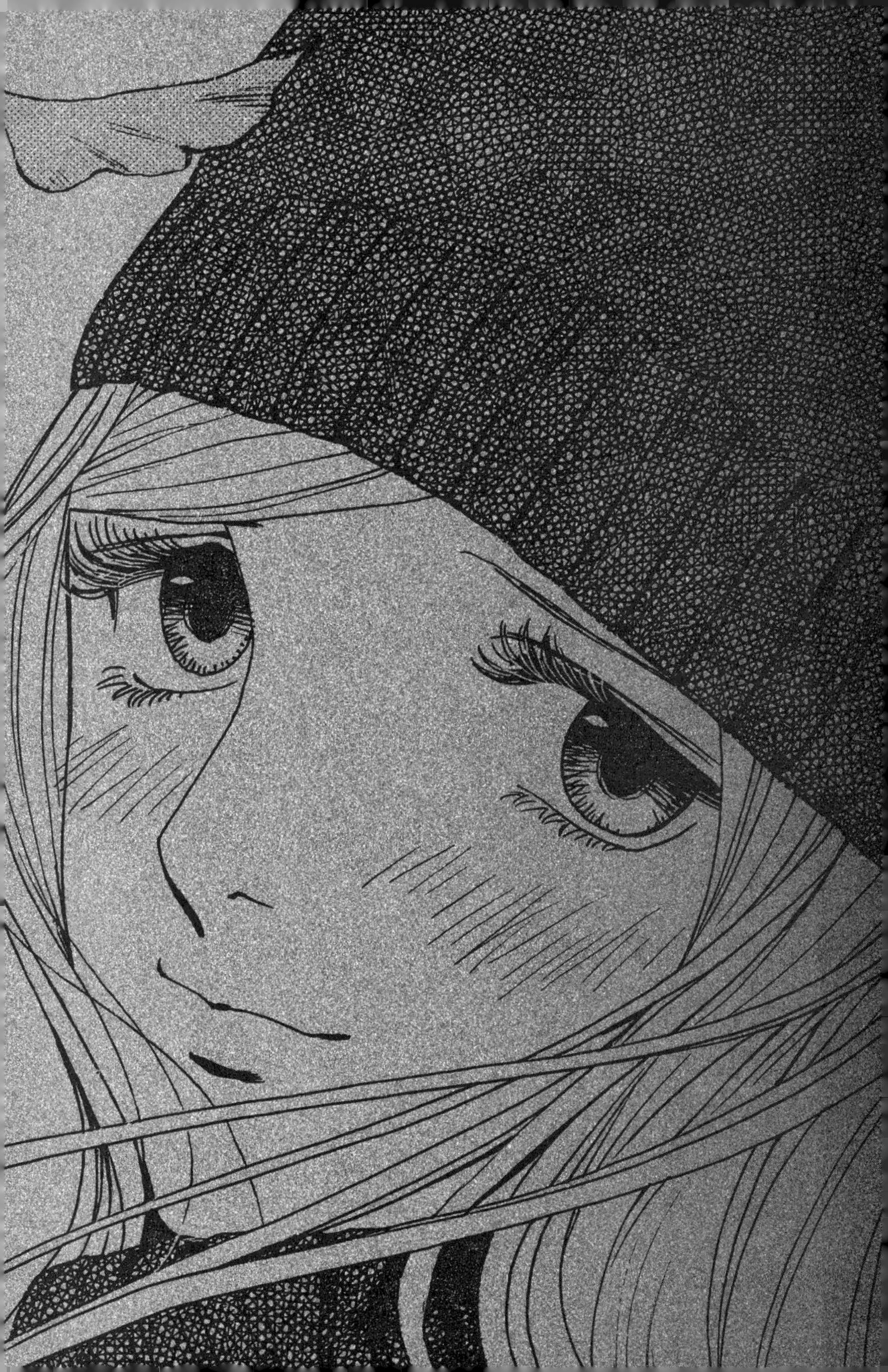

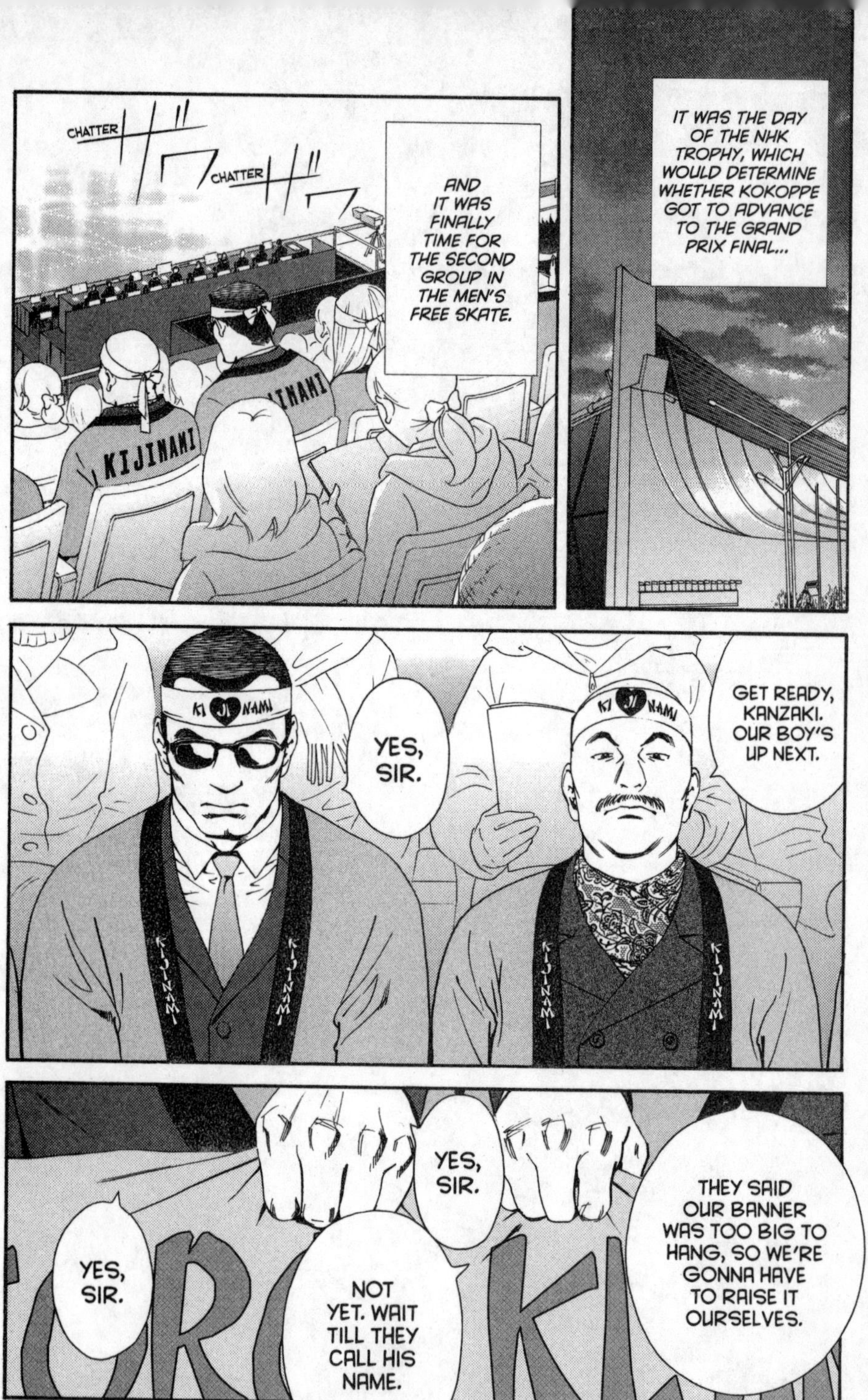
IT WAS THE DAY OF THE NHK TROPHY, WHICH WOULD DETERMINE WHETHER KOKOPPE GOT TO ADVANCE TO THE GRAND PRIX FINAL...
CHATTER ザワ
CHATTER ザワ
AND IT WAS FINALLY TIME FOR THE SECOND GROUP IN THE MEN'S FREE SKATE.
KIJINAMI
GET READY, KANZAKI. OUR BOY'S UP NEXT.
YES, SIR.
THEY SAID OUR BANNER WAS TOO BIG TO HANG, SO WE'RE GONNA HAVE TO RAISE IT OURSELVES.
YES, SIR.
NOT YET. WAIT TILL THEY CALL HIS NAME.
YES, SIR.

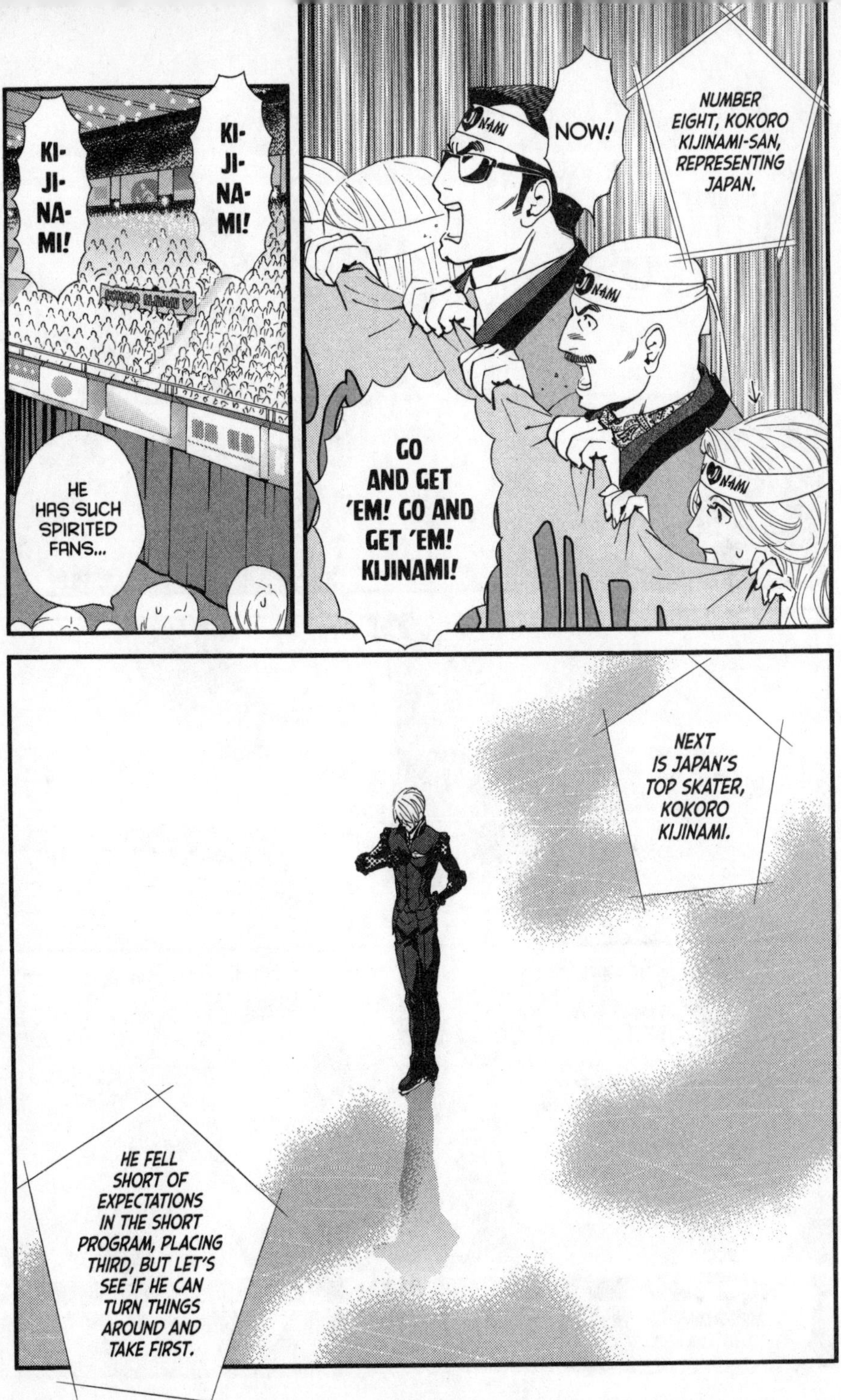
NUMBER EIGHT, KOKORO KIJINAMI-SAN, REPRESENTING JAPAN.
NOW!
GO AND GET 'EM! GO AND GET 'EM! KIJINAMI!
KI-JI-NA-MI!
KI-JI-NA-MI!
HE HAS SUCH SPIRITED FANS...
NEXT IS JAPAN'S TOP SKATER, KOKORO KIJINAMI.
HE FELL SHORT OF EXPECTATIONS IN THE SHORT PROGRAM, PLACING THIRD, BUT LET'S SEE IF HE CAN TURN THINGS AROUND AND TAKE FIRST.

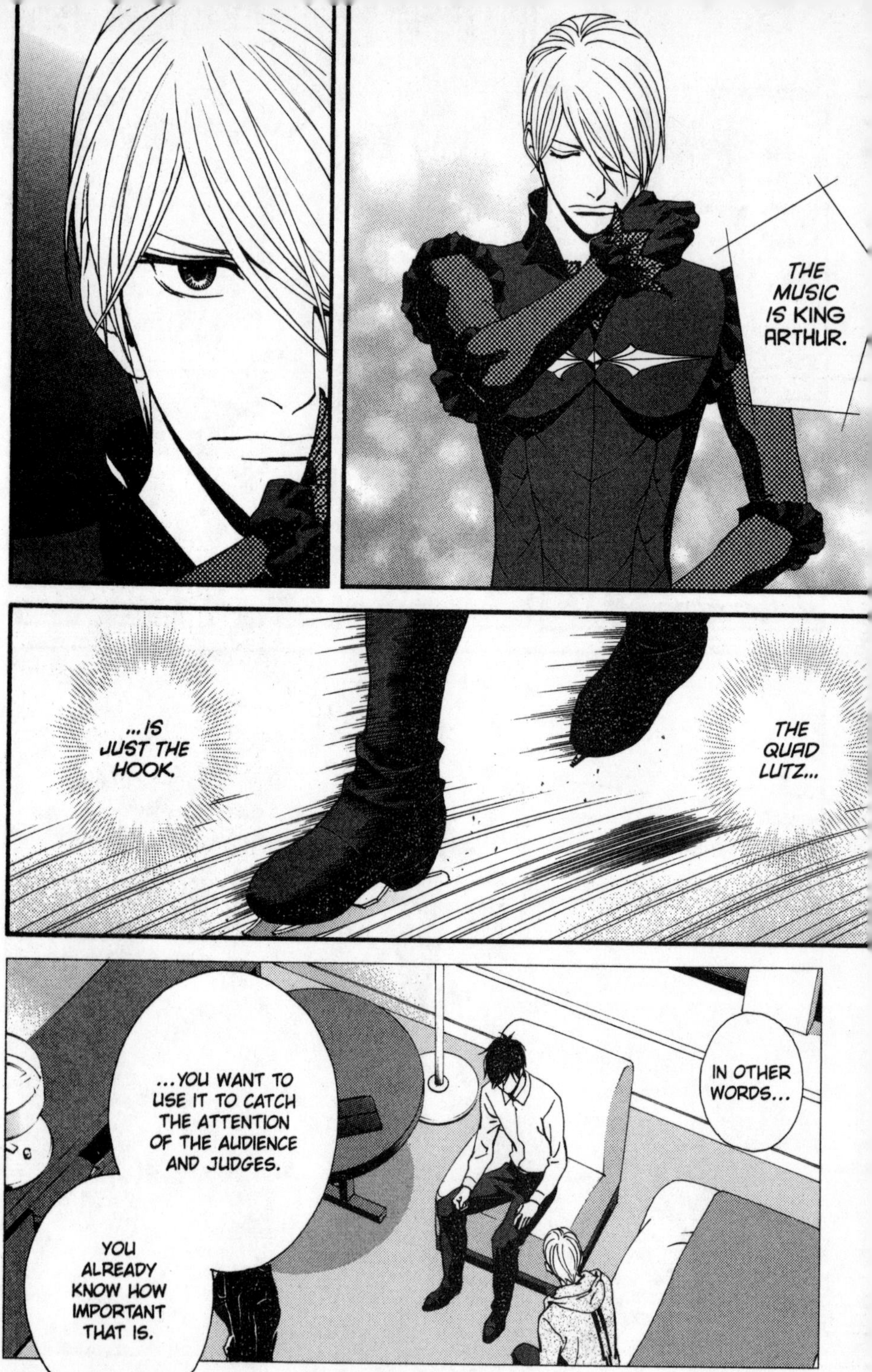
THE MUSIC IS KING ARTHUR.
THE QUAD LUTZ...
...IS JUST THE HOOK.
IN OTHER WORDS...
...YOU WANT TO USE IT TO CATCH THE ATTENTION OF THE AUDIENCE AND JUDGES.
YOU ALREADY KNOW HOW IMPORTANT THAT IS.

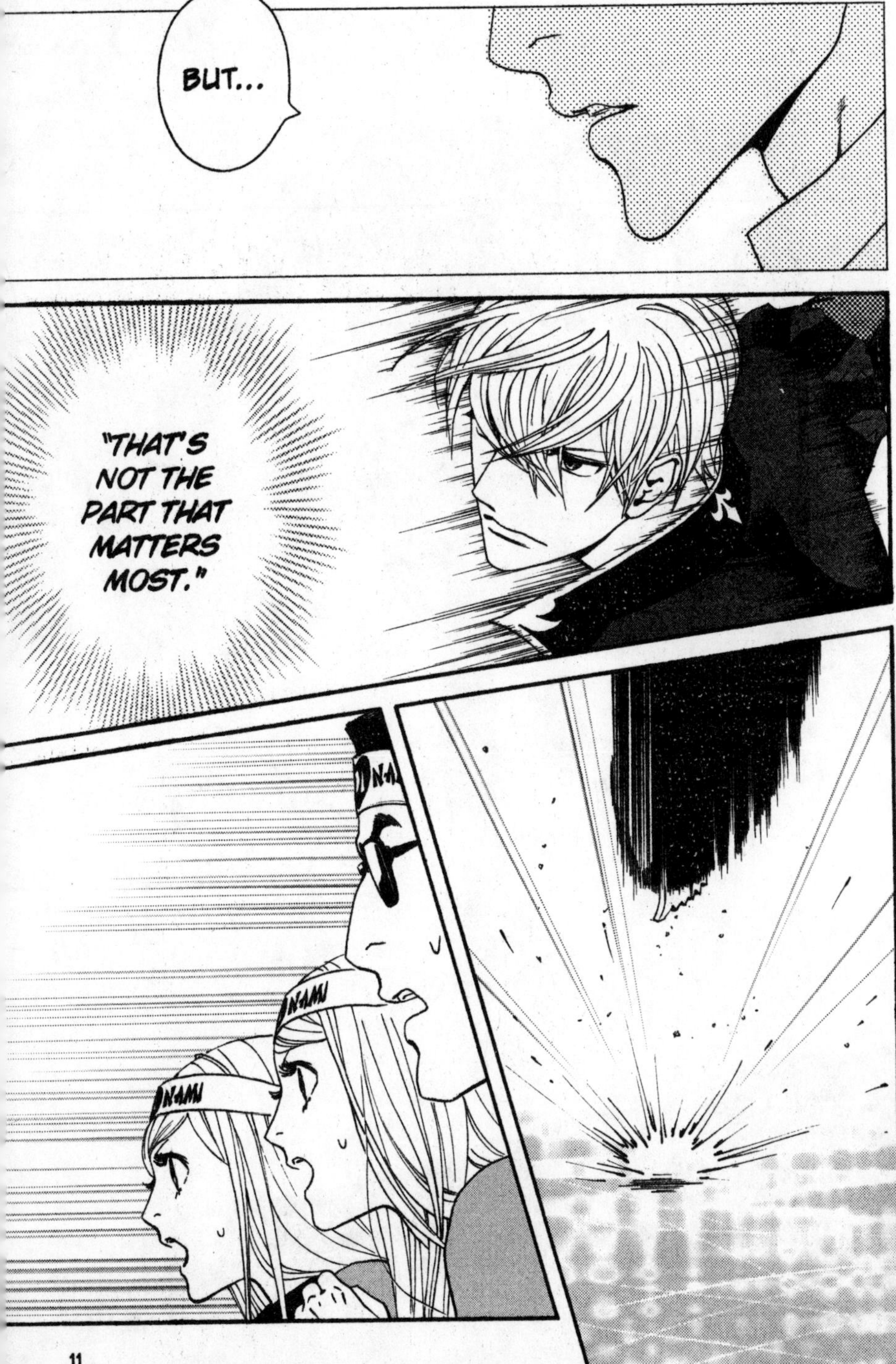

BUT...
"THAT'S NOT THE PART THAT MATTERS MOST."
NAMI
NAMI
NAMI

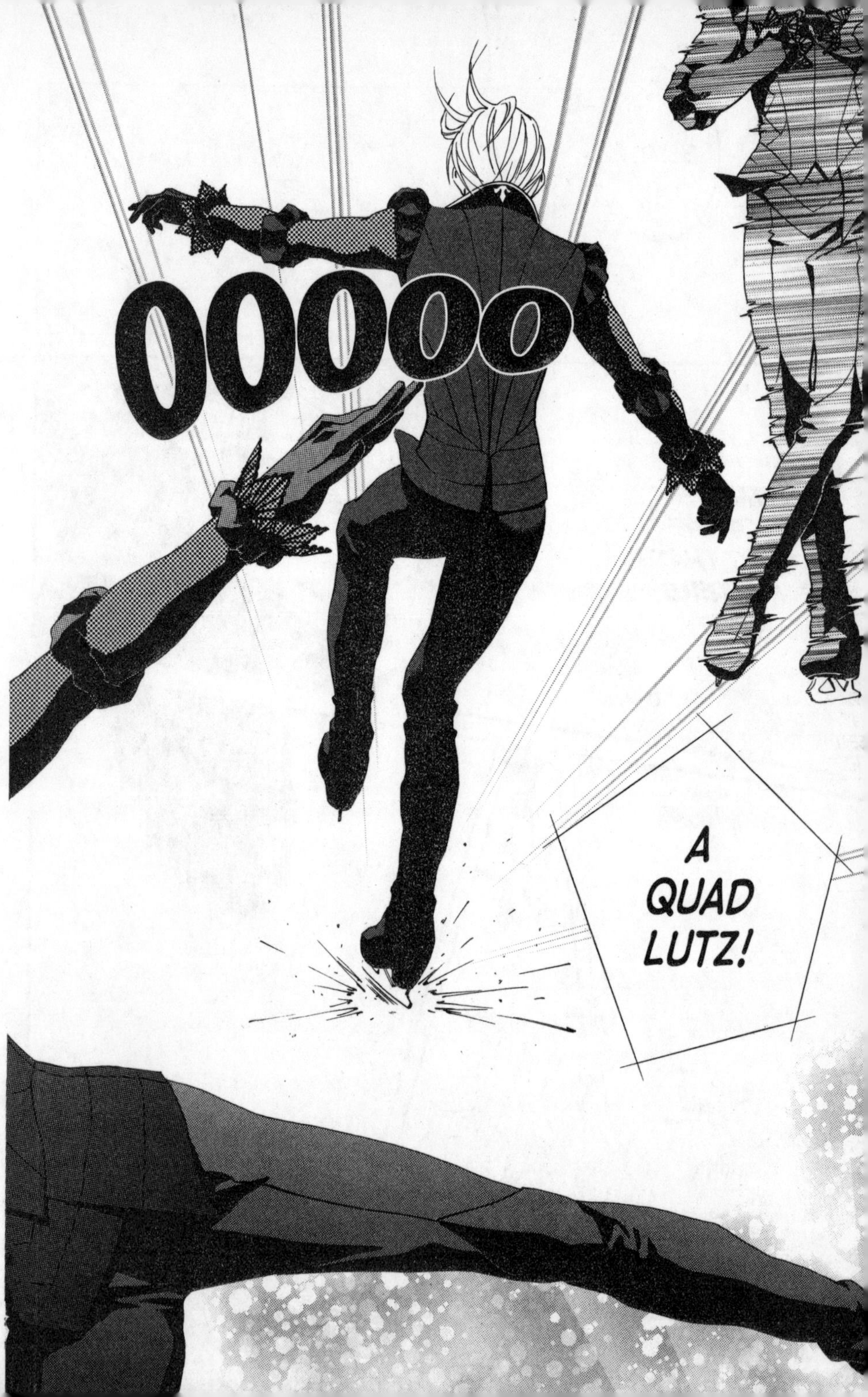
OOOOOO
A QUAD LUTZ!

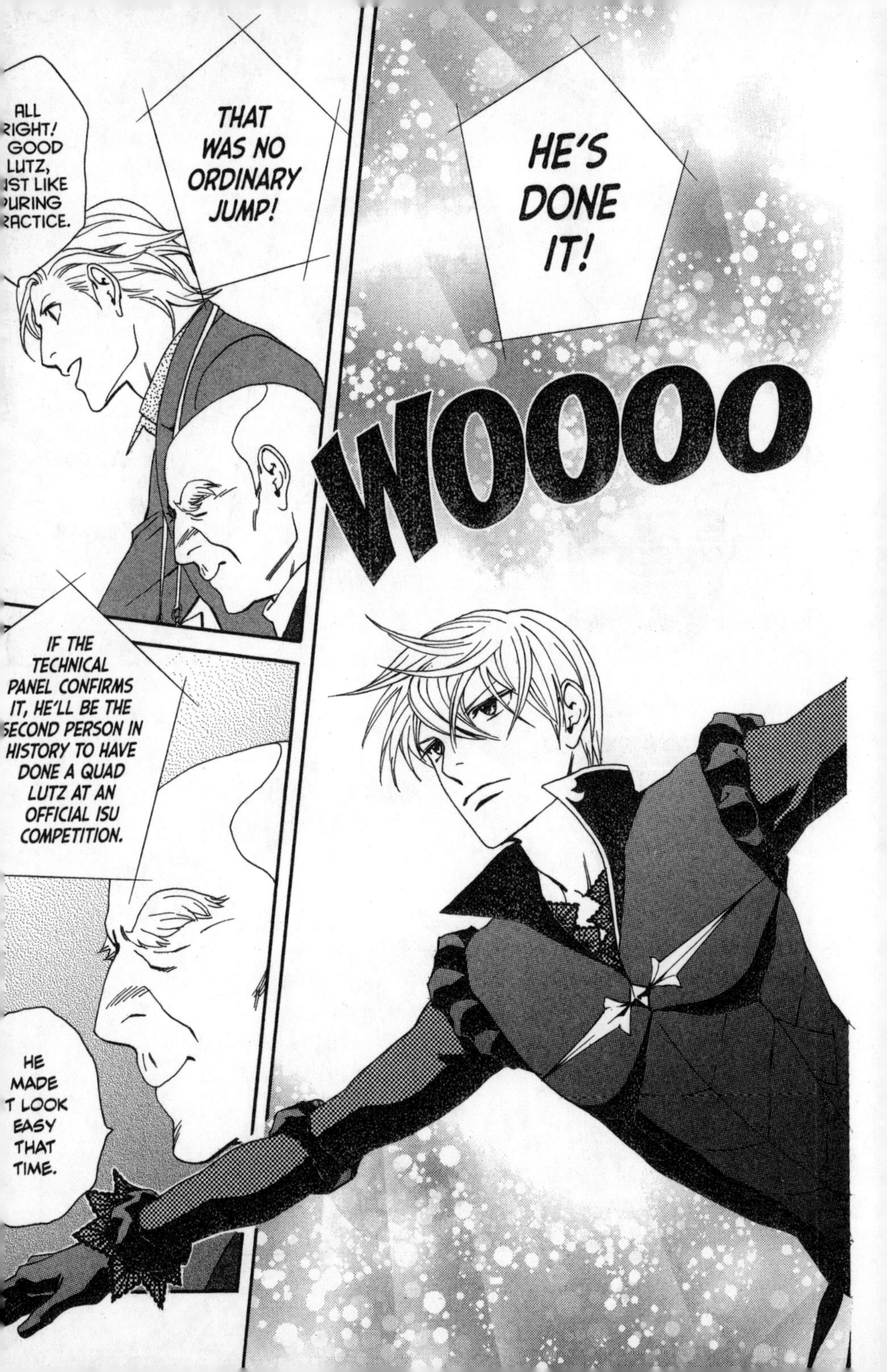
HE'S DONE IT!
WOOOOO
THAT WAS NO ORDINARY JUMP!
ALL RIGHT! GOOD LUTZ, JUST LIKE DURING PRACTICE.
IF THE TECHNICAL PANEL CONFIRMS IT, HE'LL BE THE SECOND PERSON IN HISTORY TO HAVE DONE A QUAD LUTZ AT AN OFFICIAL ISU COMPETITION.
HE MADE IT LOOK EASY THAT TIME.

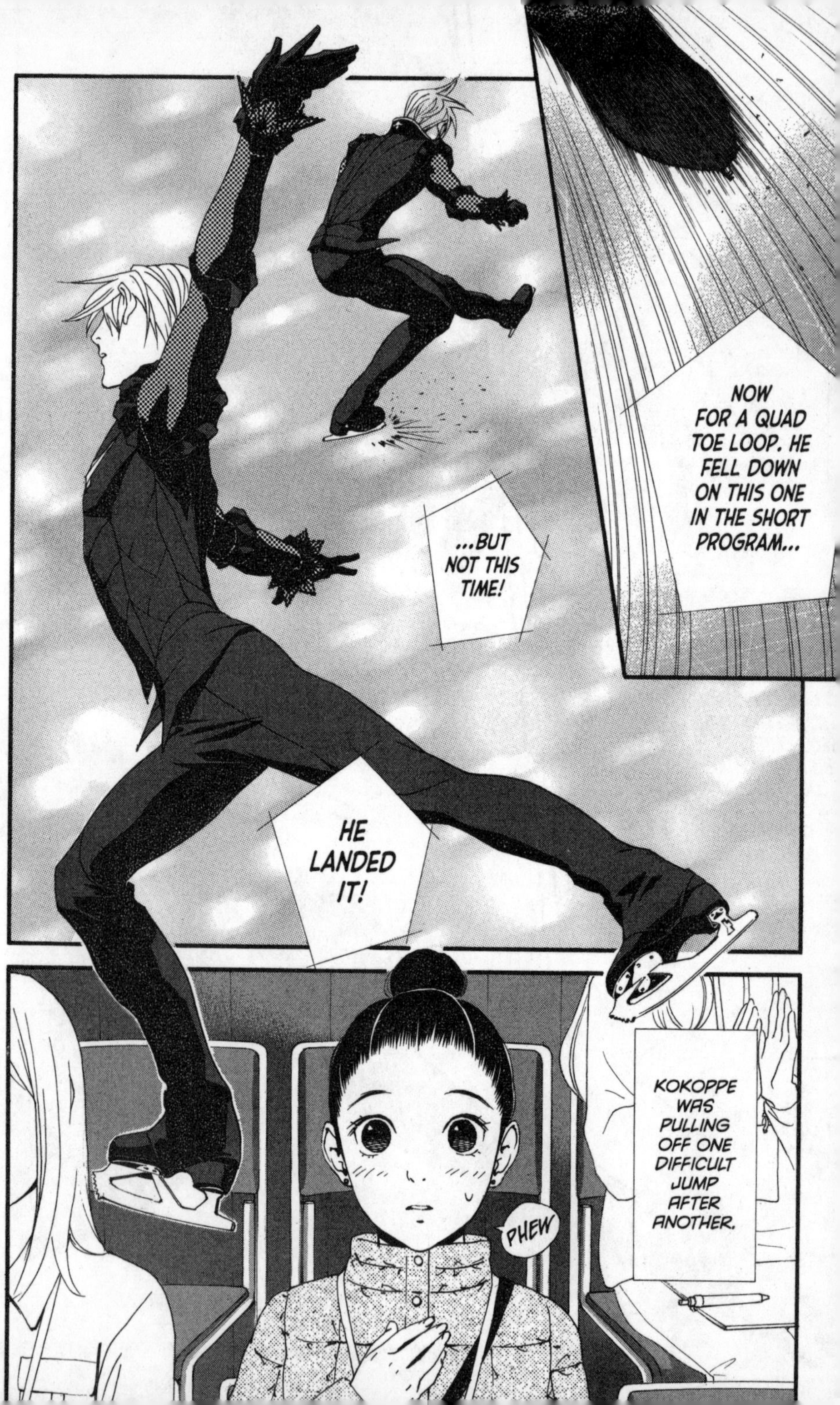
NOW FOR A QUAD TOE LOOP. HE FELL DOWN ON THIS ONE IN THE SHORT PROGRAM...
...BUT NOT THIS TIME!
HE LANDED IT!
KOKOPPE WAS PULLING OFF ONE DIFFICULT JUMP AFTER ANOTHER.
PHEW

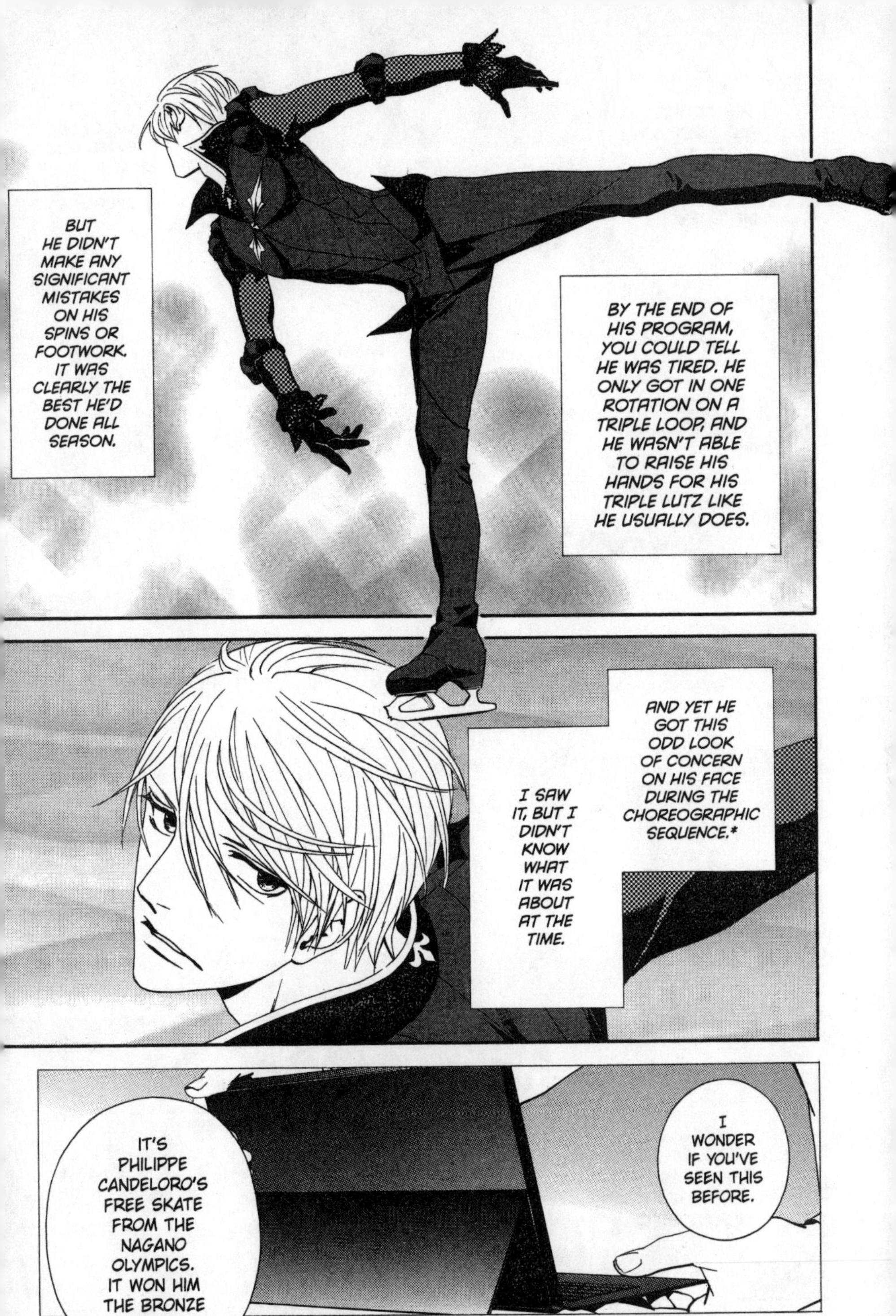
BY THE END OF HIS PROGRAM, YOU COULD TELL HE WAS TIRED. HE ONLY GOT IN ONE ROTATION ON A TRIPLE LOOP, AND HE WASN'T ABLE TO RAISE HIS HANDS FOR HIS TRIPLE LUTZ LIKE HE USUALLY DOES.
BUT HE DIDN'T MAKE ANY SIGNIFICANT MISTAKES ON HIS SPINS OR FOOTWORK. IT WAS CLEARLY THE BEST HE'D DONE ALL SEASON.
AND YET HE GOT THIS ODD LOOK OF CONCERN ON HIS FACE DURING THE CHOREOGRAPHIC SEQUENCE.*
I SAW IT, BUT I DIDN'T KNOW WHAT IT WAS ABOUT AT THE TIME.
I WONDER IF YOU'VE SEEN THIS BEFORE.
IT'S PHILIPPE CANDELORO'S FREE SKATE FROM THE NAGANO OLYMPICS. IT WON HIM THE BRONZE MEDAL.

*CHOREOGRAPHIC SEQUENCE: A FREELY COMPOSED STEP SEQUENCE THAT'S SCORED AS A WHOLE

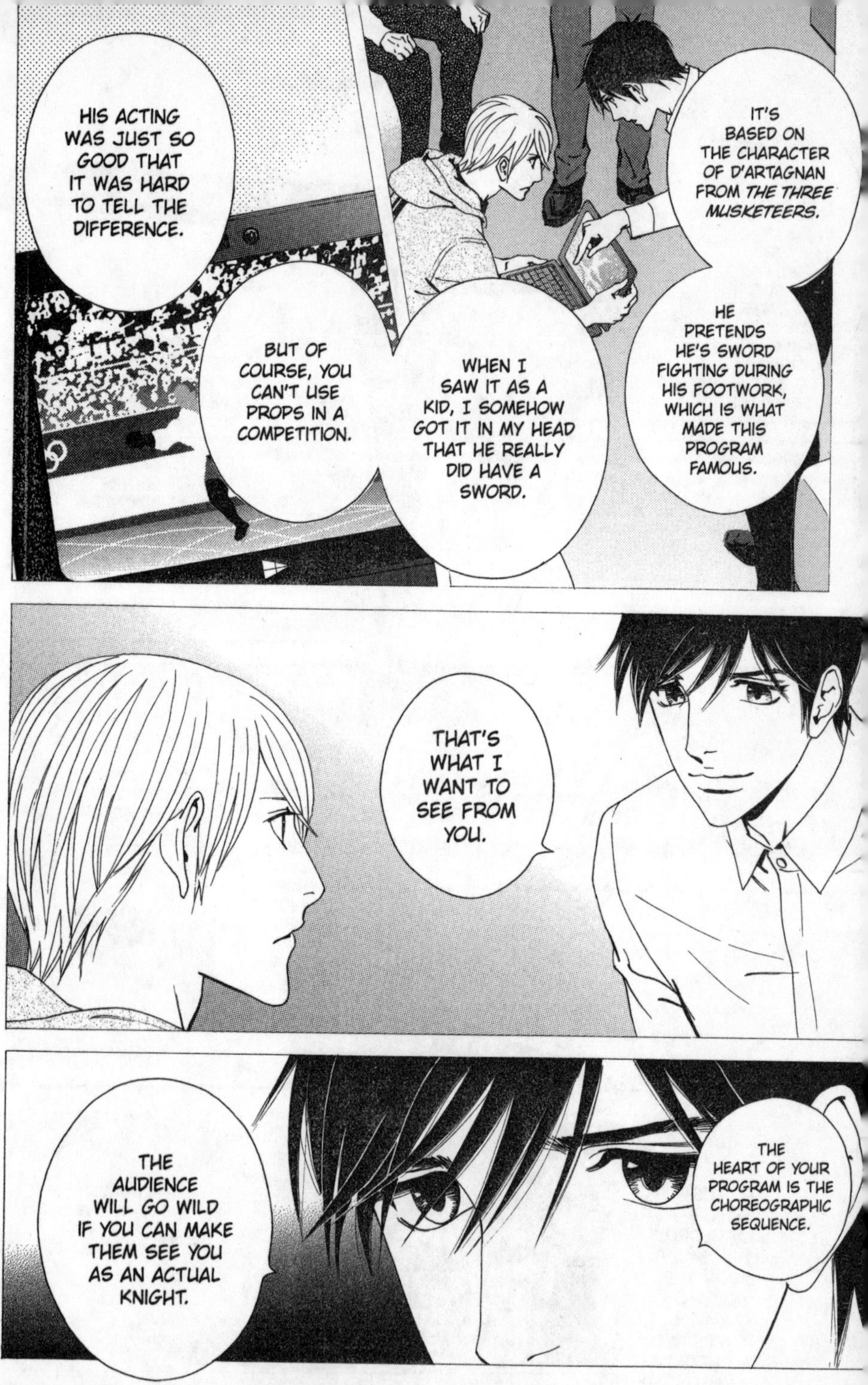
IT'S BASED ON THE CHARACTER OF D'ARTAGNAN FROM *THE THREE MUSKETEERS.*
HE PRETENDS HE'S SWORD FIGHTING DURING HIS FOOTWORK, WHICH IS WHAT MADE THIS PROGRAM FAMOUS.
WHEN I SAW IT AS A KID, I SOMEHOW GOT IT IN MY HEAD THAT HE REALLY DID HAVE A SWORD.
HIS ACTING WAS JUST SO GOOD THAT IT WAS HARD TO TELL THE DIFFERENCE.
BUT OF COURSE, YOU CAN'T USE PROPS IN A COMPETITION.
THAT'S WHAT I WANT TO SEE FROM YOU.
THE HEART OF YOUR PROGRAM IS THE CHOREOGRAPHIC SEQUENCE.
THE AUDIENCE WILL GO WILD IF YOU CAN MAKE THEM SEE YOU AS AN ACTUAL KNIGHT.

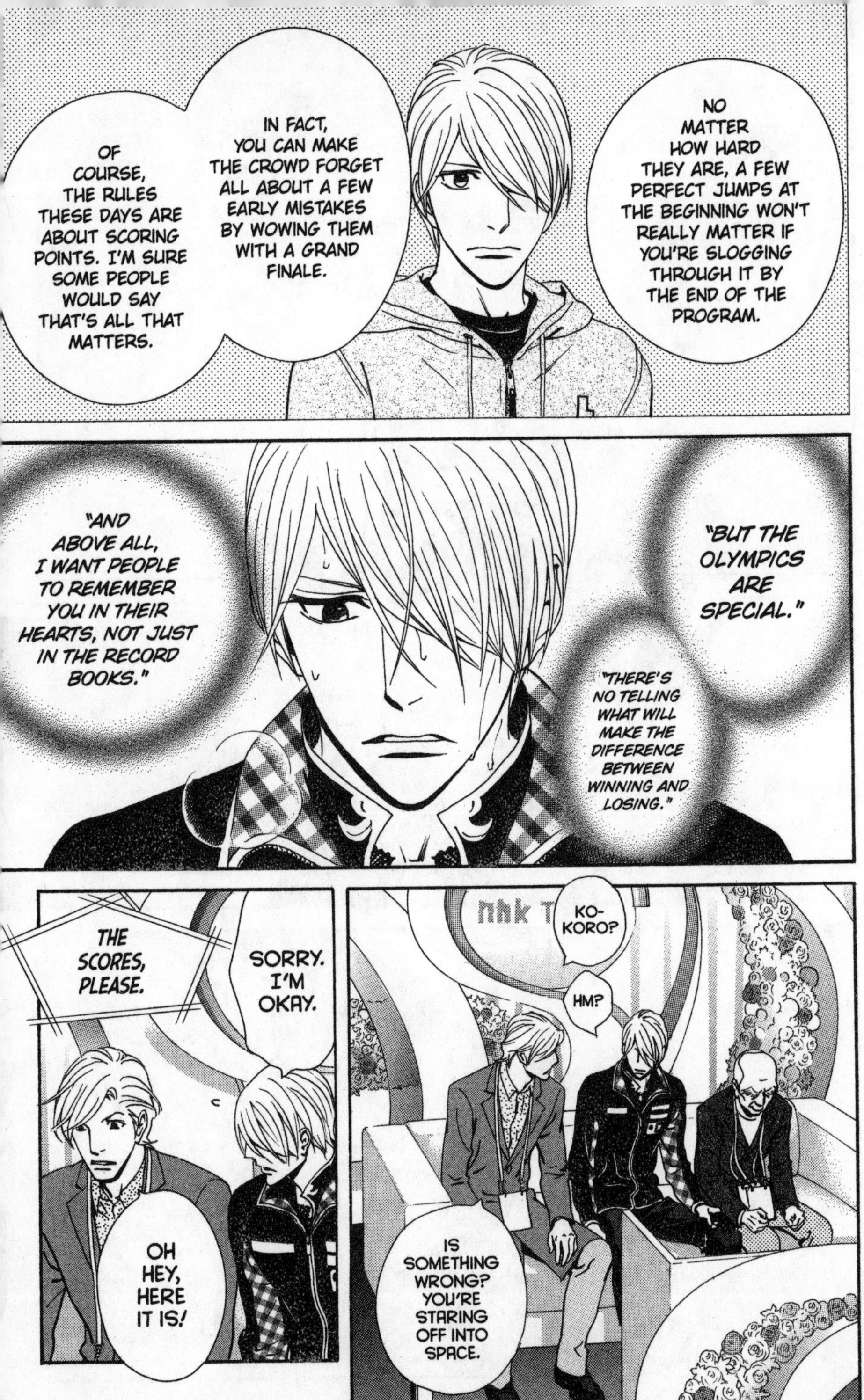
NO MATTER HOW HARD THEY ARE, A FEW PERFECT JUMPS AT THE BEGINNING WON'T REALLY MATTER IF YOU'RE SLOGGING THROUGH IT BY THE END OF THE PROGRAM.
IN FACT, YOU CAN MAKE THE CROWD FORGET ALL ABOUT A FEW EARLY MISTAKES BY WOWING THEM WITH A GRAND FINALE.
OF COURSE, THE RULES THESE DAYS ARE ABOUT SCORING POINTS. I'M SURE SOME PEOPLE WOULD SAY THAT'S ALL THAT MATTERS.
"BUT THE OLYMPICS ARE SPECIAL."
"THERE'S NO TELLING WHAT WILL MAKE THE DIFFERENCE BETWEEN WINNING AND LOSING."
"AND ABOVE ALL, I WANT PEOPLE TO REMEMBER YOU IN THEIR HEARTS, NOT JUST IN THE RECORD BOOKS."
nhk
KO-KORO?
HM?
IS SOMETHING WRONG? YOU'RE STARING OFF INTO SPACE.
SORRY. I'M OKAY.
THE SCORES, PLEASE.
OH HEY, HERE IT IS!

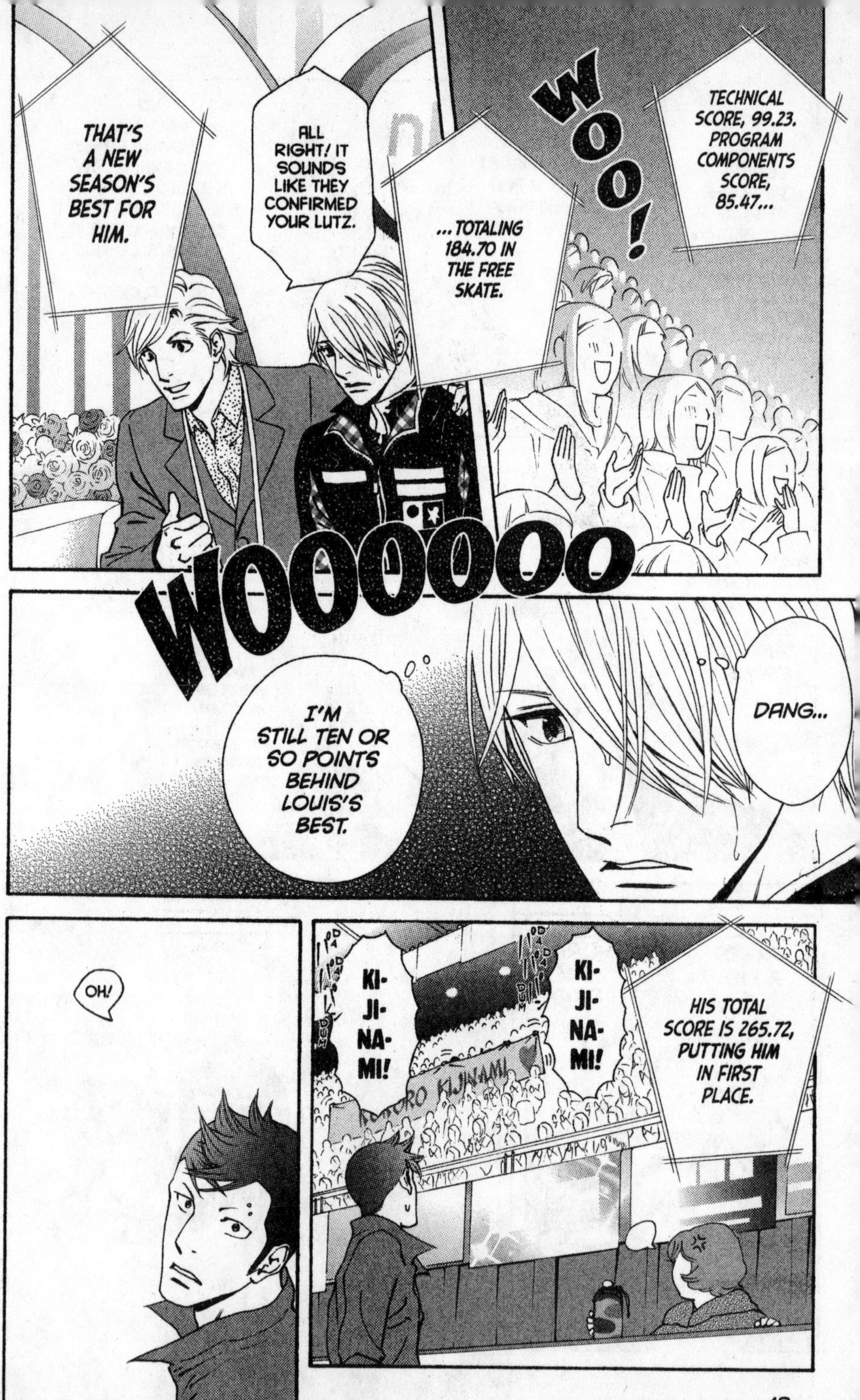
TECHNICAL SCORE, 99.23. PROGRAM COMPONENTS SCORE, 85.47...
WOO!
...TOTALING 184.70 IN THE FREE SKATE.
ALL RIGHT! IT SOUNDS LIKE THEY CONFIRMED YOUR LUTZ.
THAT'S A NEW SEASON'S BEST FOR HIM.
WOOOOOO
DANG...
I'M STILL TEN OR SO POINTS BEHIND LOUIS'S BEST.
HIS TOTAL SCORE IS 265.72, PUTTING HIM IN FIRST PLACE.
KI-JI-NA-MI!
KI-JI-NA-MI!
OH!

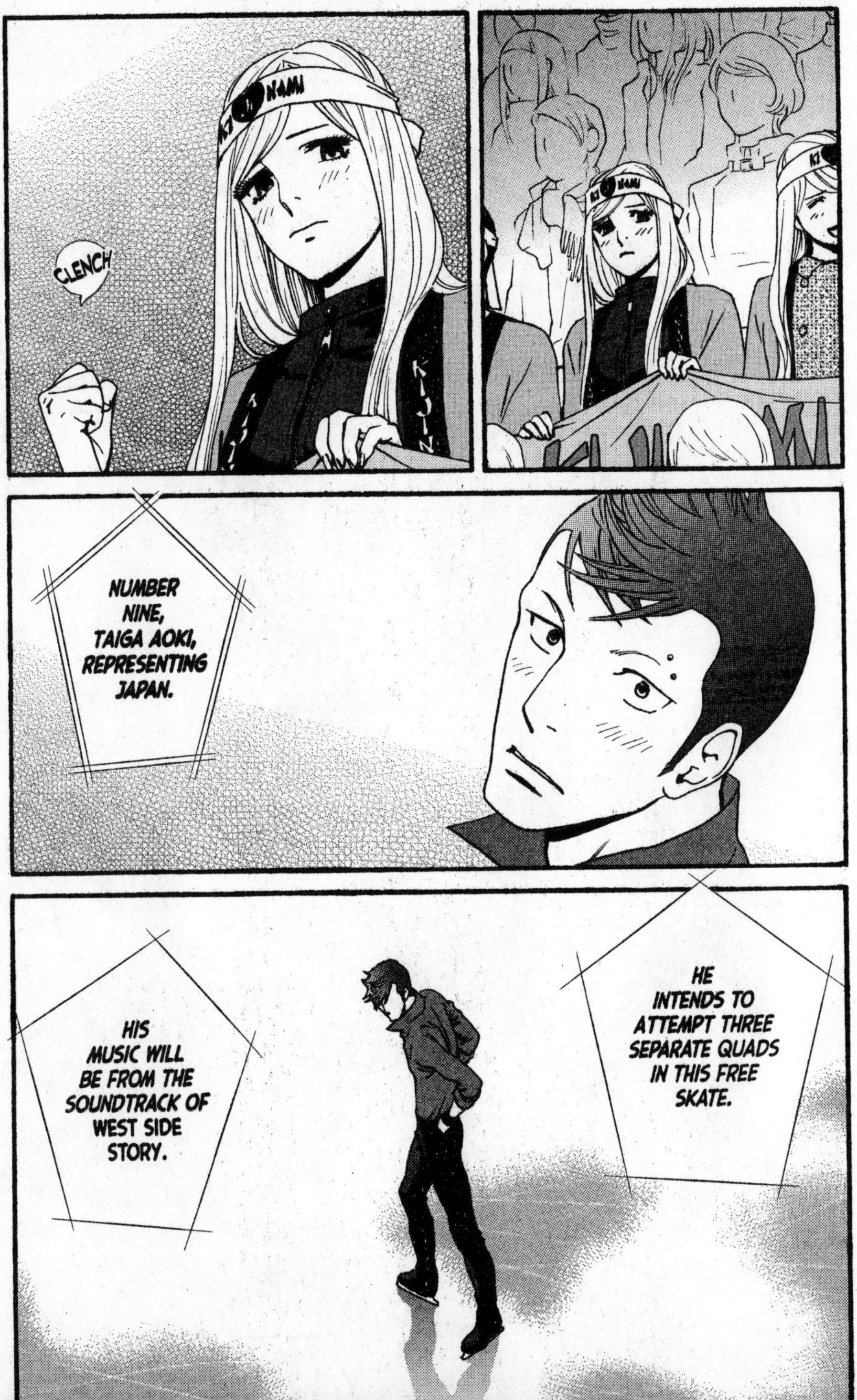
CLENCH
NUMBER NINE, TAIGA AOKI, REPRESENTING JAPAN.
HE INTENDS TO ATTEMPT THREE SEPARATE QUADS IN THIS FREE SKATE.
HIS MUSIC WILL BE FROM THE SOUNDTRACK OF WEST SIDE STORY.

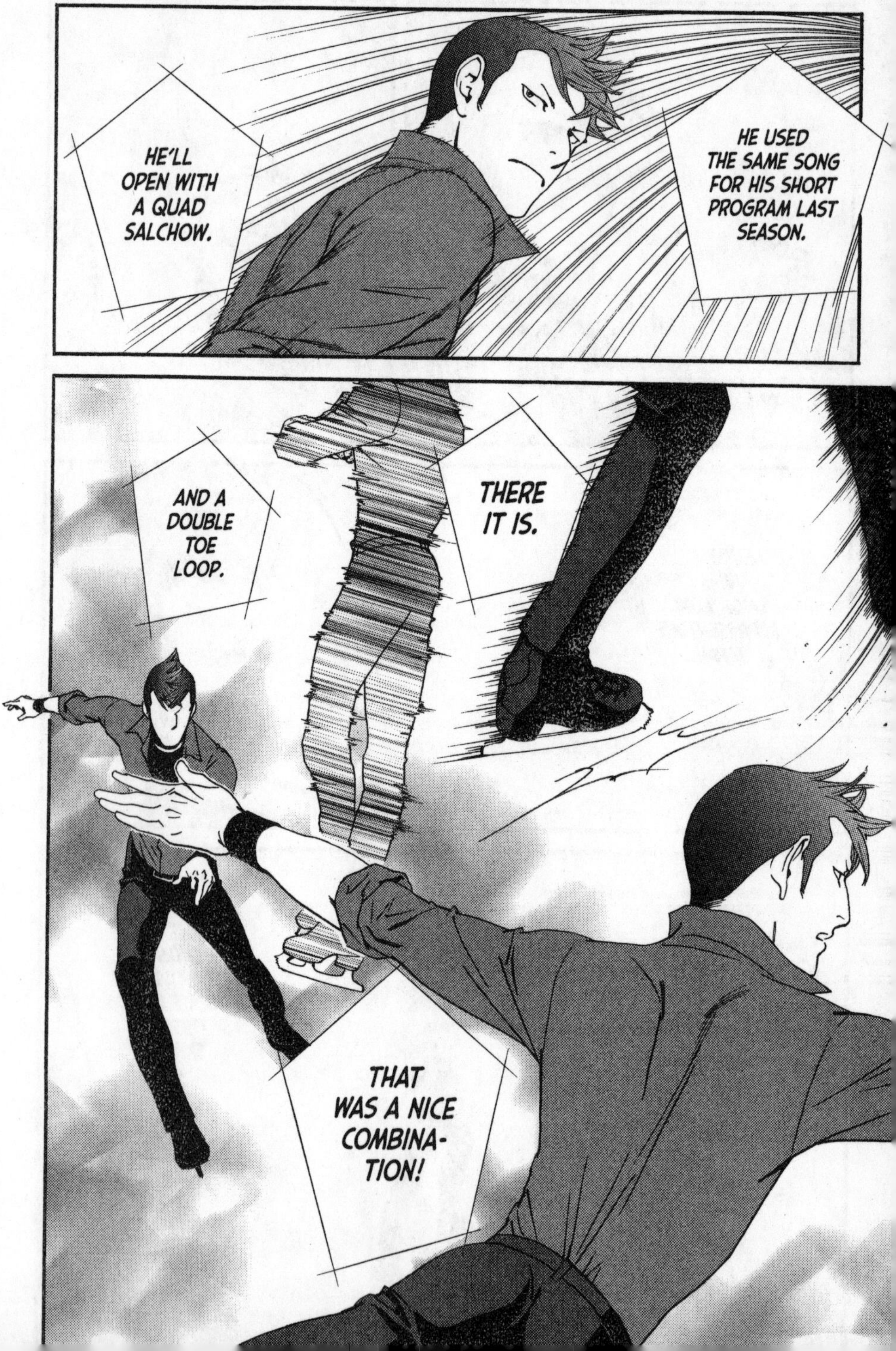
HE USED THE SAME SONG FOR HIS SHORT PROGRAM LAST SEASON.
HE'LL OPEN WITH A QUAD SALCHOW.
THERE IT IS.
AND A DOUBLE TOE LOOP.
THAT WAS A NICE COMBINA-TION!

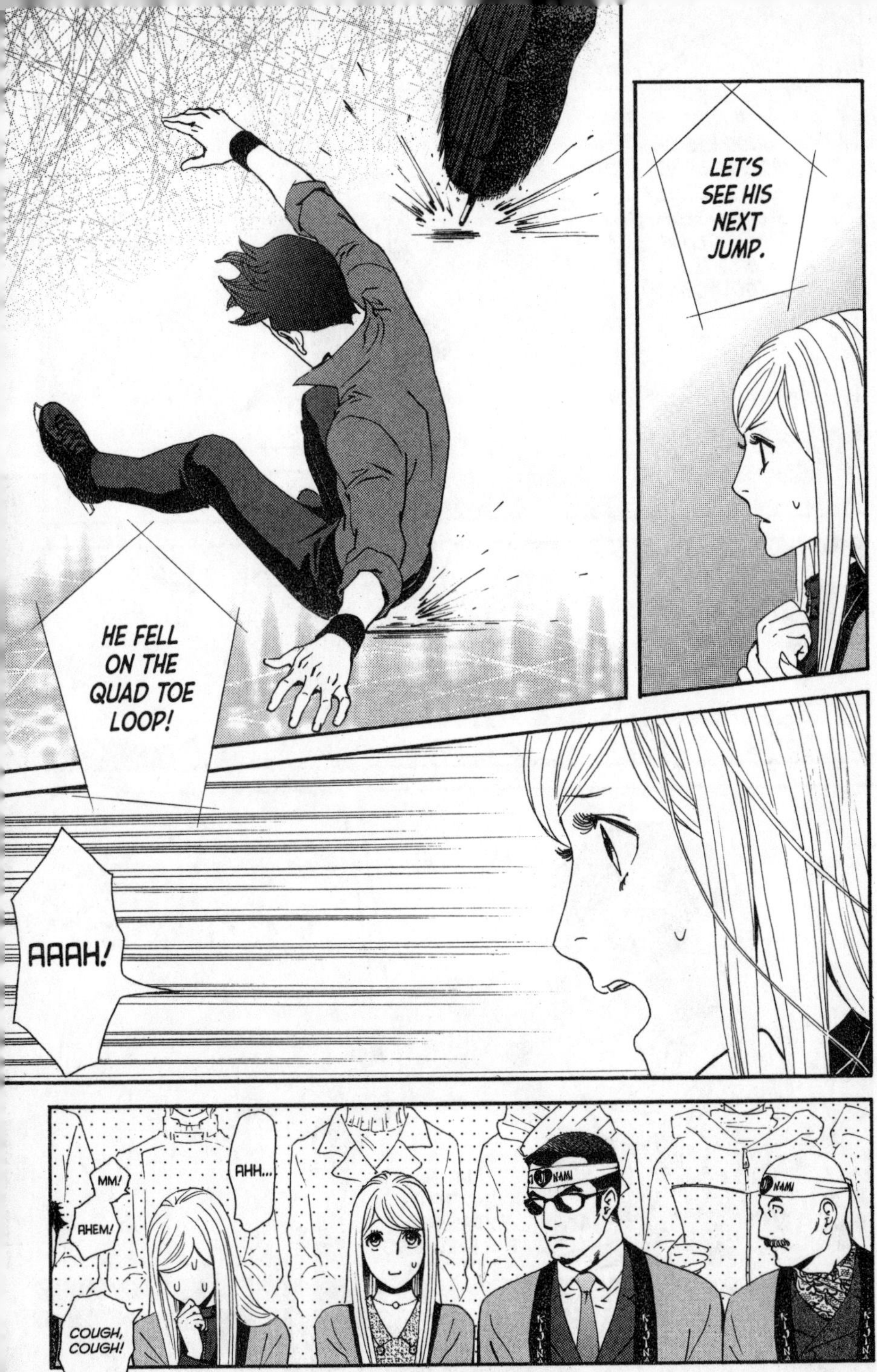

LET'S SEE HIS NEXT JUMP.
HE FELL ON THE QUAD TOE LOOP!
AAAH!
AHH...
MM!
AHEM!
COUGH, COUGH!

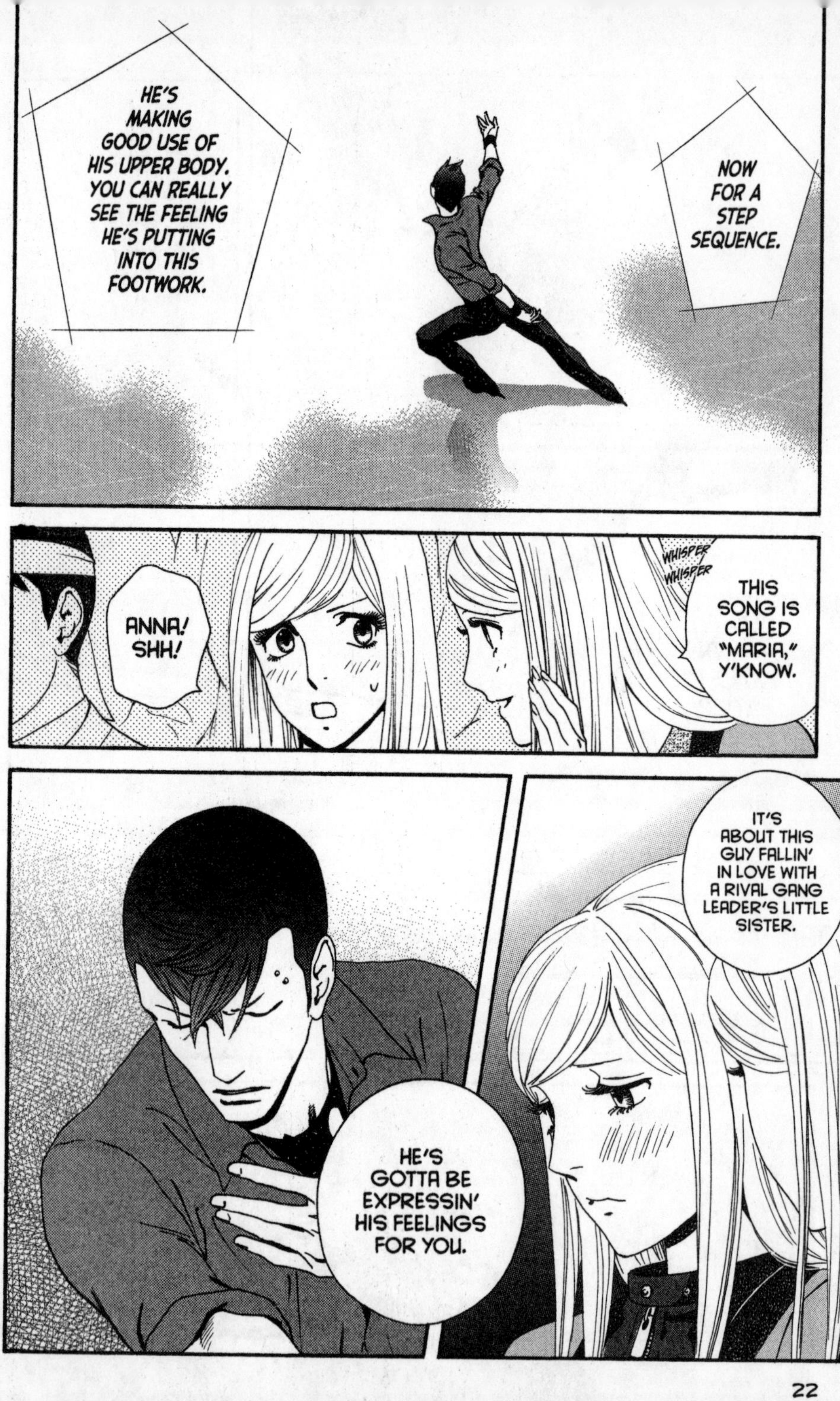
NOW FOR A STEP SEQUENCE.
HE'S MAKING GOOD USE OF HIS UPPER BODY. YOU CAN REALLY SEE THE FEELING HE'S PUTTING INTO THIS FOOTWORK.
WHISPER WHISPER
THIS SONG IS CALLED "MARIA," Y'KNOW.
ANNA! SHH!
IT'S ABOUT THIS GUY FALLIN' IN LOVE WITH A RIVAL GANG LEADER'S LITTLE SISTER.
HE'S GOTTA BE EXPRESSIN' HIS FEELINGS FOR YOU.

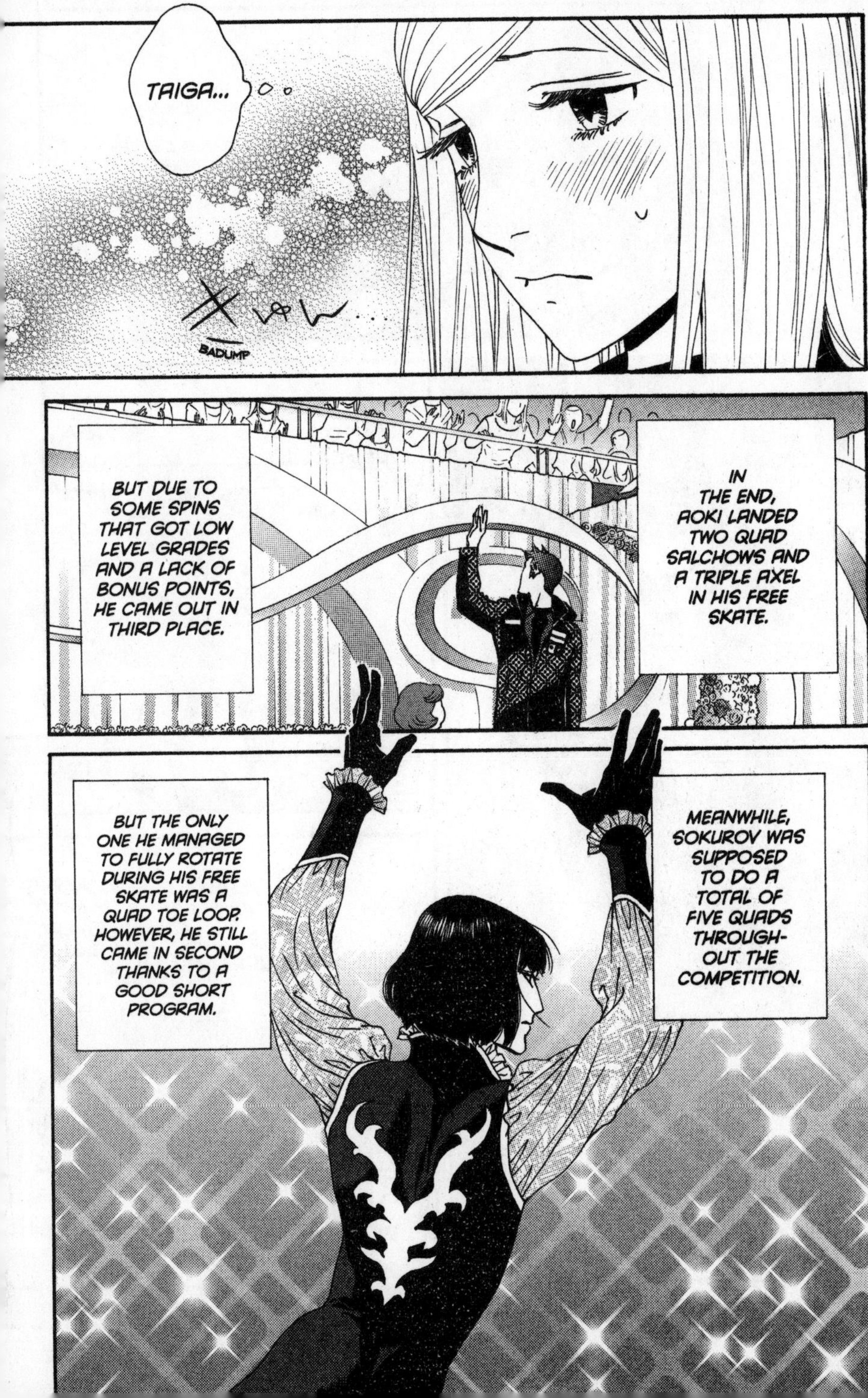
TAIGA...
BADUMP
IN THE END, AOKI LANDED TWO QUAD SALCHOWS AND A TRIPLE AXEL IN HIS FREE SKATE.
BUT DUE TO SOME SPINS THAT GOT LOW LEVEL GRADES AND A LACK OF BONUS POINTS, HE CAME OUT IN THIRD PLACE.
MEANWHILE, SOKUROV WAS SUPPOSED TO DO A TOTAL OF FIVE QUADS THROUGH-OUT THE COMPETITION.
BUT THE ONLY ONE HE MANAGED TO FULLY ROTATE DURING HIS FREE SKATE WAS A QUAD TOE LOOP. HOWEVER, HE STILL CAME IN SECOND THANKS TO A GOOD SHORT PROGRAM.

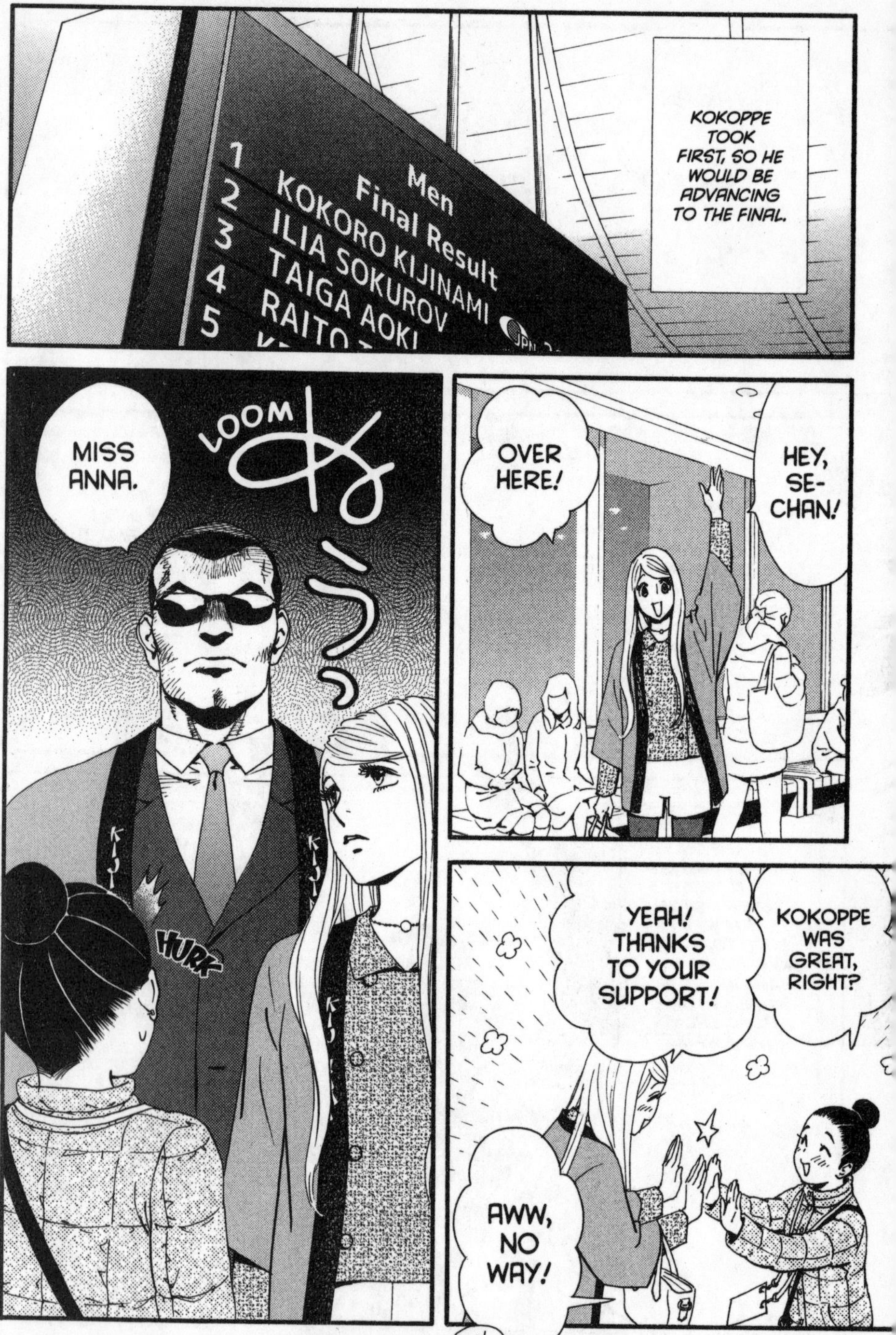
KOKOPPE TOOK FIRST, SO HE WOULD BE ADVANCING TO THE FINAL.
Men
Final Result
1 KOKORO KIJINAMI
2 ILIA SOKUROV
3 TAIGA AOKI
4 RAITO
HEY, SE-CHAN!
OVER HERE!
KOKOPPE WAS GREAT, RIGHT?
YEAH! THANKS TO YOUR SUPPORT!
AWW, NO WAY!
I did drop kick him...
LOOM
MISS ANNA.
HURK

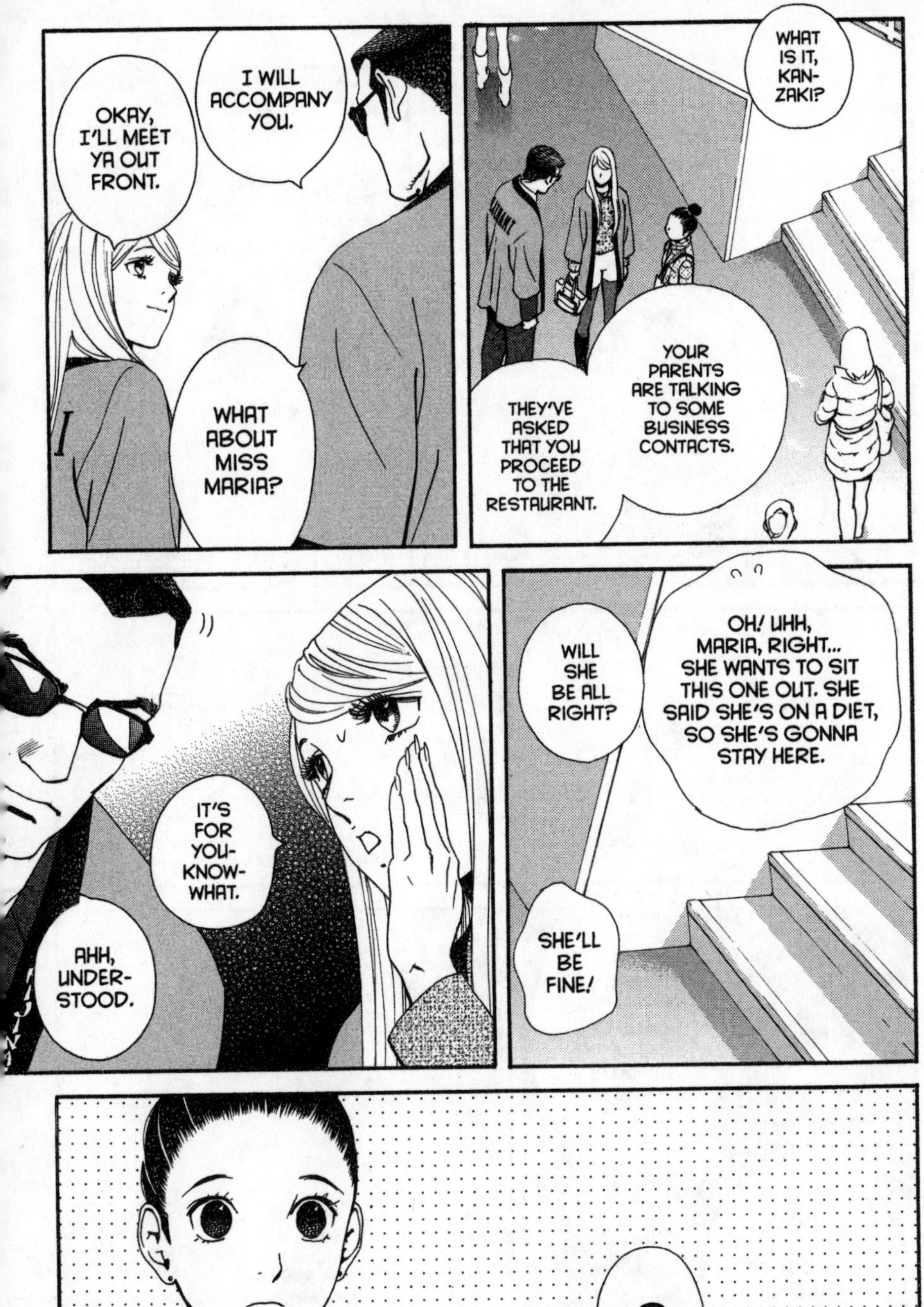
WHAT IS IT, KAN-ZAKI?
YOUR PARENTS ARE TALKING TO SOME BUSINESS CONTACTS.
THEY'VE ASKED THAT YOU PROCEED TO THE RESTAURANT.
I WILL ACCOMPANY YOU.
OKAY, I'LL MEET YA OUT FRONT.
WHAT ABOUT MISS MARIA?
OH! UHH, MARIA, RIGHT... SHE WANTS TO SIT THIS ONE OUT. SHE SAID SHE'S ON A DIET, SO SHE'S GONNA STAY HERE.
WILL SHE BE ALL RIGHT?
SHE'LL BE FINE!
IT'S FOR YOU-KNOW-WHAT.
AHH, UNDER-STOOD.
?

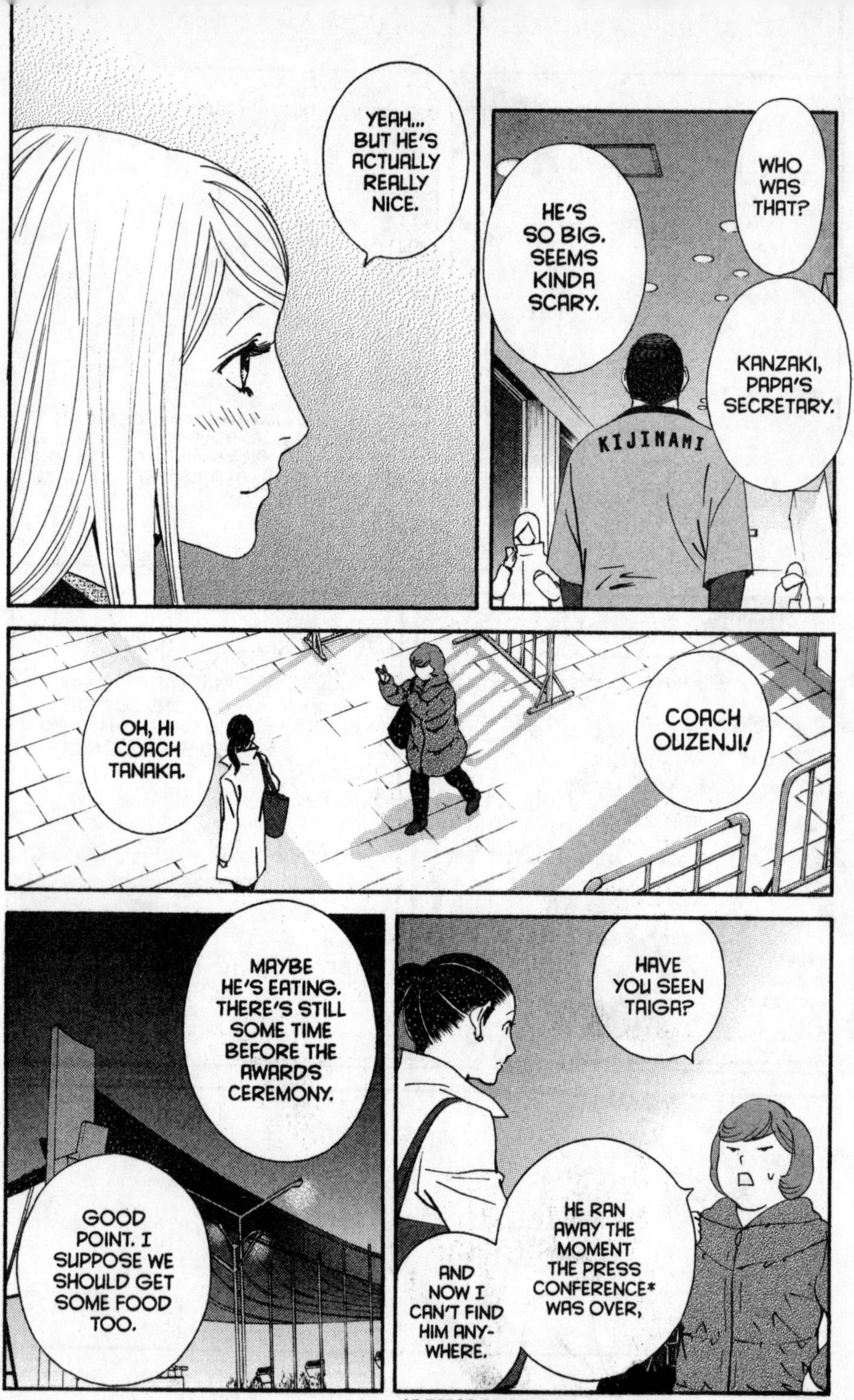
WHO WAS THAT?
KANZAKI, PAPA'S SECRETARY.
HE'S SO BIG. SEEMS KINDA SCARY.
KIJINAMI
YEAH... BUT HE'S ACTUALLY REALLY NICE.
COACH OUZENJI!
OH, HI COACH TANAKA.
HAVE YOU SEEN TAIGA?
HE RAN AWAY THE MOMENT THE PRESS CONFERENCE* WAS OVER,
AND NOW I CAN'T FIND HIM ANY-WHERE.
MAYBE HE'S EATING. THERE'S STILL SOME TIME BEFORE THE AWARDS CEREMONY.
GOOD POINT. I SUPPOSE WE SHOULD GET SOME FOOD TOO.

*A PRESS CONFERENCE IS HELD FOR THE TOP THREE PLACING SKATERS.

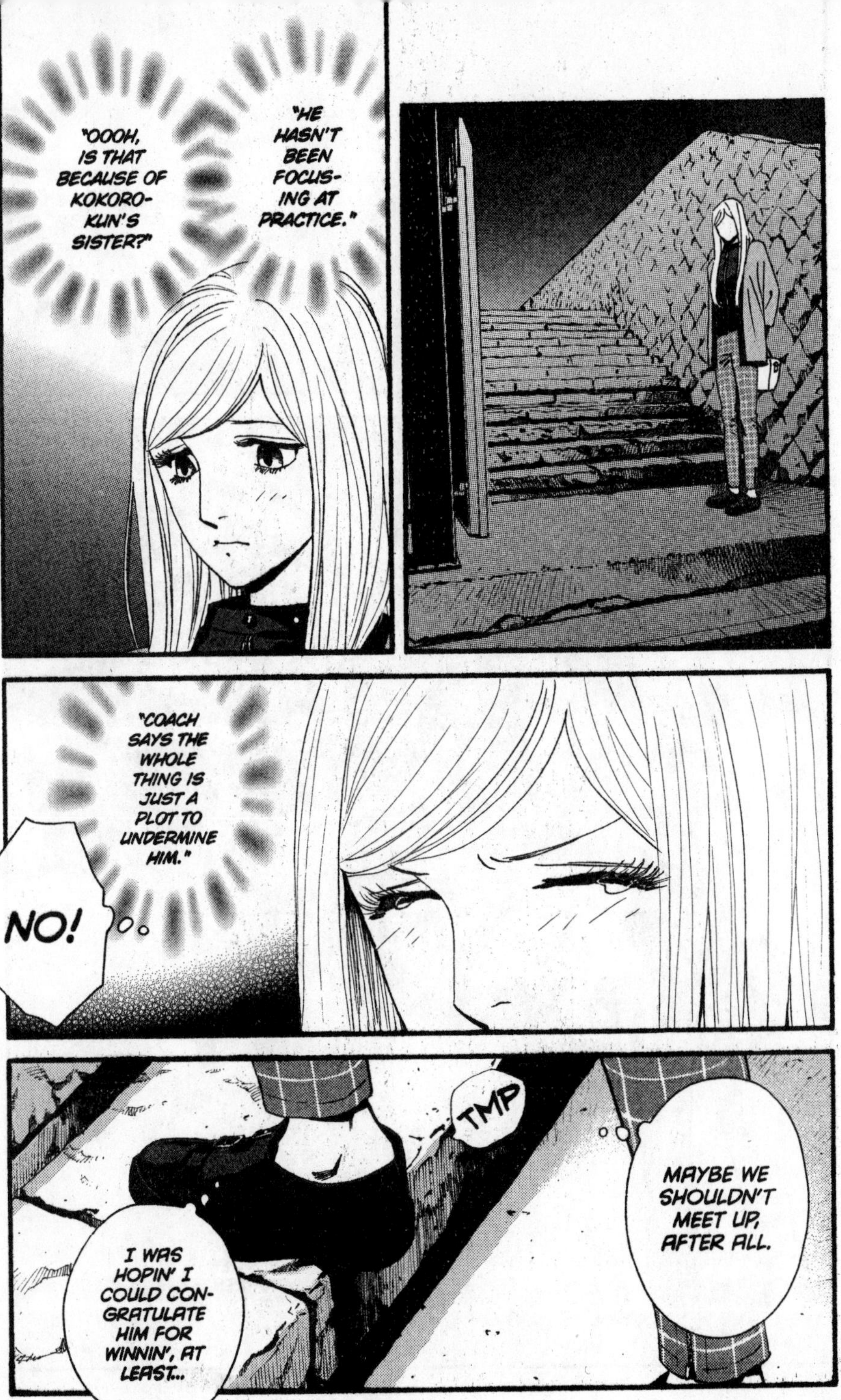
"HE HASN'T BEEN FOCUS-ING AT PRACTICE."
"OOOH, IS THAT BECAUSE OF KOKORO-KUN'S SISTER?"
"COACH SAYS THE WHOLE THING IS JUST A PLOT TO UNDERMINE HIM."
NO!
TMP
MAYBE WE SHOULDN'T MEET UP, AFTER ALL.
I WAS HOPIN' I COULD CON-GRATULATE HIM FOR WINNIN', AT LEAST...

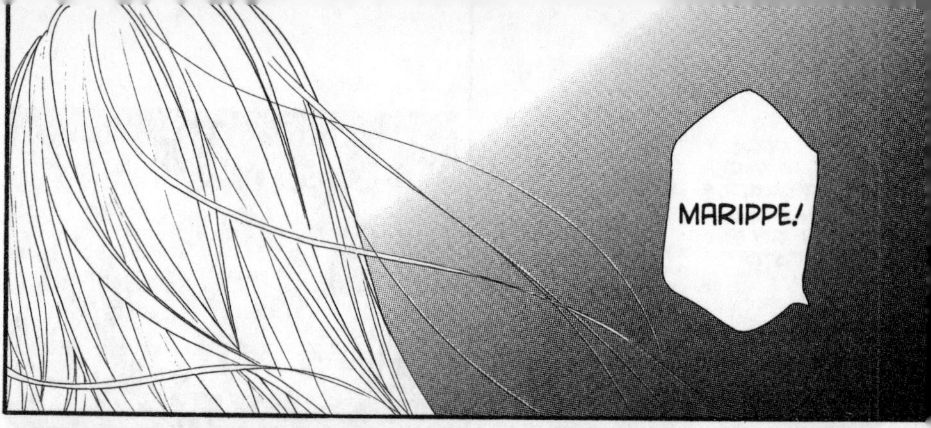
MARIPPE!
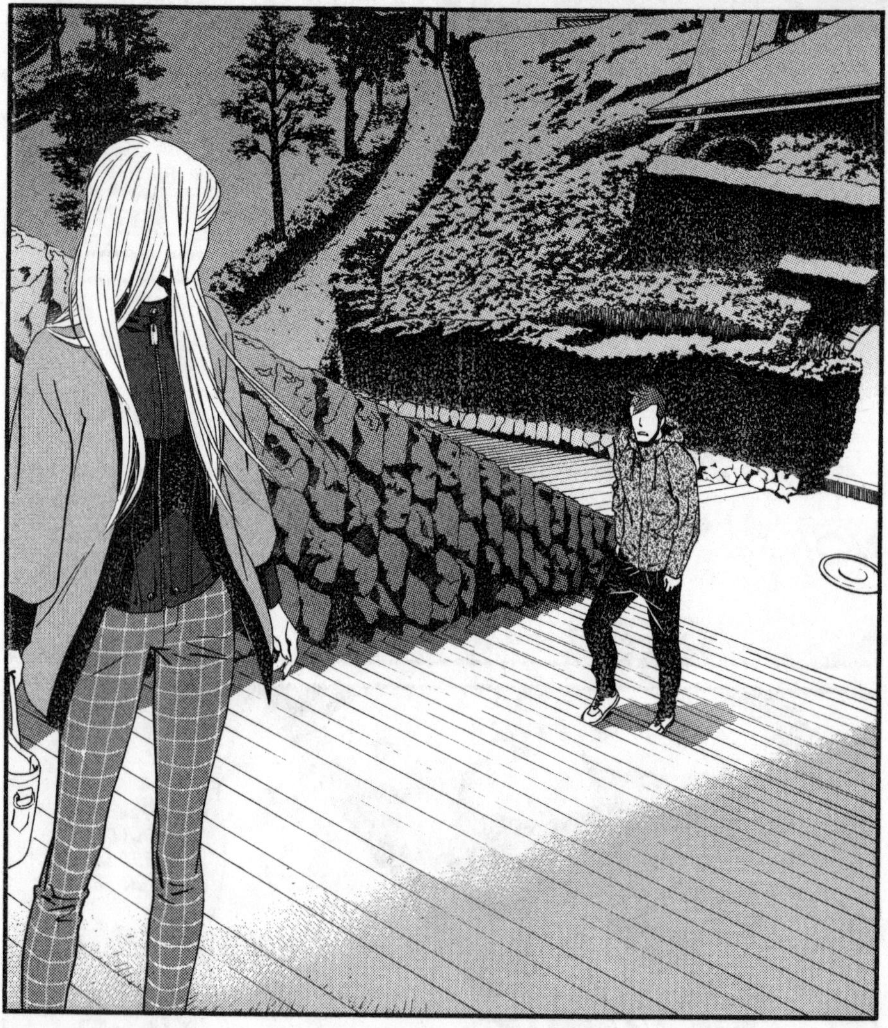

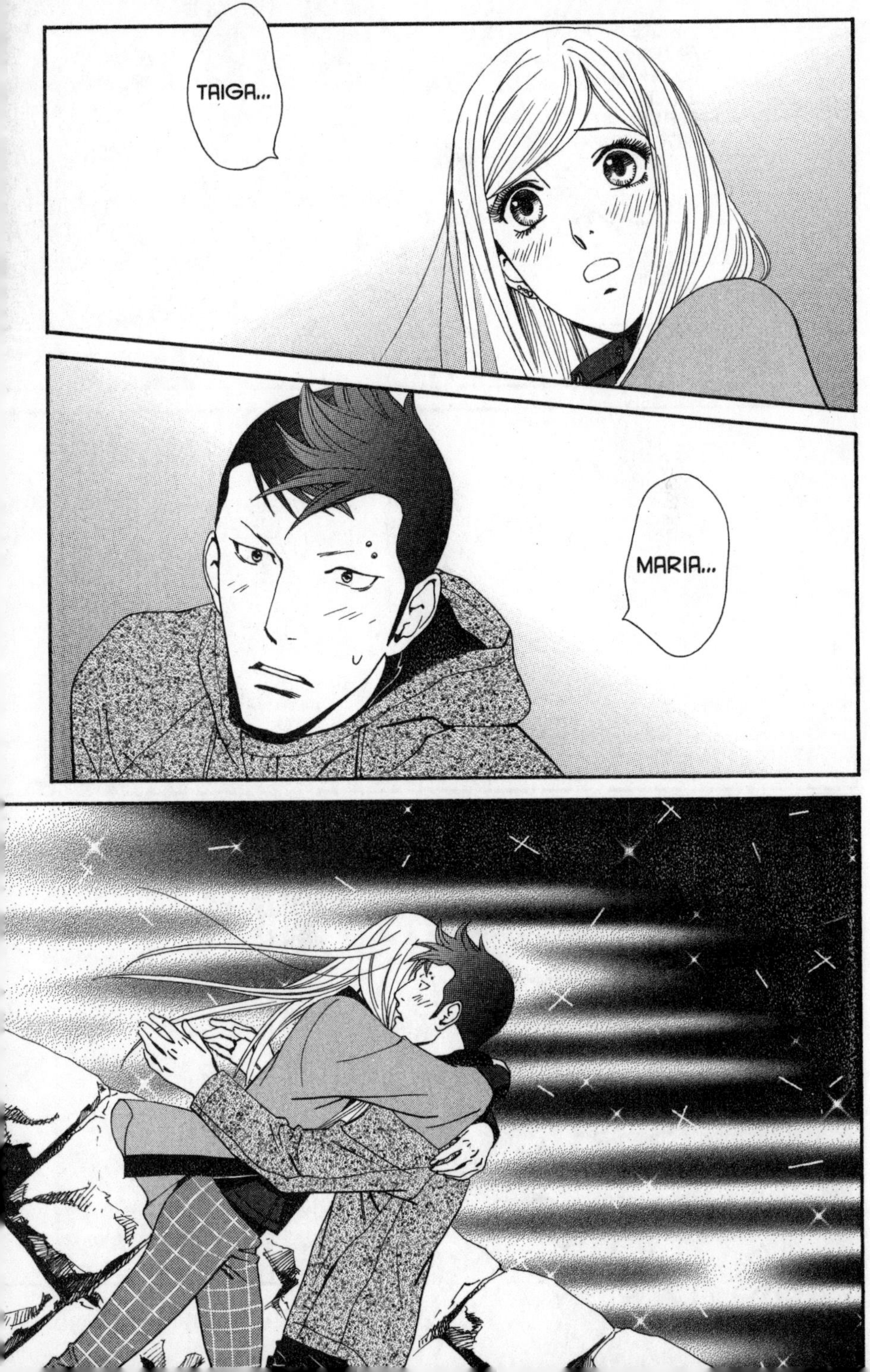
TAIGA...
MARIA...

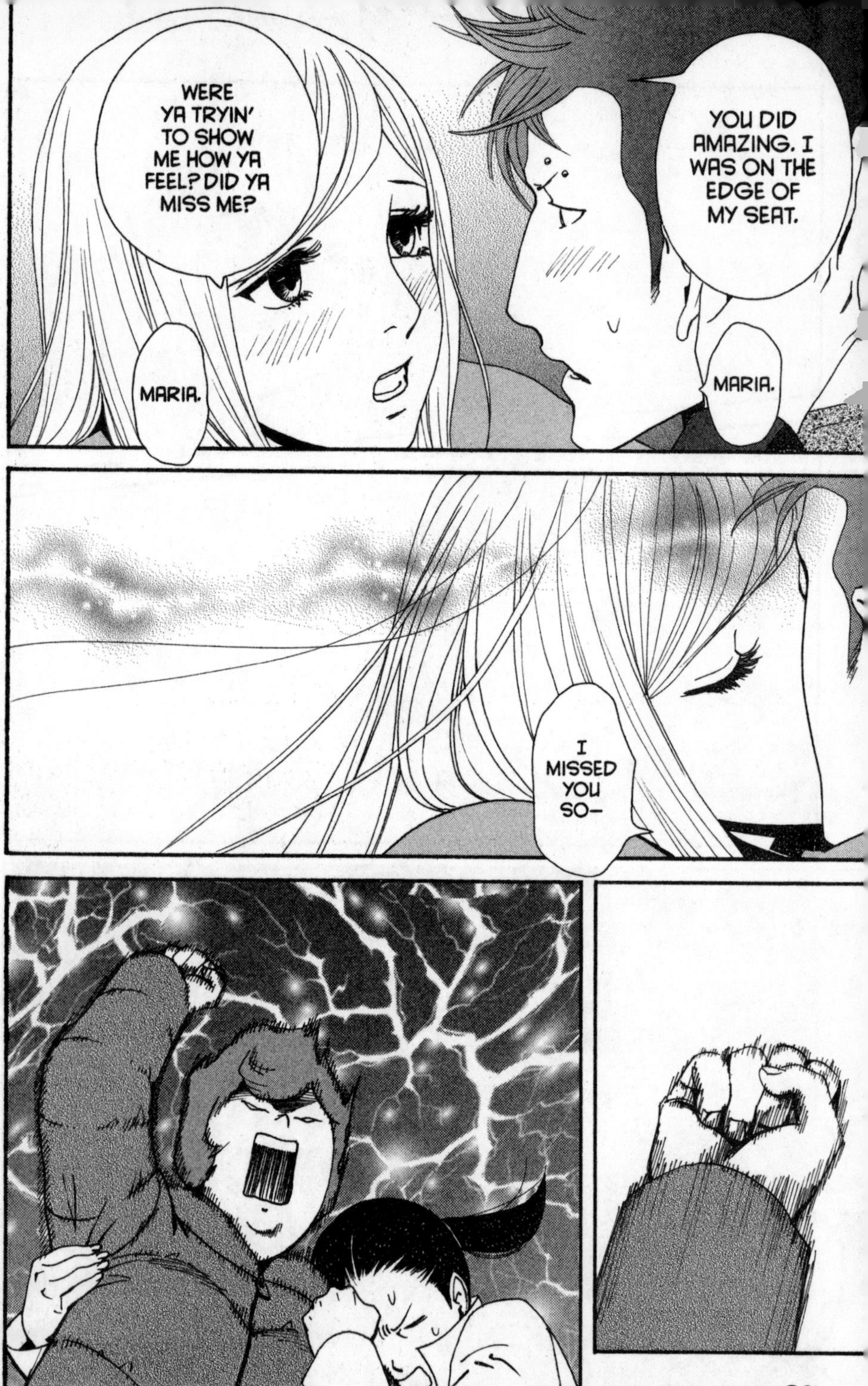
YOU DID AMAZING. I WAS ON THE EDGE OF MY SEAT.
WERE YA TRYIN' TO SHOW ME HOW YA FEEL? DID YA MISS ME?
MARIA.
MARIA.
I MISSED YOU SO—

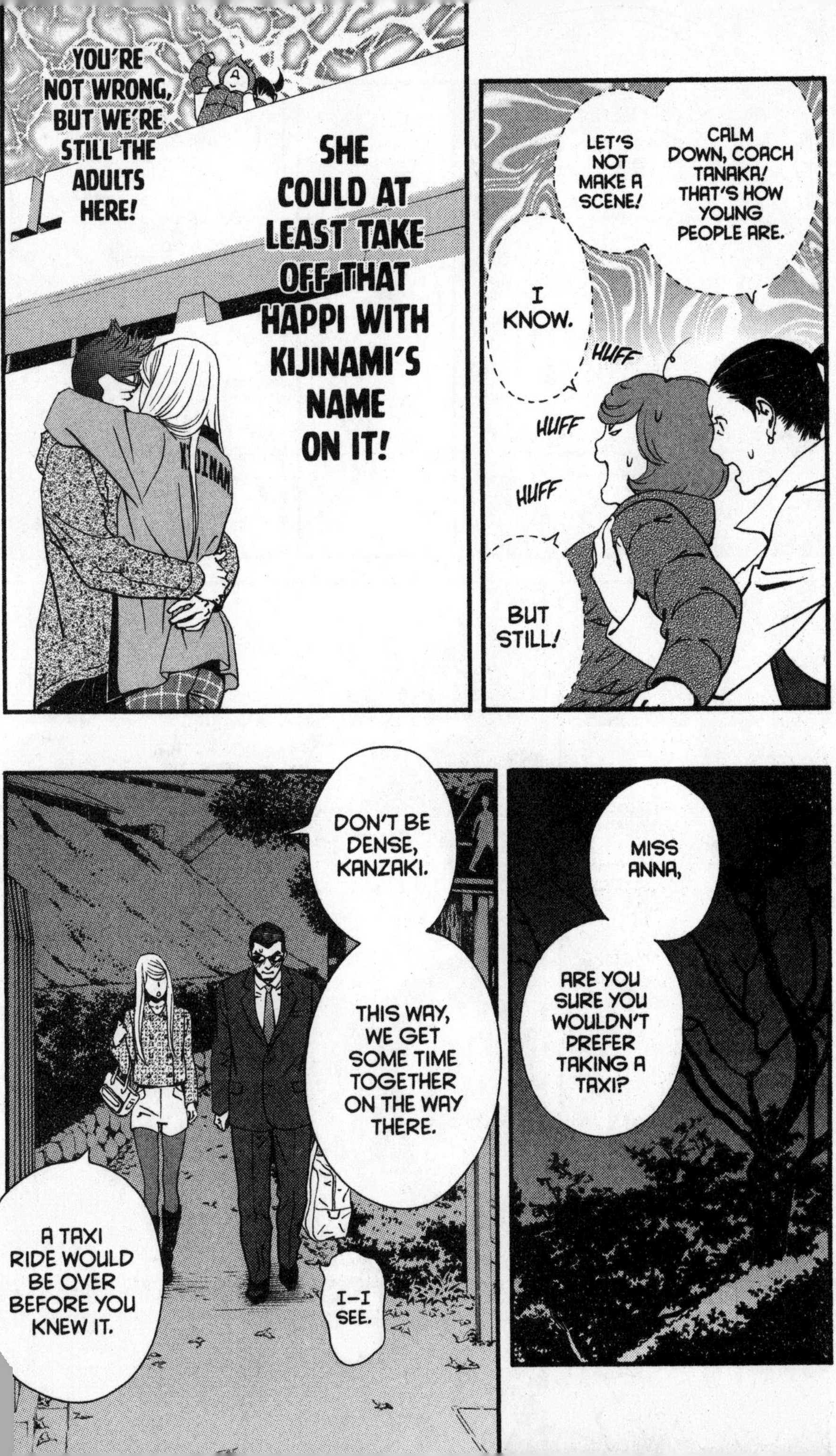
LET'S NOT MAKE A SCENE!
CALM DOWN, COACH TANAKA! THAT'S HOW YOUNG PEOPLE ARE.
I KNOW.
HUFF
HUFF
HUFF
BUT STILL!
YOU'RE NOT WRONG, BUT WE'RE STILL THE ADULTS HERE!
SHE COULD AT LEAST TAKE OFF THAT HAPPI WITH KIJINAMI'S NAME ON IT!
MISS ANNA,
ARE YOU SURE YOU WOULDN'T PREFER TAKING A TAXI?
DON'T BE DENSE, KANZAKI.
THIS WAY, WE GET SOME TIME TOGETHER ON THE WAY THERE.
A TAXI RIDE WOULD BE OVER BEFORE YOU KNEW IT.
I—I SEE.

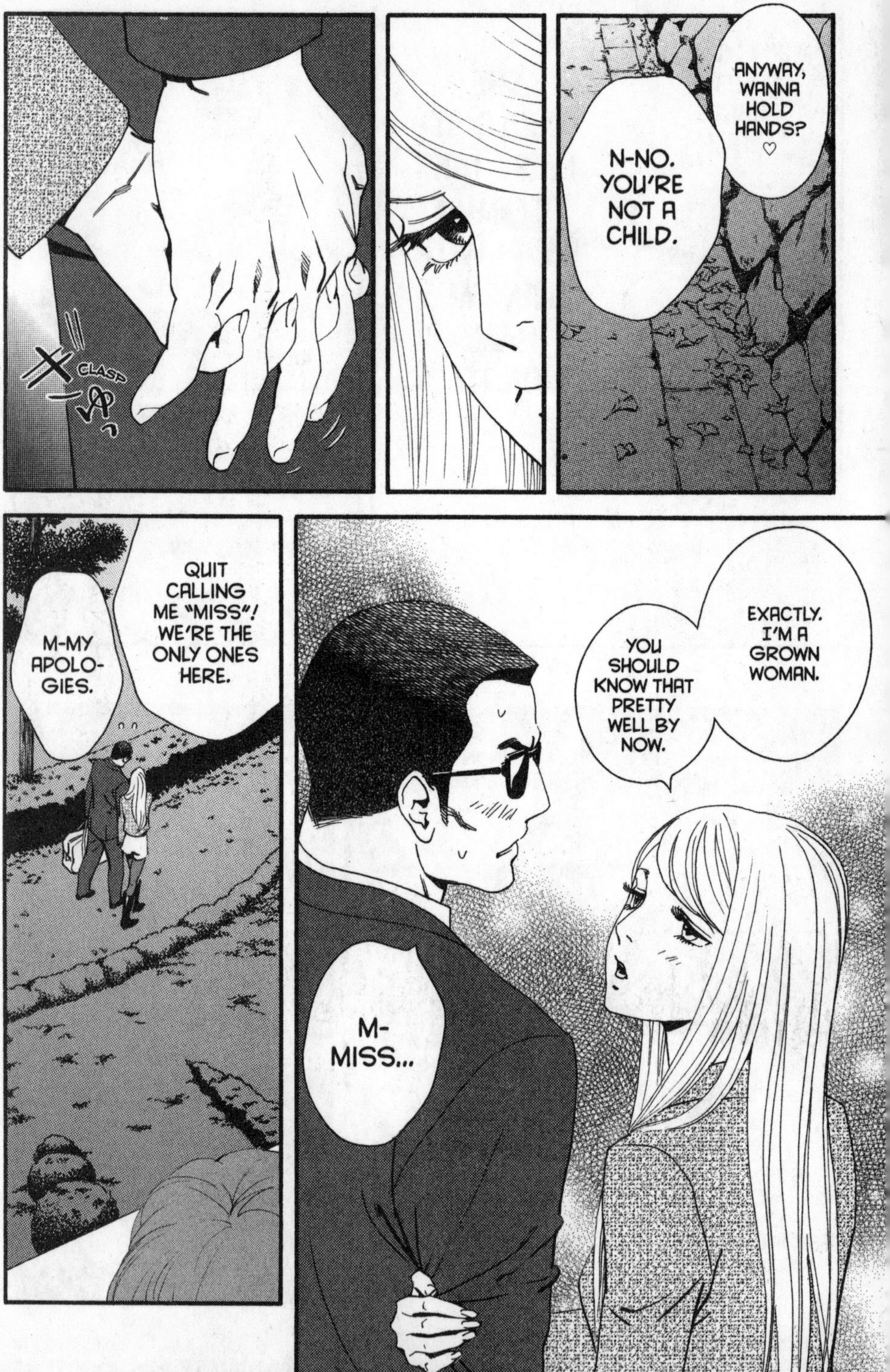
ANYWAY, WANNA HOLD HANDS? ♡
N-NO. YOU'RE NOT A CHILD.
CLASP
EXACTLY. I'M A GROWN WOMAN.
YOU SHOULD KNOW THAT PRETTY WELL BY NOW.
M-MISS...
QUIT CALLING ME "MISS"! WE'RE THE ONLY ONES HERE.
M-MY APOLOGIES.

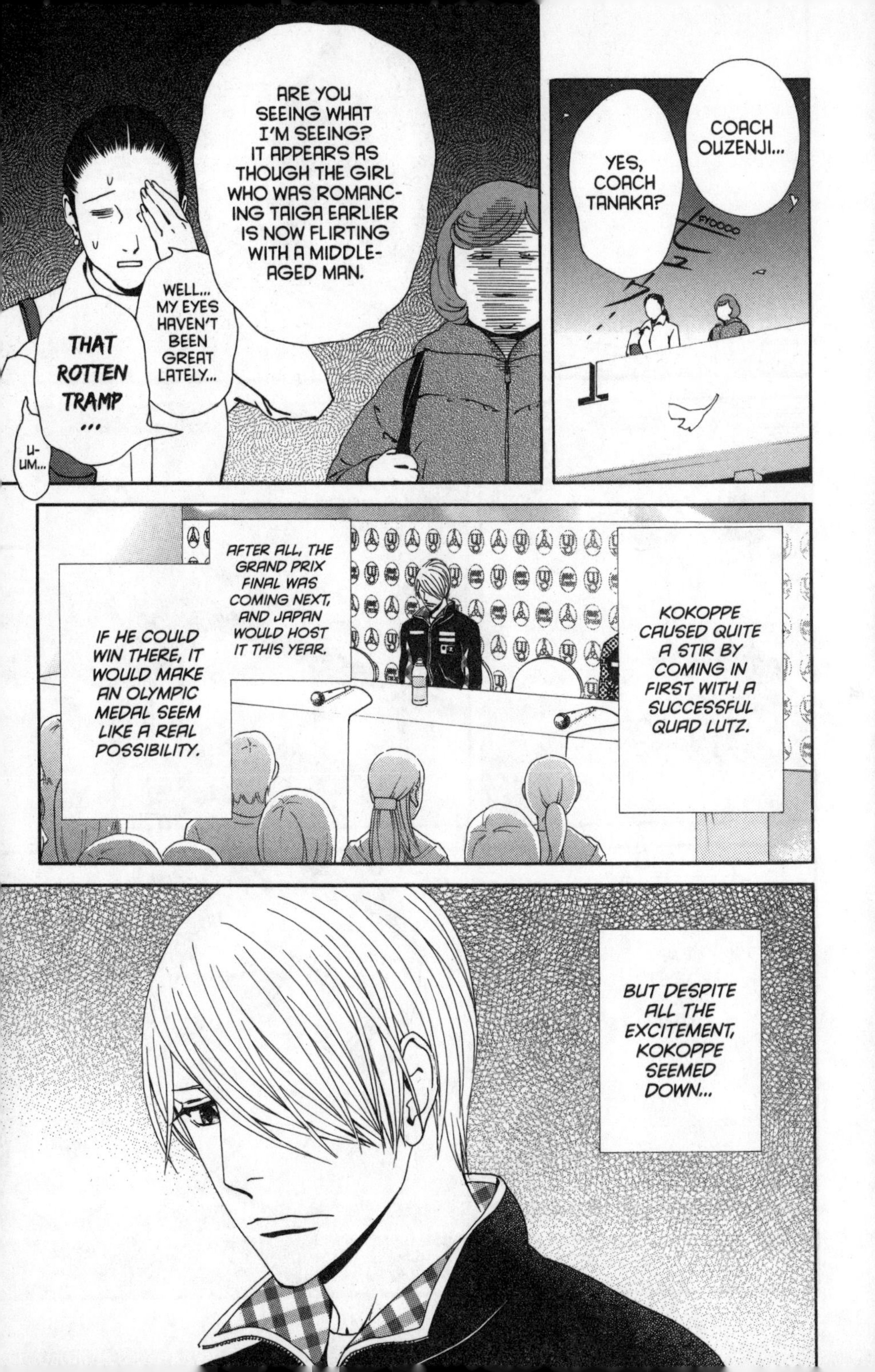
COACH OUZENJI...
YES, COACH TANAKA?
PYOOOO
ARE YOU SEEING WHAT I'M SEEING? IT APPEARS AS THOUGH THE GIRL WHO WAS ROMANCING TAIGA EARLIER IS NOW FLIRTING WITH A MIDDLE-AGED MAN.
WELL... MY EYES HAVEN'T BEEN GREAT LATELY...
THAT ROTTEN TRAMP...
U-UM...
KOKOPPE CAUSED QUITE A STIR BY COMING IN FIRST WITH A SUCCESSFUL QUAD LUTZ.
AFTER ALL, THE GRAND PRIX FINAL WAS COMING NEXT, AND JAPAN WOULD HOST IT THIS YEAR.
IF HE COULD WIN THERE, IT WOULD MAKE AN OLYMPIC MEDAL SEEM LIKE A REAL POSSIBILITY.
BUT DESPITE ALL THE EXCITEMENT, KOKOPPE SEEMED DOWN...

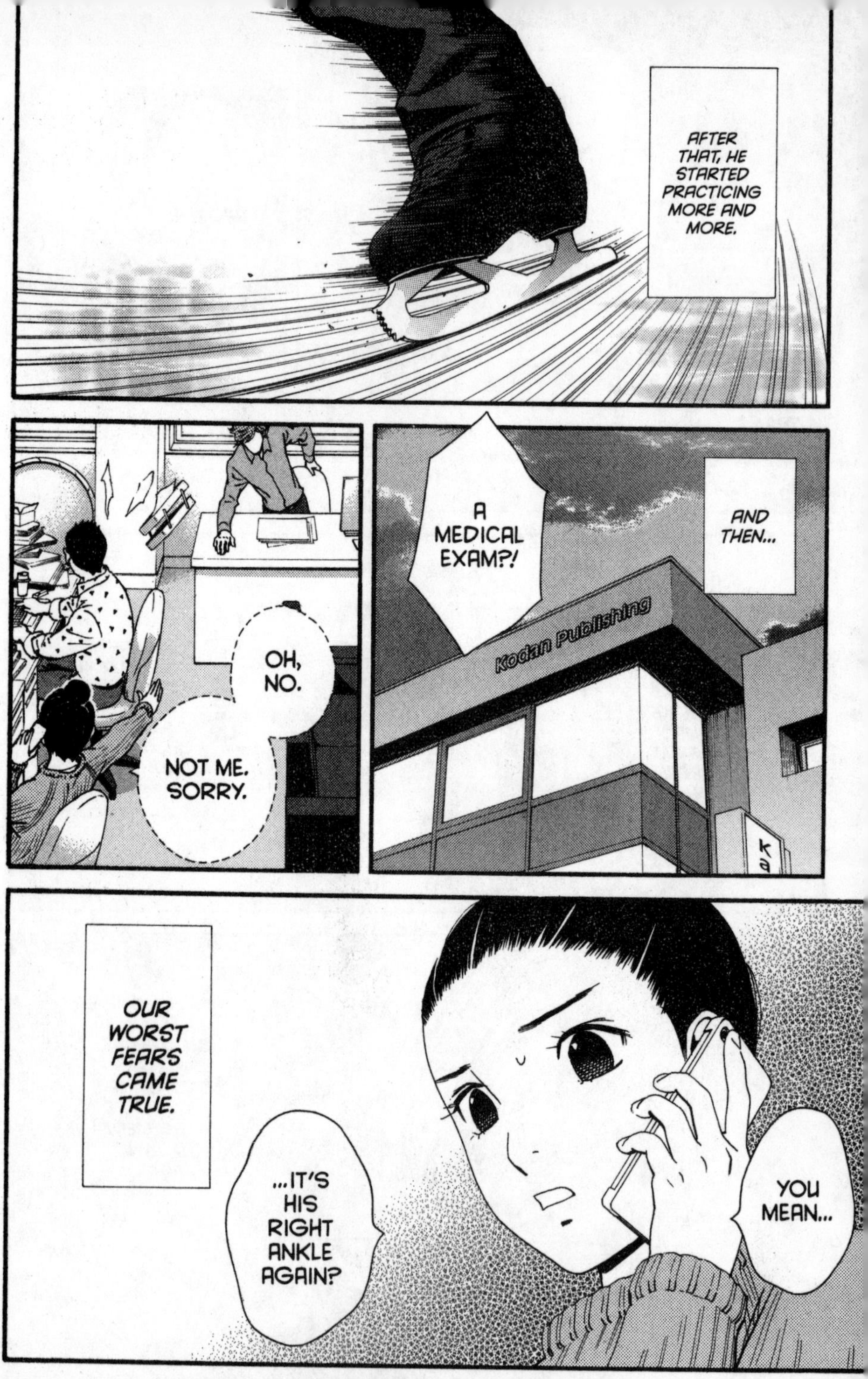
AFTER THAT, HE STARTED PRACTICING MORE AND MORE.
AND THEN...
A MEDICAL EXAM?!
Kodan Publishing
OH, NO.
NOT ME. SORRY.
YOU MEAN...
...IT'S HIS RIGHT ANKLE AGAIN?
OUR WORST FEARS CAME TRUE.

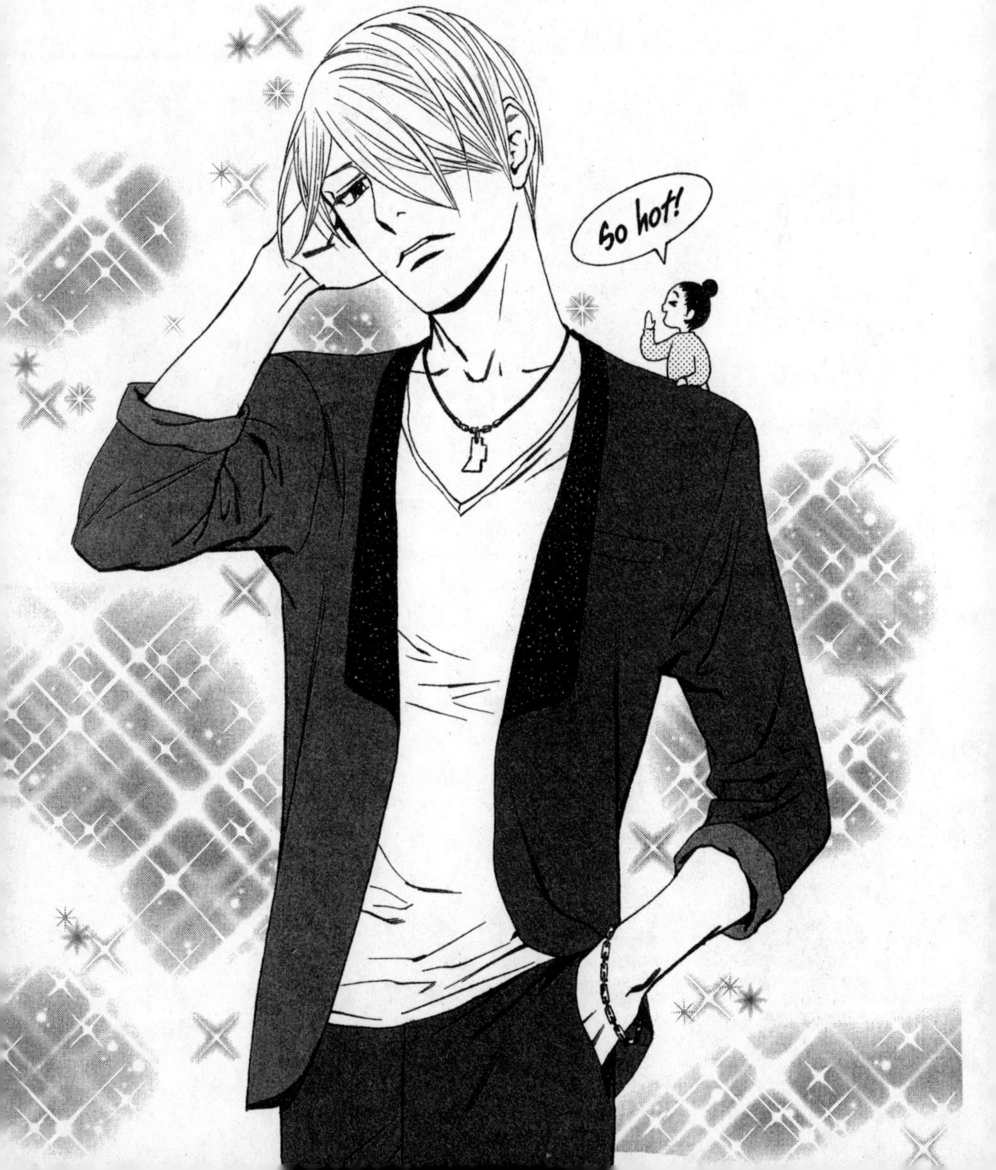
So hot!

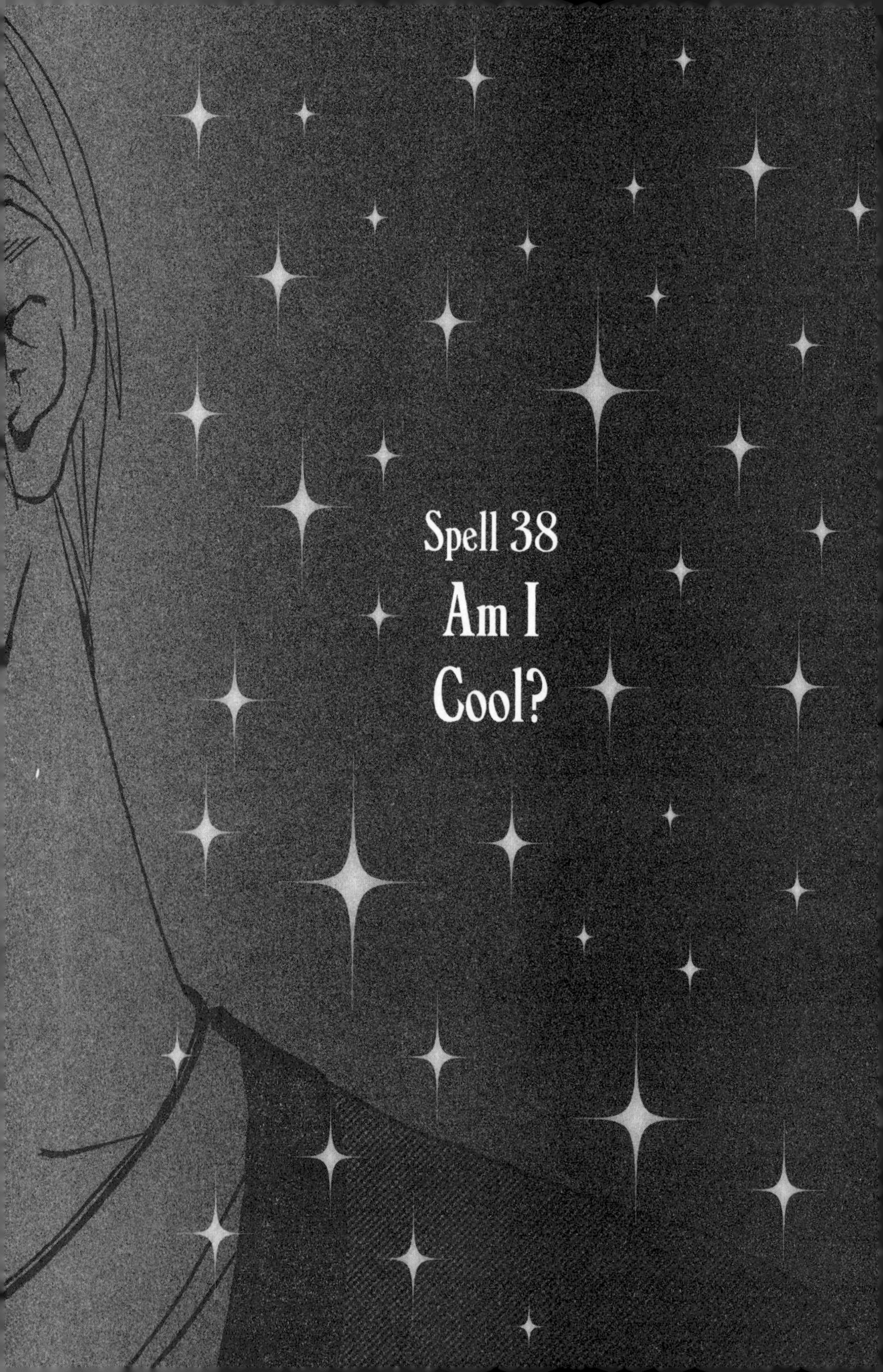
Spell 38
Am I
Cool?

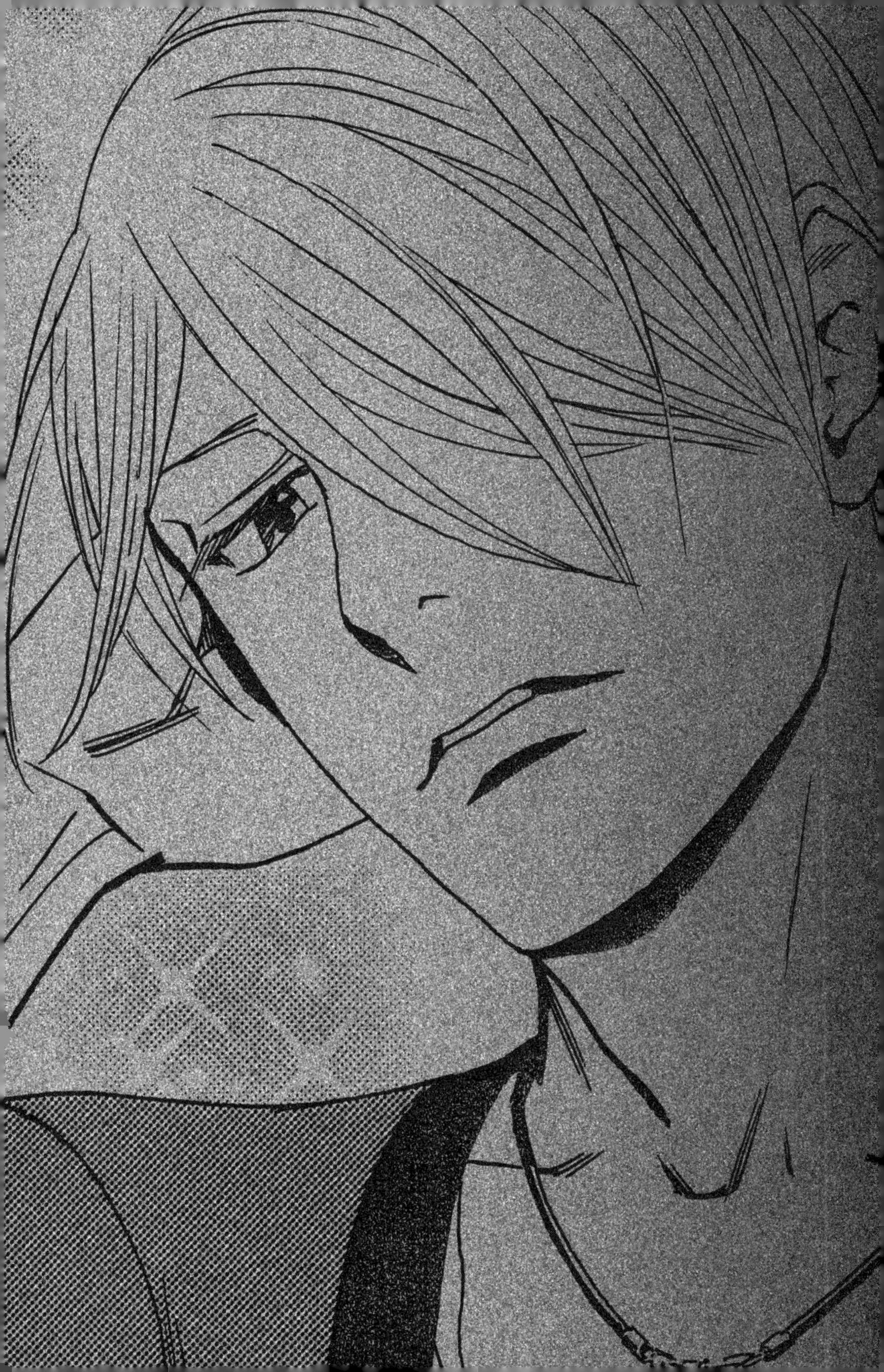

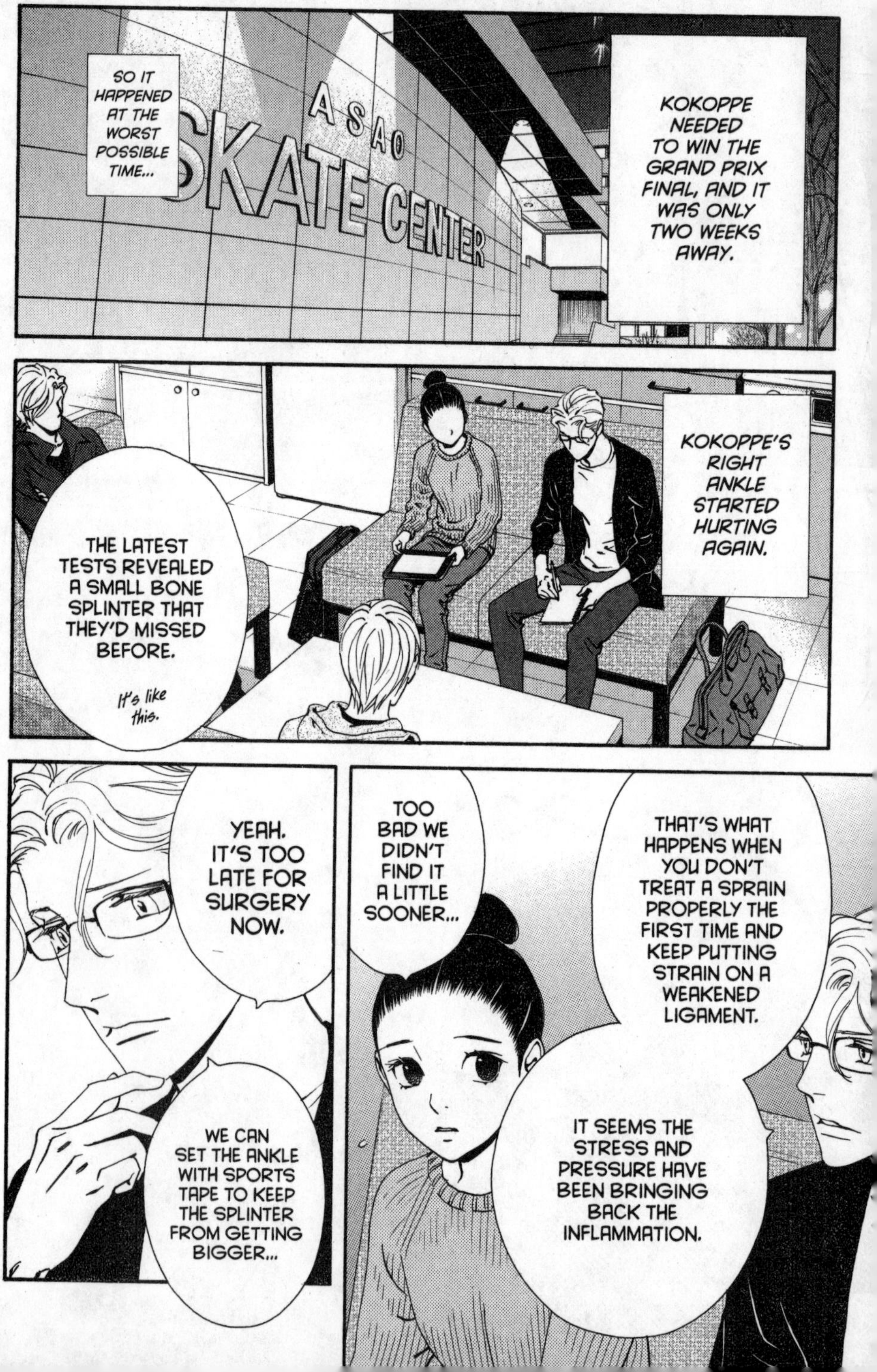
KOKOPPE NEEDED TO WIN THE GRAND PRIX FINAL, AND IT WAS ONLY TWO WEEKS AWAY.
SO IT HAPPENED AT THE WORST POSSIBLE TIME...
ASAO SKATE CENTER
KOKOPPE'S RIGHT ANKLE STARTED HURTING AGAIN.
THE LATEST TESTS REVEALED A SMALL BONE SPLINTER THAT THEY'D MISSED BEFORE.
It's like this.
THAT'S WHAT HAPPENS WHEN YOU DON'T TREAT A SPRAIN PROPERLY THE FIRST TIME AND KEEP PUTTING STRAIN ON A WEAKENED LIGAMENT.
TOO BAD WE DIDN'T FIND IT A LITTLE SOONER...
IT SEEMS THE STRESS AND PRESSURE HAVE BEEN BRINGING BACK THE INFLAMMATION.
YEAH. IT'S TOO LATE FOR SURGERY NOW.
WE CAN SET THE ANKLE WITH SPORTS TAPE TO KEEP THE SPLINTER FROM GETTING BIGGER...

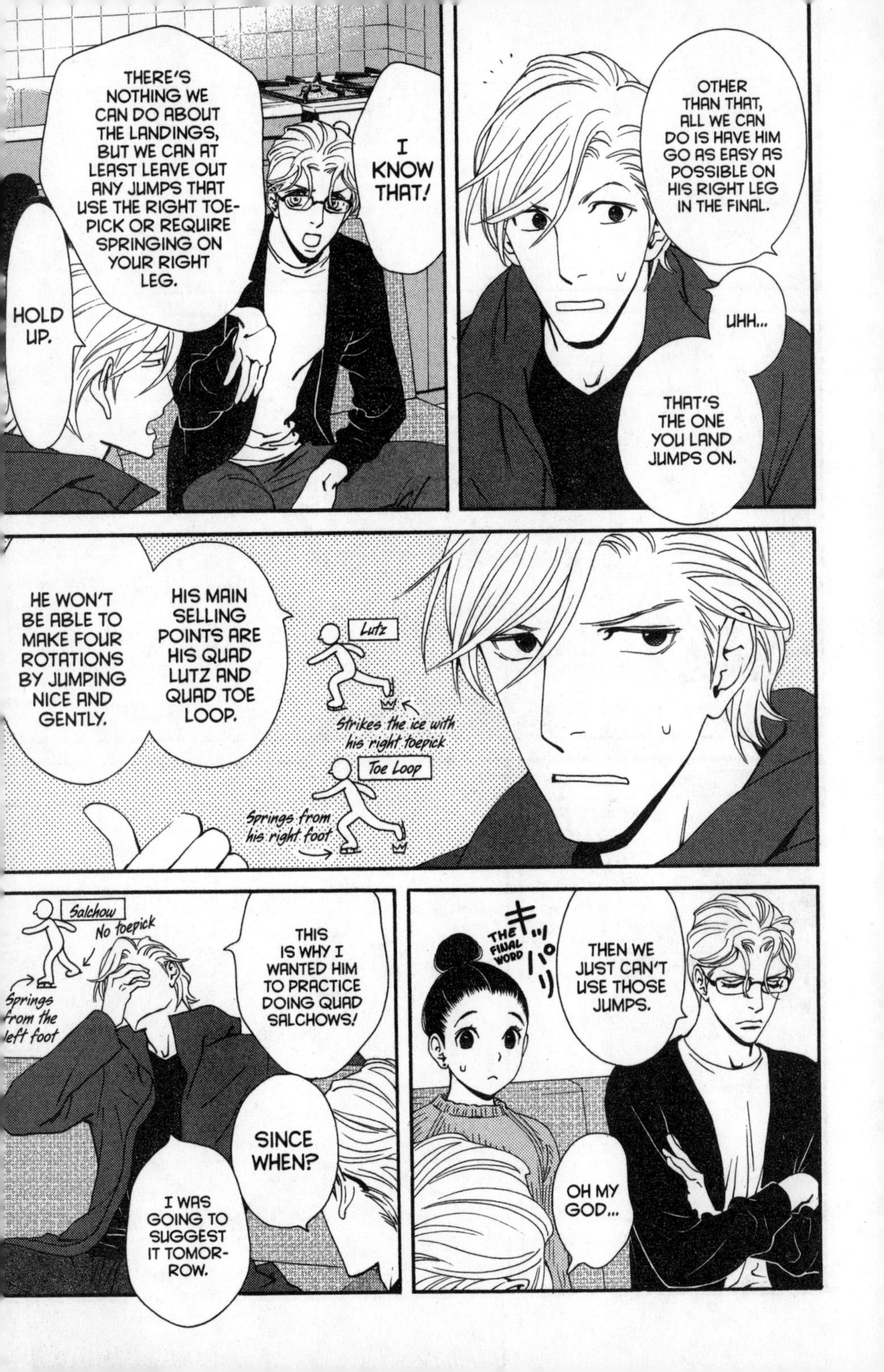
OTHER THAN THAT, ALL WE CAN DO IS HAVE HIM GO AS EASY AS POSSIBLE ON HIS RIGHT LEG IN THE FINAL.
UHH...
THAT'S THE ONE YOU LAND JUMPS ON.
THERE'S NOTHING WE CAN DO ABOUT THE LANDINGS, BUT WE CAN AT LEAST LEAVE OUT ANY JUMPS THAT USE THE RIGHT TOE-PICK OR REQUIRE SPRINGING ON YOUR RIGHT LEG.
I KNOW THAT!
HOLD UP.
HIS MAIN SELLING POINTS ARE HIS QUAD LUTZ AND QUAD TOE LOOP.
Lutz
Strikes the ice with his right toepick
Toe Loop
Springs from his right foot
HE WON'T BE ABLE TO MAKE FOUR ROTATIONS BY JUMPING NICE AND GENTLY.
THE FINAL WORD
キッパリ
THEN WE JUST CAN'T USE THOSE JUMPS.
OH MY GOD...
THIS IS WHY I WANTED HIM TO PRACTICE DOING QUAD SALCHOWS!
SINCE WHEN?
I WAS GOING TO SUGGEST IT TOMORROW.
Salchow
No toepick
Springs from the left foot

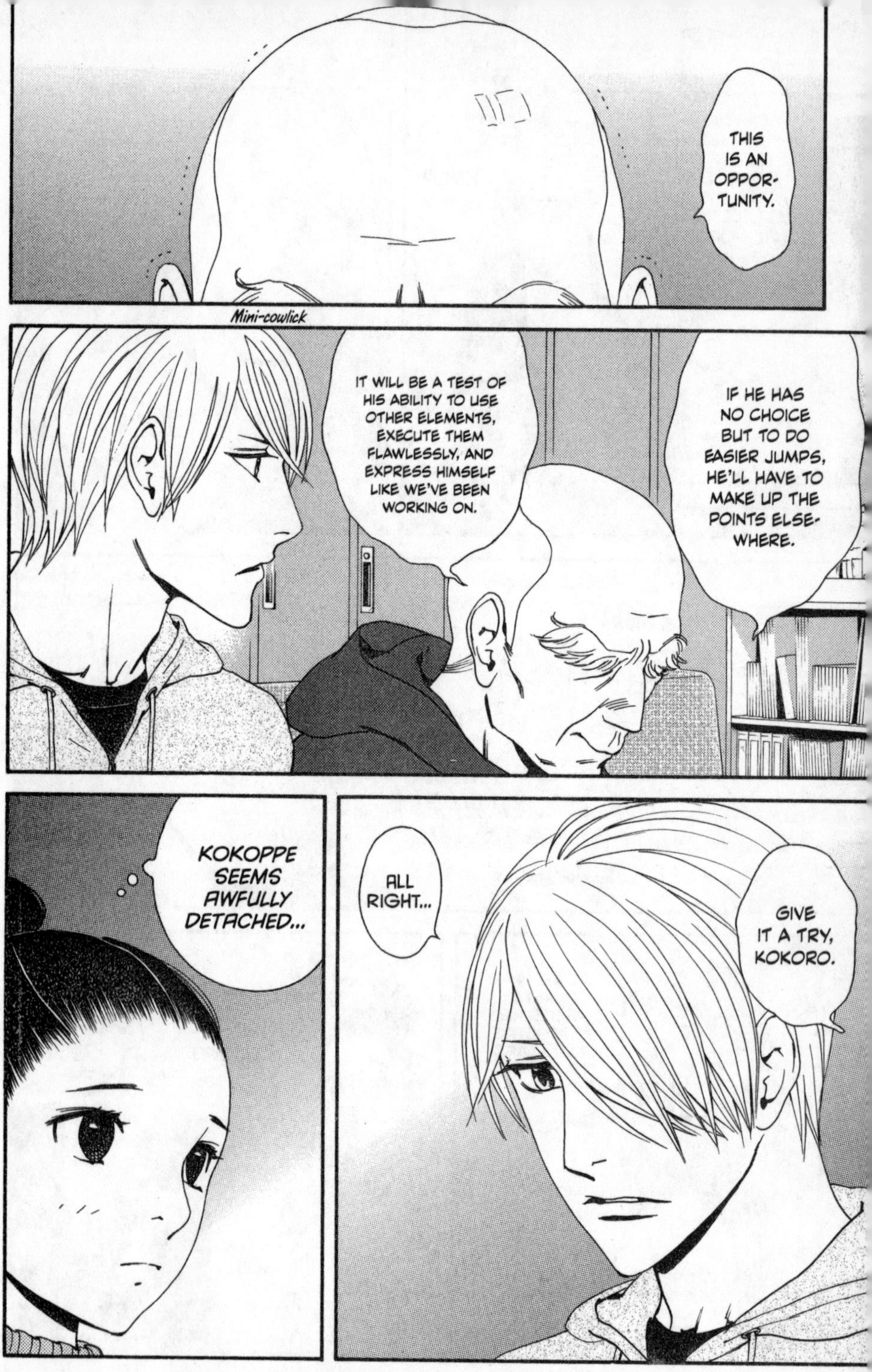
THIS IS AN OPPOR-TUNITY.
Mini-cowlick
IF HE HAS NO CHOICE BUT TO DO EASIER JUMPS, HE'LL HAVE TO MAKE UP THE POINTS ELSE-WHERE.
IT WILL BE A TEST OF HIS ABILITY TO USE OTHER ELEMENTS, EXECUTE THEM FLAWLESSLY, AND EXPRESS HIMSELF LIKE WE'VE BEEN WORKING ON.
GIVE IT A TRY, KOKORO.
ALL RIGHT...
KOKOPPE SEEMS AWFULLY DETACHED...

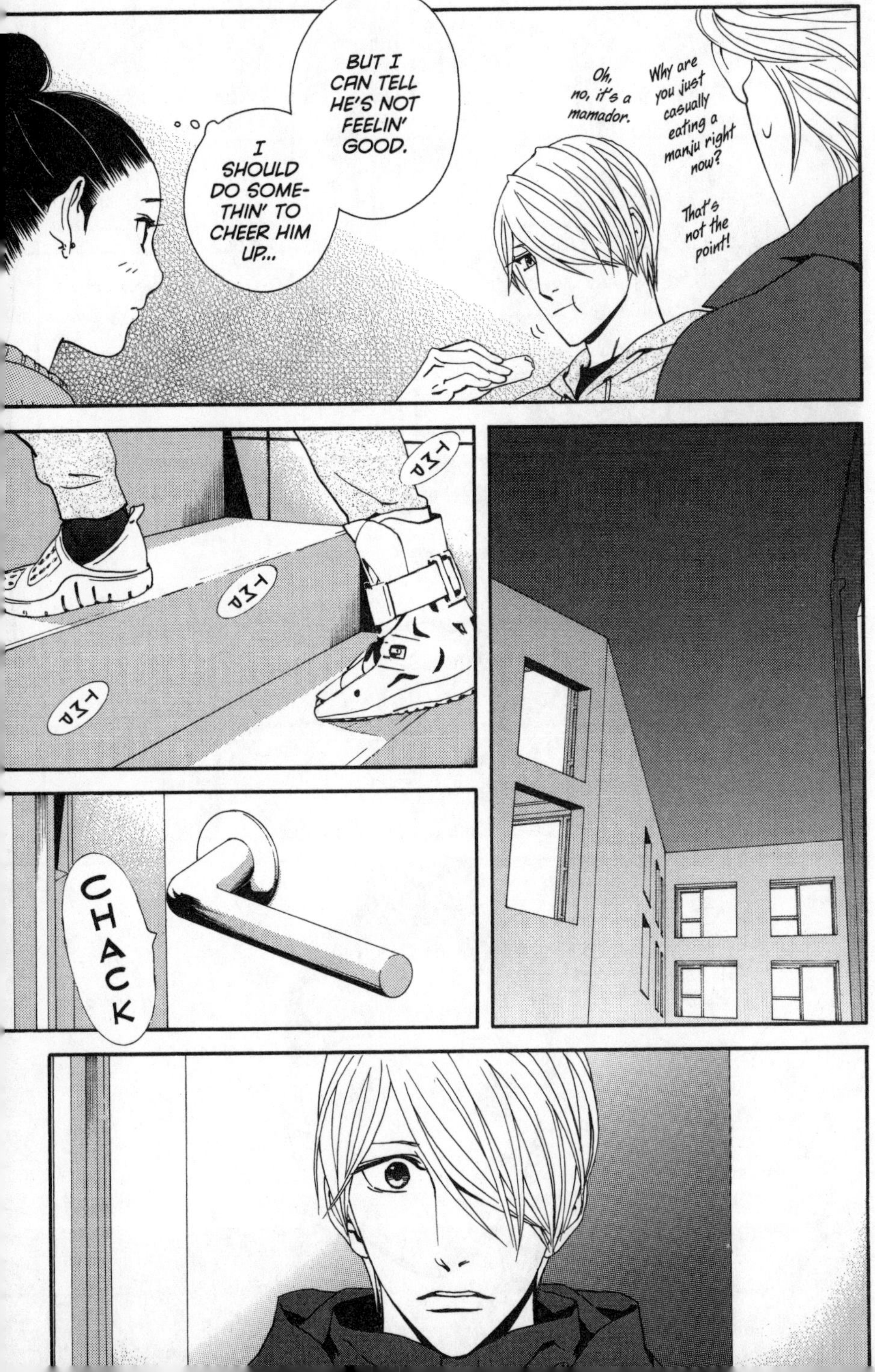
Why are you just casually eating a manju right now?
Oh, no, it's a mamador.
That's not the point!
BUT I CAN TELL HE'S NOT FEELIN' GOOD.
I SHOULD DO SOME-THIN' TO CHEER HIM UP...
TMP
TMP
TMP
CHACK

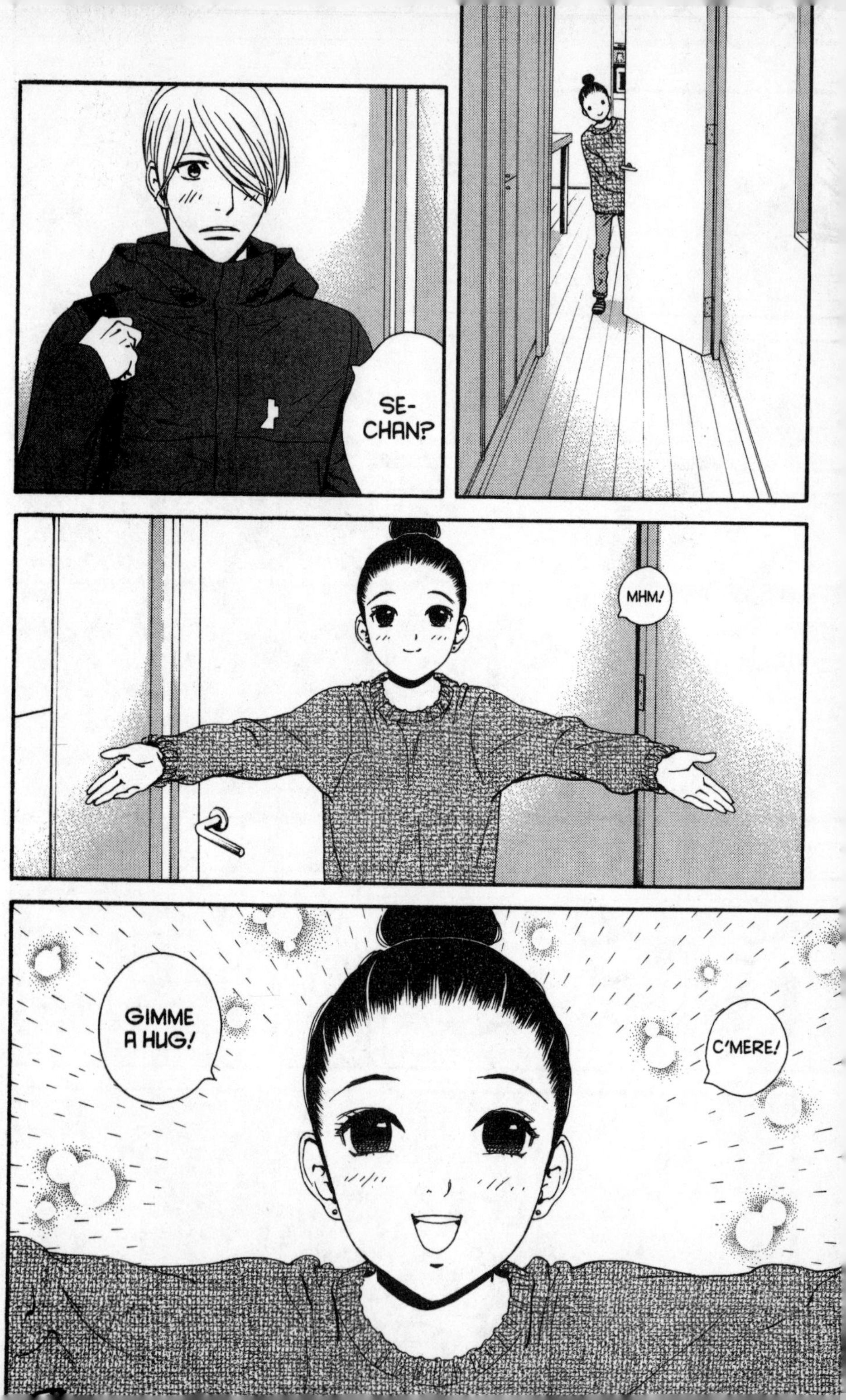
SE-CHAN?
MHM!
C'MERE!
GIMME A HUG!

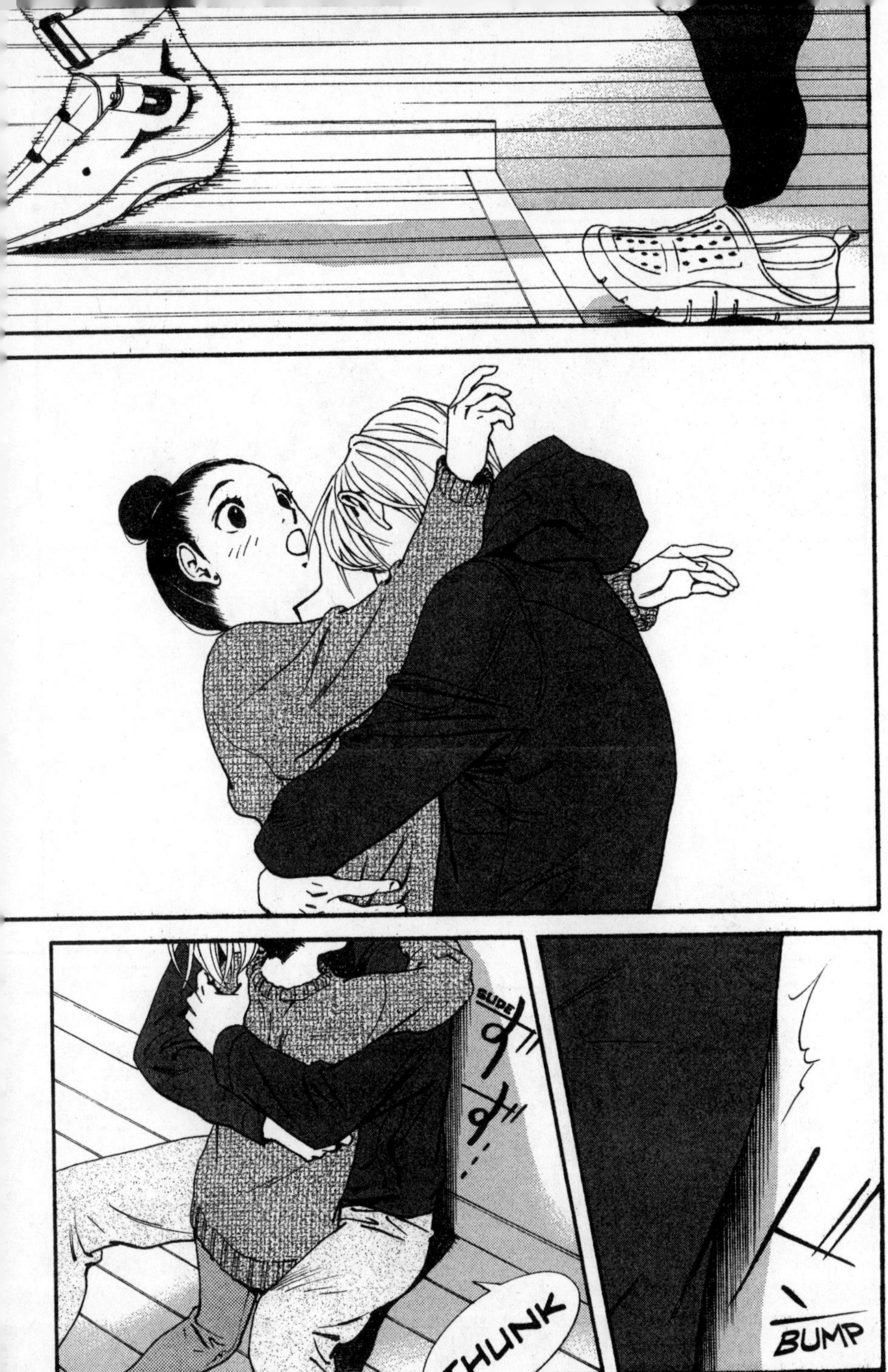
BUMP
SLIDE
THUNK

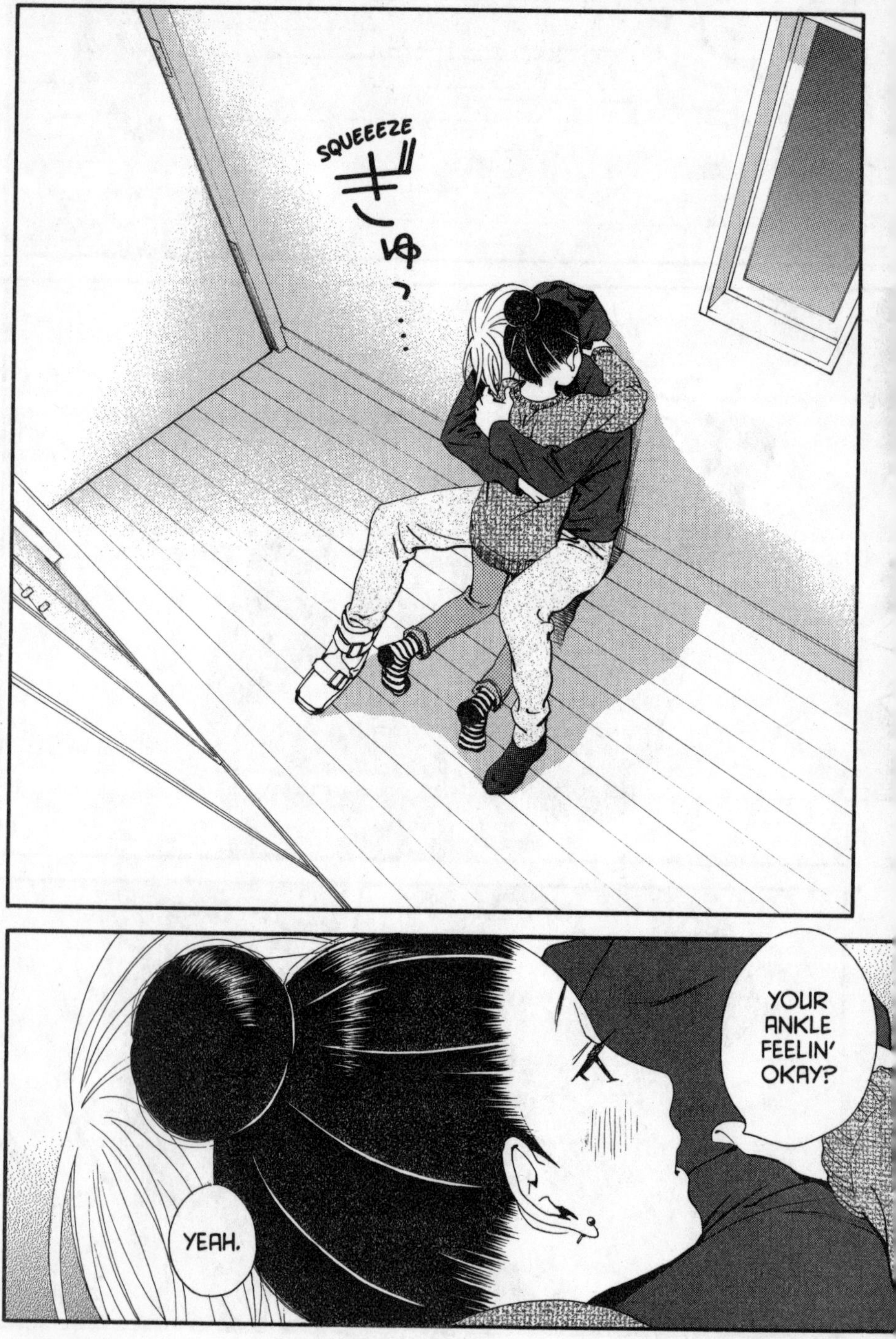
SQUEEEZE
ぎゅっ…
YOUR ANKLE FEELIN' OKAY?
YEAH.

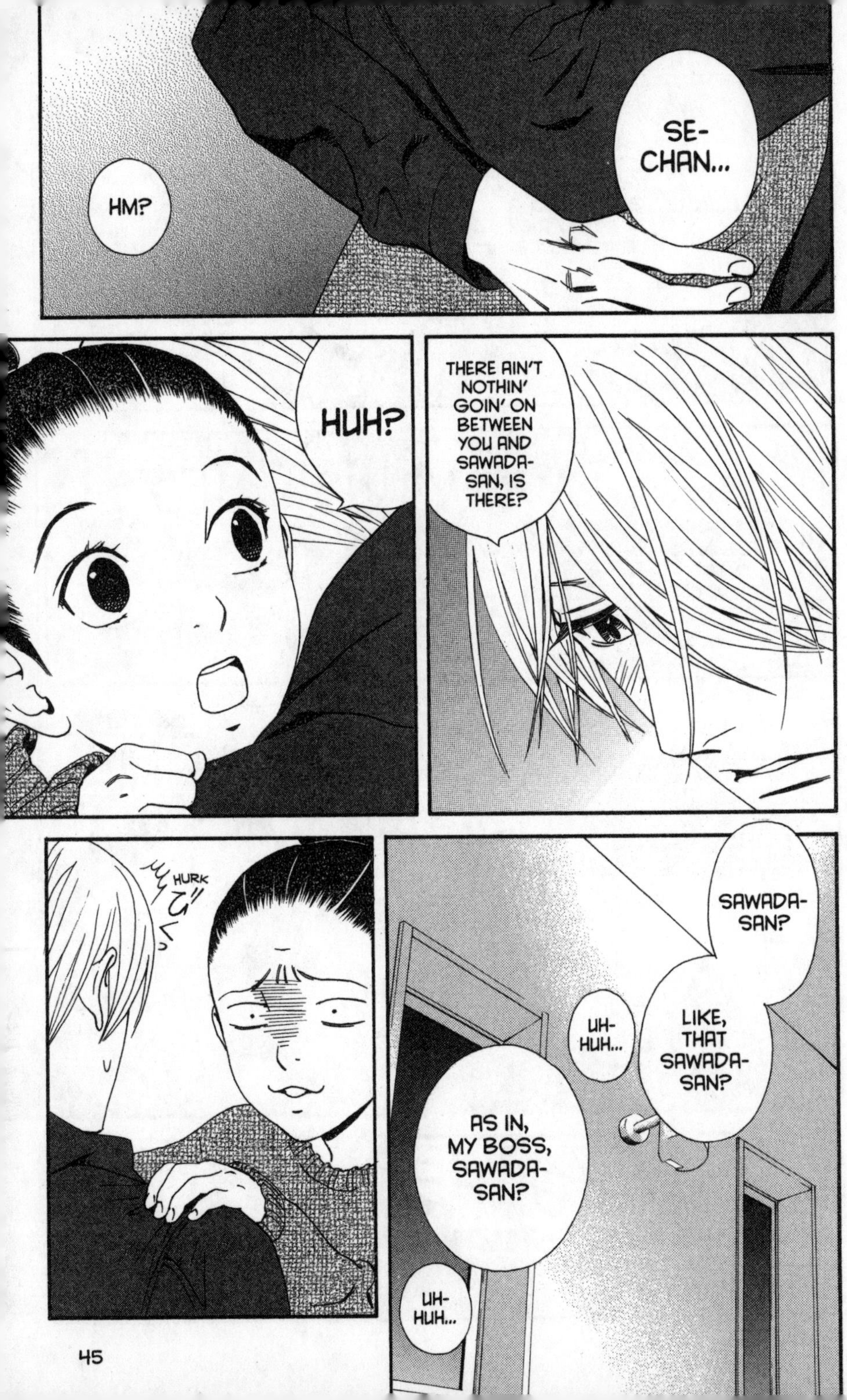
SE-CHAN...
HM?
THERE AIN'T NOTHIN' GOIN' ON BETWEEN YOU AND SAWADA-SAN, IS THERE?
HUH?
SAWADA-SAN?
LIKE, THAT SAWADA-SAN?
UH-HUH...
AS IN, MY BOSS, SAWADA-SAN?
UH-HUH...
HURK

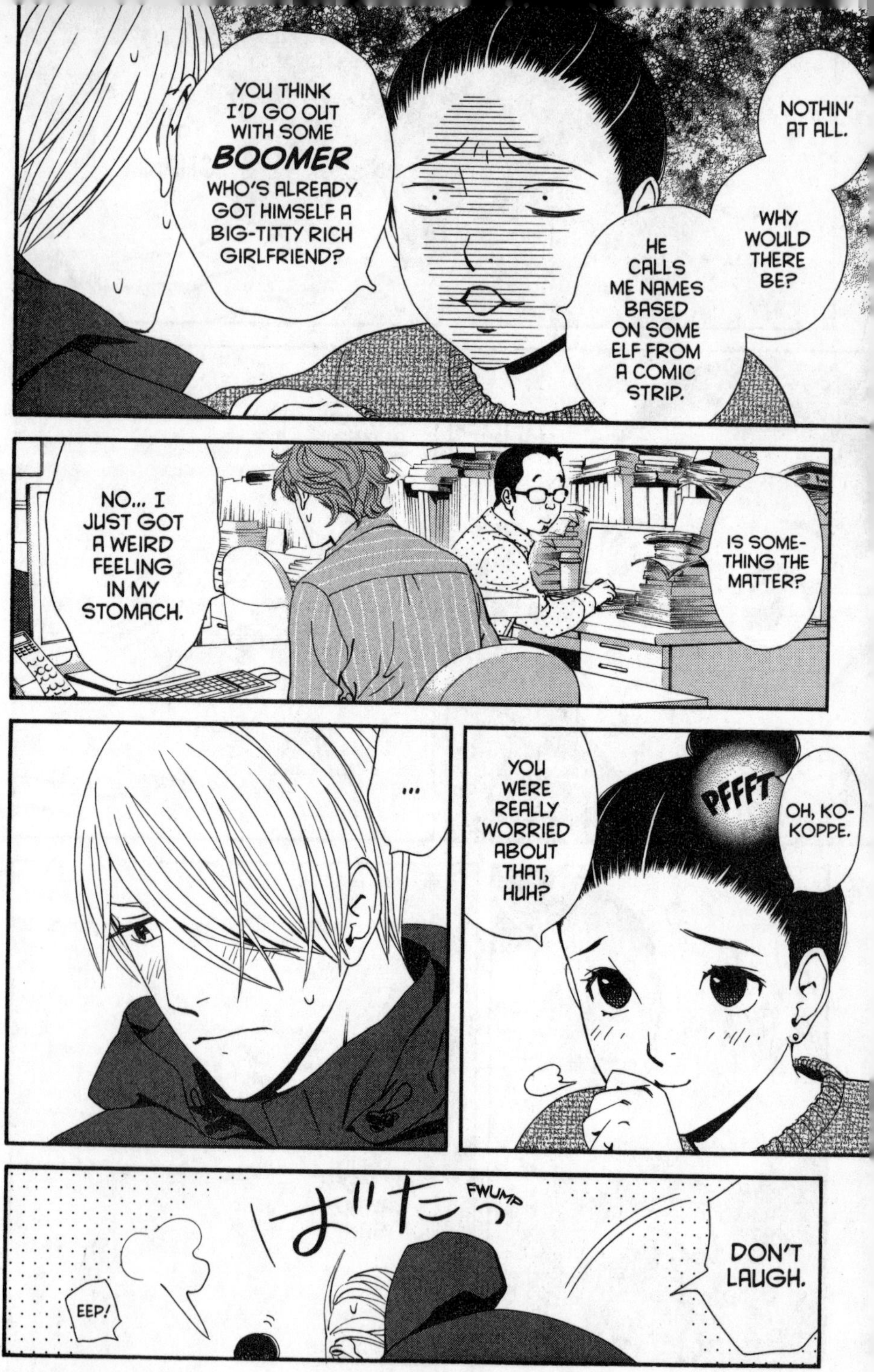
NOTHIN' AT ALL.
WHY WOULD THERE BE?
HE CALLS ME NAMES BASED ON SOME ELF FROM A COMIC STRIP.
YOU THINK I'D GO OUT WITH SOME BOOMER WHO'S ALREADY GOT HIMSELF A BIG-TITTY RICH GIRLFRIEND?
IS SOMETHING THE MATTER?
NO... I JUST GOT A WEIRD FEELING IN MY STOMACH.
PFFFT
OH, KOKOPPE.
YOU WERE REALLY WORRIED ABOUT THAT, HUH?
...
DON'T LAUGH.
FWUMP
EEP!

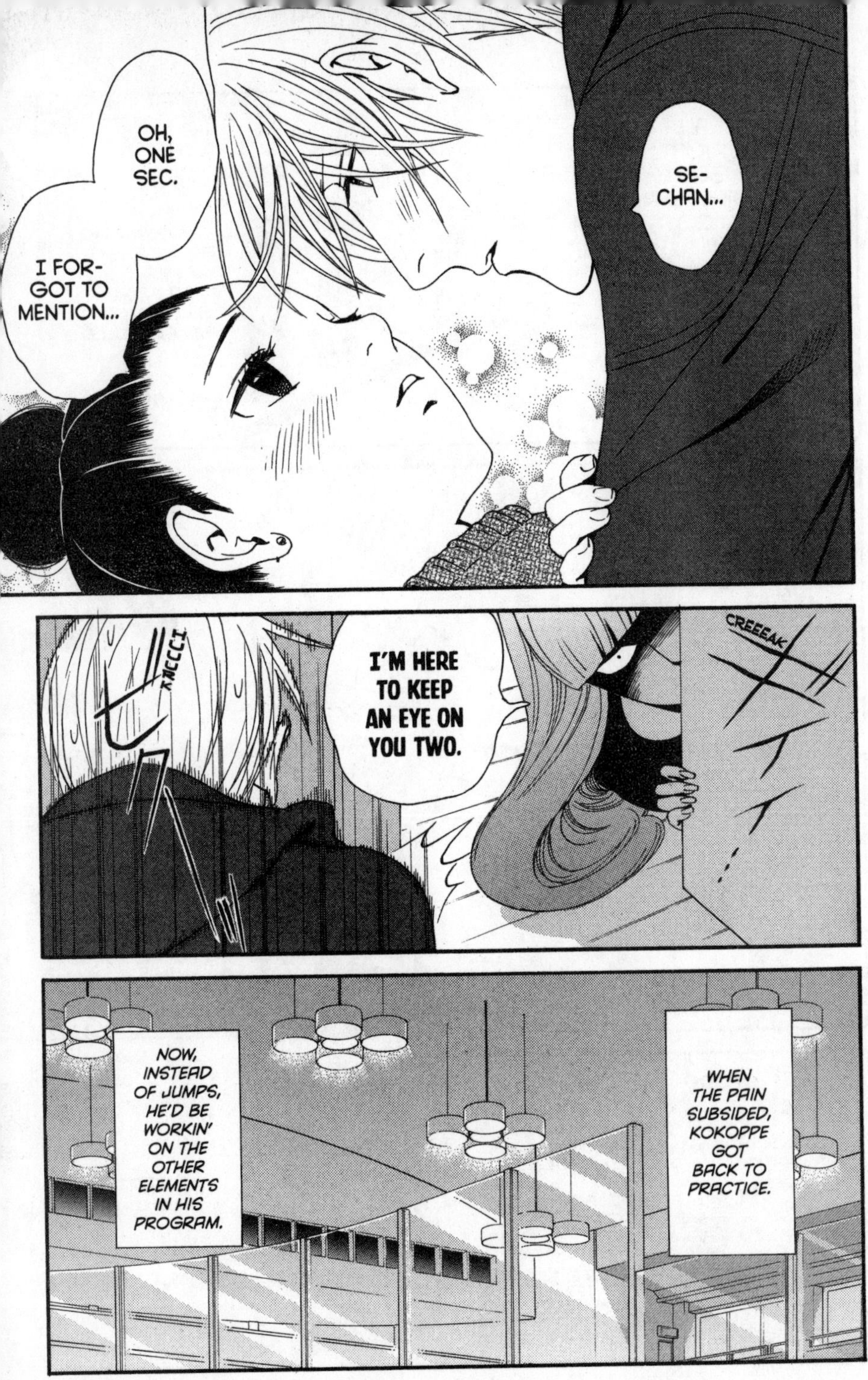
SE-CHAN...
OH, ONE SEC.
I FOR-GOT TO MENTION...
CREEEAK
I'M HERE TO KEEP AN EYE ON YOU TWO.
WHEN THE PAIN SUBSIDED, KOKOPPE GOT BACK TO PRACTICE.
NOW, INSTEAD OF JUMPS, HE'D BE WORKIN' ON THE OTHER ELEMENTS IN HIS PROGRAM.

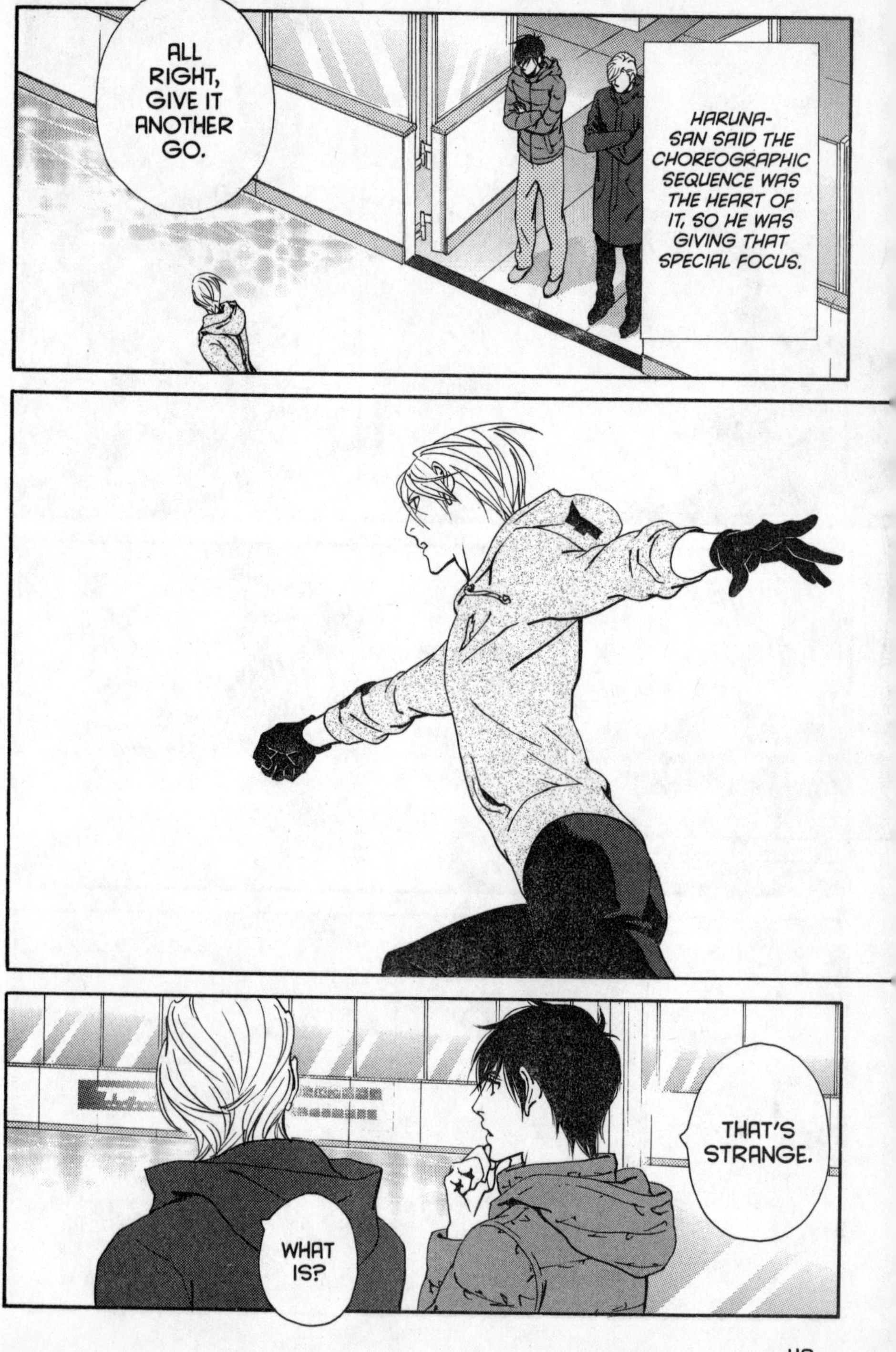
HARUNA-SAN SAID THE CHOREOGRAPHIC SEQUENCE WAS THE HEART OF IT, SO HE WAS GIVING THAT SPECIAL FOCUS.
ALL RIGHT, GIVE IT ANOTHER GO.
THAT'S STRANGE.
WHAT IS?

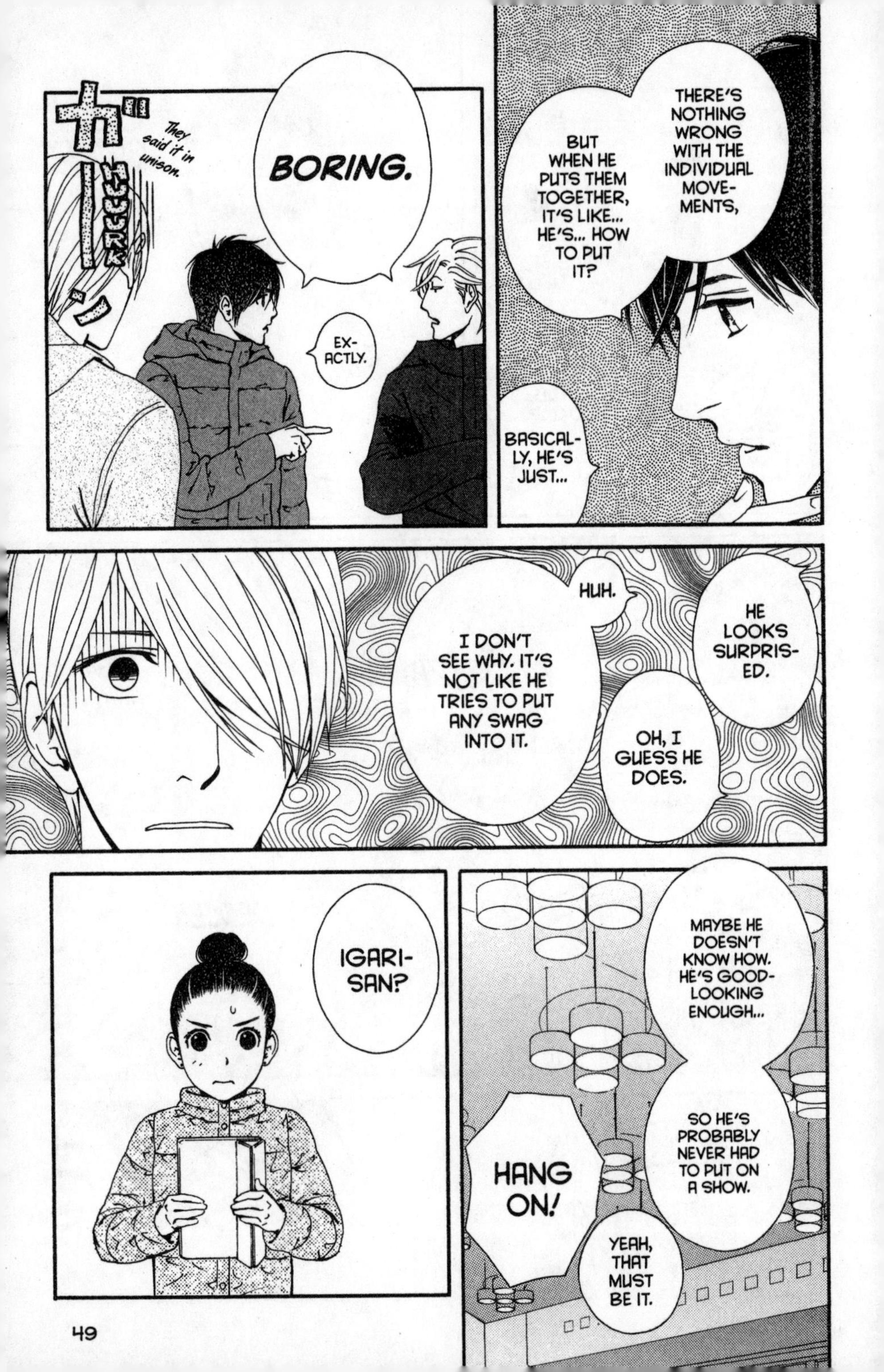
THERE'S NOTHING WRONG WITH THE INDIVIDUAL MOVEMENTS,
BUT WHEN HE PUTS THEM TOGETHER, IT'S LIKE... HE'S... HOW TO PUT IT?
BASICALLY, HE'S JUST...
BORING.
EX-ACTLY.
They said it in unison.
HUUURK
HE LOOKS SURPRISED.
HUH.
OH, I GUESS HE DOES.
I DON'T SEE WHY. IT'S NOT LIKE HE TRIES TO PUT ANY SWAG INTO IT.
MAYBE HE DOESN'T KNOW HOW. HE'S GOOD-LOOKING ENOUGH...
SO HE'S PROBABLY NEVER HAD TO PUT ON A SHOW.
YEAH, THAT MUST BE IT.
HANG ON!
IGARI-SAN?

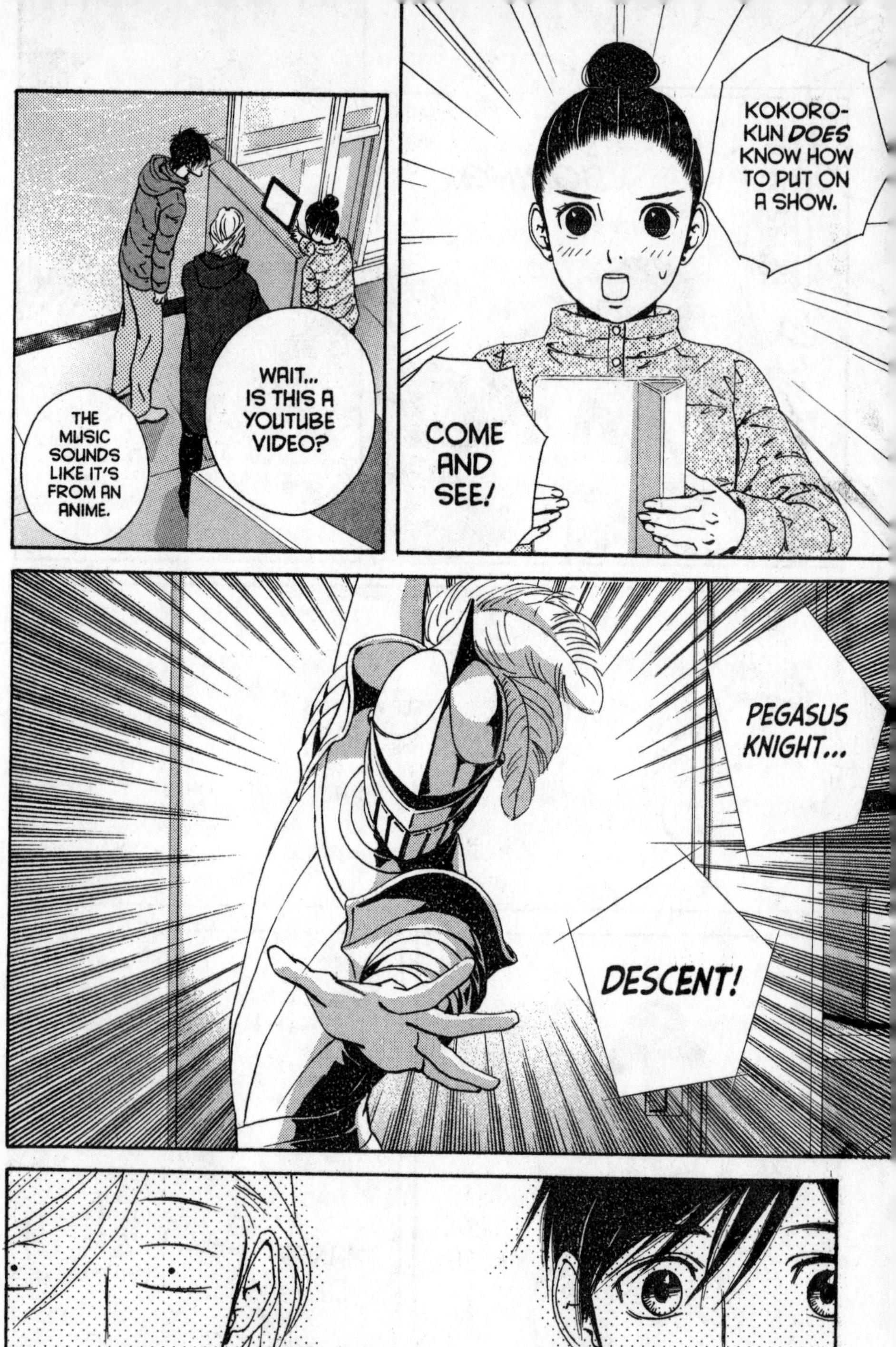
KOKORO-KUN *DOES* KNOW HOW TO PUT ON A SHOW.
COME AND SEE!
WAIT... IS THIS A YOUTUBE VIDEO?
THE MUSIC SOUNDS LIKE IT'S FROM AN ANIME.
PEGASUS KNIGHT...
DESCENT!

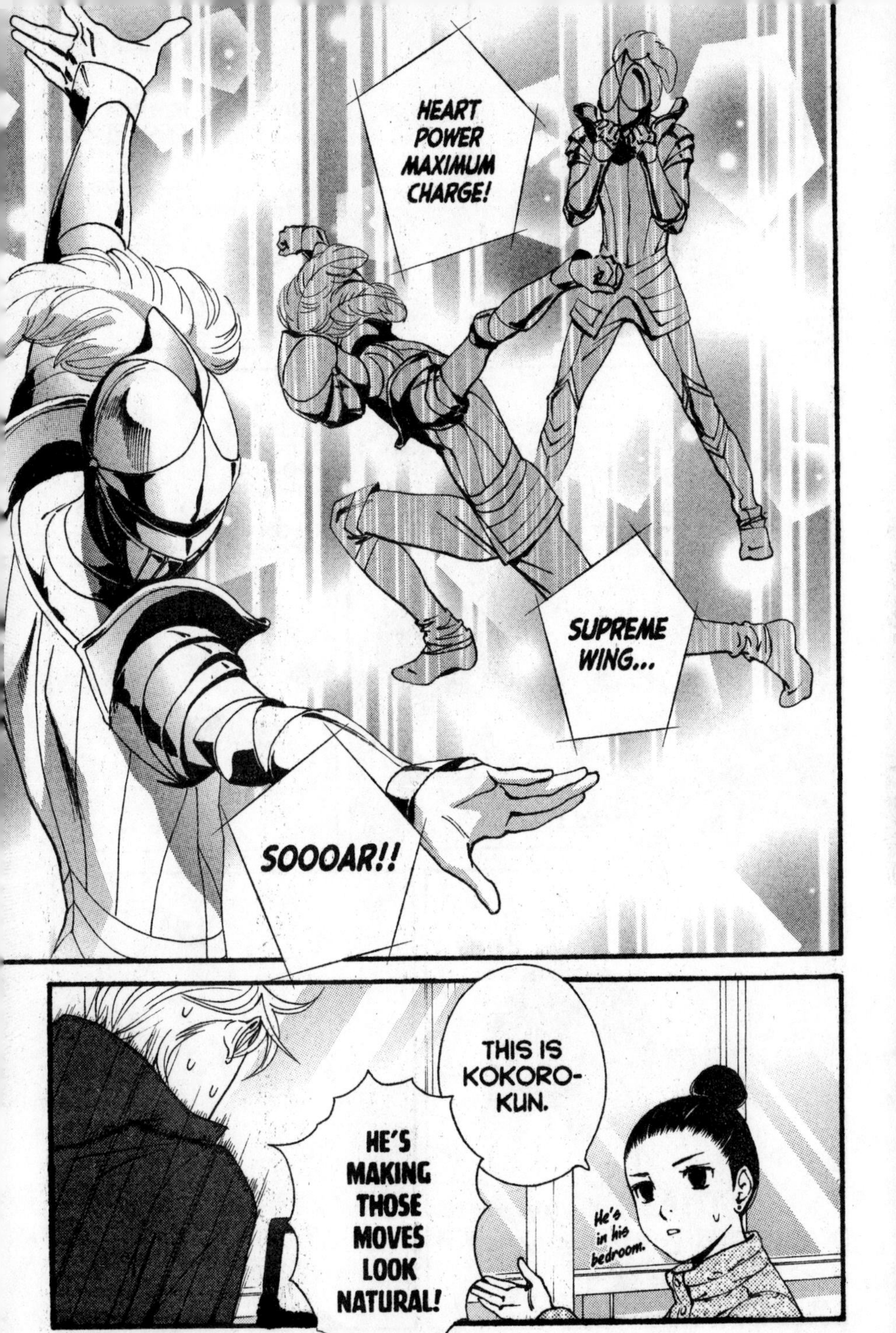
HEART POWER MAXIMUM CHARGE!
SUPREME WING...
SOOOAR!!
THIS IS KOKORO-KUN.
He's in his bedroom.
HE'S MAKING THOSE MOVES LOOK NATURAL!

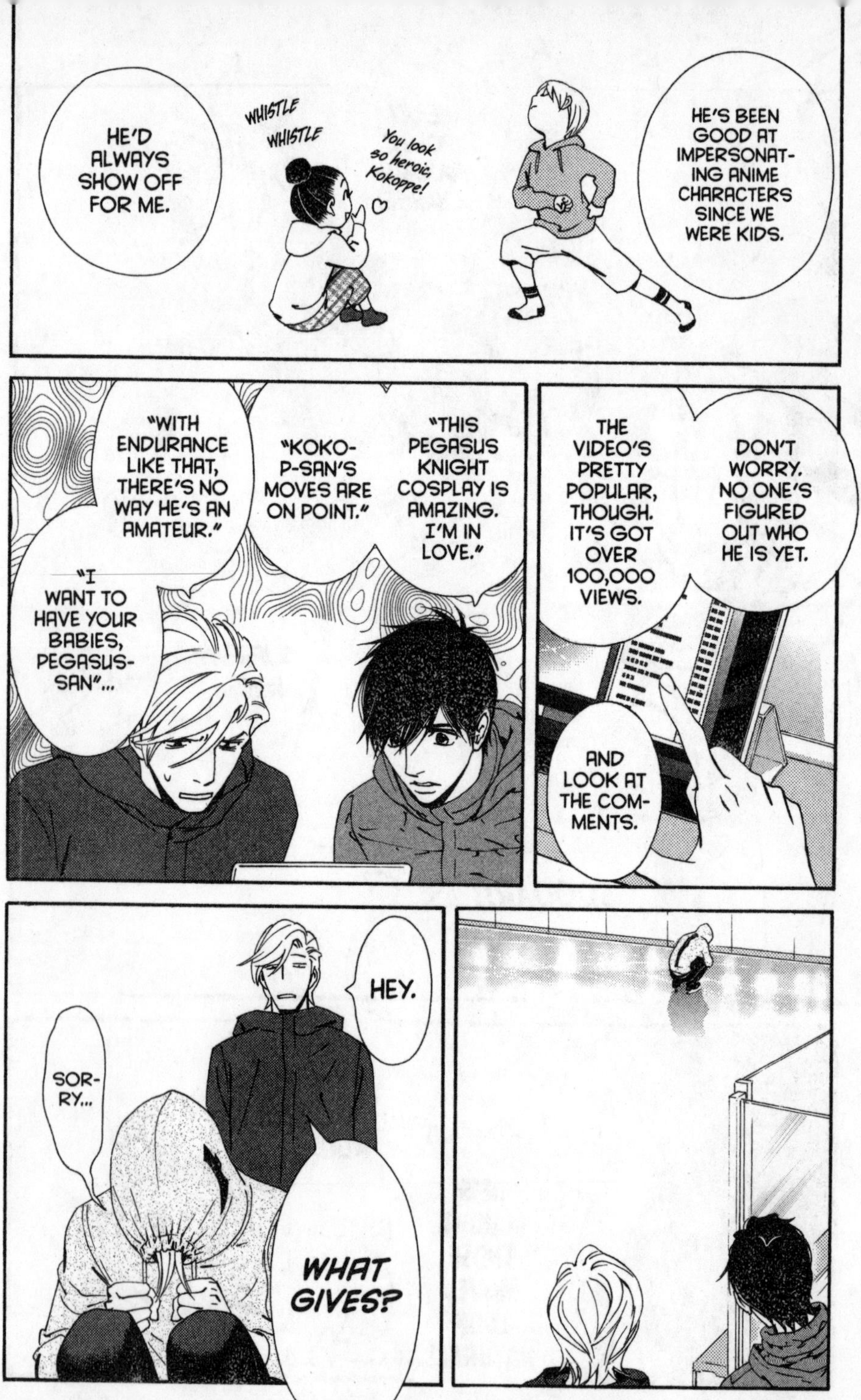
HE'S BEEN GOOD AT IMPERSONAT-ING ANIME CHARACTERS SINCE WE WERE KIDS.
You look so heroic, Kokoppe!
WHISTLE
WHISTLE
HE'D ALWAYS SHOW OFF FOR ME.
DON'T WORRY. NO ONE'S FIGURED OUT WHO HE IS YET.
THE VIDEO'S PRETTY POPULAR, THOUGH. IT'S GOT OVER 100,000 VIEWS.
AND LOOK AT THE COM-MENTS.
"THIS PEGASUS KNIGHT COSPLAY IS AMAZING. I'M IN LOVE."
"KOKO-P-SAN'S MOVES ARE ON POINT."
"WITH ENDURANCE LIKE THAT, THERE'S NO WAY HE'S AN AMATEUR."
"I WANT TO HAVE YOUR BABIES, PEGASUS-SAN"...
HEY.
WHAT GIVES?
SORRY...

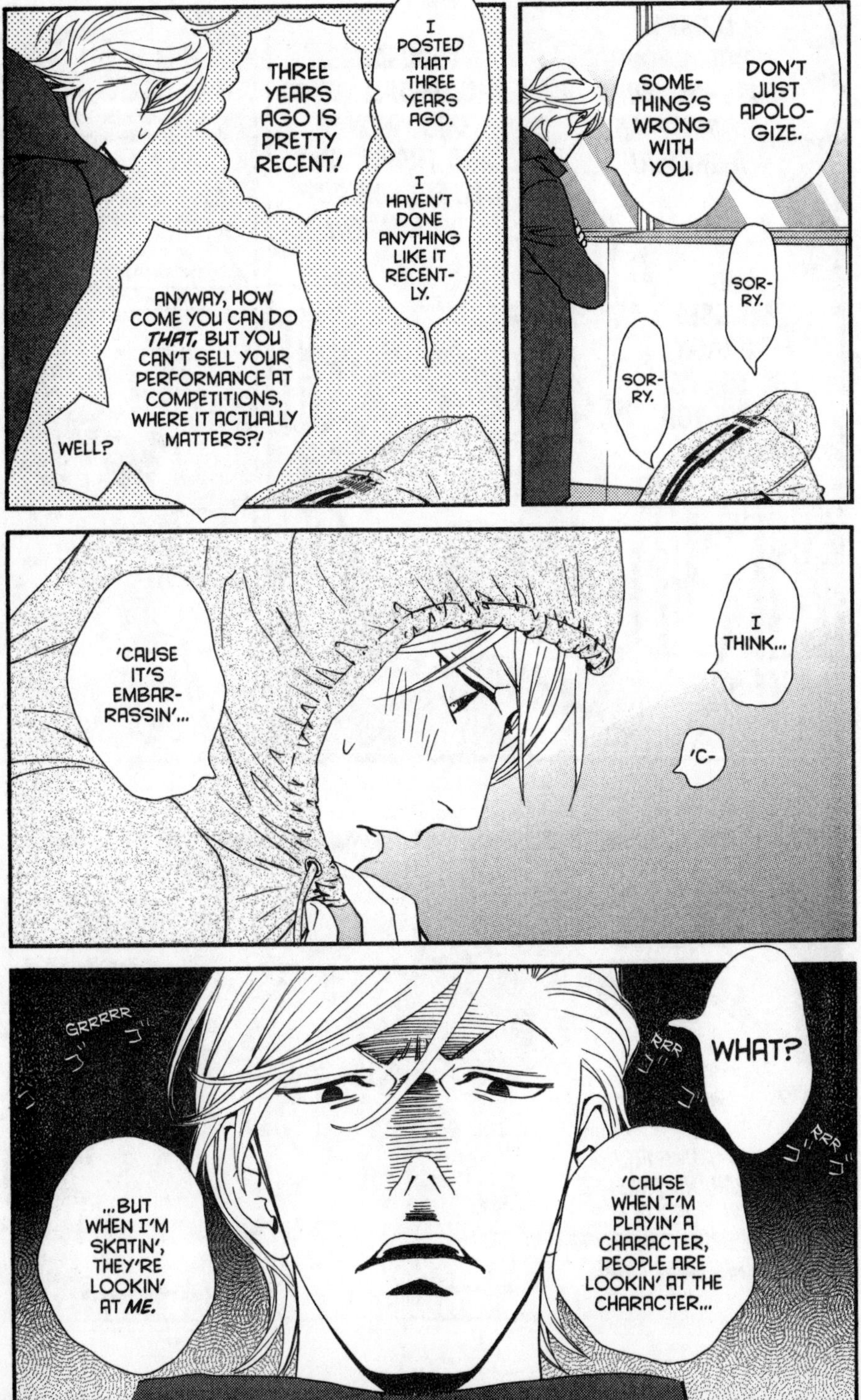
DON'T JUST APOLOGIZE.
SOMETHING'S WRONG WITH YOU.
SORRY.
SORRY.
I POSTED THAT THREE YEARS AGO.
THREE YEARS AGO IS PRETTY RECENT!
I HAVEN'T DONE ANYTHING LIKE IT RECENTLY.
ANYWAY, HOW COME YOU CAN DO *THAT,* BUT YOU CAN'T SELL YOUR PERFORMANCE AT COMPETITIONS, WHERE IT ACTUALLY MATTERS?!
WELL?
I THINK...
'C-
'CAUSE IT'S EMBARRASSIN'...
WHAT?
RRR
RRR
'CAUSE WHEN I'M PLAYIN' A CHARACTER, PEOPLE ARE LOOKIN' AT THE CHARACTER...
GRRRRR
...BUT WHEN I'M SKATIN', THEY'RE LOOKIN' AT *ME.*

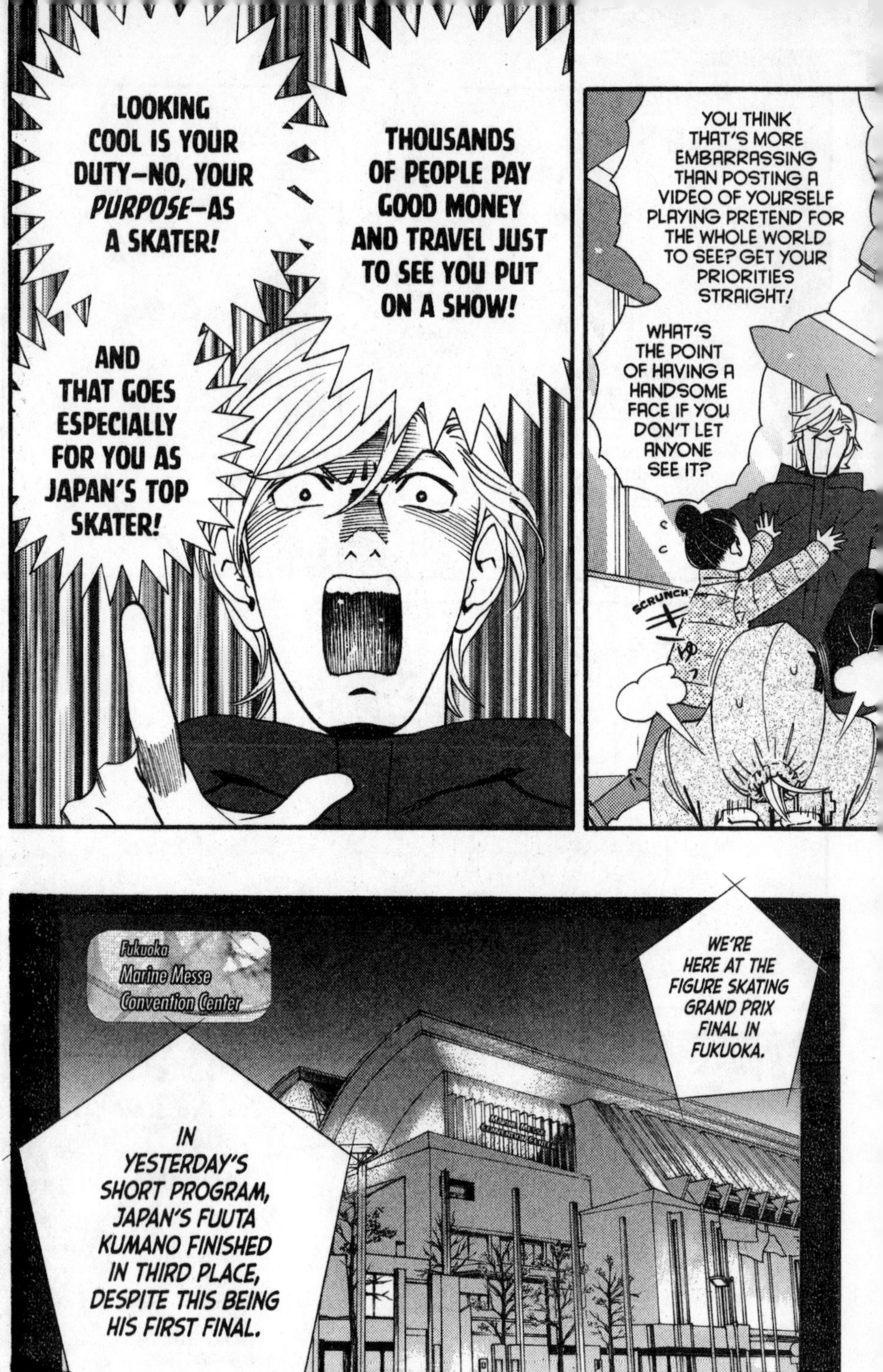
YOU THINK THAT'S MORE EMBARRASSING THAN POSTING A VIDEO OF YOURSELF PLAYING PRETEND FOR THE WHOLE WORLD TO SEE? GET YOUR PRIORITIES STRAIGHT!
WHAT'S THE POINT OF HAVING A HANDSOME FACE IF YOU DON'T LET ANYONE SEE IT?
SCRUNCH
THOUSANDS OF PEOPLE PAY GOOD MONEY AND TRAVEL JUST TO SEE YOU PUT ON A SHOW!
LOOKING COOL IS YOUR DUTY—NO, YOUR *PURPOSE*—AS A SKATER!
AND THAT GOES ESPECIALLY FOR YOU AS JAPAN'S TOP SKATER!
WE'RE HERE AT THE FIGURE SKATING GRAND PRIX FINAL IN FUKUOKA.
Fukuoka Marine Messe Convention Center
IN YESTERDAY'S SHORT PROGRAM, JAPAN'S FUUTA KUMANO FINISHED IN THIRD PLACE, DESPITE THIS BEING HIS FIRST FINAL.

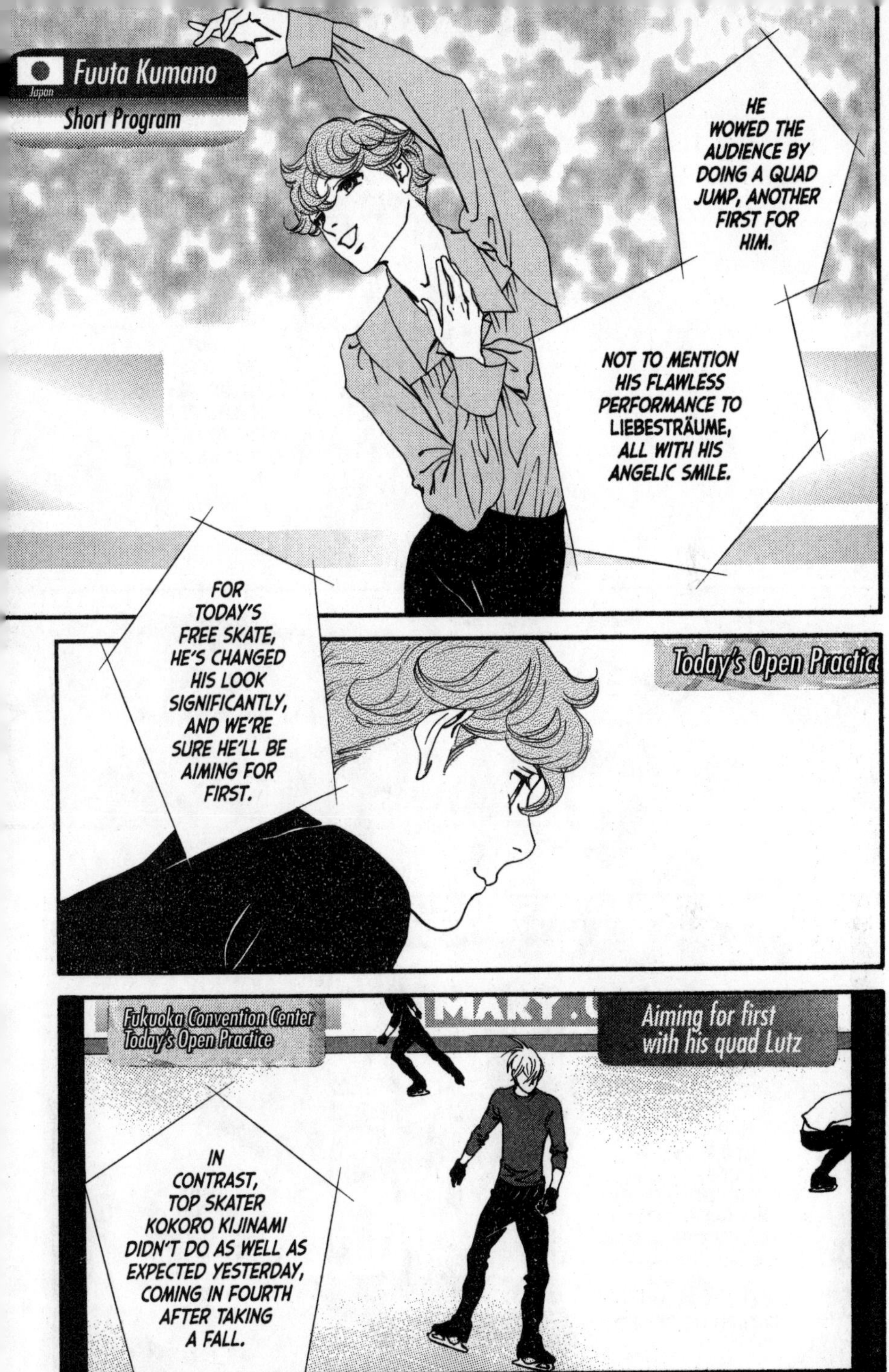
Fuuta Kumano
Japan
Short Program
HE WOWED THE AUDIENCE BY DOING A QUAD JUMP, ANOTHER FIRST FOR HIM.
NOT TO MENTION HIS FLAWLESS PERFORMANCE TO LIEBESTRÄUME, ALL WITH HIS ANGELIC SMILE.
Today's Open Practice
FOR TODAY'S FREE SKATE, HE'S CHANGED HIS LOOK SIGNIFICANTLY, AND WE'RE SURE HE'LL BE AIMING FOR FIRST.
Aiming for first with his quad Lutz
Fukuoka Convention Center Today's Open Practice
IN CONTRAST, TOP SKATER KOKORO KIJINAMI DIDN'T DO AS WELL AS EXPECTED YESTERDAY, COMING IN FOURTH AFTER TAKING A FALL.

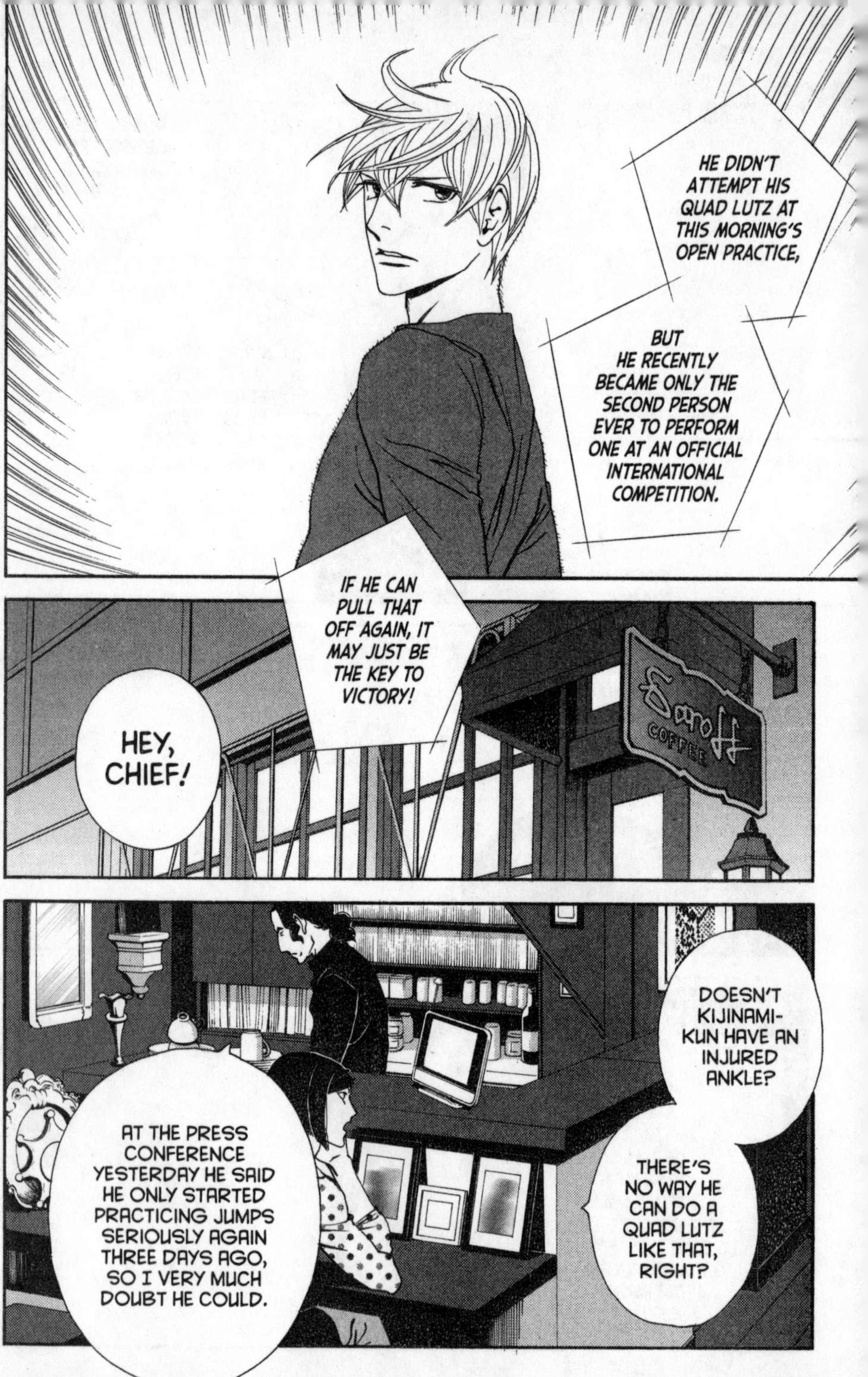
HE DIDN'T ATTEMPT HIS QUAD LUTZ AT THIS MORNING'S OPEN PRACTICE,
BUT HE RECENTLY BECAME ONLY THE SECOND PERSON EVER TO PERFORM ONE AT AN OFFICIAL INTERNATIONAL COMPETITION.
IF HE CAN PULL THAT OFF AGAIN, IT MAY JUST BE THE KEY TO VICTORY!
HEY, CHIEF!
COFFEE
DOESN'T KIJINAMI-KUN HAVE AN INJURED ANKLE?
THERE'S NO WAY HE CAN DO A QUAD LUTZ LIKE THAT, RIGHT?
AT THE PRESS CONFERENCE YESTERDAY HE SAID HE ONLY STARTED PRACTICING JUMPS SERIOUSLY AGAIN THREE DAYS AGO, SO I VERY MUCH DOUBT HE COULD.

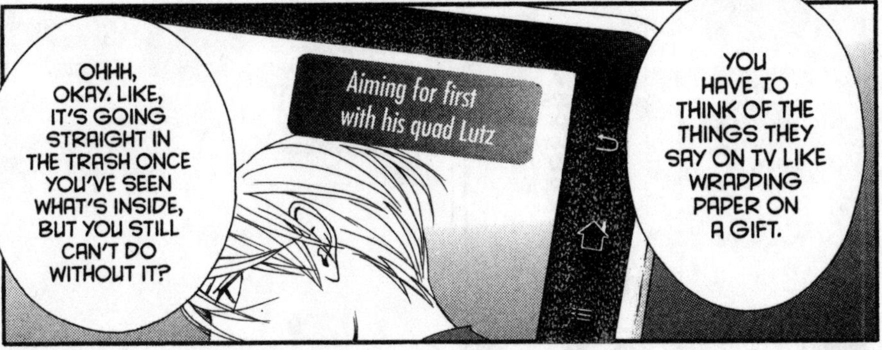
YOU HAVE TO THINK OF THE THINGS THEY SAY ON TV LIKE WRAPPING PAPER ON A GIFT.
Aiming for first with his quad Lutz
OHHH, OKAY. LIKE, IT'S GOING STRAIGHT IN THE TRASH ONCE YOU'VE SEEN WHAT'S INSIDE, BUT YOU STILL CAN'T DO WITHOUT IT?

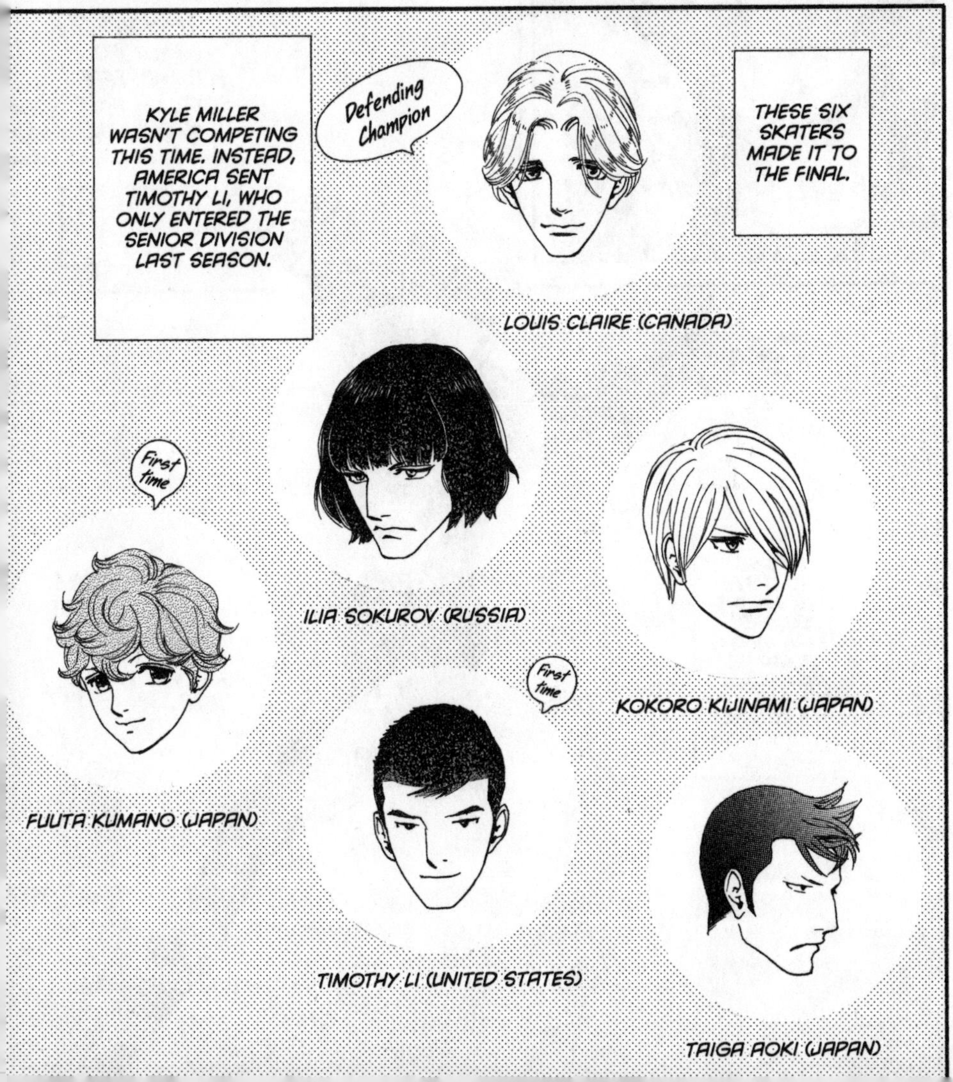
THESE SIX SKATERS MADE IT TO THE FINAL.
Defending Champion
LOUIS CLAIRE (CANADA)
KYLE MILLER WASN'T COMPETING THIS TIME. INSTEAD, AMERICA SENT TIMOTHY LI, WHO ONLY ENTERED THE SENIOR DIVISION LAST SEASON.
KOKORO KIJINAMI (JAPAN)
ILIA SOKUROV (RUSSIA)
First time
FUUTA KUMANO (JAPAN)
TAIGA AOKI (JAPAN)
First time
TIMOTHY LI (UNITED STATES)

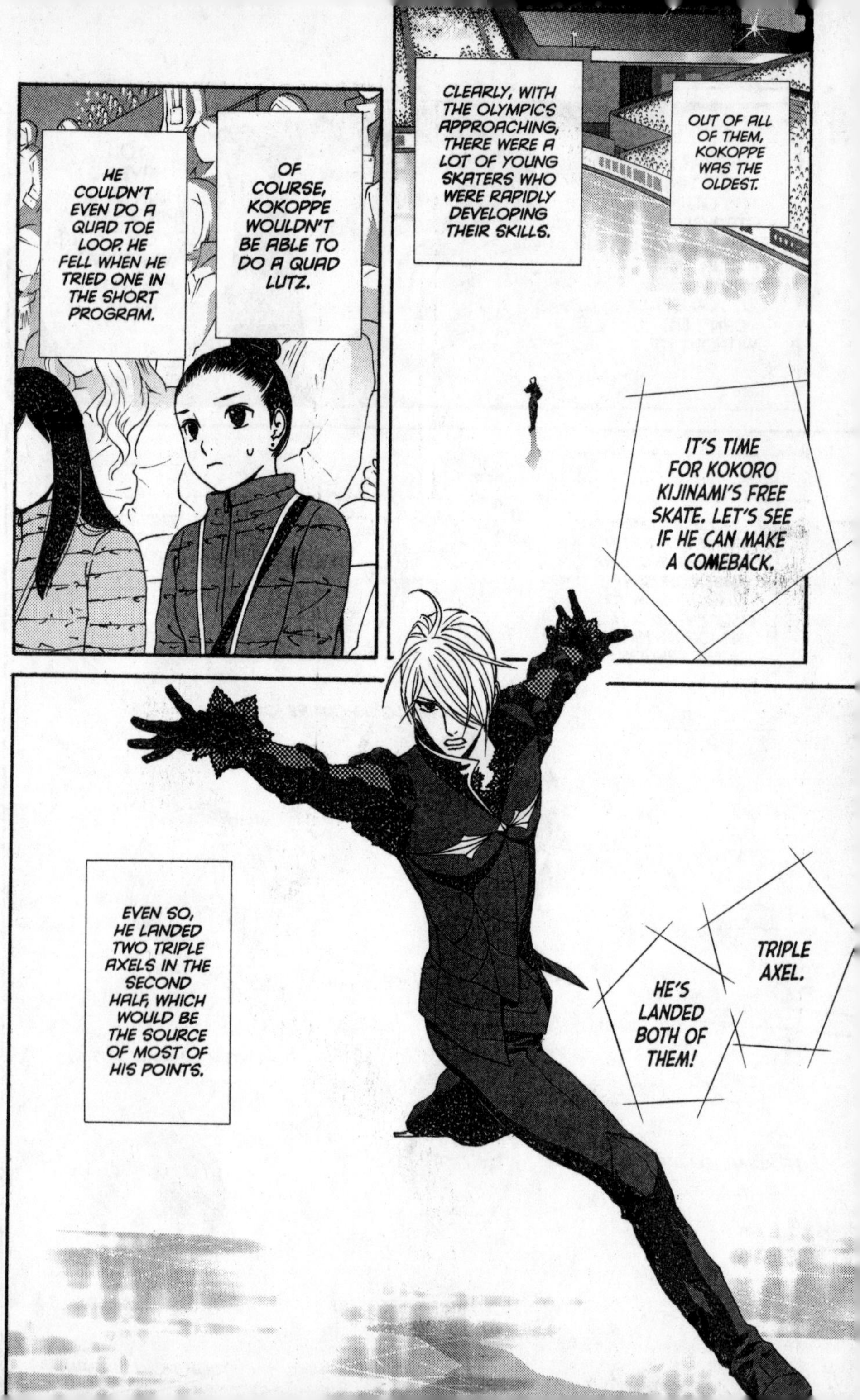
CLEARLY, WITH THE OLYMPICS APPROACHING, THERE WERE A LOT OF YOUNG SKATERS WHO WERE RAPIDLY DEVELOPING THEIR SKILLS.
OUT OF ALL OF THEM, KOKOPPE WAS THE OLDEST.
IT'S TIME FOR KOKORO KIJINAMI'S FREE SKATE. LET'S SEE IF HE CAN MAKE A COMEBACK.
OF COURSE, KOKOPPE WOULDN'T BE ABLE TO DO A QUAD LUTZ.
HE COULDN'T EVEN DO A QUAD TOE LOOP. HE FELL WHEN HE TRIED ONE IN THE SHORT PROGRAM.
TRIPLE AXEL.
HE'S LANDED BOTH OF THEM!
EVEN SO, HE LANDED TWO TRIPLE AXELS IN THE SECOND HALF, WHICH WOULD BE THE SOURCE OF MOST OF HIS POINTS.

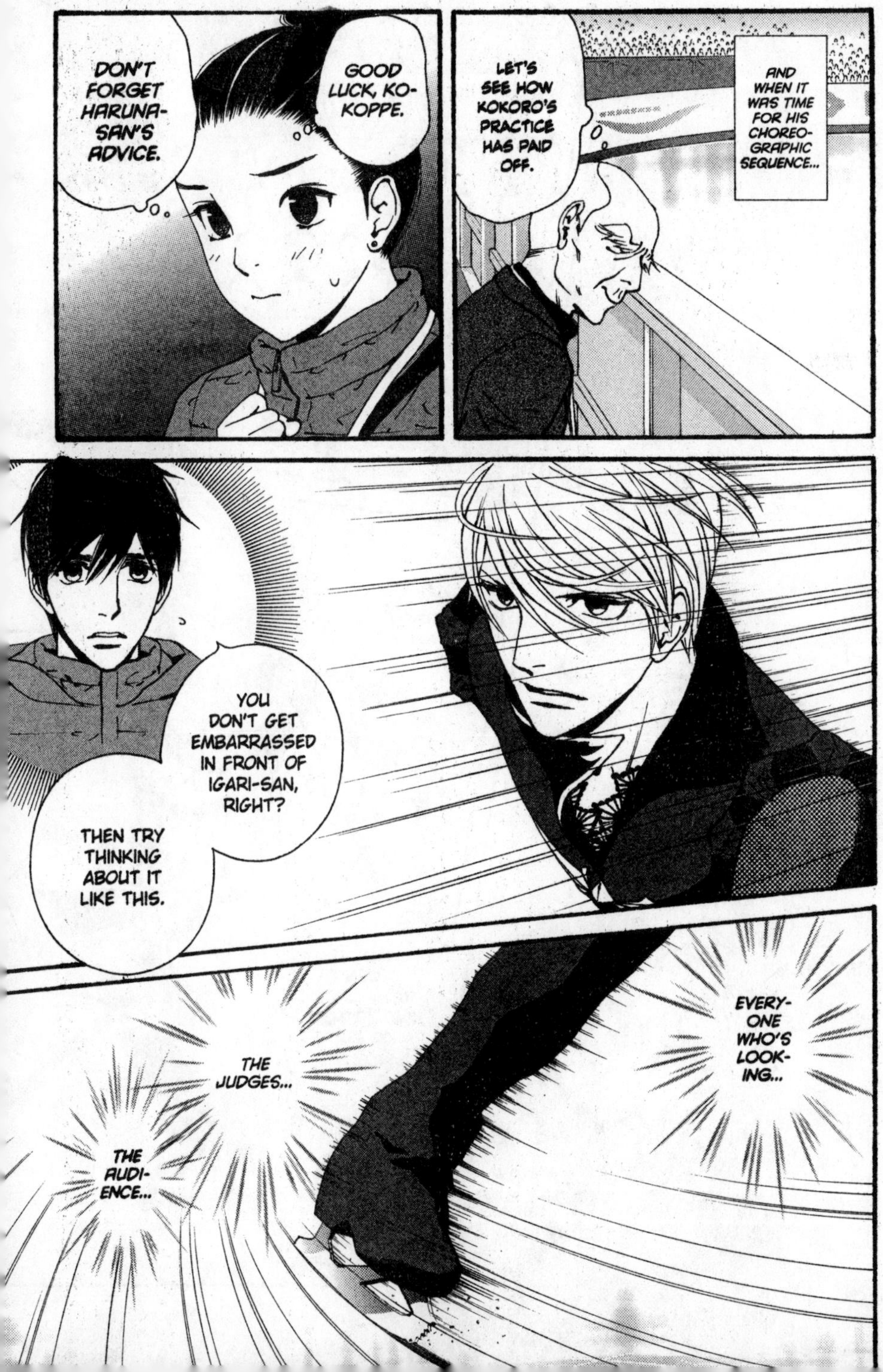
AND WHEN IT WAS TIME FOR HIS CHOREOGRAPHIC SEQUENCE...
LET'S SEE HOW KOKORO'S PRACTICE HAS PAID OFF.
GOOD LUCK, KOKOPPE.
DON'T FORGET HARUNA-SAN'S ADVICE.
YOU DON'T GET EMBARRASSED IN FRONT OF IGARI-SAN, RIGHT?
THEN TRY THINKING ABOUT IT LIKE THIS.
EVERYONE WHO'S LOOKING...
THE JUDGES...
THE AUDIENCE...

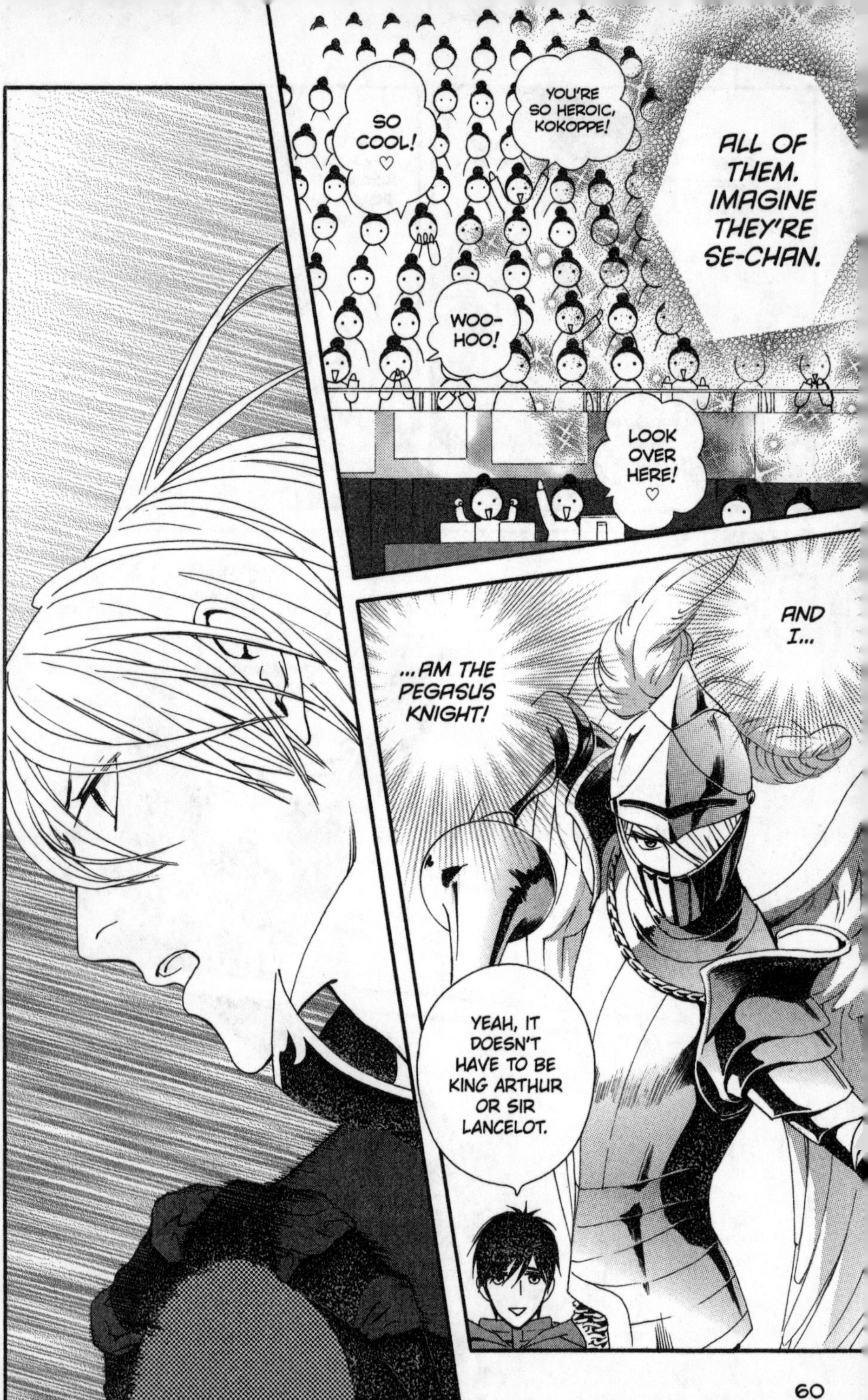
ALL OF THEM. IMAGINE THEY'RE SE-CHAN.
YOU'RE SO HEROIC, KOKOPPE!
SO COOL! ♡
WOO-HOO!
LOOK OVER HERE! ♡
AND I...
...AM THE PEGASUS KNIGHT!
YEAH, IT DOESN'T HAVE TO BE KING ARTHUR OR SIR LANCELOT.

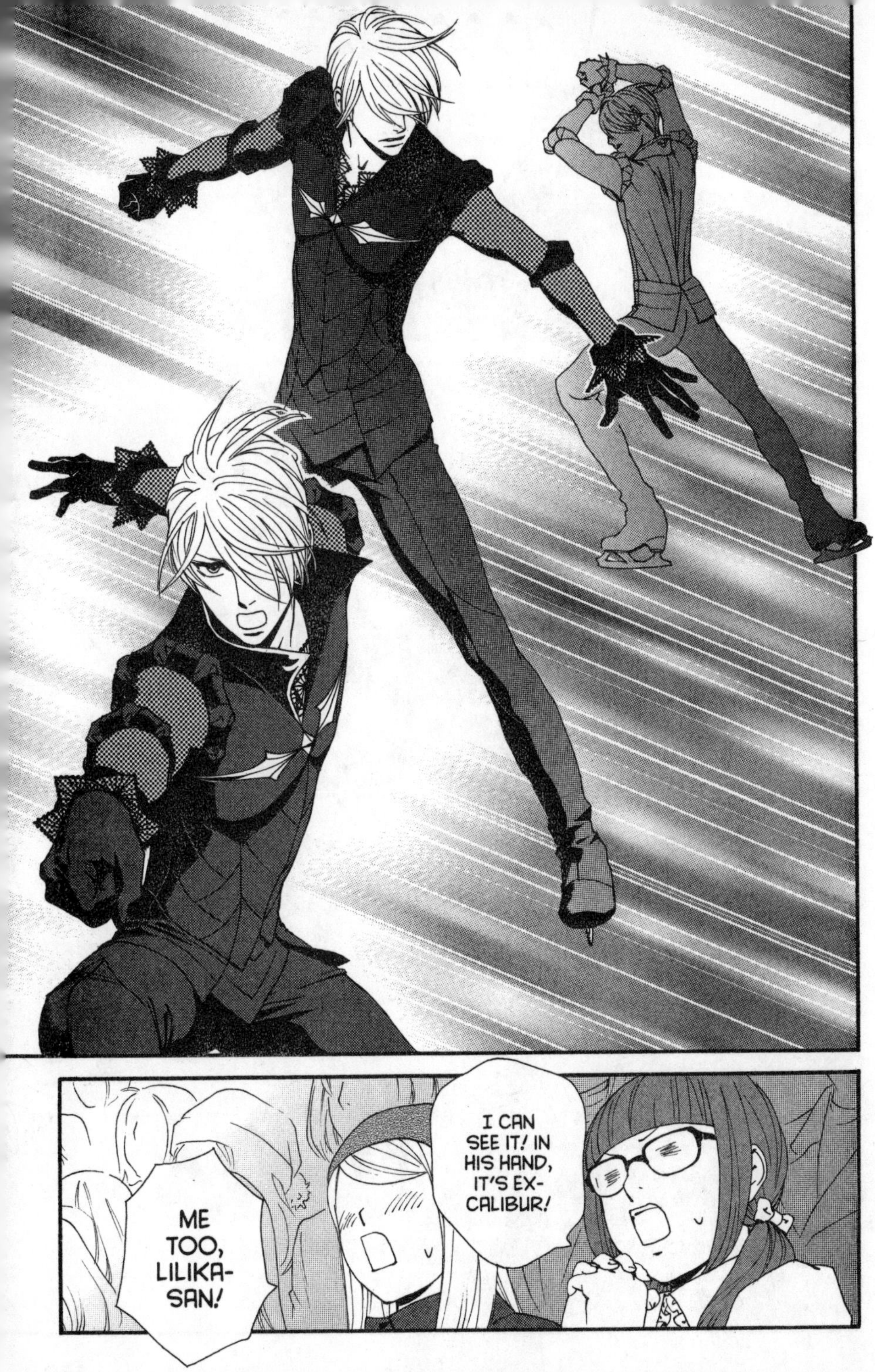
I CAN SEE IT! IN HIS HAND, IT'S EX-CALIBUR!
ME TOO, LILIKA-SAN!

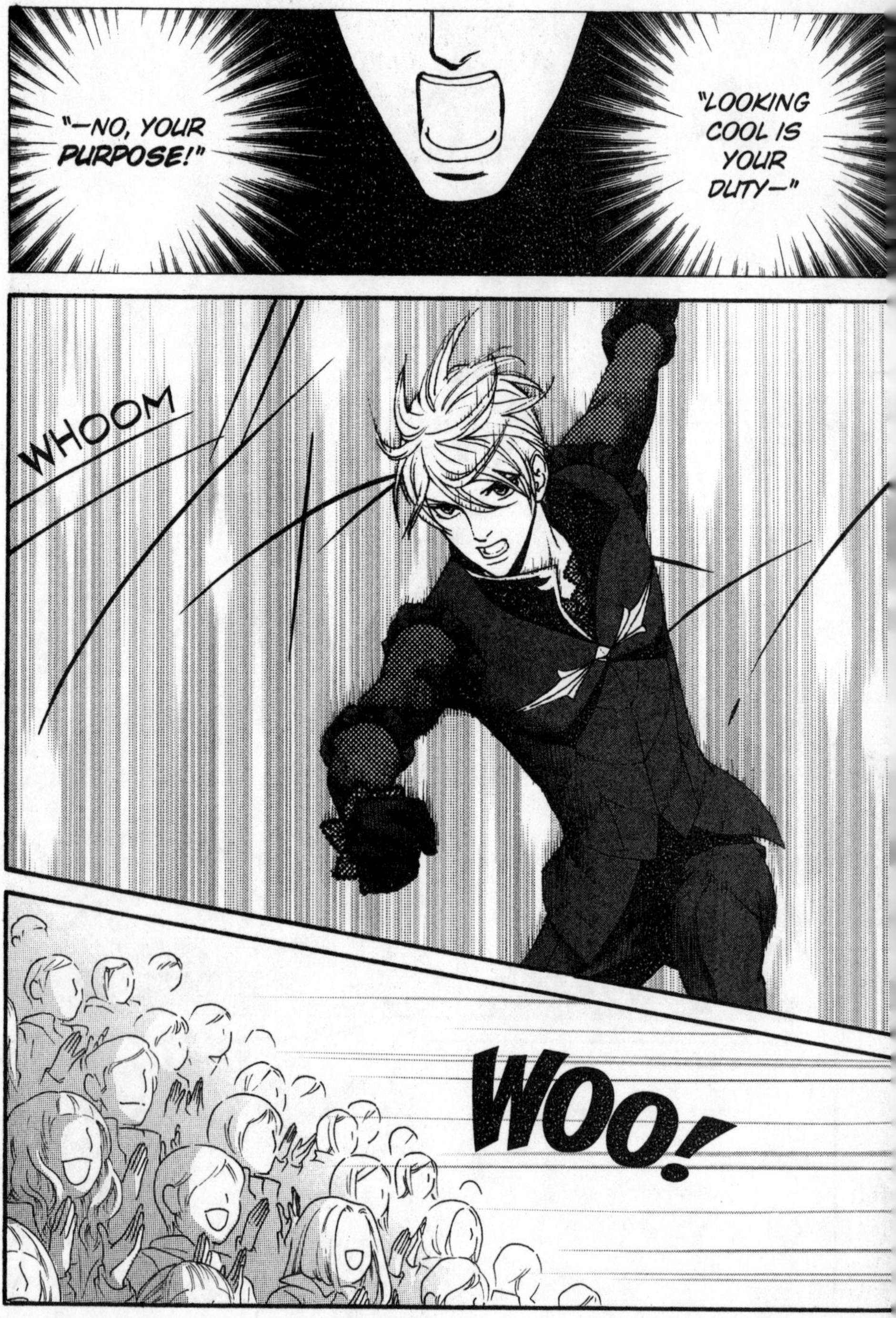
"LOOKING COOL IS YOUR DUTY—"
"—NO, YOUR PURPOSE!"
WHOOM
WOO!

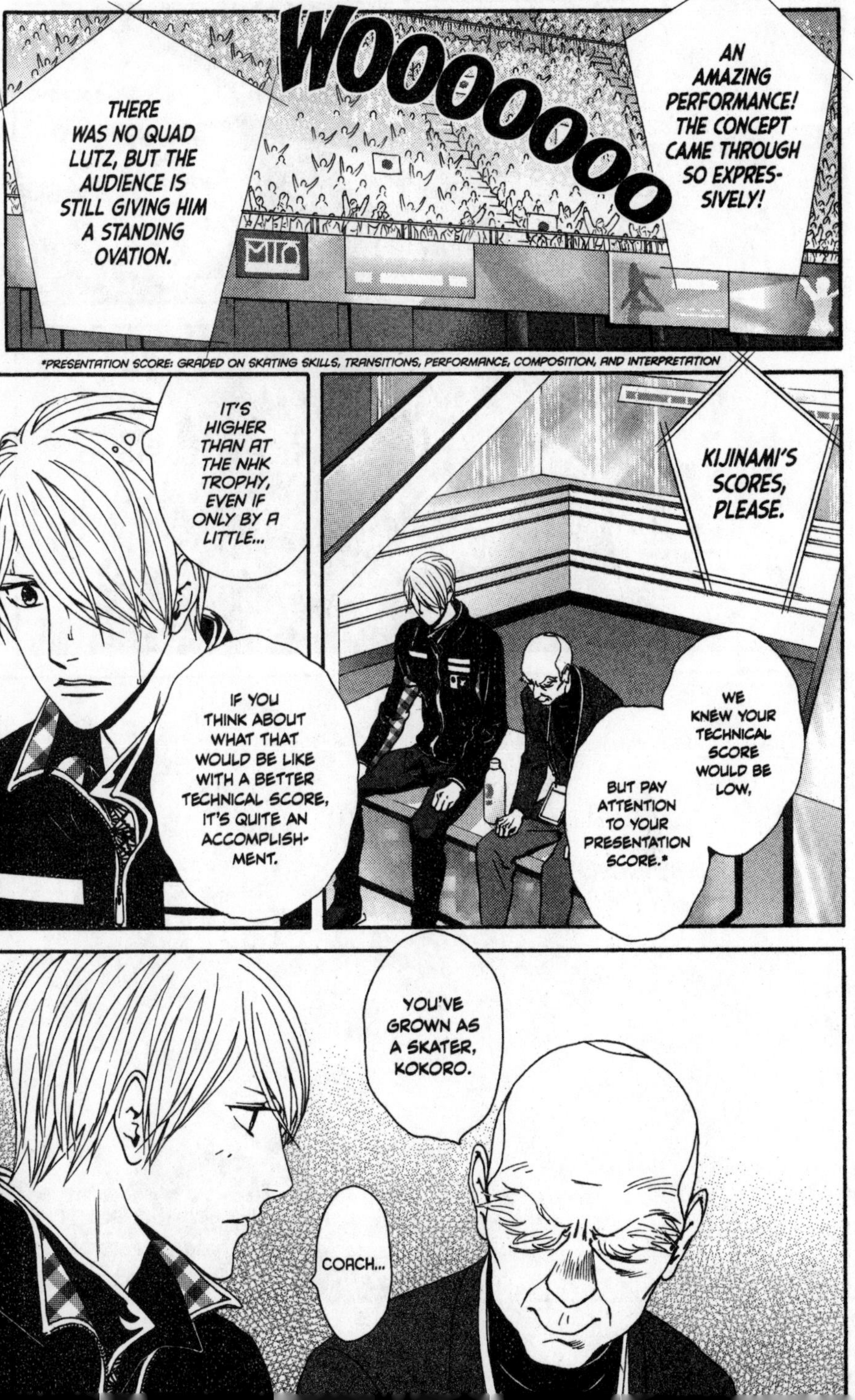
AN AMAZING PERFORMANCE! THE CONCEPT CAME THROUGH SO EXPRES-SIVELY!
WOOOOOOO
THERE WAS NO QUAD LUTZ, BUT THE AUDIENCE IS STILL GIVING HIM A STANDING OVATION.
KIJINAMI'S SCORES, PLEASE.
WE KNEW YOUR TECHNICAL SCORE WOULD BE LOW,
BUT PAY ATTENTION TO YOUR PRESENTATION SCORE.*
IT'S HIGHER THAN AT THE NHK TROPHY, EVEN IF ONLY BY A LITTLE...
IF YOU THINK ABOUT WHAT THAT WOULD BE LIKE WITH A BETTER TECHNICAL SCORE, IT'S QUITE AN ACCOMPLISH-MENT.
YOU'VE GROWN AS A SKATER, KOKORO.
COACH...

*PRESENTATION SCORE: GRADED ON SKATING SKILLS, TRANSITIONS, PERFORMANCE, COMPOSITION, AND INTERPRETATION

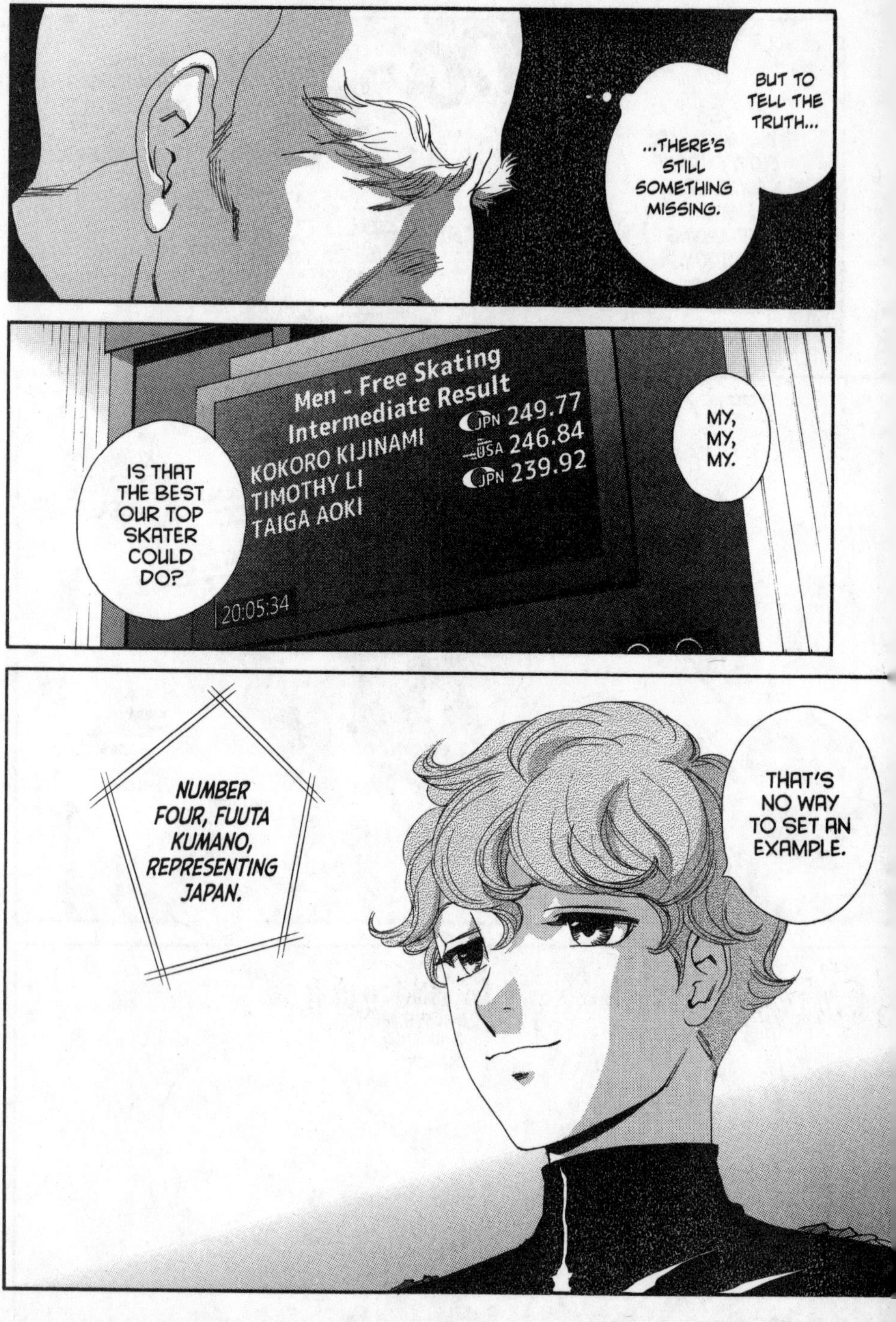
BUT TO TELL THE TRUTH...
...THERE'S STILL SOMETHING MISSING.
MY, MY, MY.
Men - Free Skating Intermediate Result
KOKORO KIJINAMI JPN 249.77
TIMOTHY LI USA 246.84
TAIGA AOKI JPN 239.92
20:05:34
IS THAT THE BEST OUR TOP SKATER COULD DO?
THAT'S NO WAY TO SET AN EXAMPLE.
NUMBER FOUR, FUUTA KUMANO, REPRESENTING JAPAN.

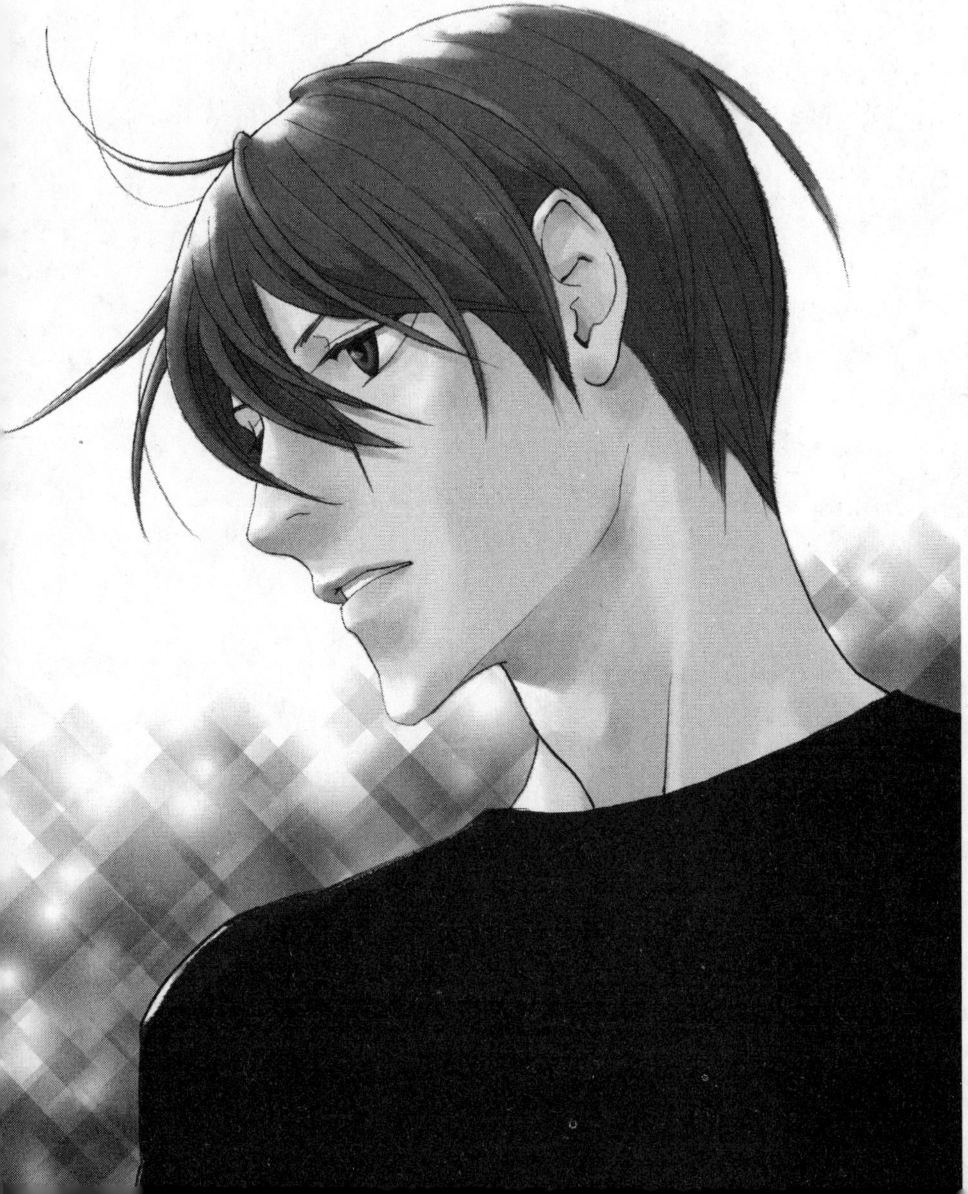

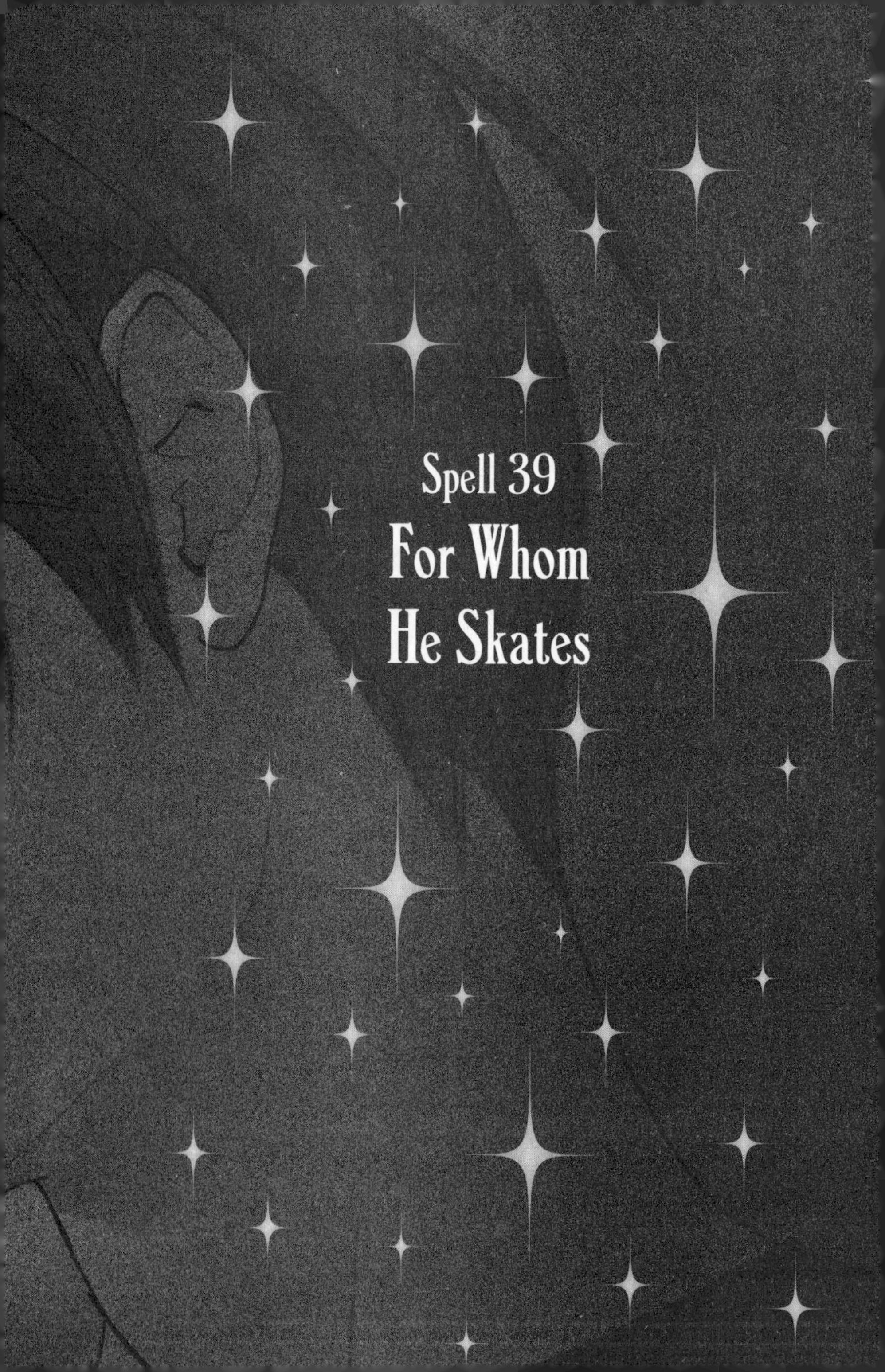
Spell 39
For Whom
He Skates

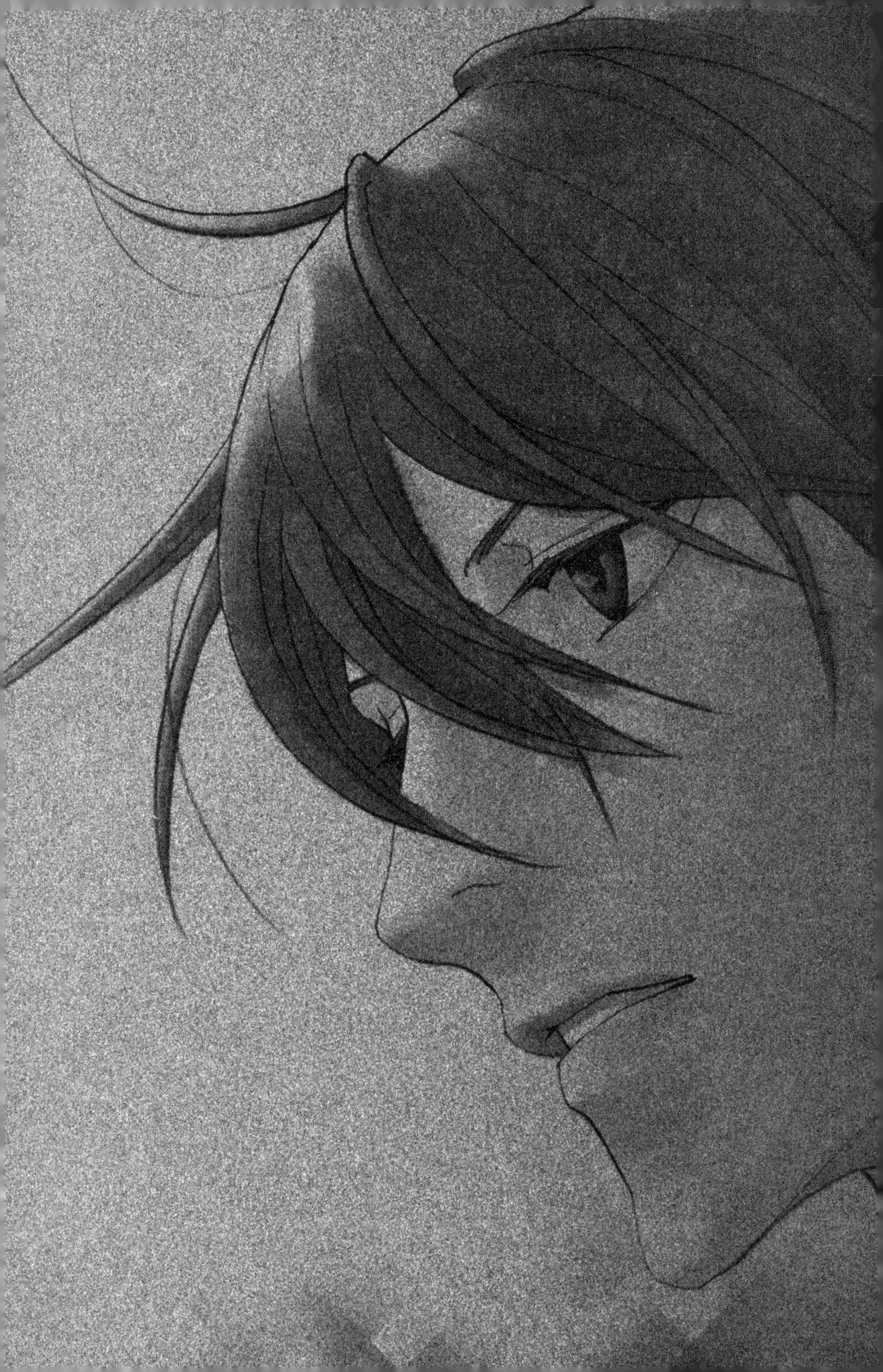

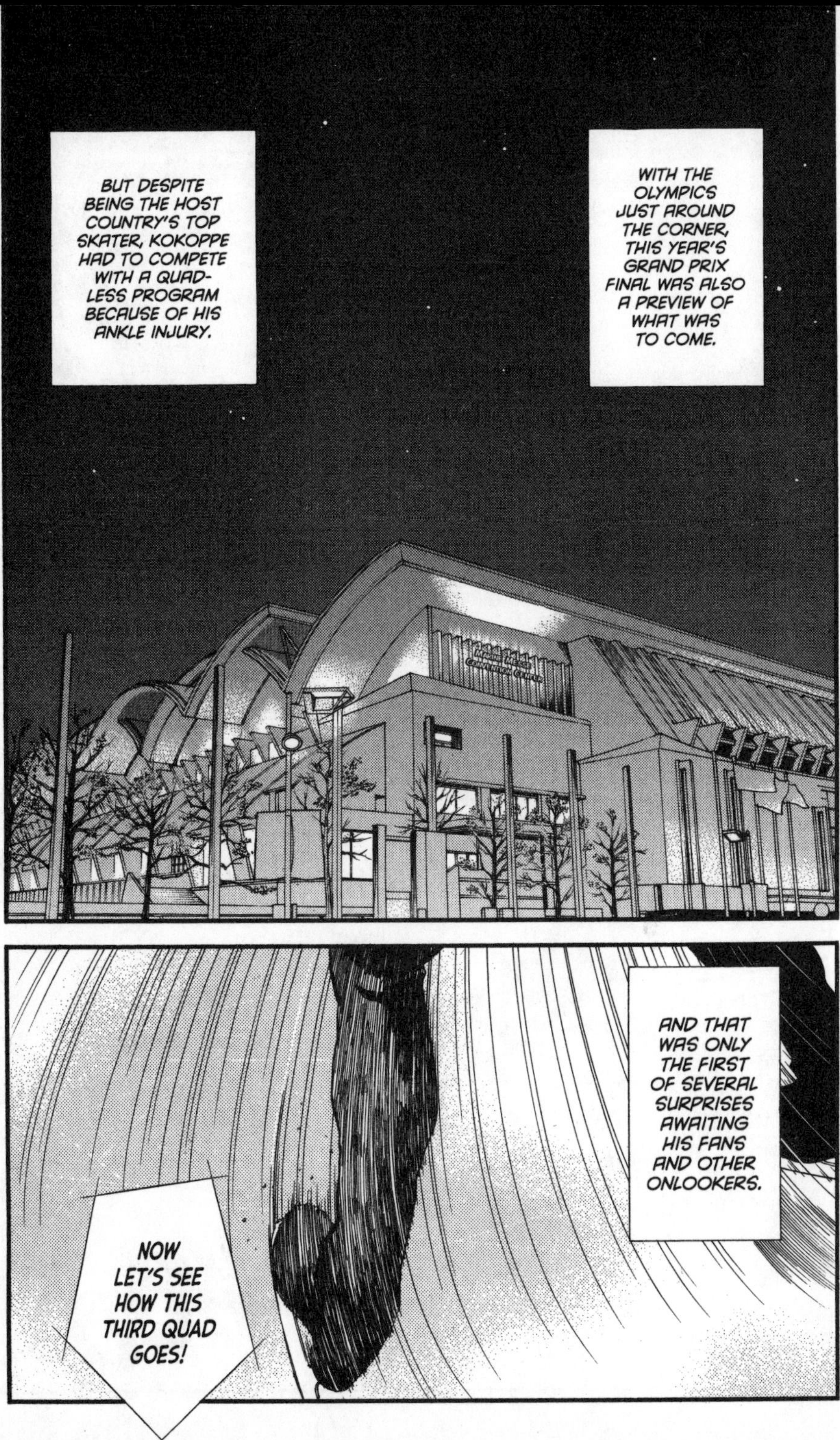
WITH THE OLYMPICS JUST AROUND THE CORNER, THIS YEAR'S GRAND PRIX FINAL WAS ALSO A PREVIEW OF WHAT WAS TO COME.
BUT DESPITE BEING THE HOST COUNTRY'S TOP SKATER, KOKOPPE HAD TO COMPETE WITH A QUAD-LESS PROGRAM BECAUSE OF HIS ANKLE INJURY.
AND THAT WAS ONLY THE FIRST OF SEVERAL SURPRISES AWAITING HIS FANS AND OTHER ONLOOKERS.
NOW LET'S SEE HOW THIS THIRD QUAD GOES!

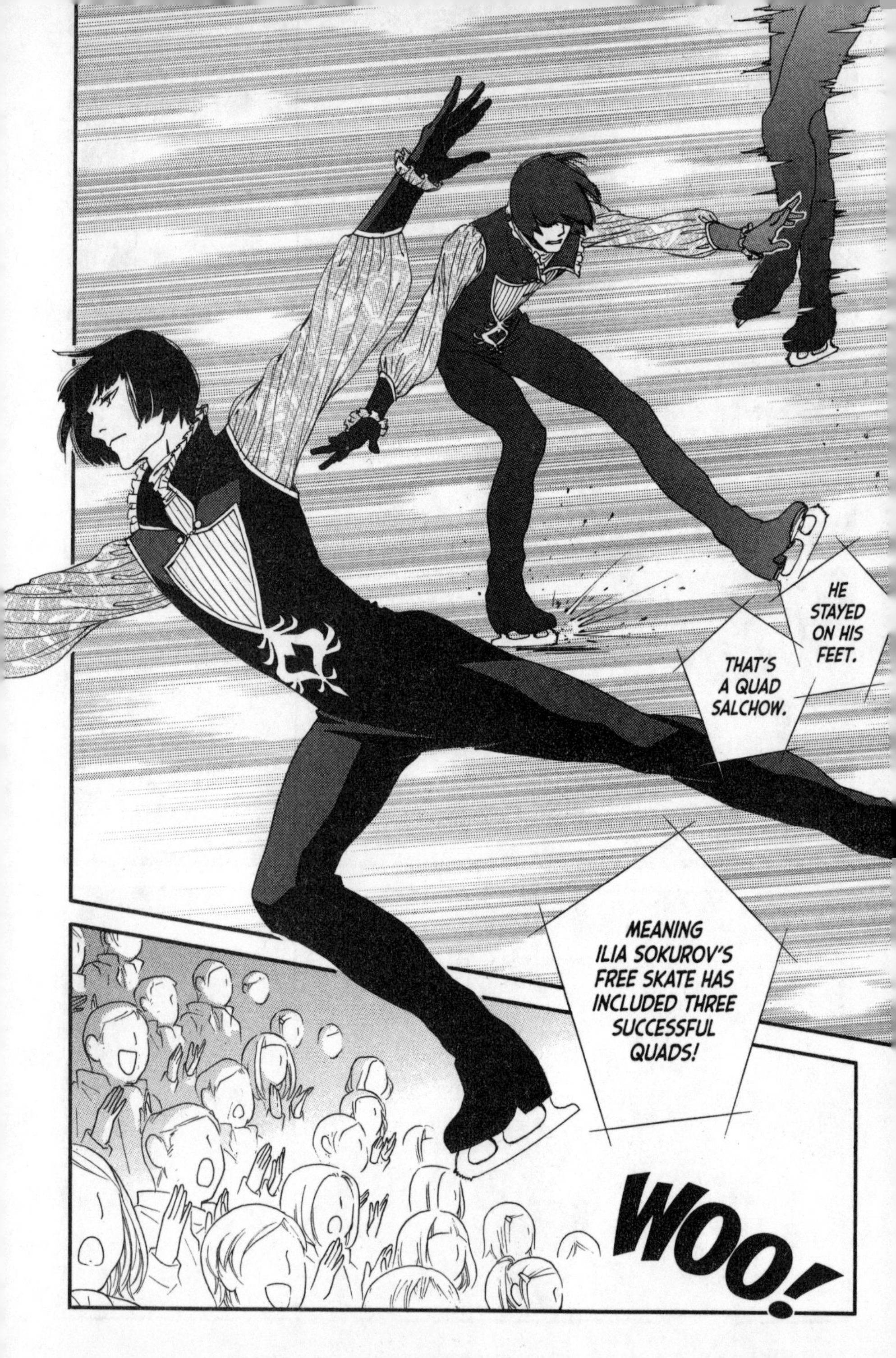
HE STAYED ON HIS FEET.
THAT'S A QUAD SALCHOW.
MEANING ILIA SOKUROV'S FREE SKATE HAS INCLUDED THREE SUCCESSFUL QUADS!
WOO!

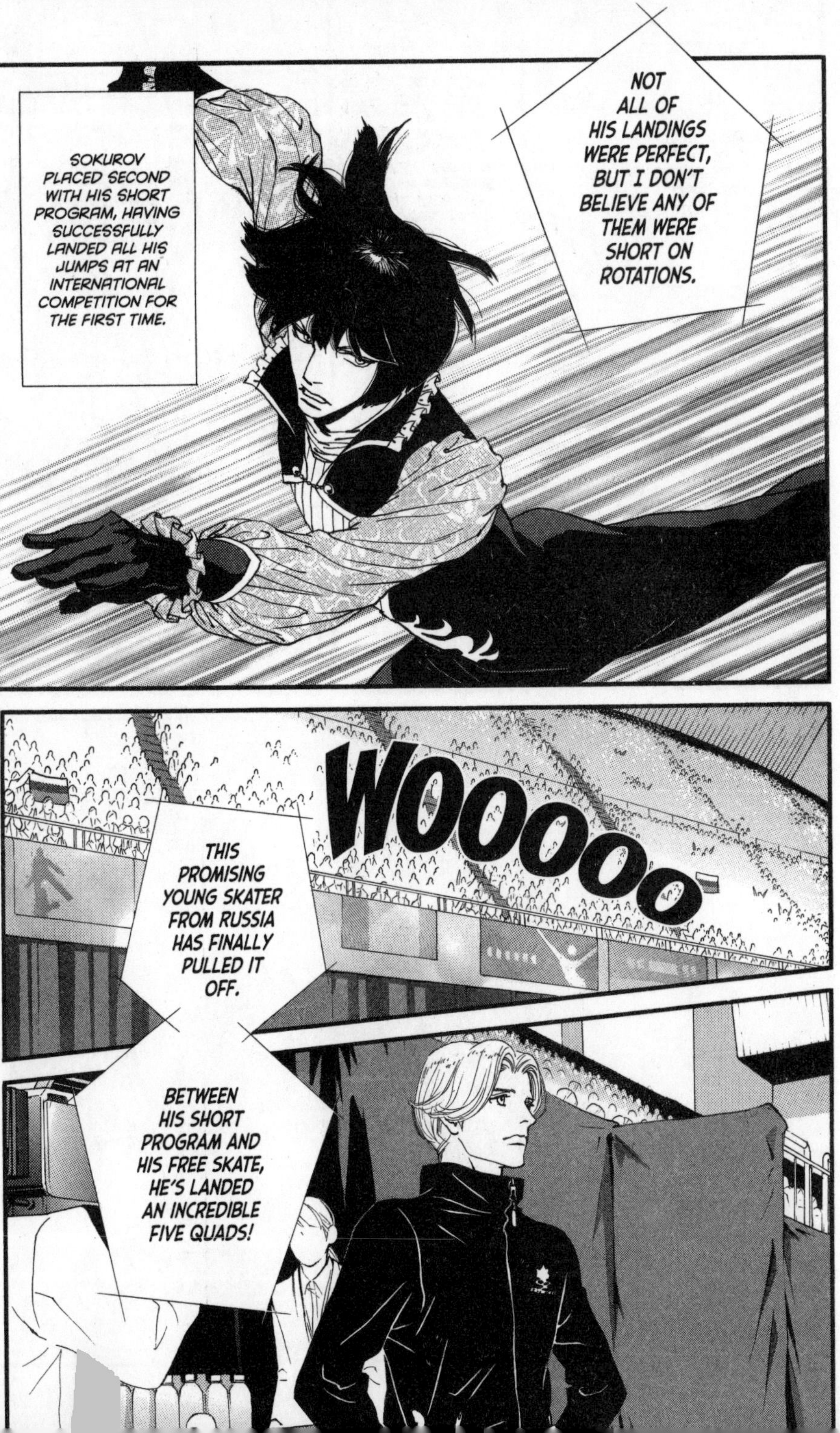
NOT ALL OF HIS LANDINGS WERE PERFECT, BUT I DON'T BELIEVE ANY OF THEM WERE SHORT ON ROTATIONS.
SOKUROV PLACED SECOND WITH HIS SHORT PROGRAM, HAVING SUCCESSFULLY LANDED ALL HIS JUMPS AT AN INTERNATIONAL COMPETITION FOR THE FIRST TIME.
WOOOOO
THIS PROMISING YOUNG SKATER FROM RUSSIA HAS FINALLY PULLED IT OFF.
BETWEEN HIS SHORT PROGRAM AND HIS FREE SKATE, HE'S LANDED AN INCREDIBLE FIVE QUADS!

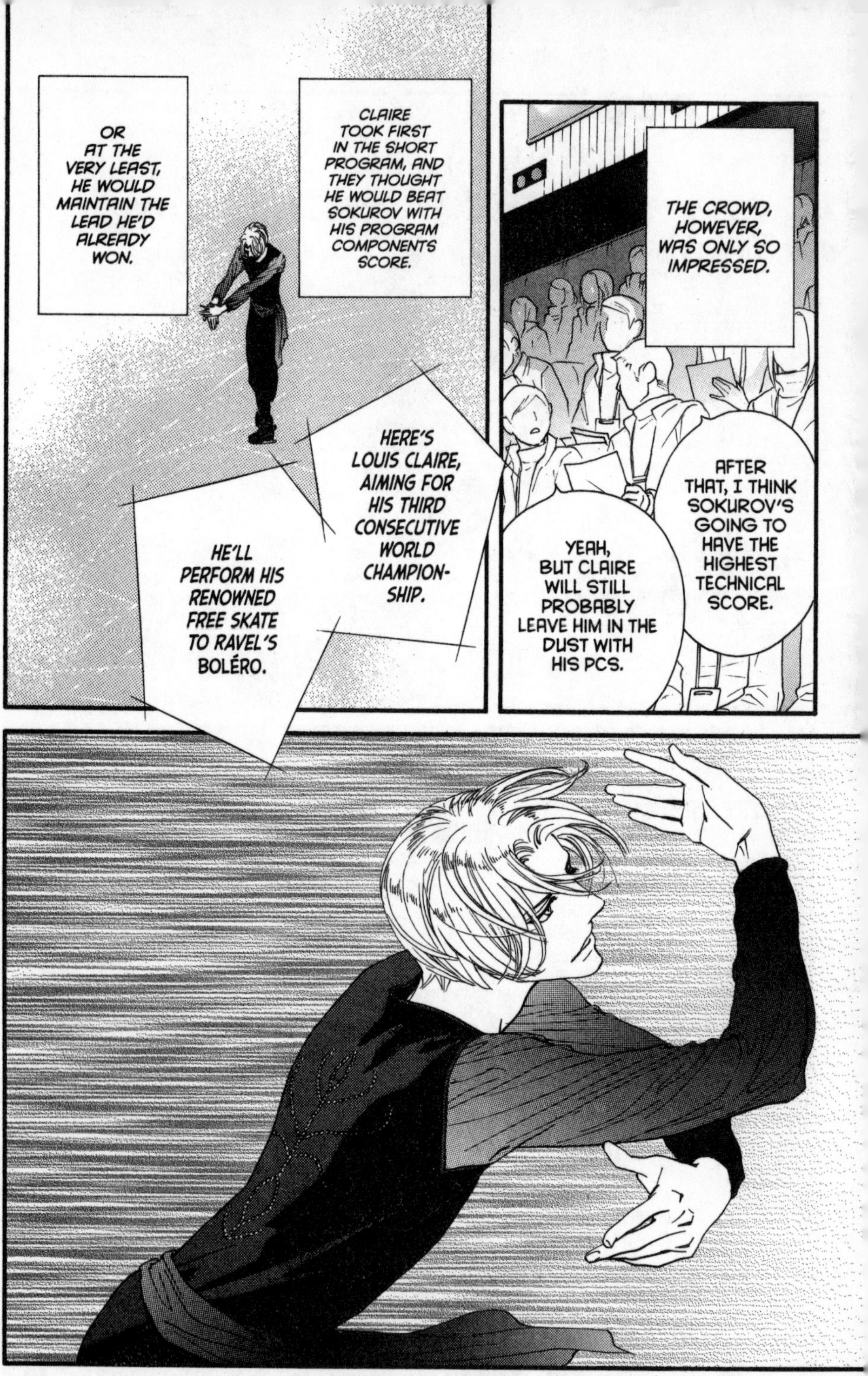
THE CROWD, HOWEVER, WAS ONLY SO IMPRESSED.
AFTER THAT, I THINK SOKUROV'S GOING TO HAVE THE HIGHEST TECHNICAL SCORE.
YEAH, BUT CLAIRE WILL STILL PROBABLY LEAVE HIM IN THE DUST WITH HIS PCS.
CLAIRE TOOK FIRST IN THE SHORT PROGRAM, AND THEY THOUGHT HE WOULD BEAT SOKUROV WITH HIS PROGRAM COMPONENTS SCORE.
OR AT THE VERY LEAST, HE WOULD MAINTAIN THE LEAD HE'D ALREADY WON.
HERE'S LOUIS CLAIRE, AIMING FOR HIS THIRD CONSECUTIVE WORLD CHAMPION-SHIP.
HE'LL PERFORM HIS RENOWNED FREE SKATE TO RAVEL'S BOLÉRO.

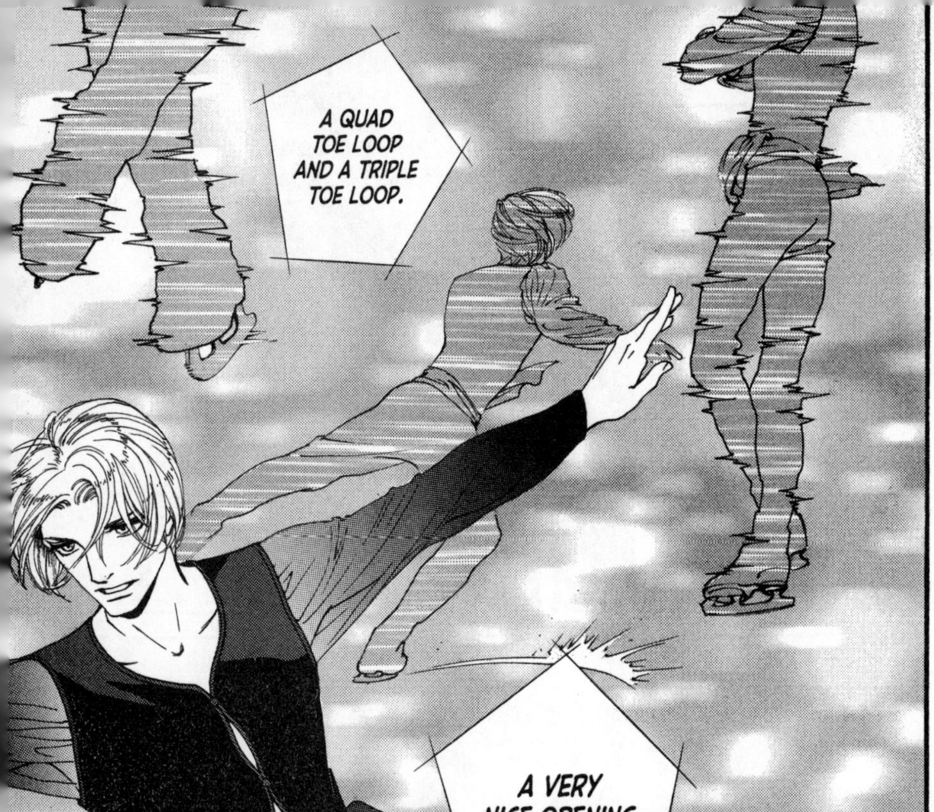
A QUAD TOE LOOP AND A TRIPLE TOE LOOP.
A VERY NICE OPENING COMBINATION!
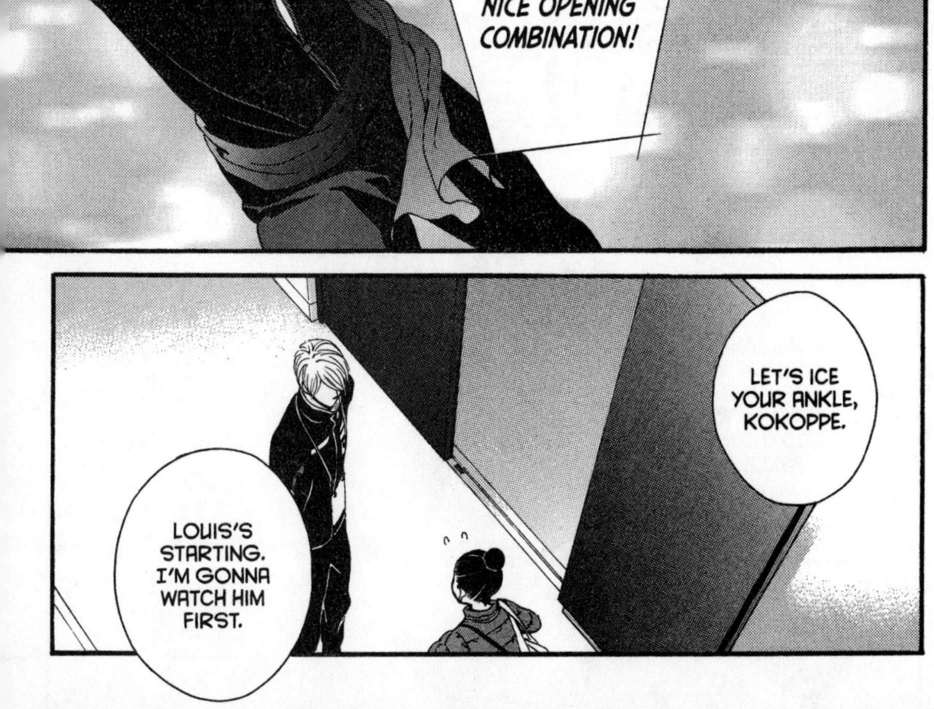
LET'S ICE YOUR ANKLE, KOKOPPE.
LOUIS'S STARTING. I'M GONNA WATCH HIM FIRST.

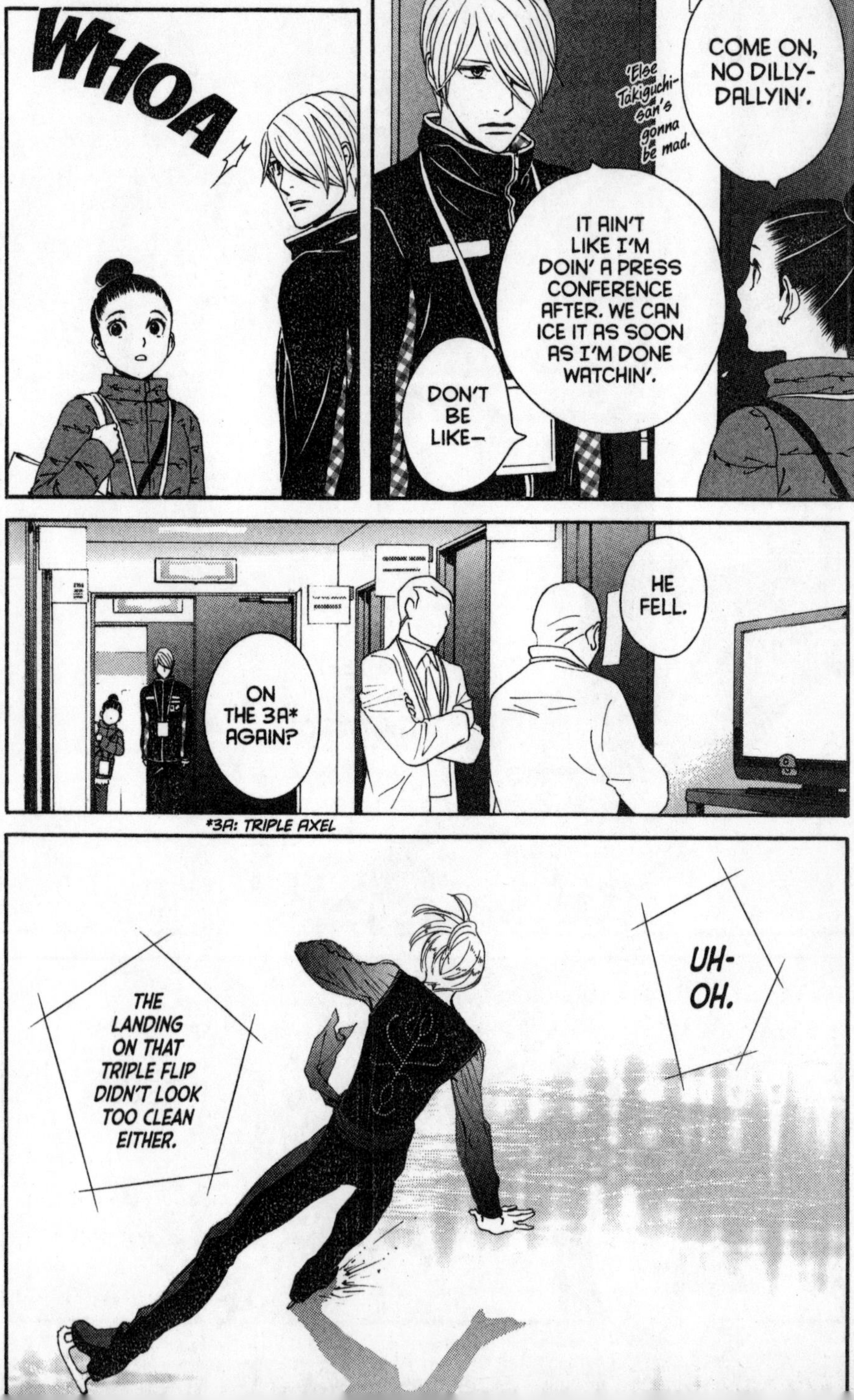
COME ON, NO DILLY-DALLYIN'.
'Else Takiguchi-san's gonna be mad.
IT AIN'T LIKE I'M DOIN' A PRESS CONFERENCE AFTER. WE CAN ICE IT AS SOON AS I'M DONE WATCHIN'.
DON'T BE LIKE—
WHOA
HE FELL.
ON THE 3A* AGAIN?
UH-OH.
THE LANDING ON THAT TRIPLE FLIP DIDN'T LOOK TOO CLEAN EITHER.

*3A: TRIPLE AXEL

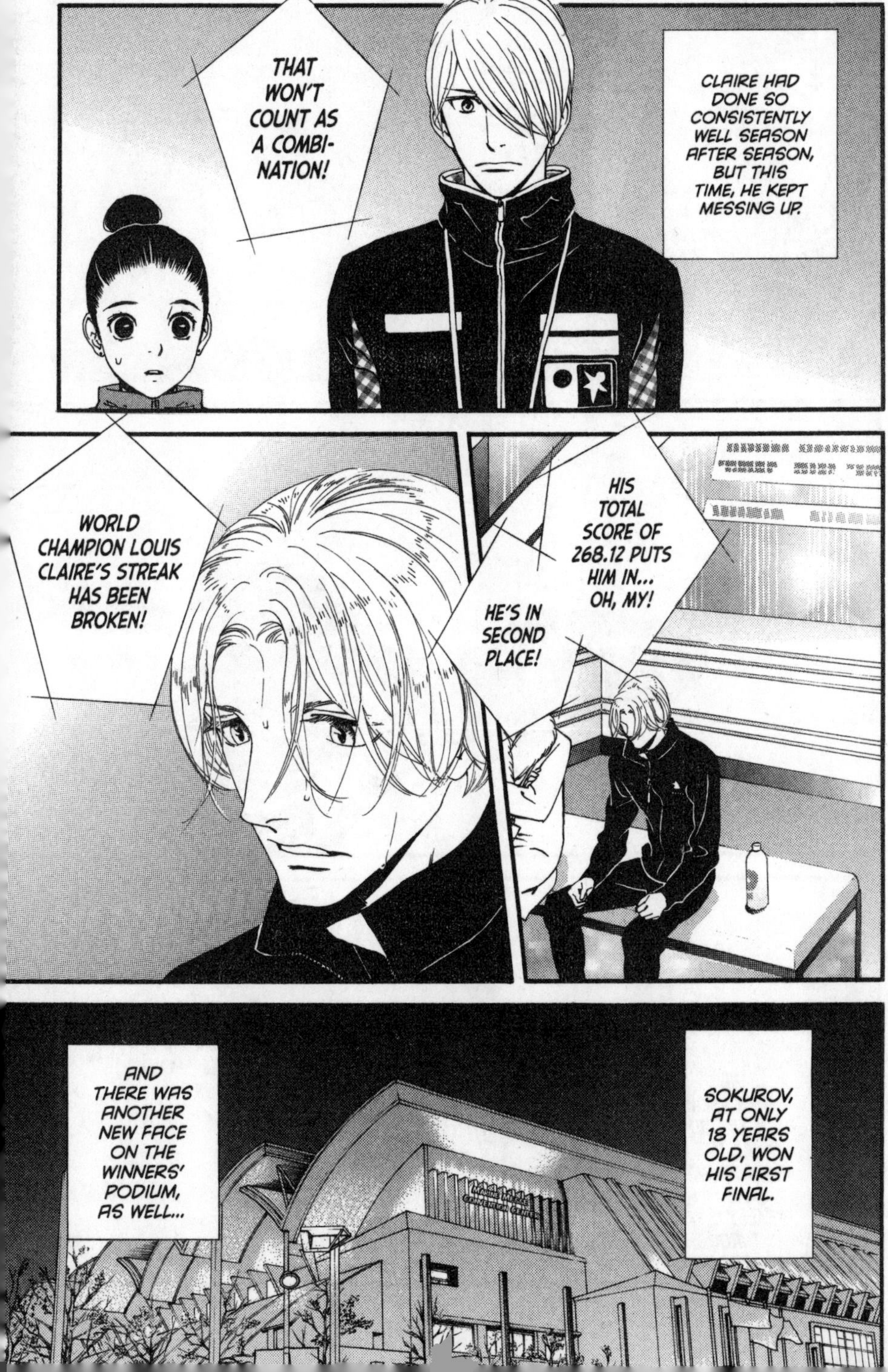
CLAIRE HAD DONE SO CONSISTENTLY WELL SEASON AFTER SEASON, BUT THIS TIME, HE KEPT MESSING UP.
THAT WON'T COUNT AS A COMBI-NATION!
HIS TOTAL SCORE OF 268.12 PUTS HIM IN... OH, MY!
HE'S IN SECOND PLACE!
WORLD CHAMPION LOUIS CLAIRE'S STREAK HAS BEEN BROKEN!
SOKUROV, AT ONLY 18 YEARS OLD, WON HIS FIRST FINAL.
AND THERE WAS ANOTHER NEW FACE ON THE WINNERS' PODIUM, AS WELL...

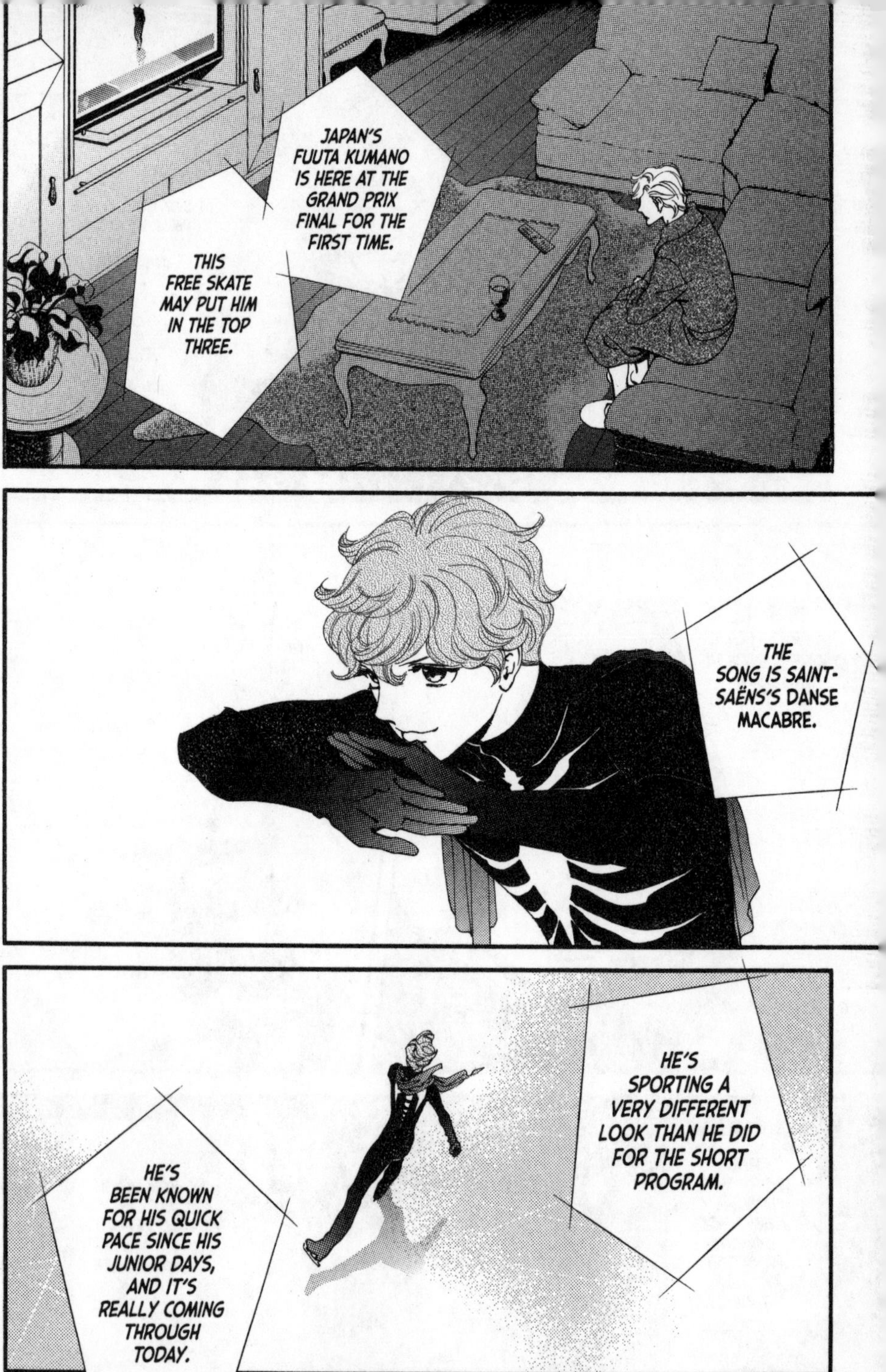
JAPAN'S FUUTA KUMANO IS HERE AT THE GRAND PRIX FINAL FOR THE FIRST TIME.
THIS FREE SKATE MAY PUT HIM IN THE TOP THREE.
THE SONG IS SAINT-SAËNS'S DANSE MACABRE.
HE'S SPORTING A VERY DIFFERENT LOOK THAN HE DID FOR THE SHORT PROGRAM.
HE'S BEEN KNOWN FOR HIS QUICK PACE SINCE HIS JUNIOR DAYS, AND IT'S REALLY COMING THROUGH TODAY.

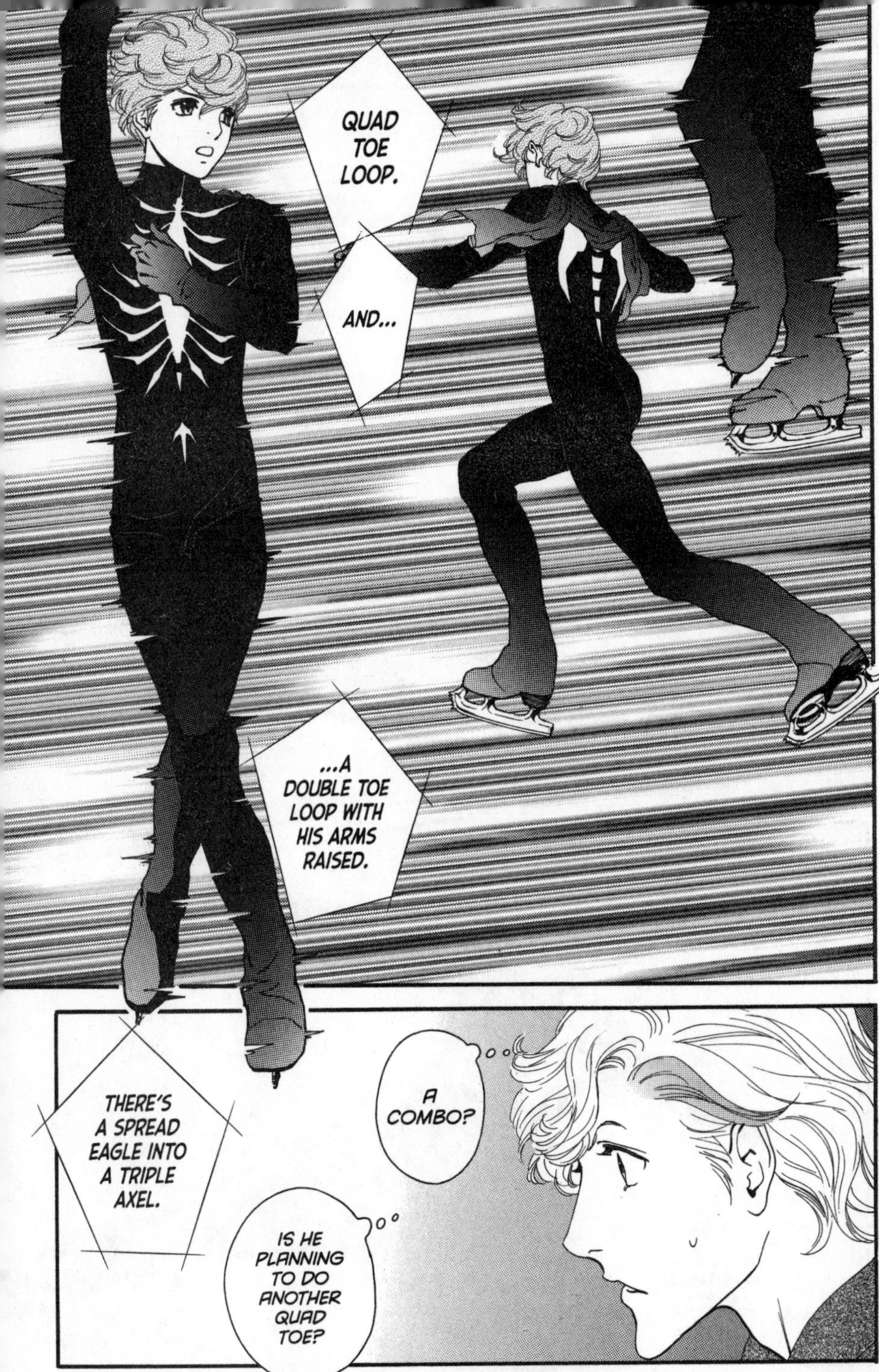
QUAD TOE LOOP.
AND...
...A DOUBLE TOE LOOP WITH HIS ARMS RAISED.
A COMBO?
IS HE PLANNING TO DO ANOTHER QUAD TOE?
THERE'S A SPREAD EAGLE INTO A TRIPLE AXEL.

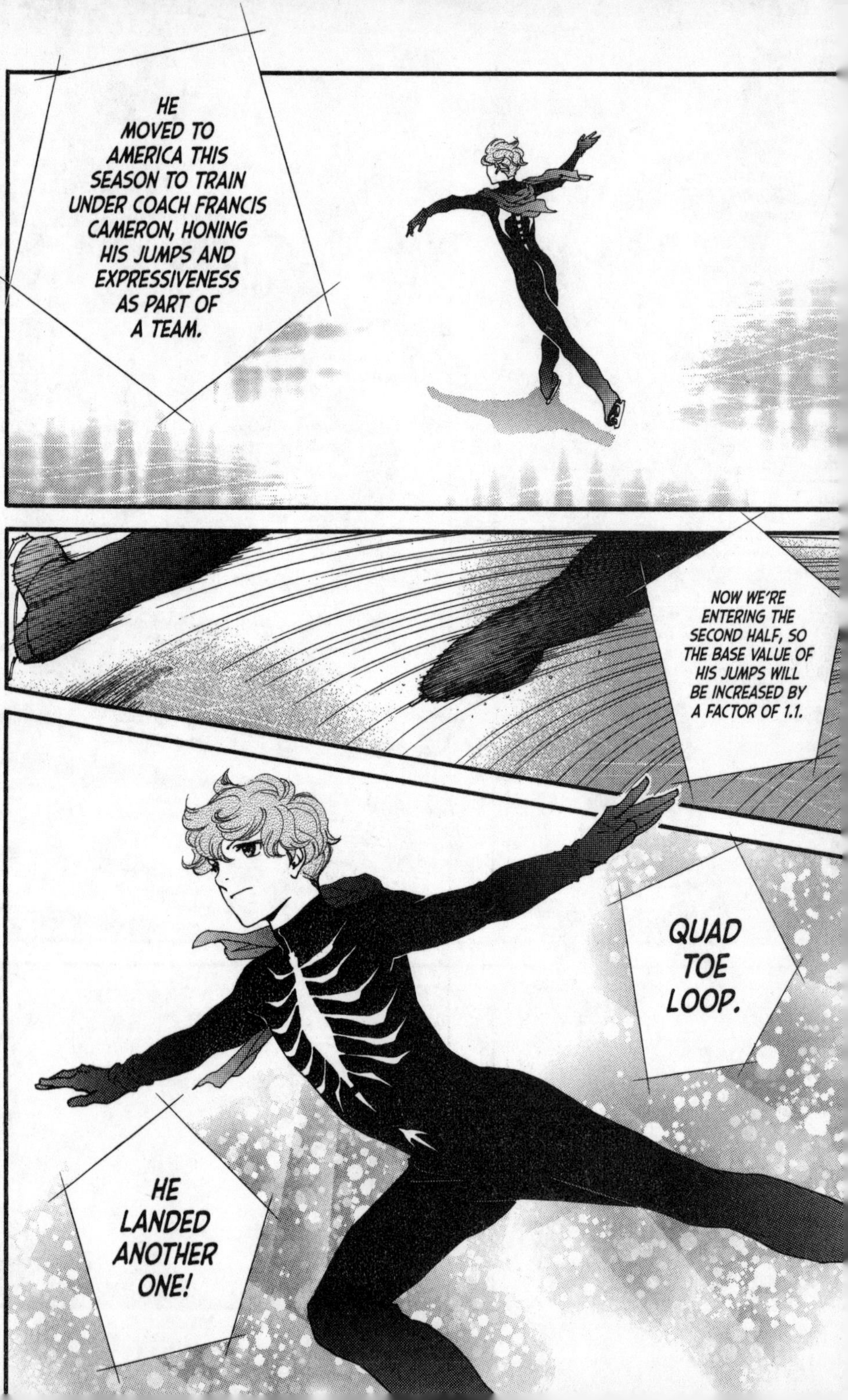
HE MOVED TO AMERICA THIS SEASON TO TRAIN UNDER COACH FRANCIS CAMERON, HONING HIS JUMPS AND EXPRESSIVENESS AS PART OF A TEAM.
NOW WE'RE ENTERING THE SECOND HALF, SO THE BASE VALUE OF HIS JUMPS WILL BE INCREASED BY A FACTOR OF 1.1.
QUAD TOE LOOP.
HE LANDED ANOTHER ONE!

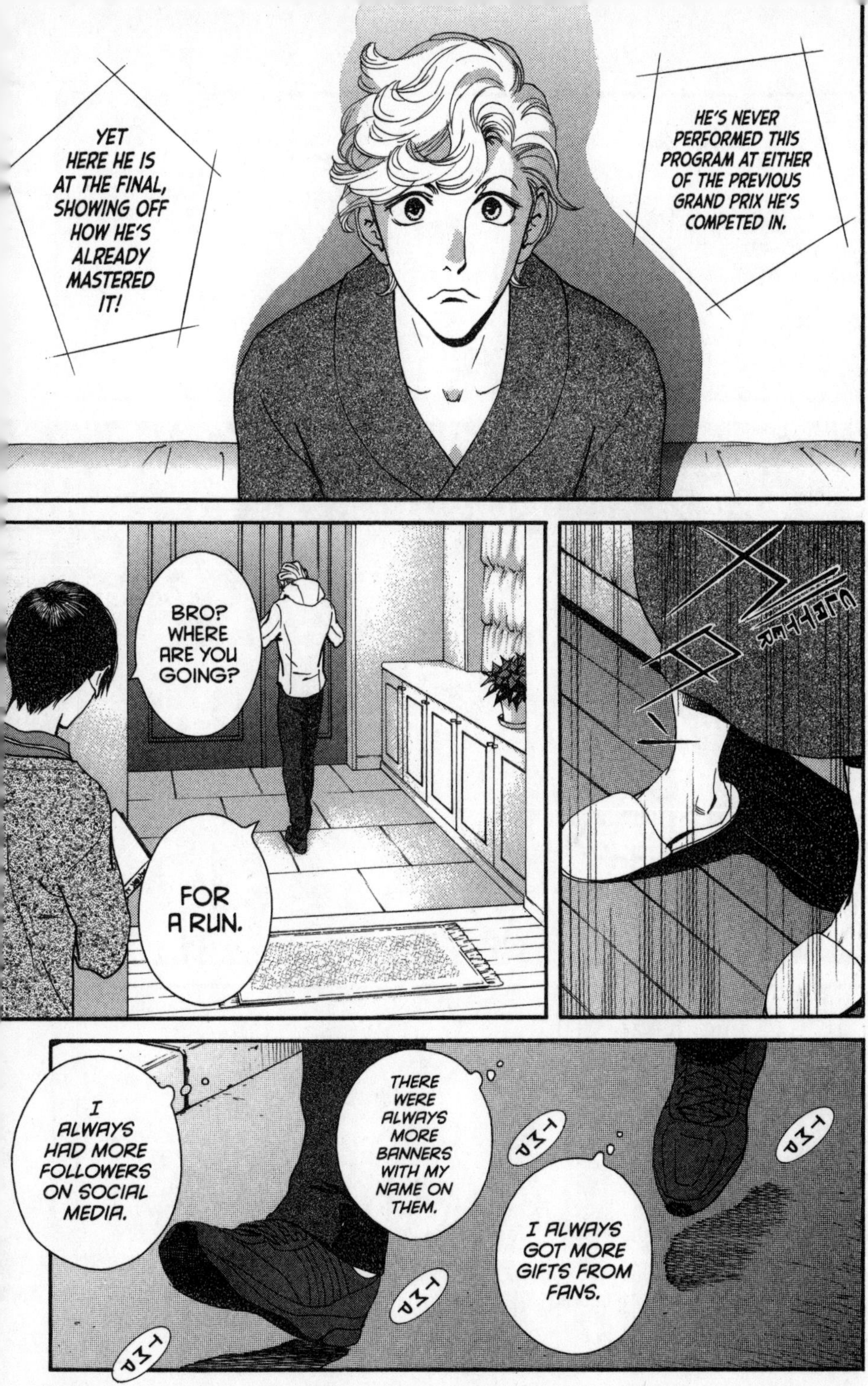
HE'S NEVER PERFORMED THIS PROGRAM AT EITHER OF THE PREVIOUS GRAND PRIX HE'S COMPETED IN.
YET HERE HE IS AT THE FINAL, SHOWING OFF HOW HE'S ALREADY MASTERED IT!
CLATTER
BRO? WHERE ARE YOU GOING?
FOR A RUN.
TMP
TMP
I ALWAYS GOT MORE GIFTS FROM FANS.
THERE WERE ALWAYS MORE BANNERS WITH MY NAME ON THEM.
I ALWAYS HAD MORE FOLLOWERS ON SOCIAL MEDIA.
TMP
TMP

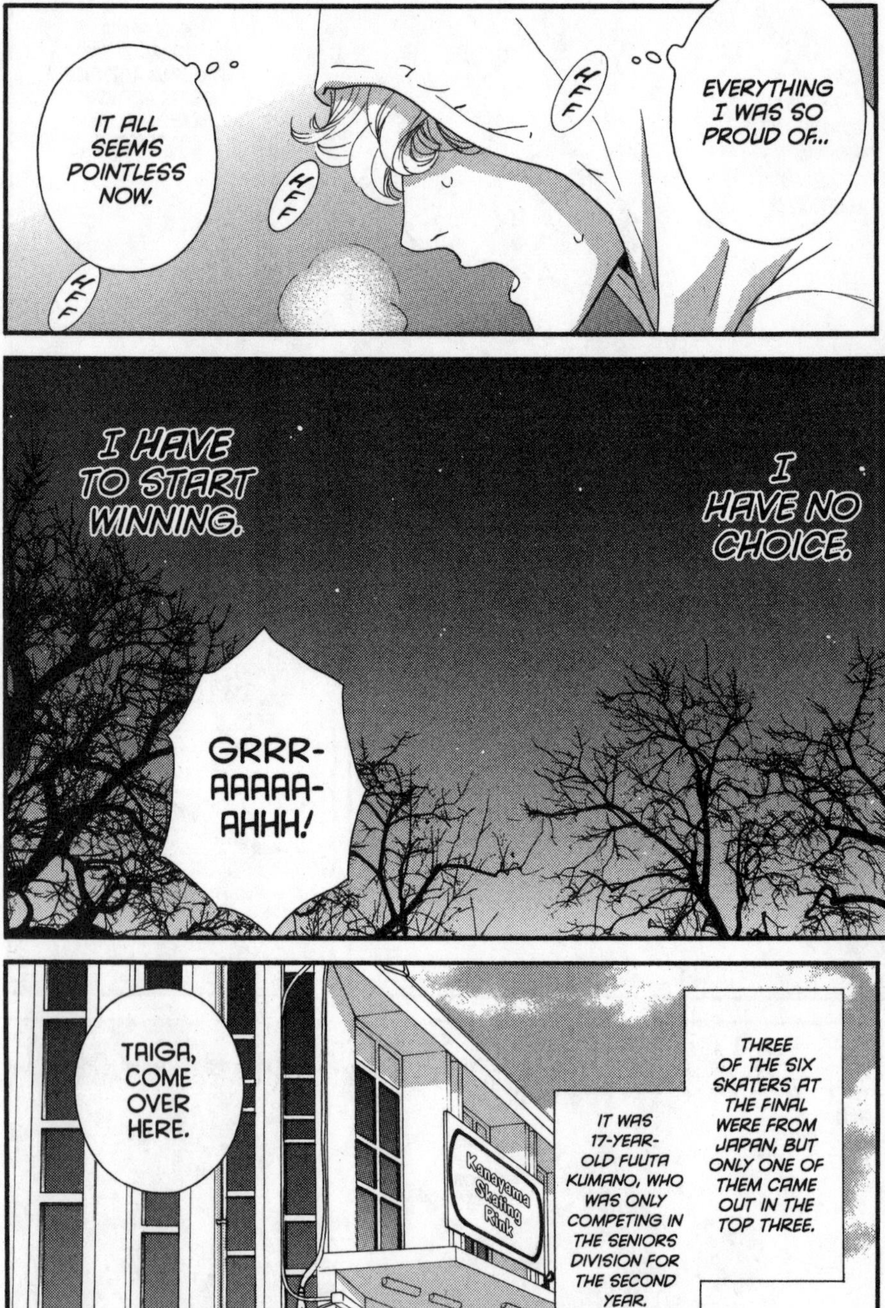
EVERYTHING I WAS SO PROUD OF...
HFF
HFF
IT ALL SEEMS POINTLESS NOW.
HFF
I HAVE NO CHOICE.
I HAVE TO START WINNING.
GRRR-AAAAA-AHHH!
THREE OF THE SIX SKATERS AT THE FINAL WERE FROM JAPAN, BUT ONLY ONE OF THEM CAME OUT IN THE TOP THREE.
IT WAS 17-YEAR-OLD FUUTA KUMANO, WHO WAS ONLY COMPETING IN THE SENIORS DIVISION FOR THE SECOND YEAR.
Kanayama Skating Rink
TAIGA, COME OVER HERE.

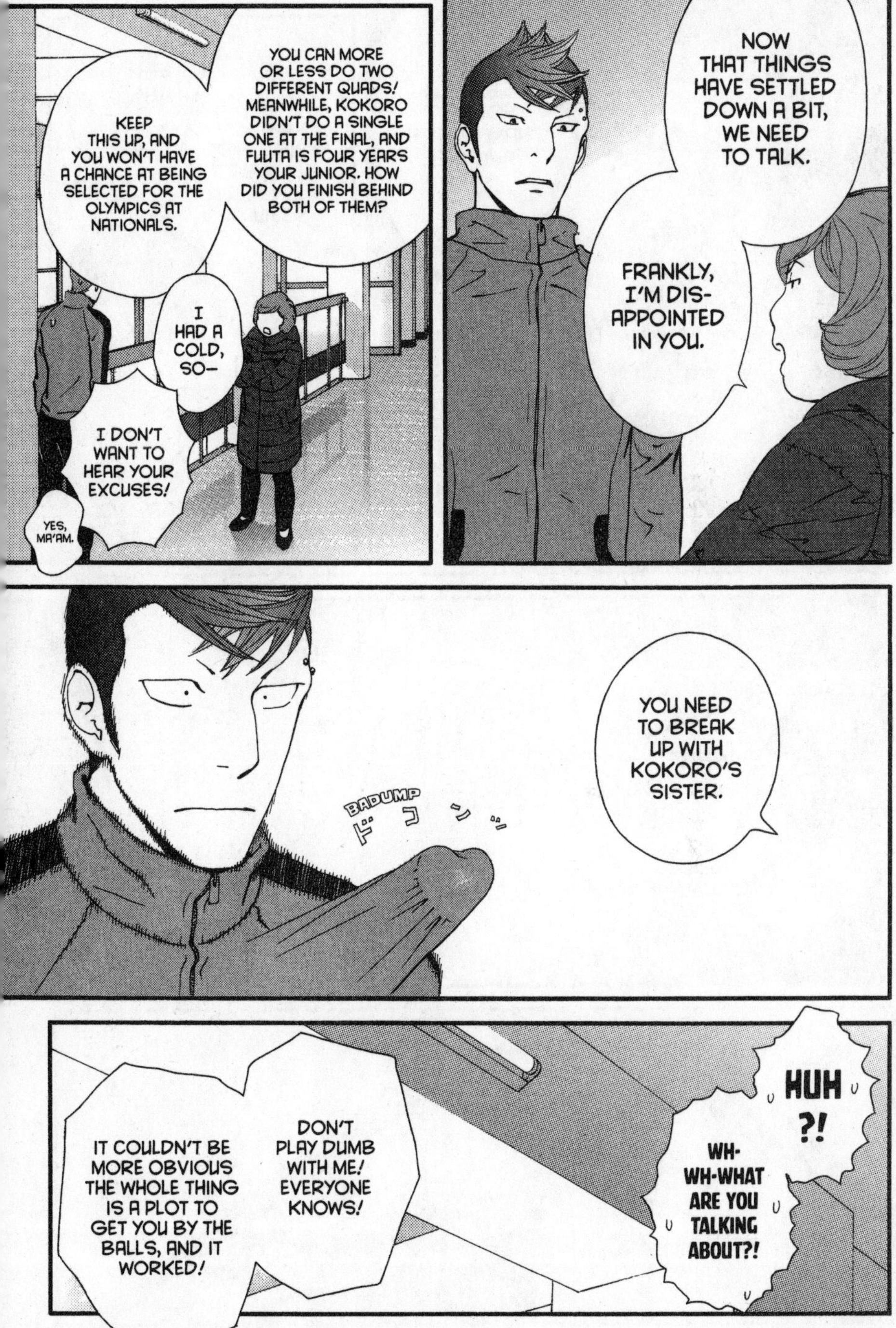
NOW THAT THINGS HAVE SETTLED DOWN A BIT, WE NEED TO TALK.
FRANKLY, I'M DIS-APPOINTED IN YOU.
YOU CAN MORE OR LESS DO TWO DIFFERENT QUADS! MEANWHILE, KOKORO DIDN'T DO A SINGLE ONE AT THE FINAL, AND FUUTA IS FOUR YEARS YOUR JUNIOR. HOW DID YOU FINISH BEHIND BOTH OF THEM?
KEEP THIS UP, AND YOU WON'T HAVE A CHANCE AT BEING SELECTED FOR THE OLYMPICS AT NATIONALS.
I HAD A COLD, SO—
I DON'T WANT TO HEAR YOUR EXCUSES!
YES, MA'AM.
YOU NEED TO BREAK UP WITH KOKORO'S SISTER.
BADUMP
HUH?!
WH-WH-WHAT ARE YOU TALKING ABOUT?!
DON'T PLAY DUMB WITH ME! EVERYONE KNOWS!
IT COULDN'T BE MORE OBVIOUS THE WHOLE THING IS A PLOT TO GET YOU BY THE BALLS, AND IT WORKED!

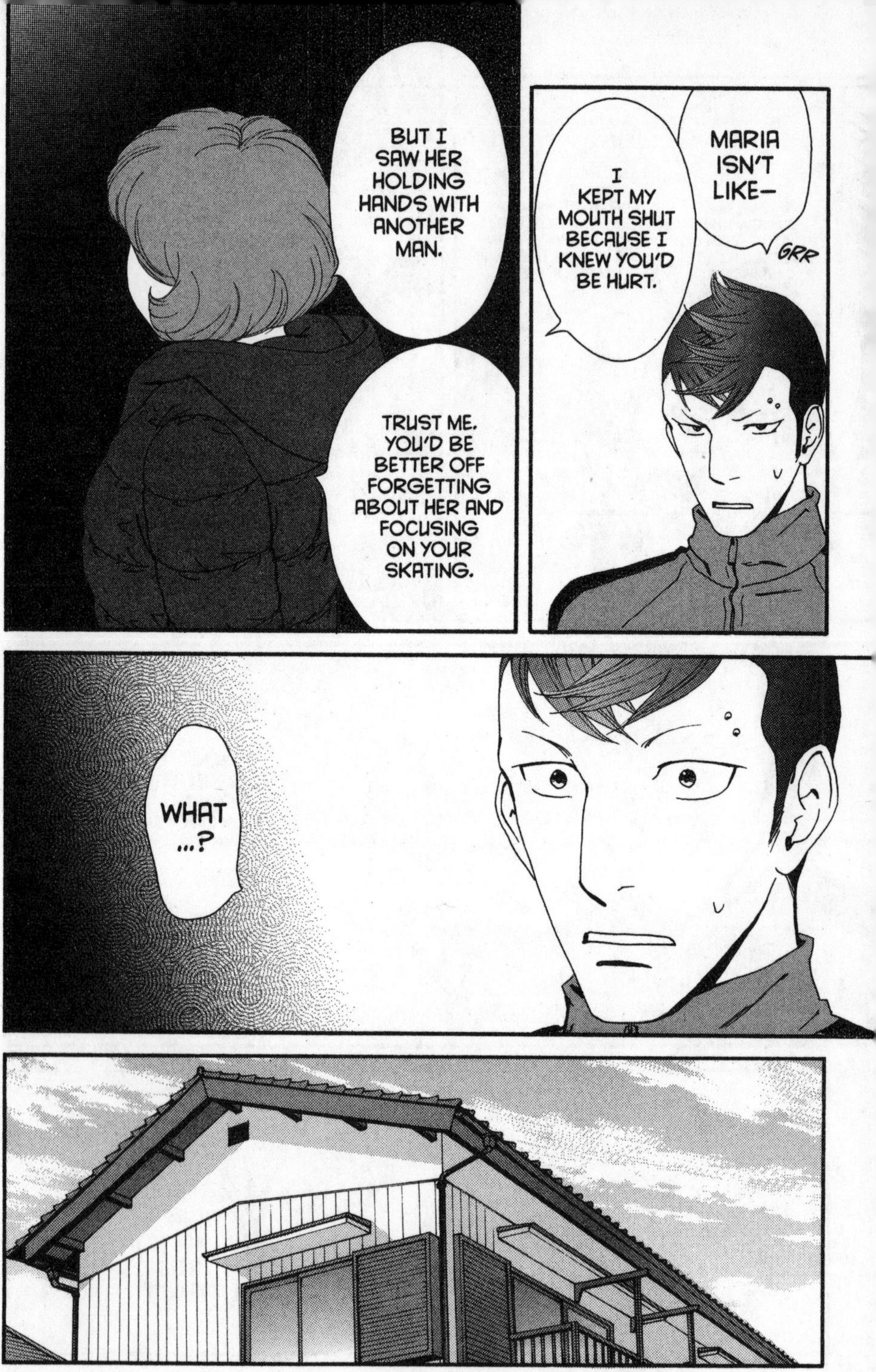
MARIA ISN'T LIKE—
GRR
I KEPT MY MOUTH SHUT BECAUSE I KNEW YOU'D BE HURT.
BUT I SAW HER HOLDING HANDS WITH ANOTHER MAN.
TRUST ME. YOU'D BE BETTER OFF FORGETTING ABOUT HER AND FOCUSING ON YOUR SKATING.
WHAT ...?

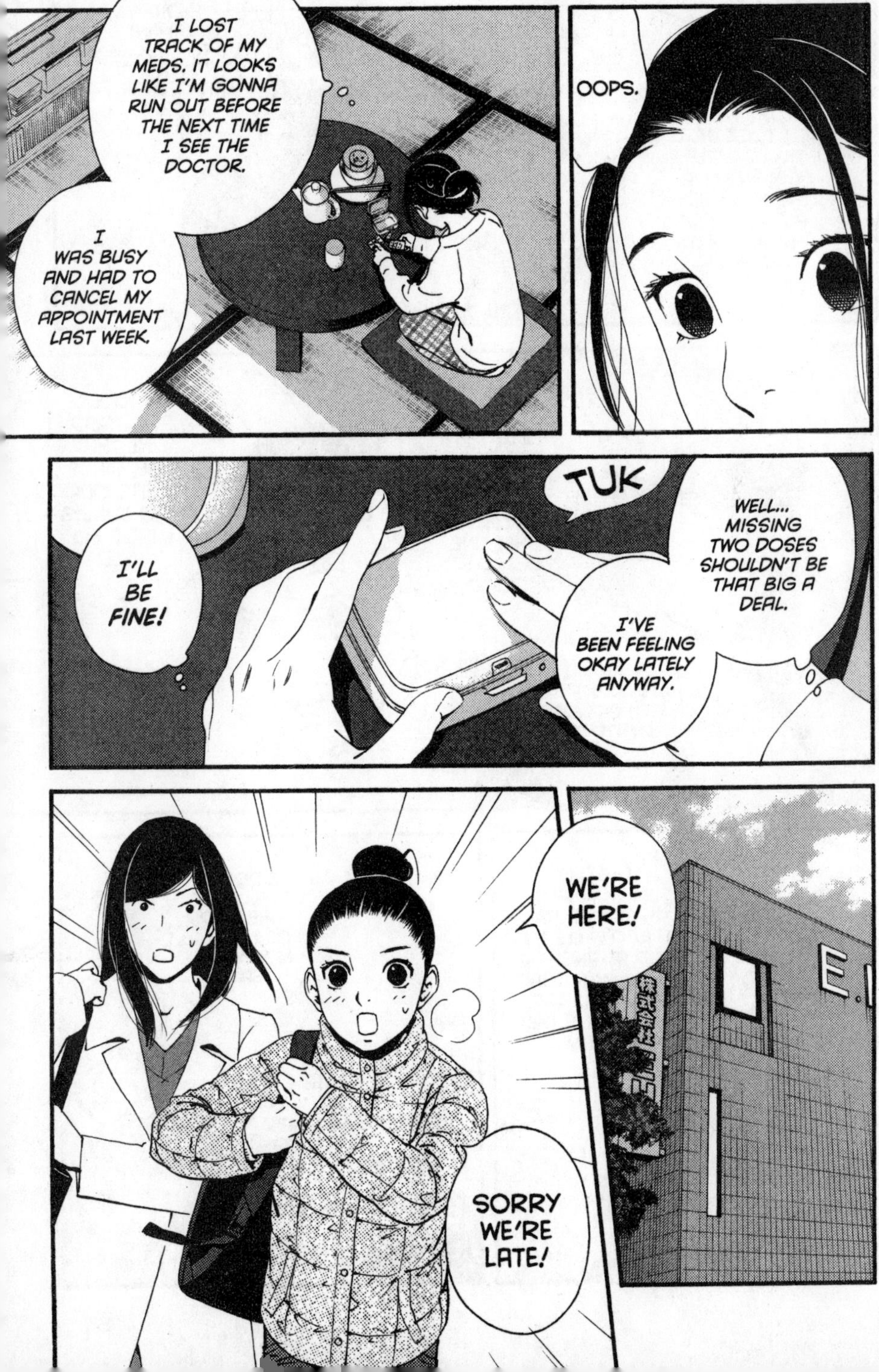
OOPS.
I LOST TRACK OF MY MEDS. IT LOOKS LIKE I'M GONNA RUN OUT BEFORE THE NEXT TIME I SEE THE DOCTOR.
I WAS BUSY AND HAD TO CANCEL MY APPOINTMENT LAST WEEK.
TUK
WELL... MISSING TWO DOSES SHOULDN'T BE THAT BIG A DEAL.
I'VE BEEN FEELING OKAY LATELY ANYWAY.
I'LL BE FINE!
WE'RE HERE!
SORRY WE'RE LATE!

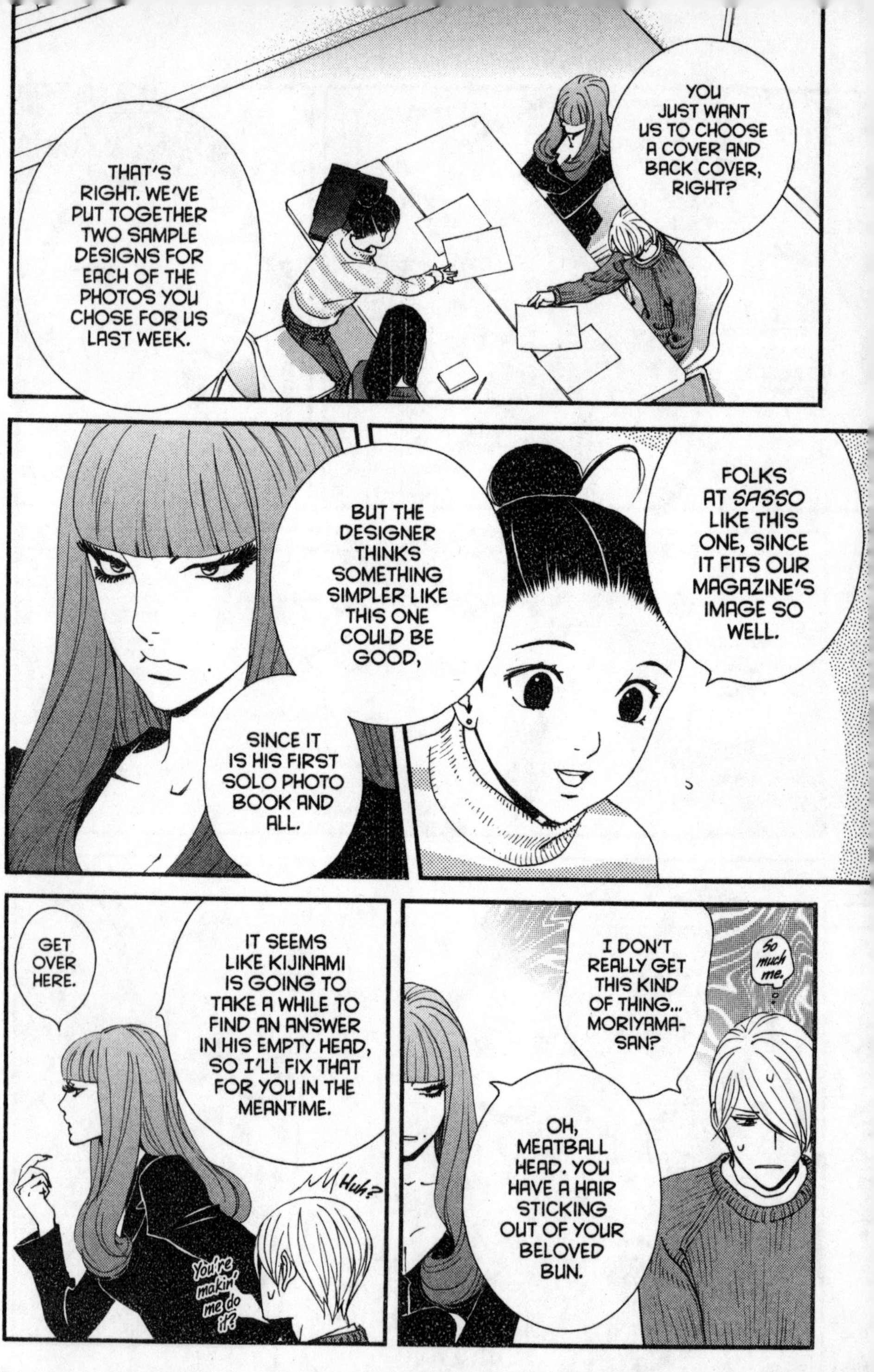
YOU JUST WANT US TO CHOOSE A COVER AND BACK COVER, RIGHT?
THAT'S RIGHT. WE'VE PUT TOGETHER TWO SAMPLE DESIGNS FOR EACH OF THE PHOTOS YOU CHOSE FOR US LAST WEEK.
FOLKS AT *SASSO* LIKE THIS ONE, SINCE IT FITS OUR MAGAZINE'S IMAGE SO WELL.
BUT THE DESIGNER THINKS SOMETHING SIMPLER LIKE THIS ONE COULD BE GOOD,
SINCE IT IS HIS FIRST SOLO PHOTO BOOK AND ALL.
So much me.
I DON'T REALLY GET THIS KIND OF THING... MORIYAMA-SAN?
OH, MEATBALL HEAD. YOU HAVE A HAIR STICKING OUT OF YOUR BELOVED BUN.
IT SEEMS LIKE KIJINAMI IS GOING TO TAKE A WHILE TO FIND AN ANSWER IN HIS EMPTY HEAD, SO I'LL FIX THAT FOR YOU IN THE MEANTIME.
GET OVER HERE.
Huh?
You're makin' me do it?

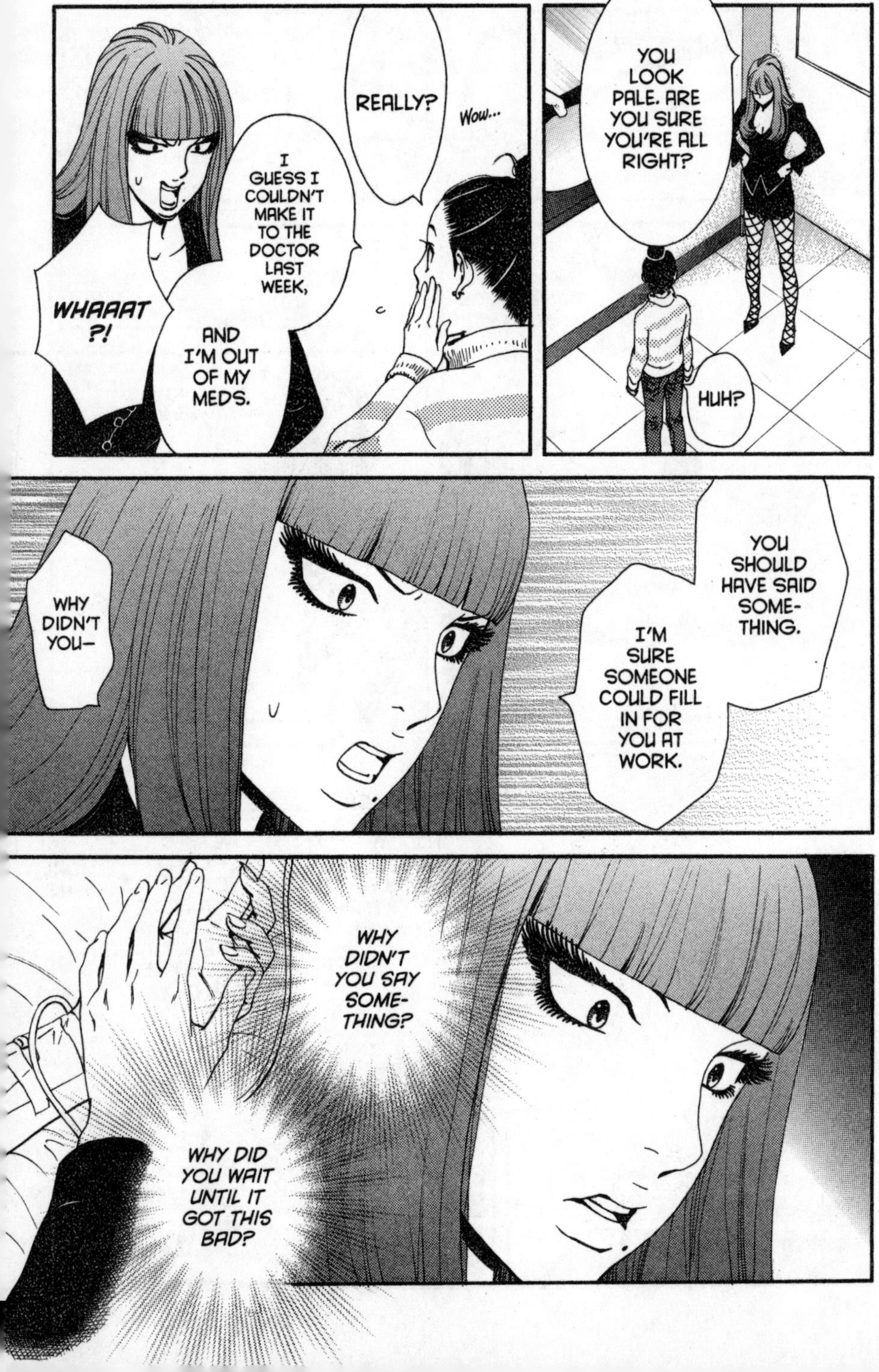
YOU LOOK PALE. ARE YOU SURE YOU'RE ALL RIGHT?
HUH?
REALLY?
Wow...
I GUESS I COULDN'T MAKE IT TO THE DOCTOR LAST WEEK,
AND I'M OUT OF MY MEDS.
WHAAAT?!
YOU SHOULD HAVE SAID SOME-THING.
I'M SURE SOMEONE COULD FILL IN FOR YOU AT WORK.
WHY DIDN'T YOU—
WHY DIDN'T YOU SAY SOME-THING?
WHY DID YOU WAIT UNTIL IT GOT THIS BAD?

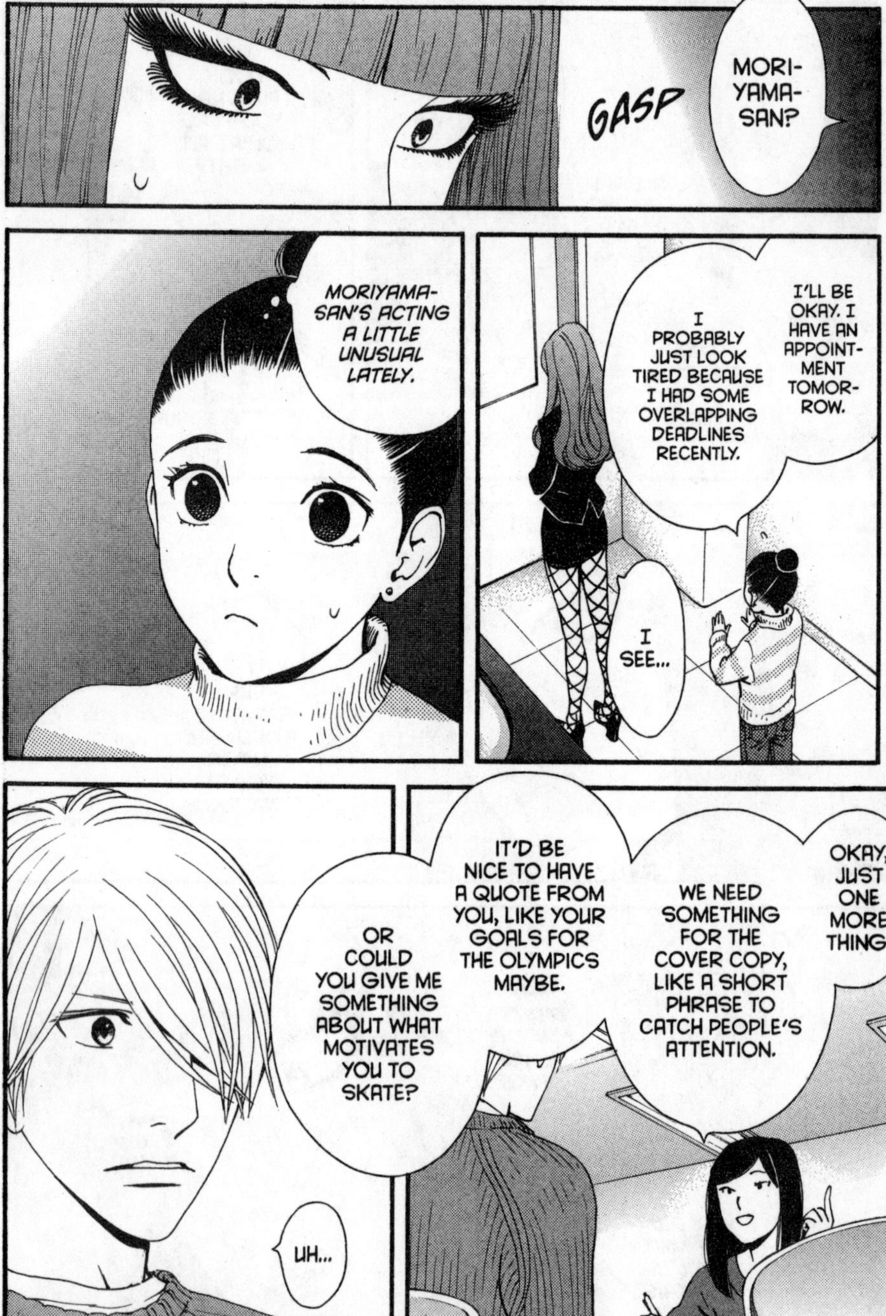
MORI-YAMA-SAN?
GASP
I'LL BE OKAY. I HAVE AN APPOINTMENT TOMORROW.
I PROBABLY JUST LOOK TIRED BECAUSE I HAD SOME OVERLAPPING DEADLINES RECENTLY.
I SEE...
MORIYAMA-SAN'S ACTING A LITTLE UNUSUAL LATELY.
OKAY, JUST ONE MORE THING.
WE NEED SOMETHING FOR THE COVER COPY, LIKE A SHORT PHRASE TO CATCH PEOPLE'S ATTENTION.
IT'D BE NICE TO HAVE A QUOTE FROM YOU, LIKE YOUR GOALS FOR THE OLYMPICS MAYBE.
OR COULD YOU GIVE ME SOMETHING ABOUT WHAT MOTIVATES YOU TO SKATE?
UH...

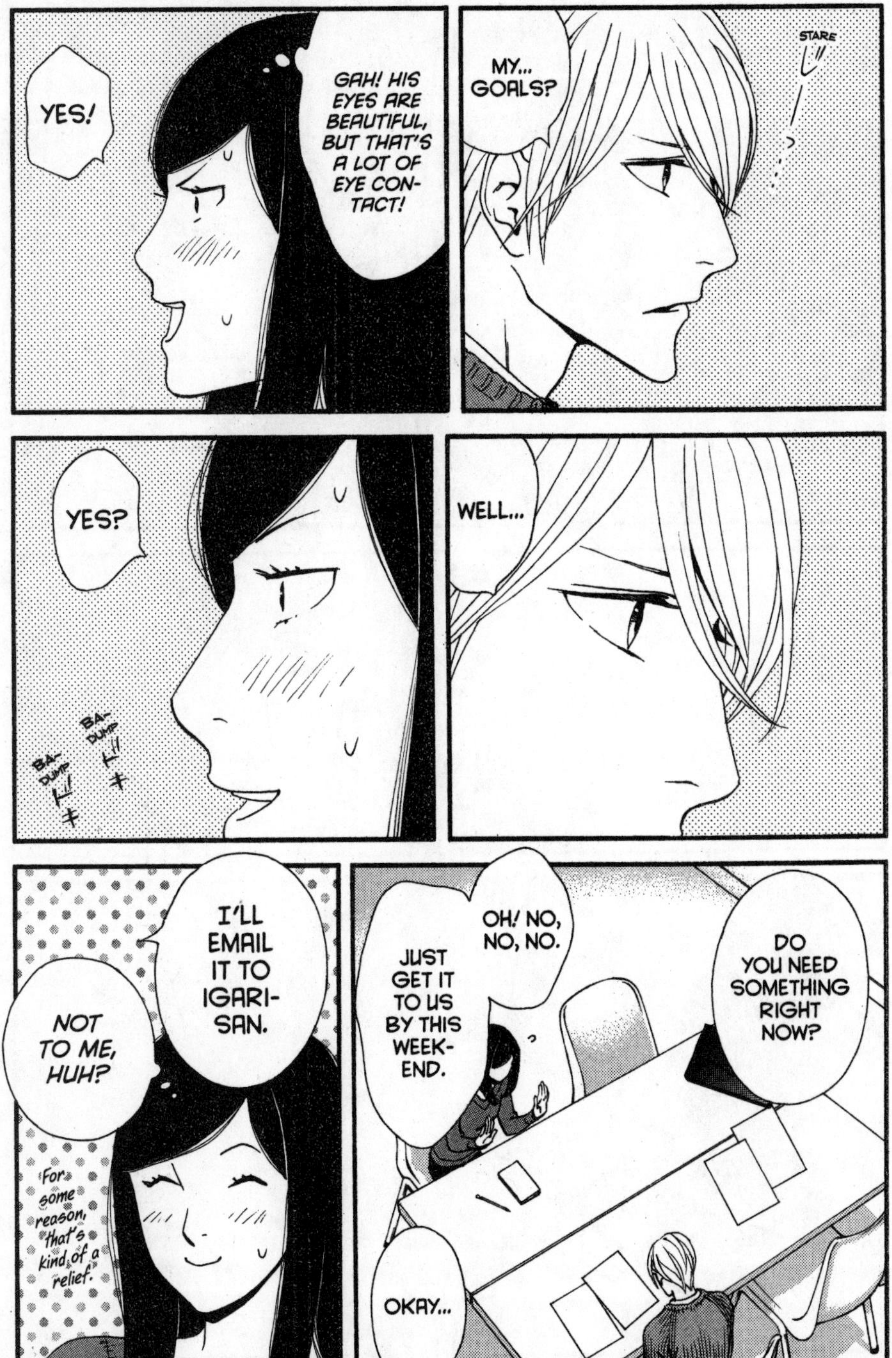
STARE
MY... GOALS?
GAH! HIS EYES ARE BEAUTIFUL, BUT THAT'S A LOT OF EYE CONTACT!
YES!
WELL...
YES?
BA-DUMP
BA-DUMP
DO YOU NEED SOMETHING RIGHT NOW?
OH! NO, NO, NO.
JUST GET IT TO US BY THIS WEEK-END.
OKAY...
I'LL EMAIL IT TO IGARI-SAN.
NOT TO ME, HUH?
For some reason, that's kind of a relief.

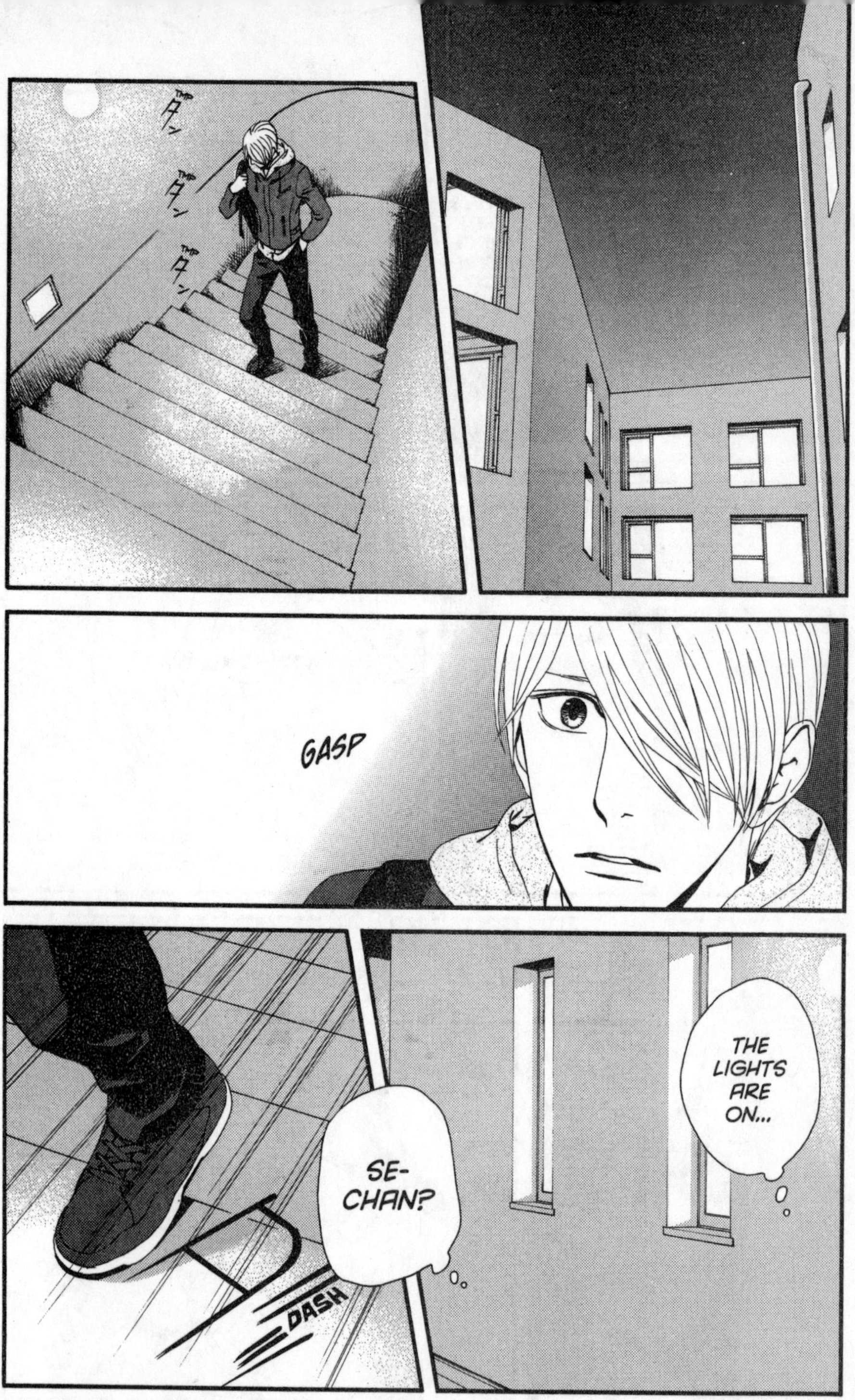
THP
THP
THP
GASP
THE LIGHTS ARE ON...
SE-CHAN?
DASH

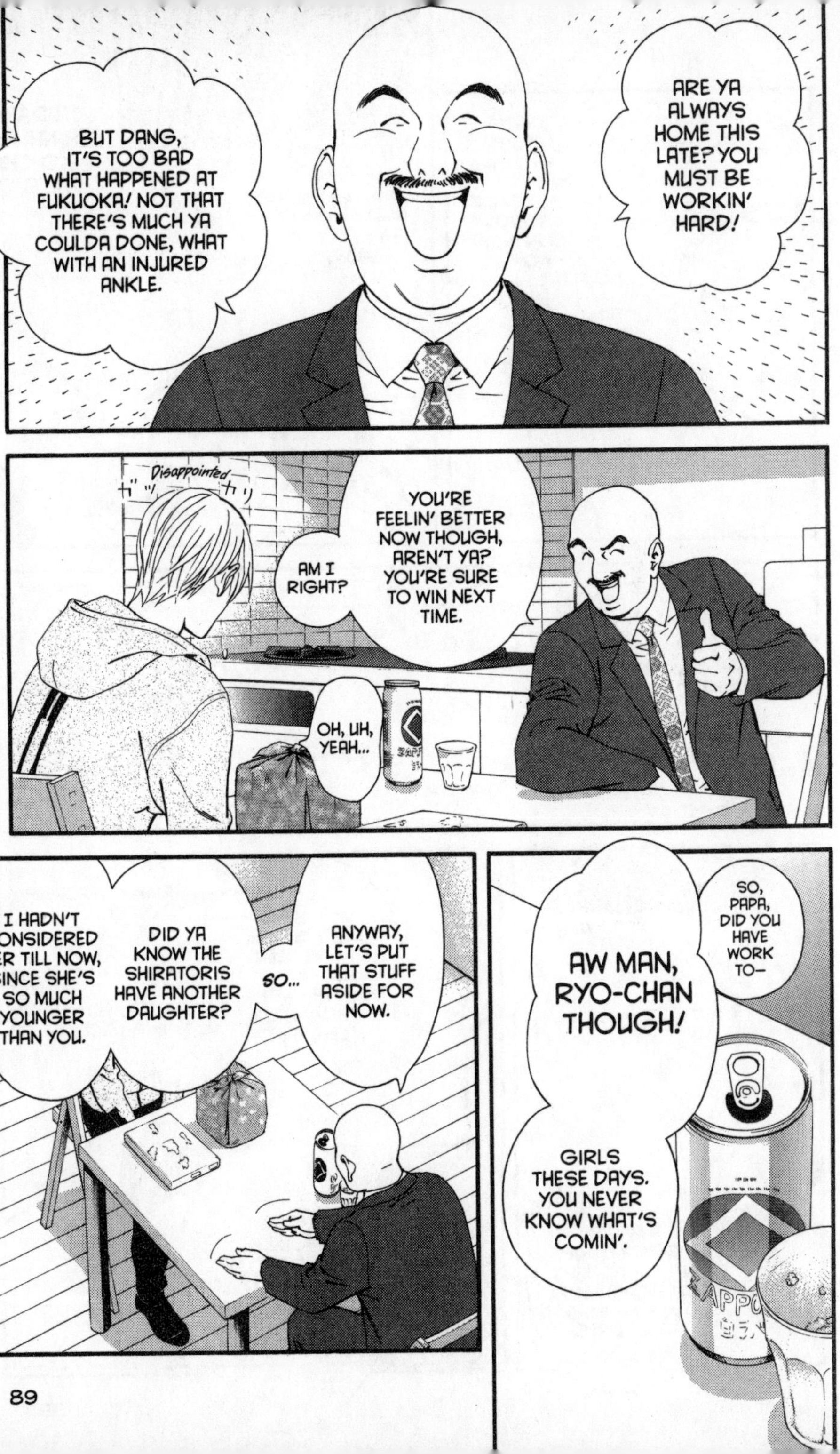
ARE YA ALWAYS HOME THIS LATE? YOU MUST BE WORKIN' HARD!
BUT DANG, IT'S TOO BAD WHAT HAPPENED AT FUKUOKA! NOT THAT THERE'S MUCH YA COULDA DONE, WHAT WITH AN INJURED ANKLE.
YOU'RE FEELIN' BETTER NOW THOUGH, AREN'T YA? YOU'RE SURE TO WIN NEXT TIME.
AM I RIGHT?
ガッ カリ
Disappointed
OH, UH, YEAH...
SO, PAPA, DID YOU HAVE WORK TO—
AW MAN, RYO-CHAN THOUGH!
GIRLS THESE DAYS. YOU NEVER KNOW WHAT'S COMIN'.
ANYWAY, LET'S PUT THAT STUFF ASIDE FOR NOW.
SO...
DID YA KNOW THE SHIRATORIS HAVE ANOTHER DAUGHTER?
I HADN'T CONSIDERED HER TILL NOW, SINCE SHE'S SO MUCH YOUNGER THAN YOU.

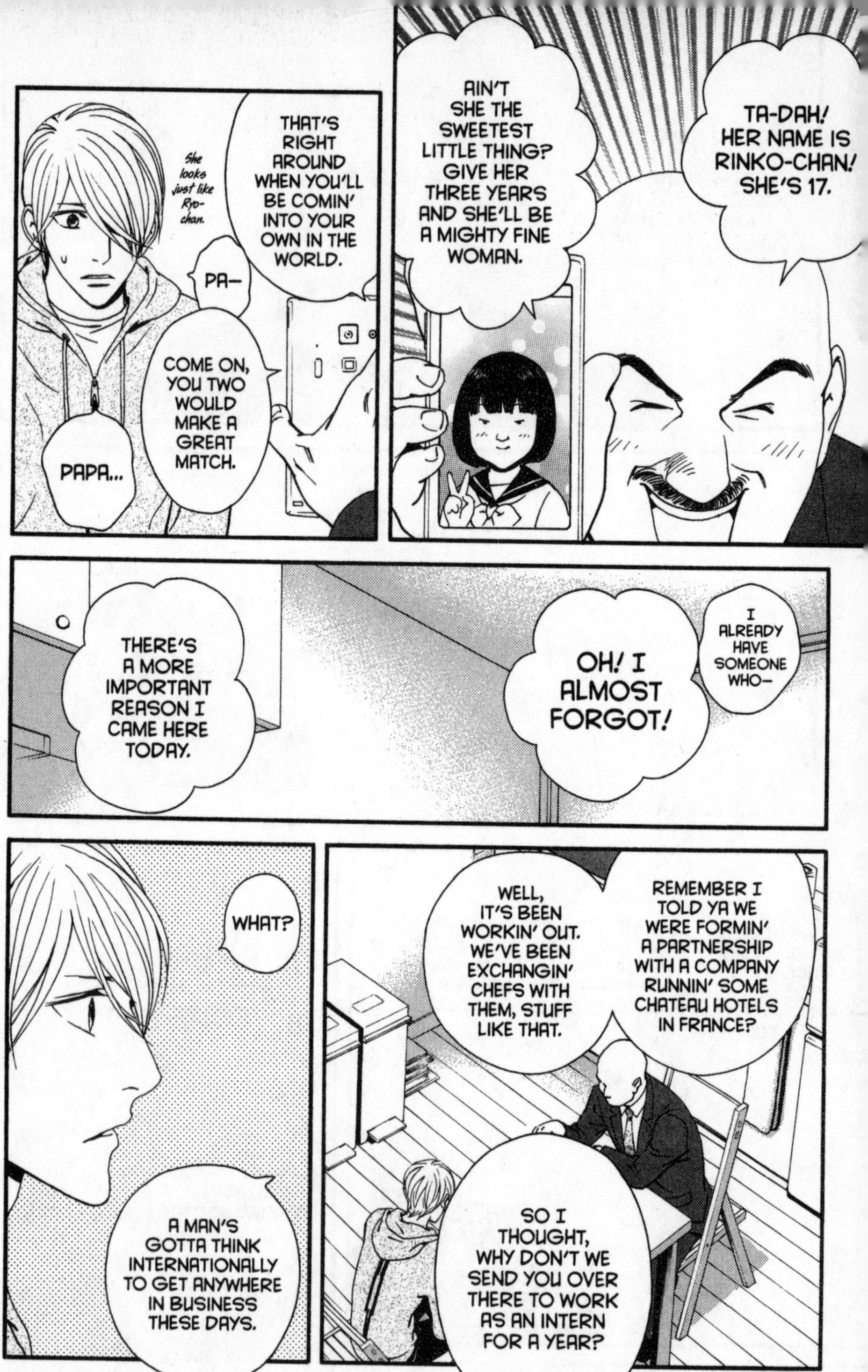
TA-DAH! HER NAME IS RINKO-CHAN! SHE'S 17.
AIN'T SHE THE SWEETEST LITTLE THING? GIVE HER THREE YEARS AND SHE'LL BE A MIGHTY FINE WOMAN.
THAT'S RIGHT AROUND WHEN YOU'LL BE COMIN' INTO YOUR OWN IN THE WORLD.
She looks just like Ryo-chan.
PA—
COME ON, YOU TWO WOULD MAKE A GREAT MATCH.
PAPA...
I ALREADY HAVE SOMEONE WHO—
OH! I ALMOST FORGOT!
THERE'S A MORE IMPORTANT REASON I CAME HERE TODAY.
REMEMBER I TOLD YA WE WERE FORMIN' A PARTNERSHIP WITH A COMPANY RUNNIN' SOME CHATEAU HOTELS IN FRANCE?
WELL, IT'S BEEN WORKIN' OUT. WE'VE BEEN EXCHANGIN' CHEFS WITH THEM, STUFF LIKE THAT.
SO I THOUGHT, WHY DON'T WE SEND YOU OVER THERE TO WORK AS AN INTERN FOR A YEAR?
WHAT?
A MAN'S GOTTA THINK INTERNATIONALLY TO GET ANYWHERE IN BUSINESS THESE DAYS.

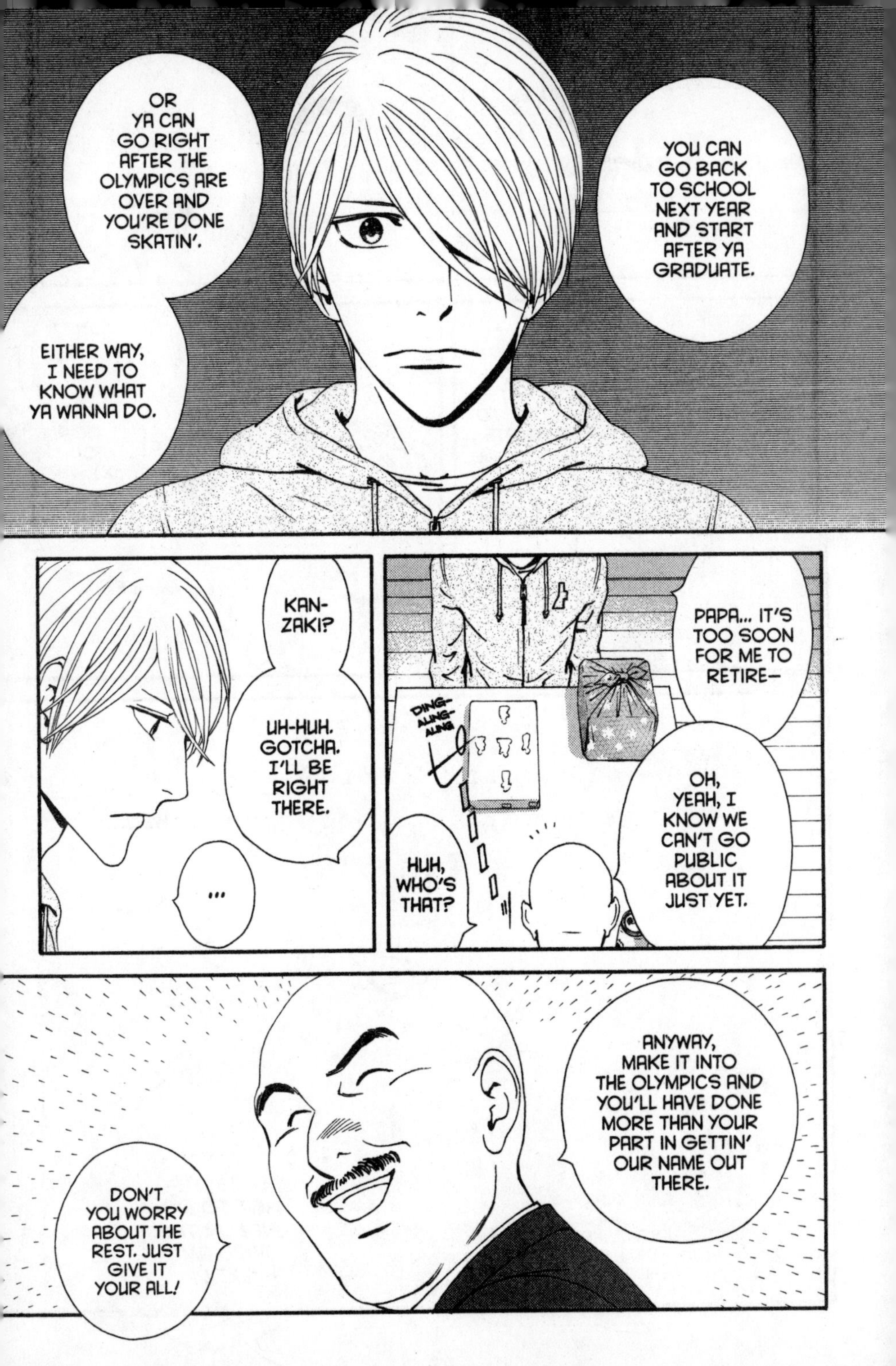
YOU CAN GO BACK TO SCHOOL NEXT YEAR AND START AFTER YA GRADUATE.
OR YA CAN GO RIGHT AFTER THE OLYMPICS ARE OVER AND YOU'RE DONE SKATIN'.
EITHER WAY, I NEED TO KNOW WHAT YA WANNA DO.
PAPA... IT'S TOO SOON FOR ME TO RETIRE–
DING-ALING-ALING
OH, YEAH, I KNOW WE CAN'T GO PUBLIC ABOUT IT JUST YET.
HUH, WHO'S THAT?
KAN-ZAKI?
UH-HUH. GOTCHA. I'LL BE RIGHT THERE.
...
ANYWAY, MAKE IT INTO THE OLYMPICS AND YOU'LL HAVE DONE MORE THAN YOUR PART IN GETTIN' OUR NAME OUT THERE.
DON'T YOU WORRY ABOUT THE REST. JUST GIVE IT YOUR ALL!

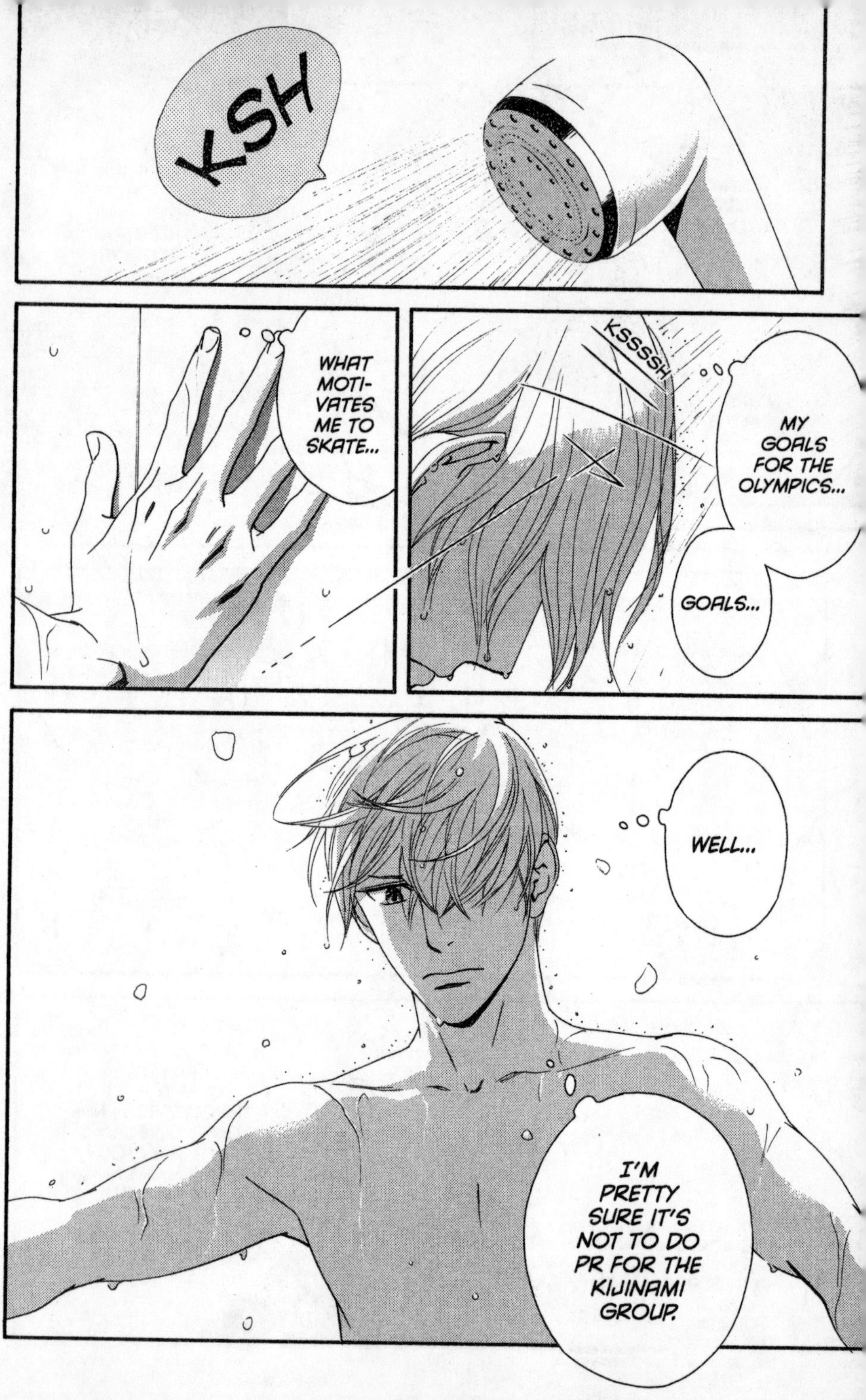
KSH
KSSSSH
MY GOALS FOR THE OLYMPICS...
GOALS...
WHAT MOTI-VATES ME TO SKATE...
WELL...
I'M PRETTY SURE IT'S NOT TO DO PR FOR THE KIJINAMI GROUP.

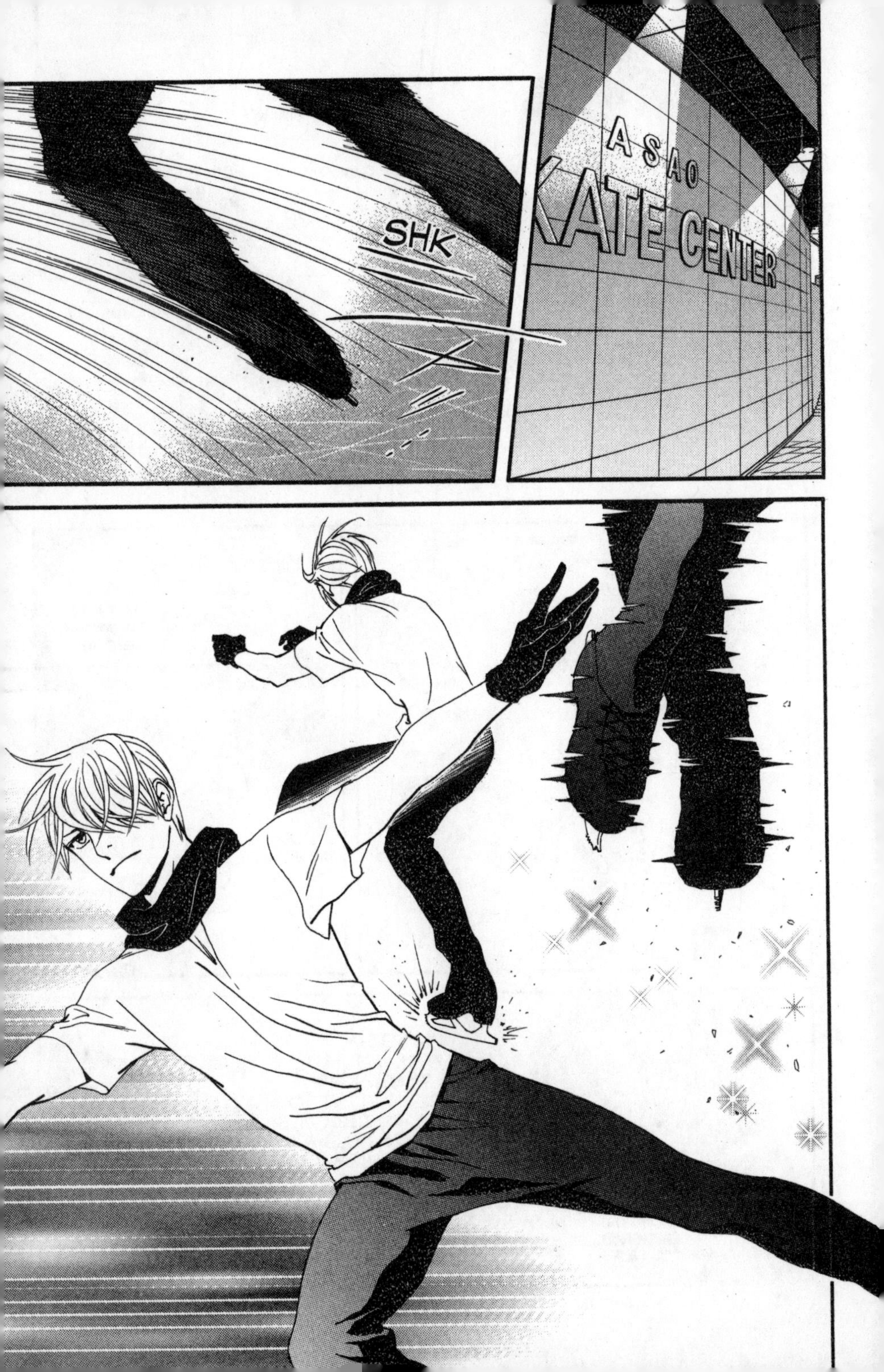
ASAO
KATE CENTER
SHK

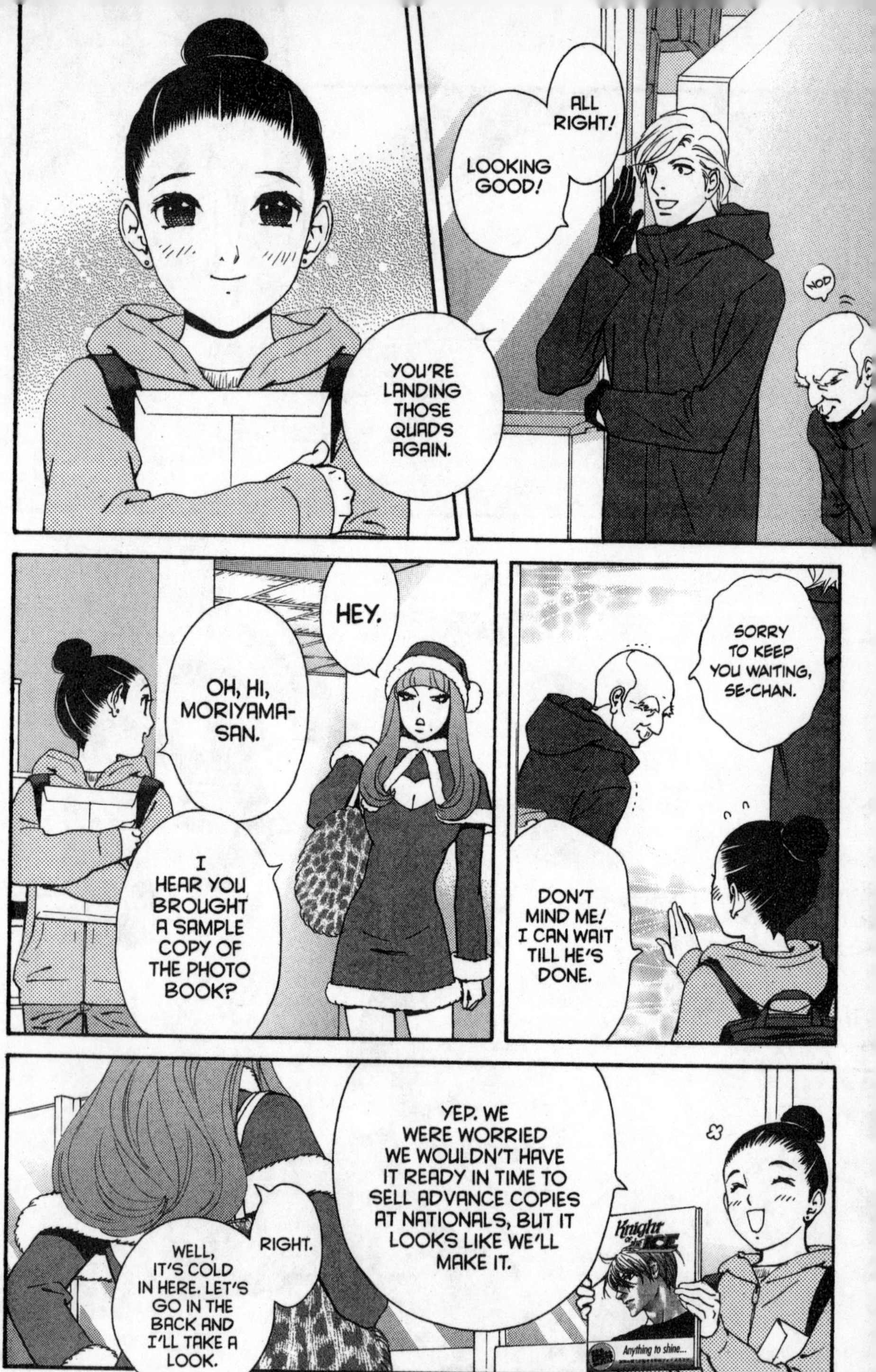
ALL RIGHT!
LOOKING GOOD!
NOD
YOU'RE LANDING THOSE QUADS AGAIN.
SORRY TO KEEP YOU WAITING, SE-CHAN.
DON'T MIND ME! I CAN WAIT TILL HE'S DONE.
HEY.
OH, HI, MORIYAMA-SAN.
I HEAR YOU BROUGHT A SAMPLE COPY OF THE PHOTO BOOK?
YEP. WE WERE WORRIED WE WOULDN'T HAVE IT READY IN TIME TO SELL ADVANCE COPIES AT NATIONALS, BUT IT LOOKS LIKE WE'LL MAKE IT.
Knight of the ICE
Anything to shine...
RIGHT.
WELL, IT'S COLD IN HERE. LET'S GO IN THE BACK AND I'LL TAKE A LOOK.
Moriyama had to come up with this herself.

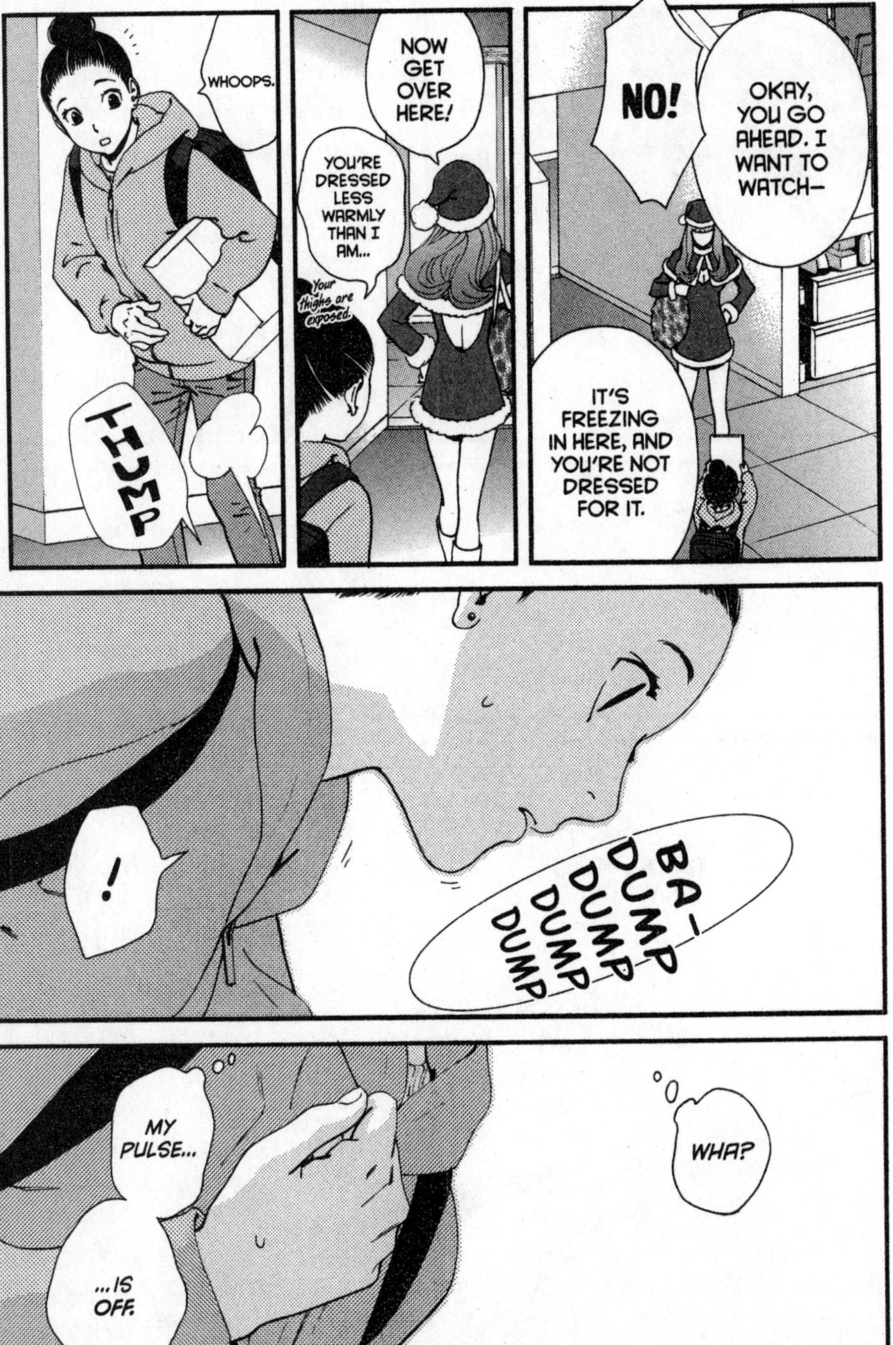
OKAY, YOU GO AHEAD. I WANT TO WATCH—
NO!
IT'S FREEZING IN HERE, AND YOU'RE NOT DRESSED FOR IT.
NOW GET OVER HERE!
YOU'RE DRESSED LESS WARMLY THAN I AM...
Your thighs are exposed.
WHOOPS.
THUMP
BA-DUMP DUMP DUMP DUMP DUMP
!
WHA?
MY PULSE...
...IS OFF.

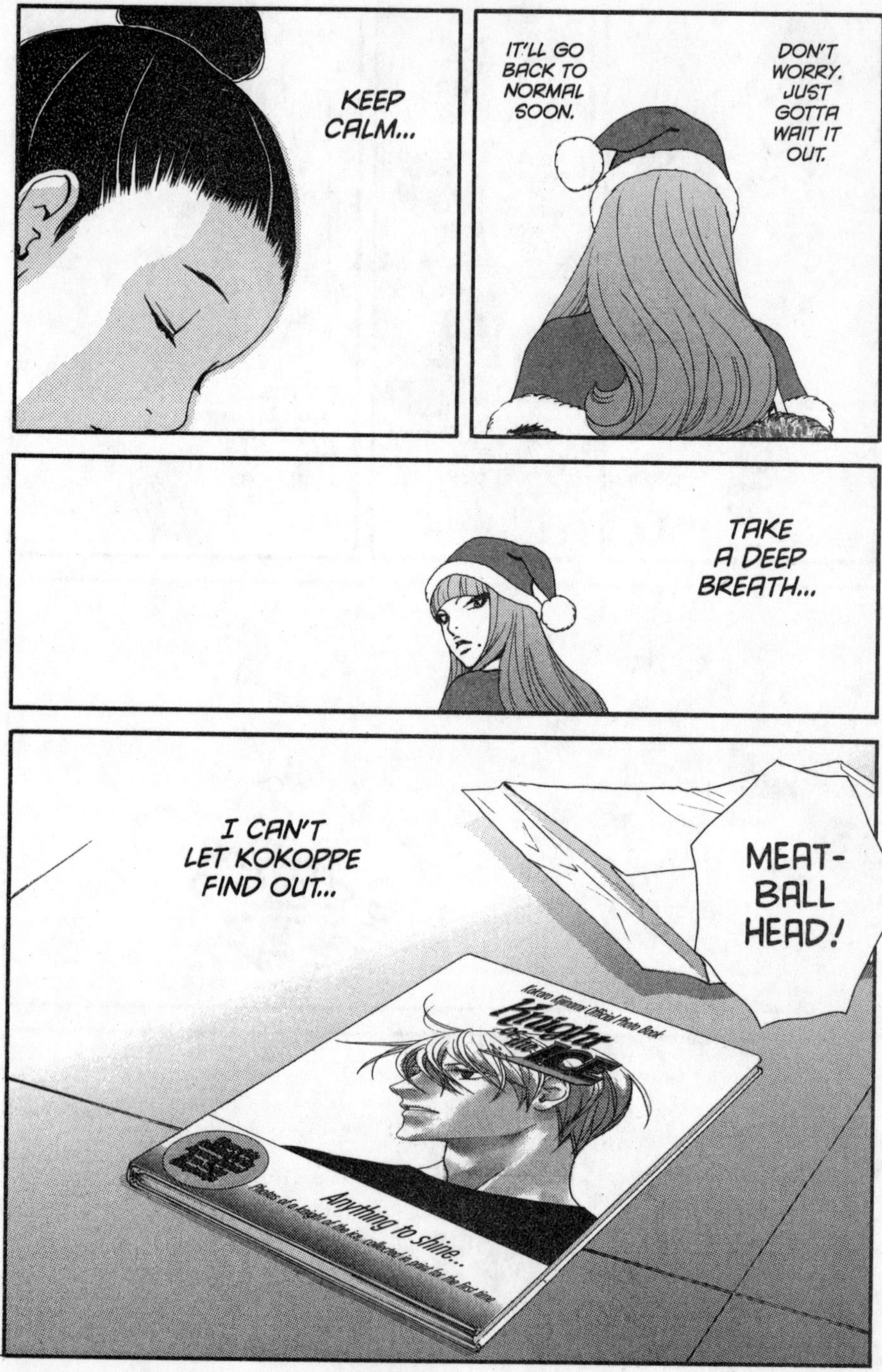
DON'T WORRY. JUST GOTTA WAIT IT OUT.
IT'LL GO BACK TO NORMAL SOON.
KEEP CALM...
TAKE A DEEP BREATH...
MEAT-BALL HEAD!
I CAN'T LET KOKOPPE FIND OUT...
Kokoro Kijinami Official Photo Book
Knight of the Ice
Anything to shine...
Photos of a knight of the ice, collected in print for the first time.

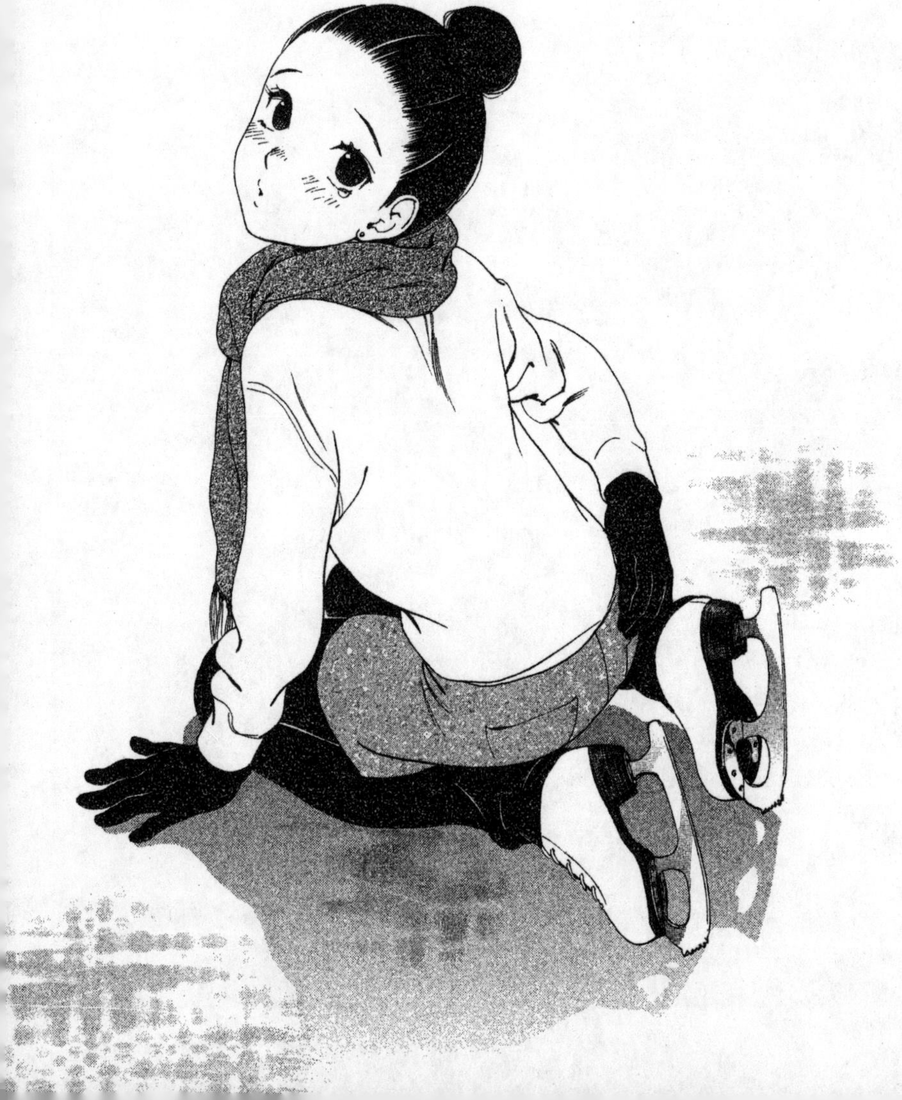

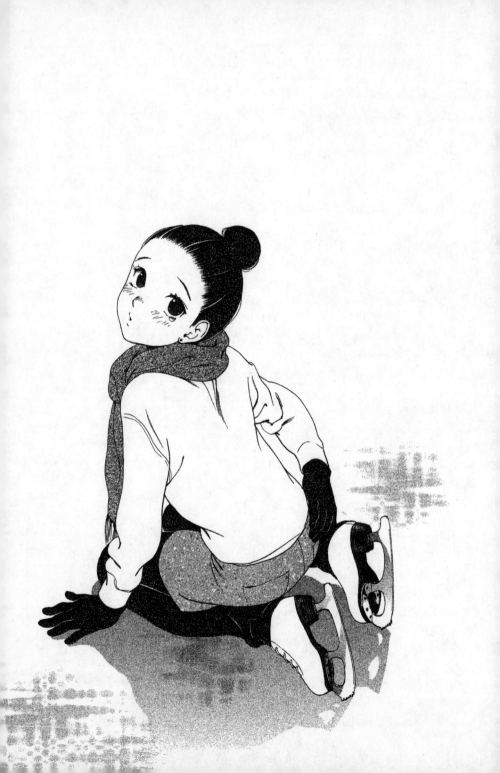

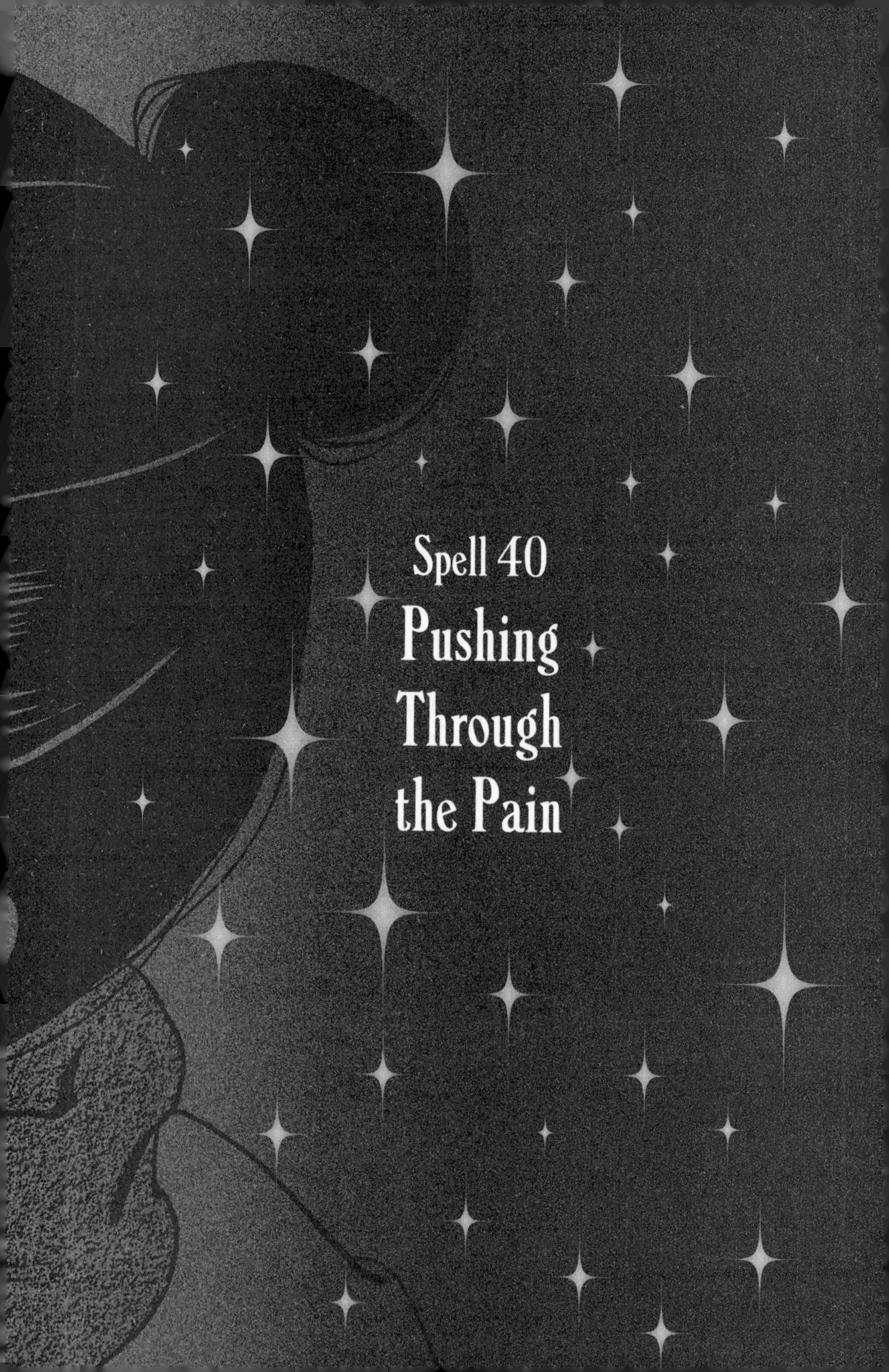
Spell 40
Pushing Through the Pain

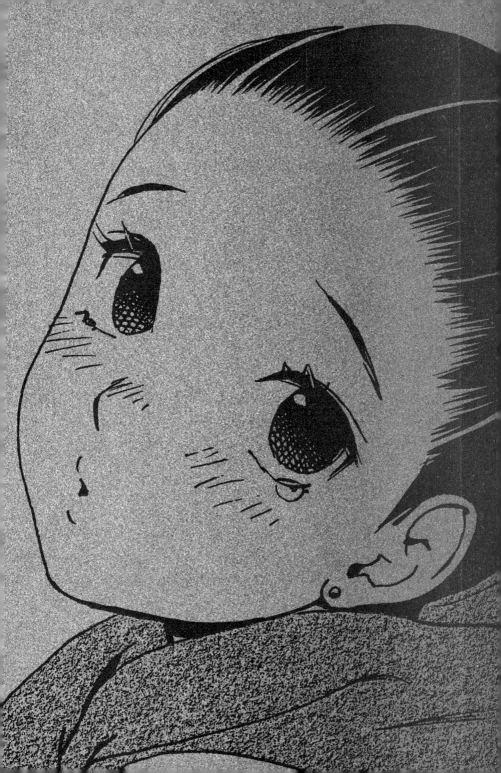

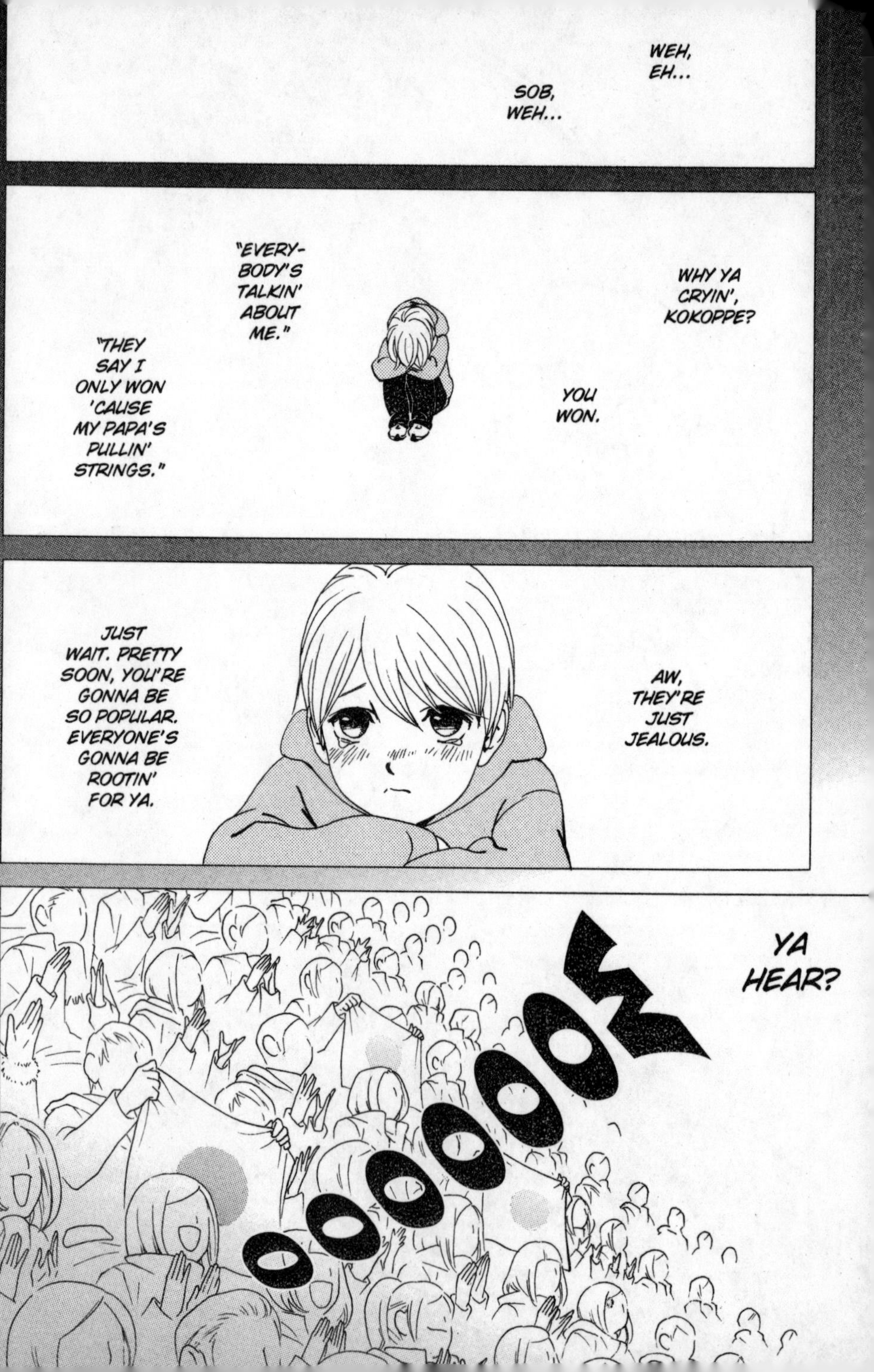
WEH, EH...
SOB, WEH...
WHY YA CRYIN', KOKOPPE?
YOU WON.
"EVERY-BODY'S TALKIN' ABOUT ME."
"THEY SAY I ONLY WON 'CAUSE MY PAPA'S PULLIN' STRINGS."
AW, THEY'RE JUST JEALOUS.
JUST WAIT. PRETTY SOON, YOU'RE GONNA BE SO POPULAR. EVERYONE'S GONNA BE ROOTIN' FOR YA.
YA HEAR?

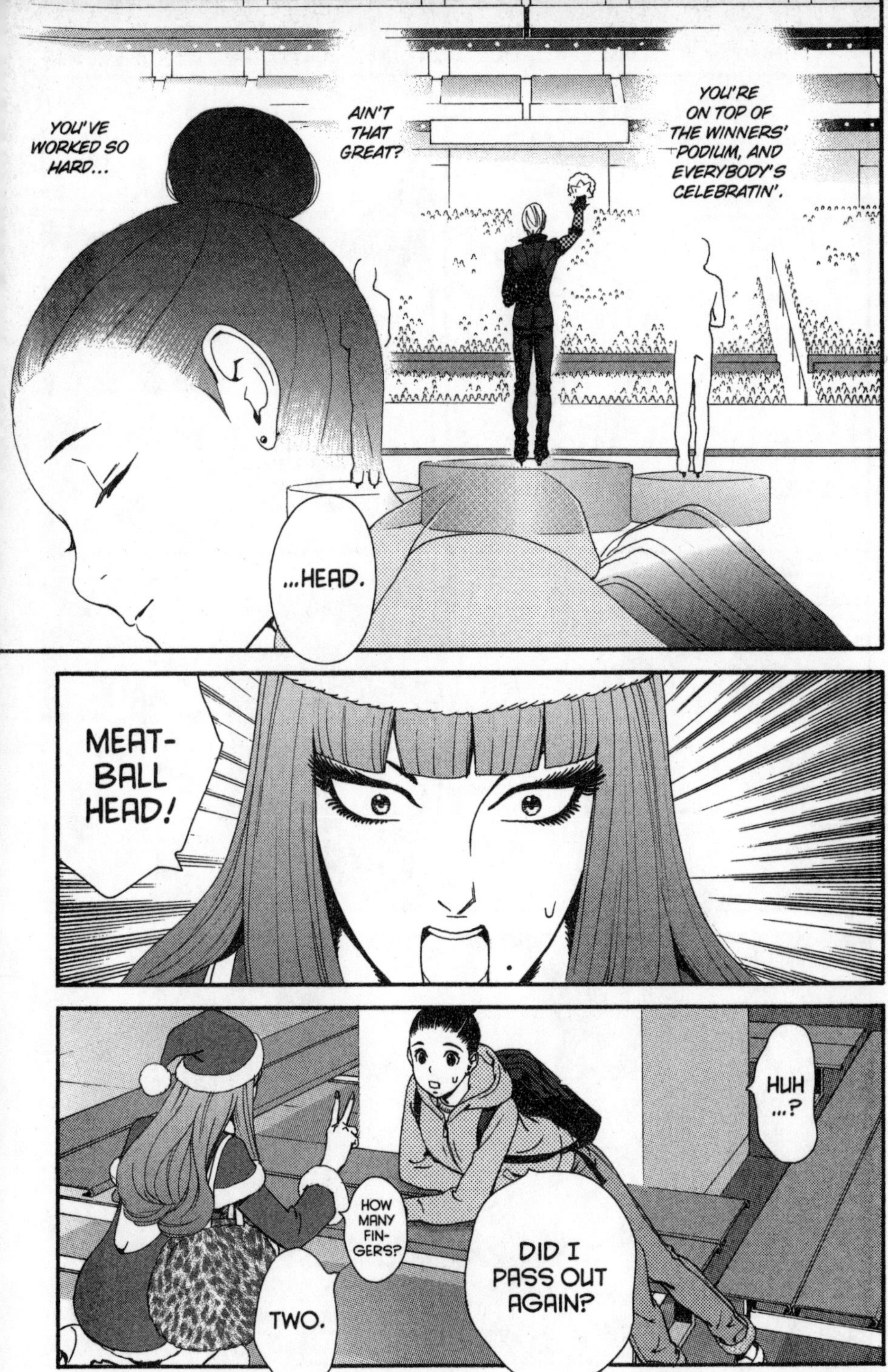
YOU'RE ON TOP OF THE WINNERS' PODIUM, AND EVERYBODY'S CELEBRATIN'.
AIN'T THAT GREAT?
YOU'VE WORKED SO HARD...
...HEAD.
MEAT-BALL HEAD!
HUH ...?
DID I PASS OUT AGAIN?
HOW MANY FIN-GERS?
TWO.

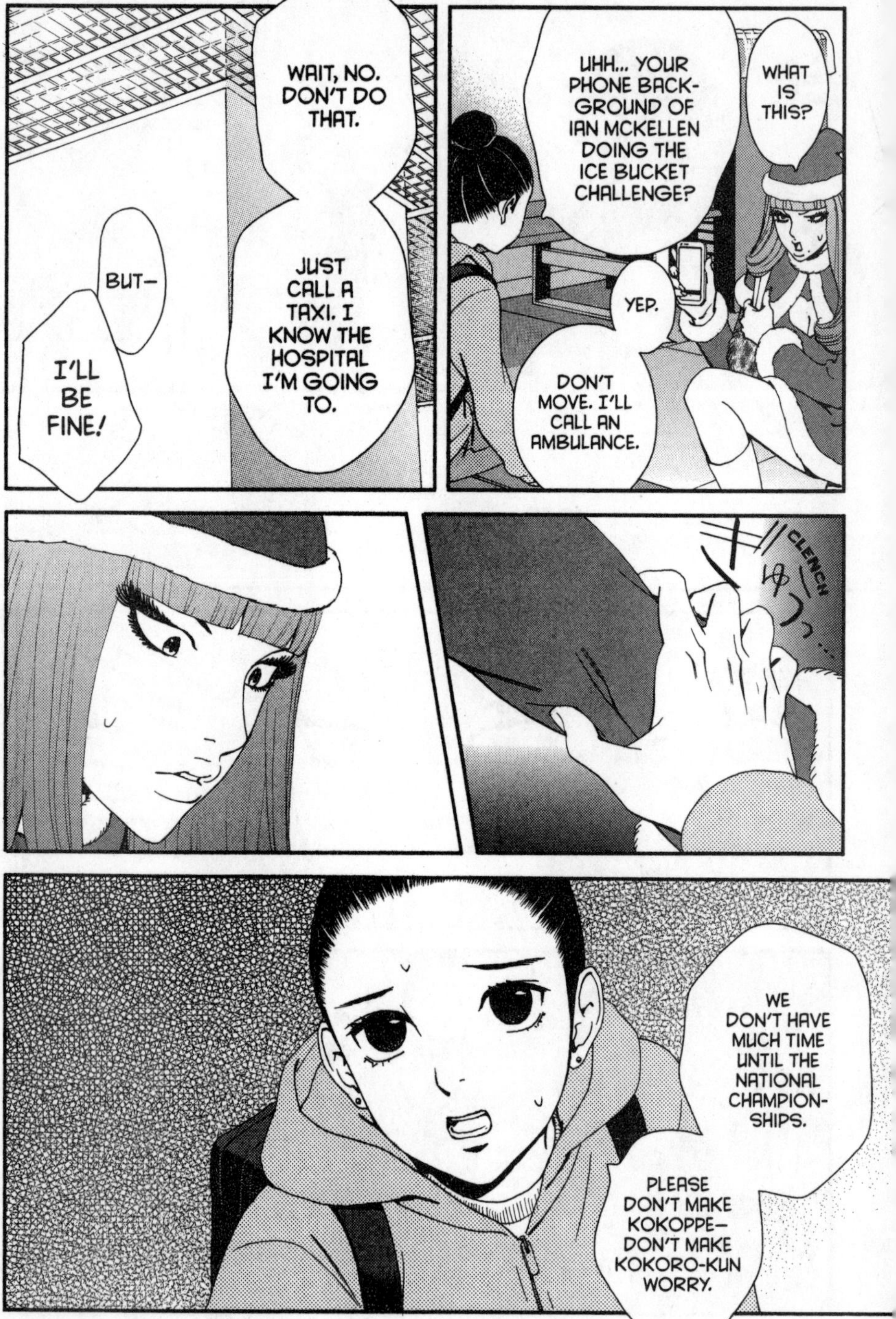
WHAT IS THIS?
UHH... YOUR PHONE BACKGROUND OF IAN MCKELLEN DOING THE ICE BUCKET CHALLENGE?
YEP.
DON'T MOVE. I'LL CALL AN AMBULANCE.
WAIT, NO. DON'T DO THAT.
JUST CALL A TAXI. I KNOW THE HOSPITAL I'M GOING TO.
BUT—
I'LL BE FINE!
CLENCH
WE DON'T HAVE MUCH TIME UNTIL THE NATIONAL CHAMPIONSHIPS.
PLEASE DON'T MAKE KOKOPPE— DON'T MAKE KOKORO-KUN WORRY.

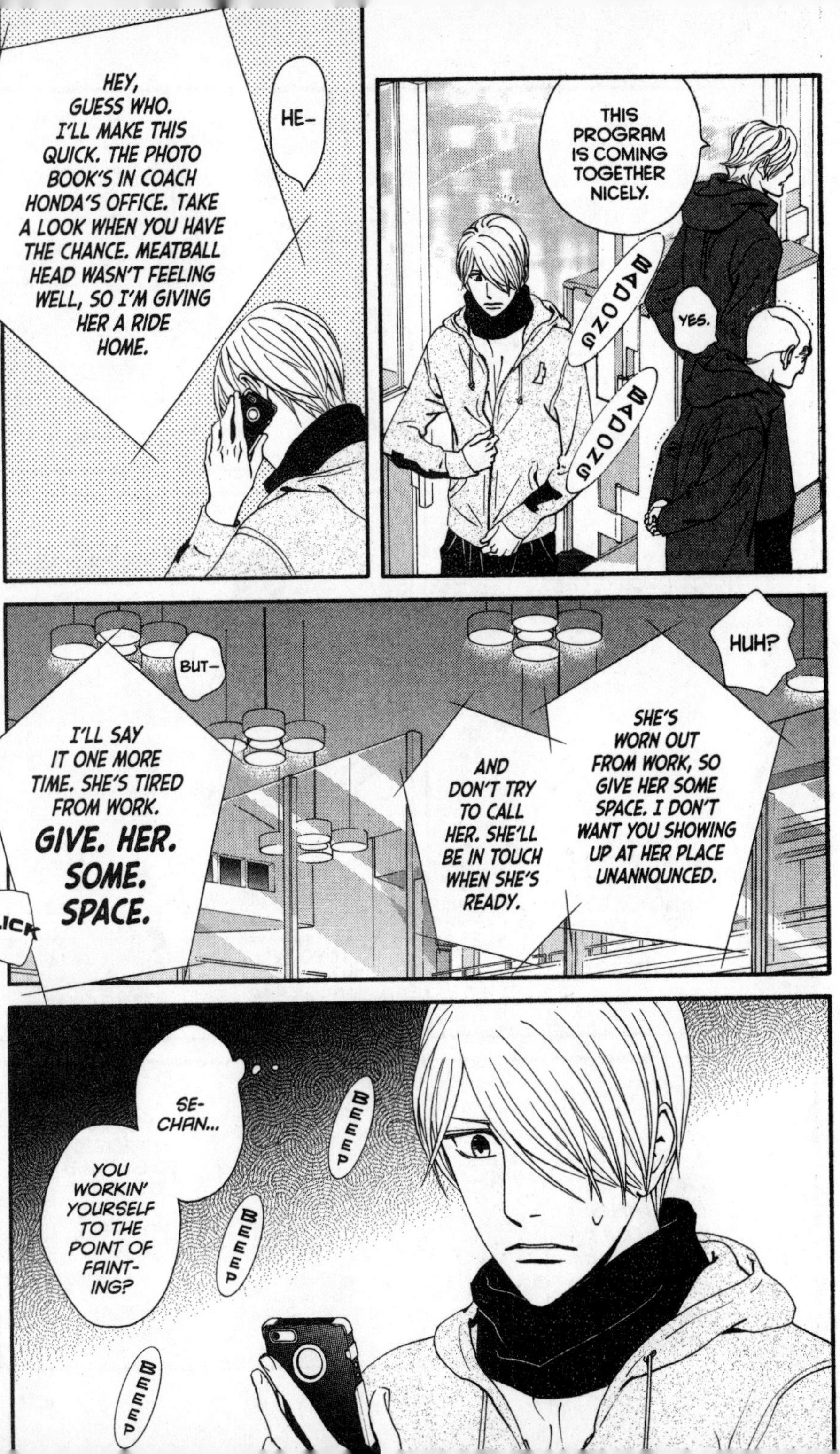

THIS PROGRAM IS COMING TOGETHER NICELY.
BADONG
BADONG
YES.
HE-
HEY, GUESS WHO. I'LL MAKE THIS QUICK. THE PHOTO BOOK'S IN COACH HONDA'S OFFICE. TAKE A LOOK WHEN YOU HAVE THE CHANCE. MEATBALL HEAD WASN'T FEELING WELL, SO I'M GIVING HER A RIDE HOME.
HUH?
SHE'S WORN OUT FROM WORK, SO GIVE HER SOME SPACE. I DON'T WANT YOU SHOWING UP AT HER PLACE UNANNOUNCED.
AND DON'T TRY TO CALL HER. SHE'LL BE IN TOUCH WHEN SHE'S READY.
BUT-
I'LL SAY IT ONE MORE TIME. SHE'S TIRED FROM WORK. GIVE. HER. SOME. SPACE.
CLICK
SE-CHAN...
BEEEP
BEEEP
BEEEP
YOU WORKIN' YOURSELF TO THE POINT OF FAINT-ING?

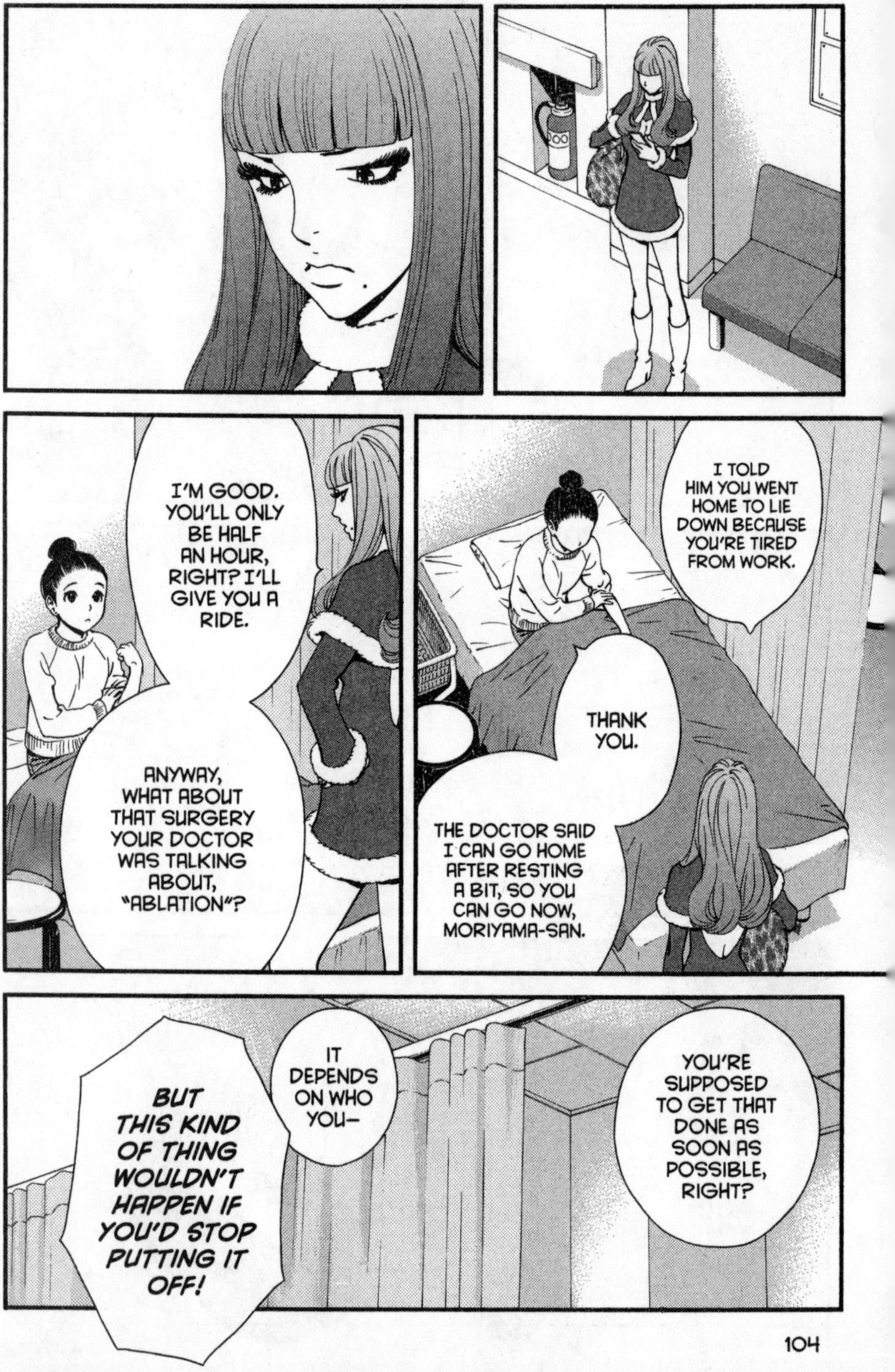
I TOLD HIM YOU WENT HOME TO LIE DOWN BECAUSE YOU'RE TIRED FROM WORK.
THANK YOU.
THE DOCTOR SAID I CAN GO HOME AFTER RESTING A BIT, SO YOU CAN GO NOW, MORIYAMA-SAN.
I'M GOOD. YOU'LL ONLY BE HALF AN HOUR, RIGHT? I'LL GIVE YOU A RIDE.
ANYWAY, WHAT ABOUT THAT SURGERY YOUR DOCTOR WAS TALKING ABOUT, "ABLATION"?
YOU'RE SUPPOSED TO GET THAT DONE AS SOON AS POSSIBLE, RIGHT?
IT DEPENDS ON WHO YOU—
BUT THIS KIND OF THING WOULDN'T HAPPEN IF YOU'D STOP PUTTING IT OFF!

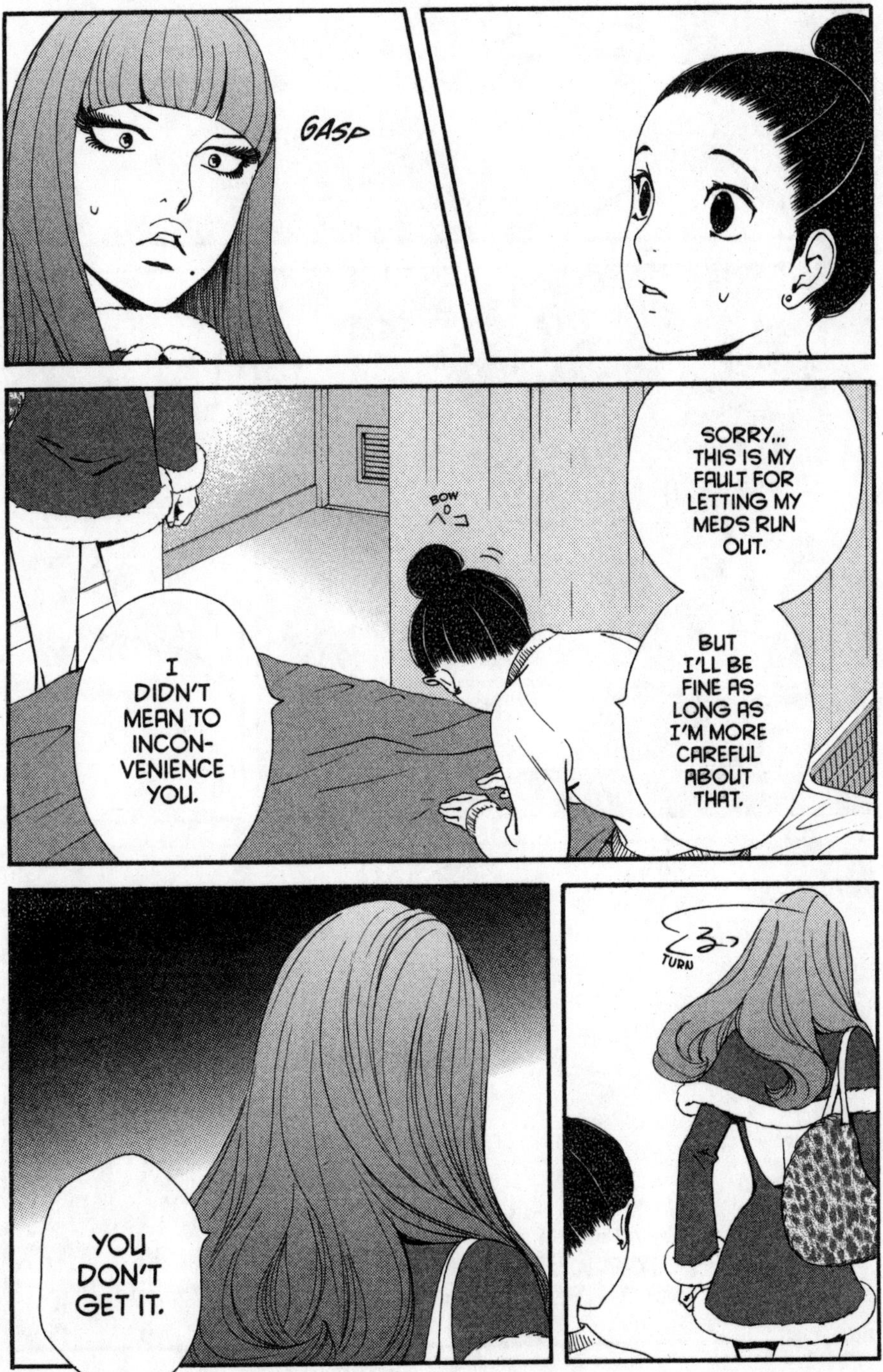
GASP
SORRY... THIS IS MY FAULT FOR LETTING MY MEDS RUN OUT.
BUT I'LL BE FINE AS LONG AS I'M MORE CAREFUL ABOUT THAT.
BOW
I DIDN'T MEAN TO INCON-VENIENCE YOU.
TURN
YOU DON'T GET IT.

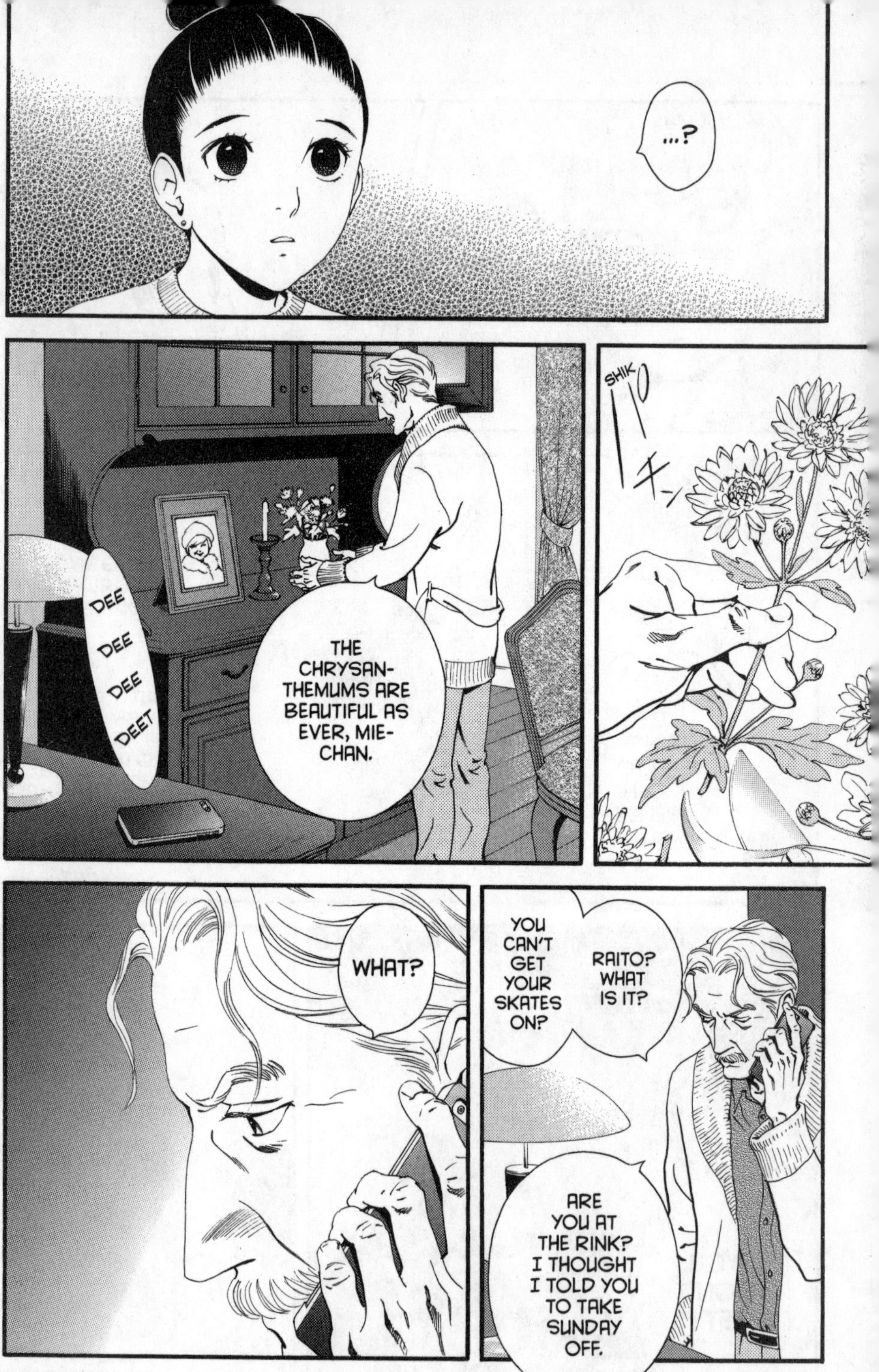
...?
SHIK
DEE DEE DEE DEET
THE CHRYSANTHEMUMS ARE BEAUTIFUL AS EVER, MIE-CHAN.
RAITO? WHAT IS IT?
YOU CAN'T GET YOUR SKATES ON?
ARE YOU AT THE RINK? I THOUGHT I TOLD YOU TO TAKE SUNDAY OFF.
WHAT?

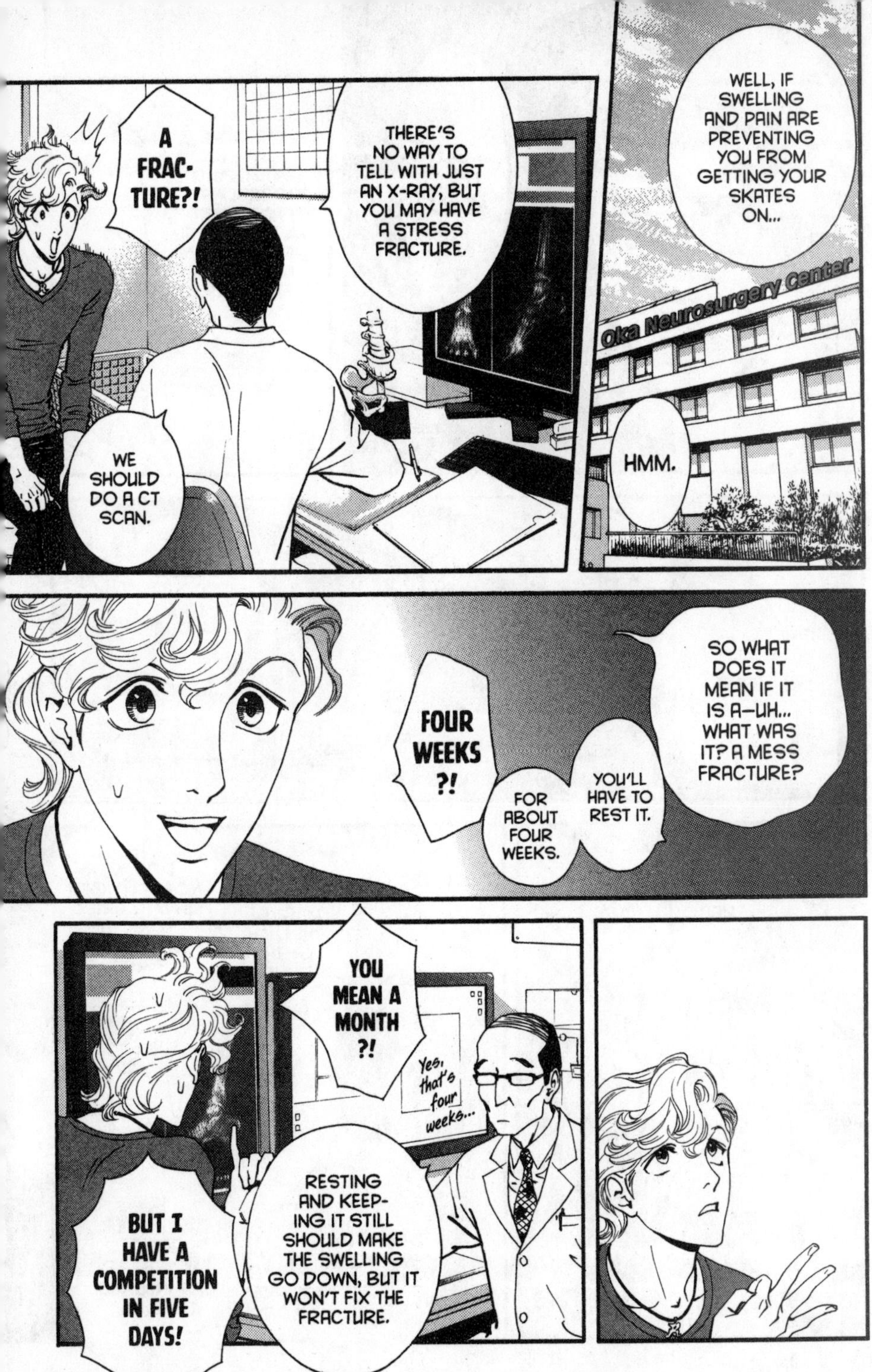
WELL, IF SWELLING AND PAIN ARE PREVENTING YOU FROM GETTING YOUR SKATES ON...
Oka Neurosurgery Center
HMM.
THERE'S NO WAY TO TELL WITH JUST AN X-RAY, BUT YOU MAY HAVE A STRESS FRACTURE.
A FRAC-TURE?!
WE SHOULD DO A CT SCAN.
SO WHAT DOES IT MEAN IF IT IS A—UH... WHAT WAS IT? A MESS FRACTURE?
YOU'LL HAVE TO REST IT.
FOR ABOUT FOUR WEEKS.
FOUR WEEKS ?!
YOU MEAN A MONTH ?!
Yes, that's four weeks...
RESTING AND KEEP-ING IT STILL SHOULD MAKE THE SWELLING GO DOWN, BUT IT WON'T FIX THE FRACTURE.
BUT I HAVE A COMPETITION IN FIVE DAYS!

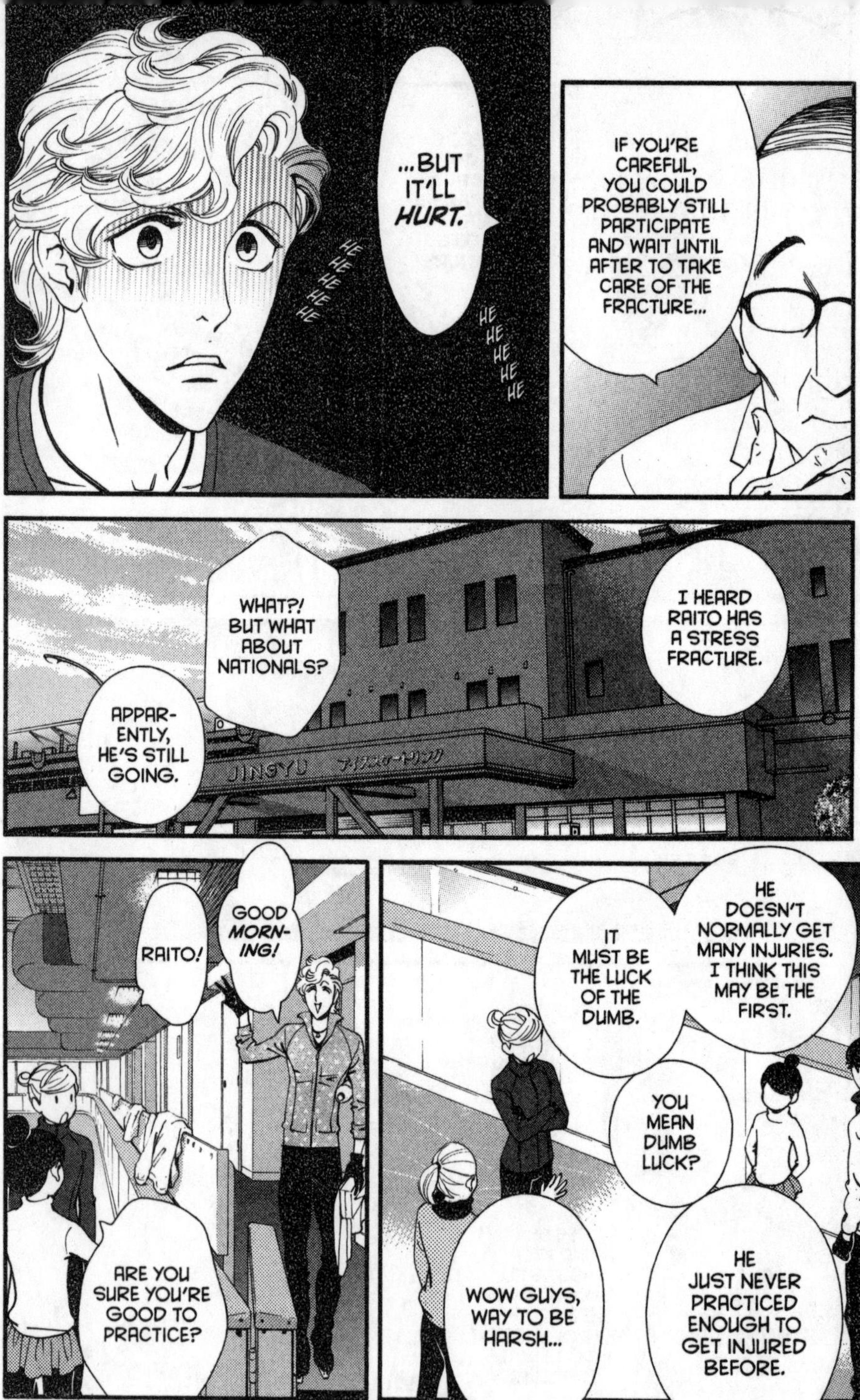
IF YOU'RE CAREFUL, YOU COULD PROBABLY STILL PARTICIPATE AND WAIT UNTIL AFTER TO TAKE CARE OF THE FRACTURE...
...BUT IT'LL *HURT.*
HE HE HE HE HE
HE HE HE HE HE
I HEARD RAITO HAS A STRESS FRACTURE.
WHAT?! BUT WHAT ABOUT NATIONALS?
APPARENTLY, HE'S STILL GOING.
JINGYU
HE DOESN'T NORMALLY GET MANY INJURIES. I THINK THIS MAY BE THE FIRST.
IT MUST BE THE LUCK OF THE DUMB.
YOU MEAN DUMB LUCK?
HE JUST NEVER PRACTICED ENOUGH TO GET INJURED BEFORE.
WOW GUYS, WAY TO BE HARSH...
GOOD *MORNING!*
RAITO!
ARE YOU SURE YOU'RE GOOD TO PRACTICE?

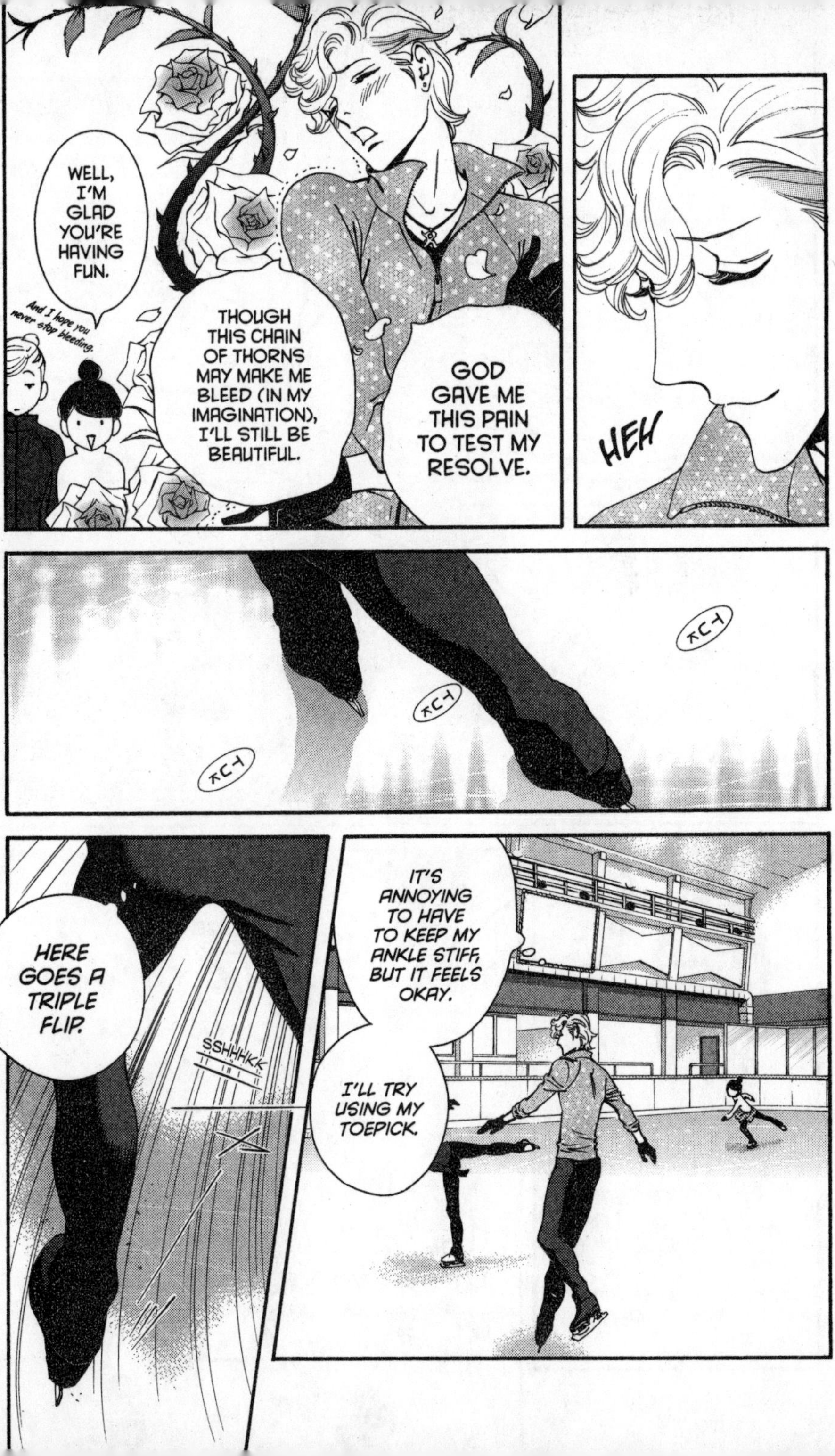
HEH
GOD GAVE ME THIS PAIN TO TEST MY RESOLVE.
THOUGH THIS CHAIN OF THORNS MAY MAKE ME BLEED (IN MY IMAGINATION), I'LL STILL BE BEAUTIFUL.
WELL, I'M GLAD YOU'RE HAVING FUN.
And I hope you never stop bleeding.
IT'S ANNOYING TO HAVE TO KEEP MY ANKLE STIFF, BUT IT FEELS OKAY.
I'LL TRY USING MY TOEPICK.
HERE GOES A TRIPLE FLIP.
SSHHHKK

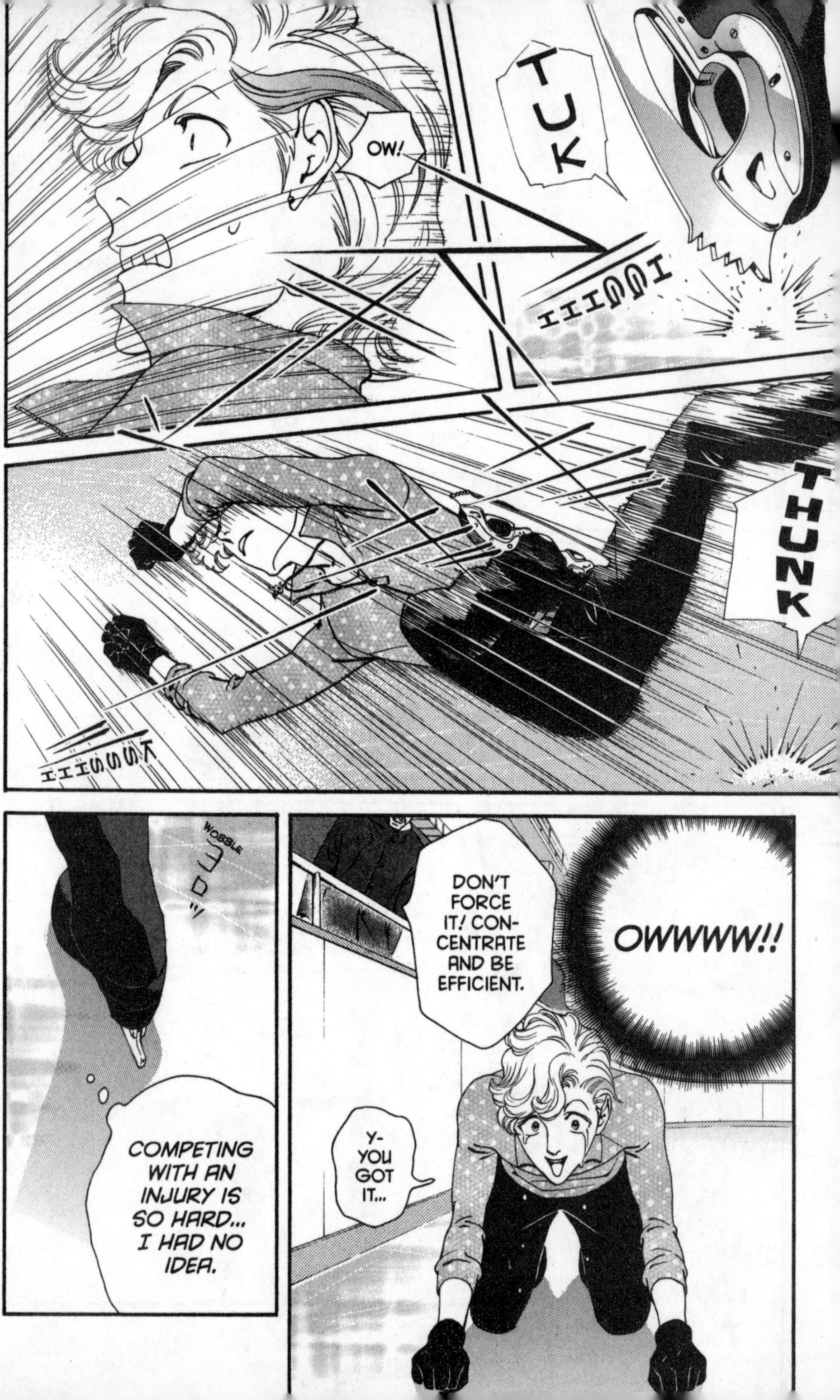
TUK
OW!
IGGIII
THUNK
OWWWW!!
DON'T FORCE IT! CONCENTRATE AND BE EFFICIENT.
Y-YOU GOT IT...
WOBBLE
COMPETING WITH AN INJURY IS SO HARD... I HAD NO IDEA.

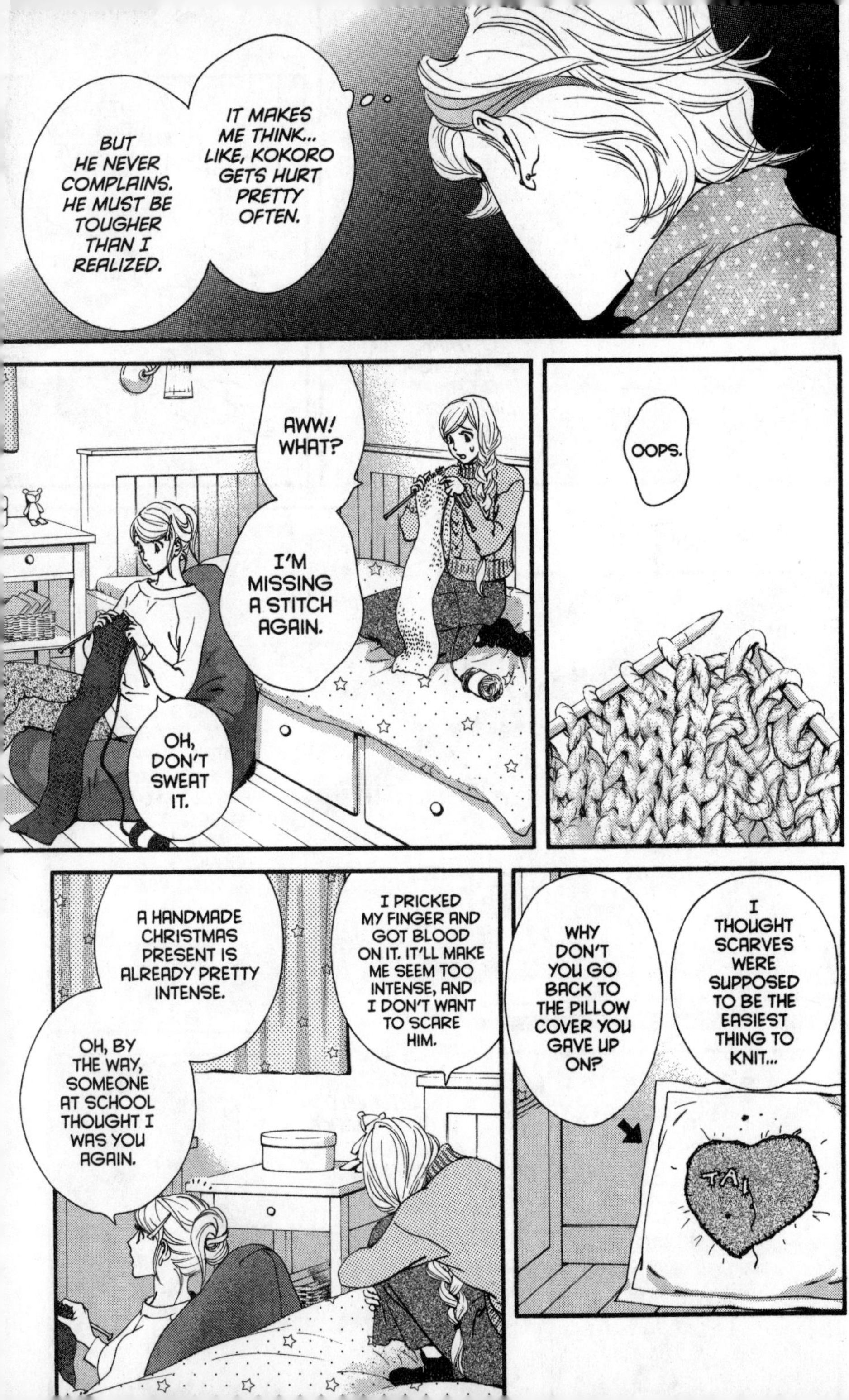
IT MAKES ME THINK... LIKE, KOKORO GETS HURT PRETTY OFTEN.
BUT HE NEVER COMPLAINS. HE MUST BE TOUGHER THAN I REALIZED.
OOPS.
AWW! WHAT?
I'M MISSING A STITCH AGAIN.
OH, DON'T SWEAT IT.
I THOUGHT SCARVES WERE SUPPOSED TO BE THE EASIEST THING TO KNIT...
WHY DON'T YOU GO BACK TO THE PILLOW COVER YOU GAVE UP ON?
TAI
I PRICKED MY FINGER AND GOT BLOOD ON IT. IT'LL MAKE ME SEEM TOO INTENSE, AND I DON'T WANT TO SCARE HIM.
A HANDMADE CHRISTMAS PRESENT IS ALREADY PRETTY INTENSE.
OH, BY THE WAY, SOMEONE AT SCHOOL THOUGHT I WAS YOU AGAIN.

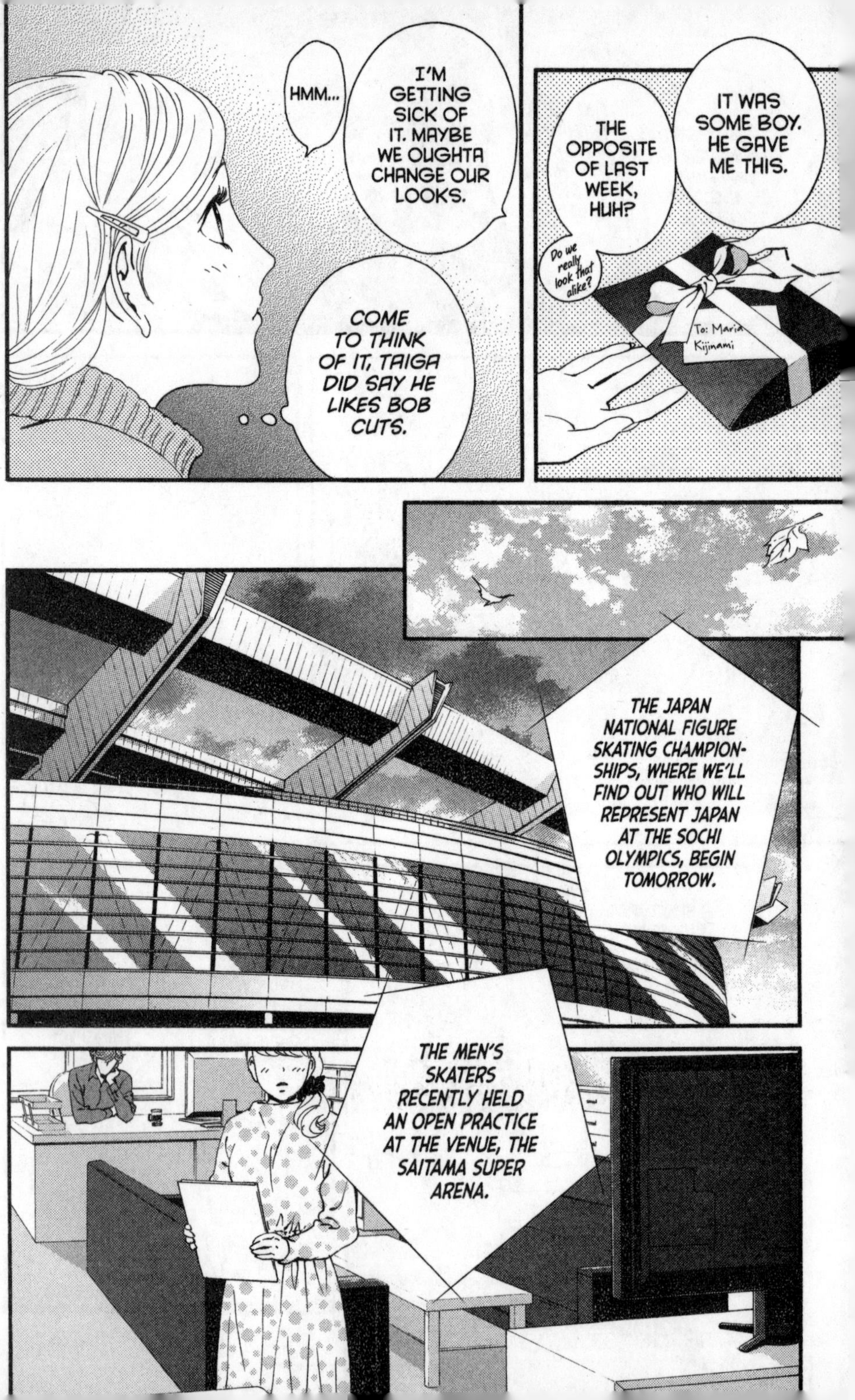
IT WAS SOME BOY. HE GAVE ME THIS.
THE OPPOSITE OF LAST WEEK, HUH?
Do we really look that alike?
To: Maria Kijinami
I'M GETTING SICK OF IT. MAYBE WE OUGHTA CHANGE OUR LOOKS.
HMM...
COME TO THINK OF IT, TAIGA DID SAY HE LIKES BOB CUTS.
THE JAPAN NATIONAL FIGURE SKATING CHAMPIONSHIPS, WHERE WE'LL FIND OUT WHO WILL REPRESENT JAPAN AT THE SOCHI OLYMPICS, BEGIN TOMORROW.
THE MEN'S SKATERS RECENTLY HELD AN OPEN PRACTICE AT THE VENUE, THE SAITAMA SUPER ARENA.

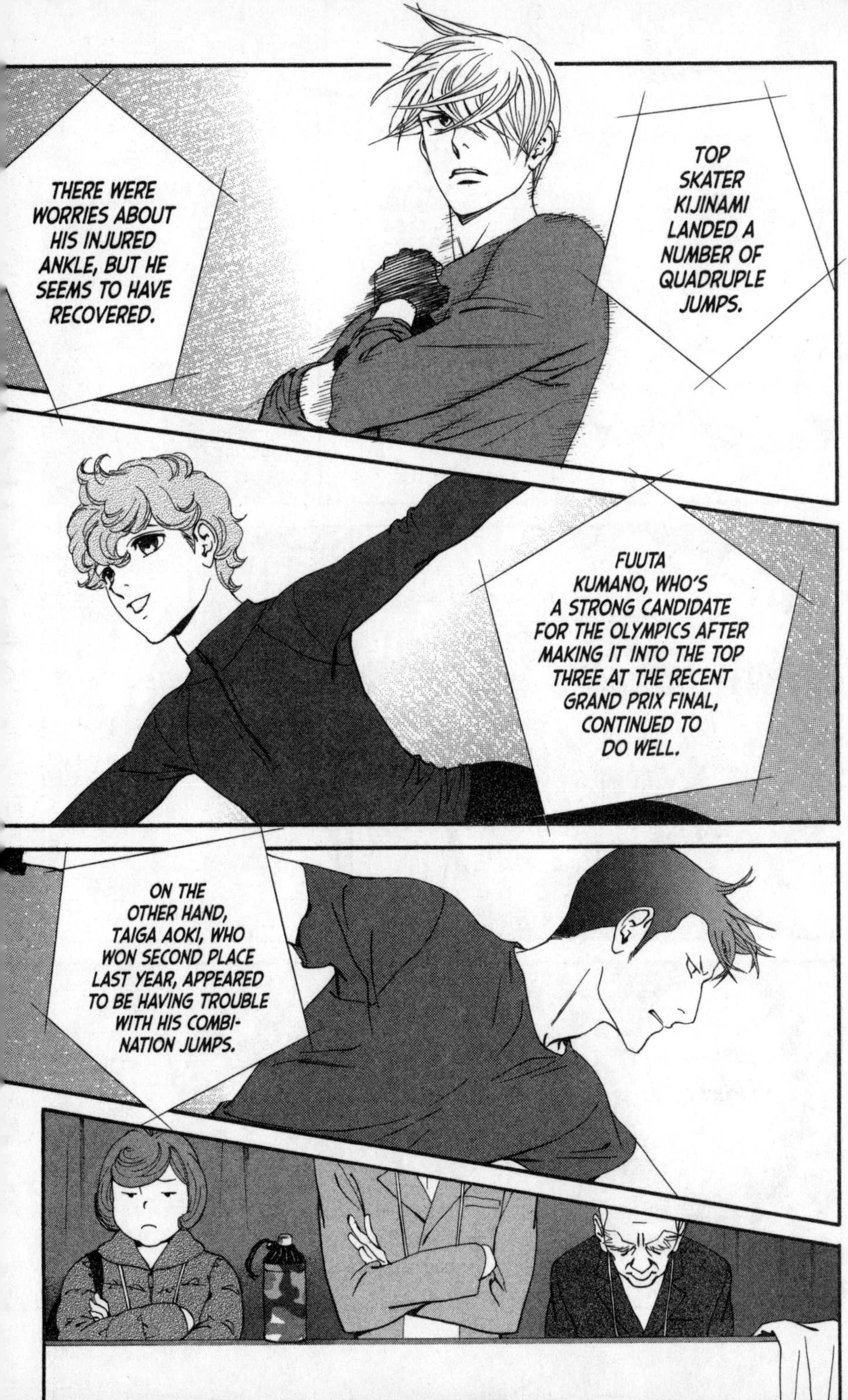
TOP SKATER KIJINAMI LANDED A NUMBER OF QUADRUPLE JUMPS.
THERE WERE WORRIES ABOUT HIS INJURED ANKLE, BUT HE SEEMS TO HAVE RECOVERED.
FUUTA KUMANO, WHO'S A STRONG CANDIDATE FOR THE OLYMPICS AFTER MAKING IT INTO THE TOP THREE AT THE RECENT GRAND PRIX FINAL, CONTINUED TO DO WELL.
ON THE OTHER HAND, TAIGA AOKI, WHO WON SECOND PLACE LAST YEAR, APPEARED TO BE HAVING TROUBLE WITH HIS COMBI-NATION JUMPS.

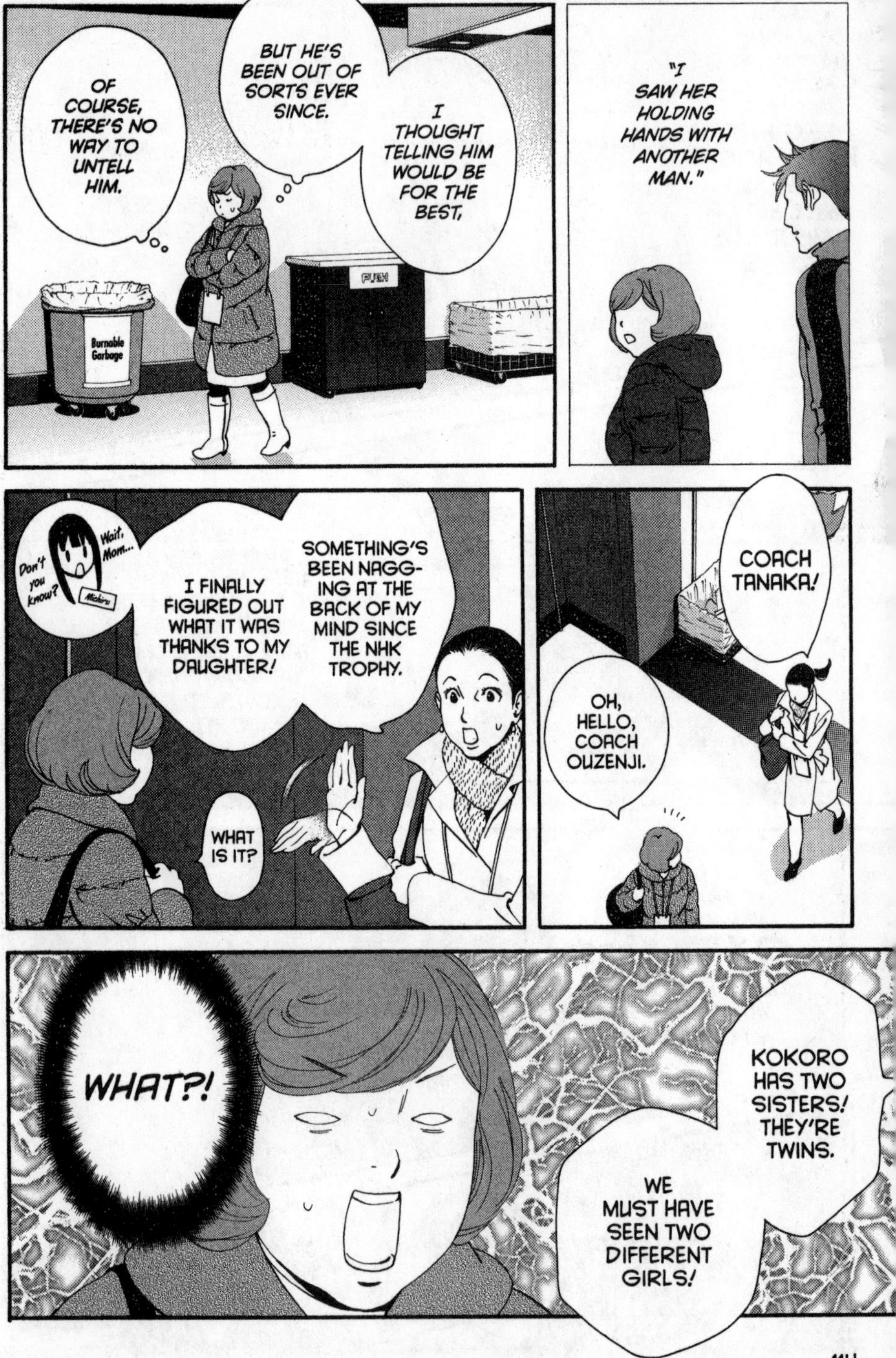
"I SAW HER HOLDING HANDS WITH ANOTHER MAN."
I THOUGHT TELLING HIM WOULD BE FOR THE BEST,
BUT HE'S BEEN OUT OF SORTS EVER SINCE.
OF COURSE, THERE'S NO WAY TO UNTELL HIM.
PUSH
Burnable Garbage
COACH TANAKA!
OH, HELLO, COACH OUZENJI.
SOMETHING'S BEEN NAGGING AT THE BACK OF MY MIND SINCE THE NHK TROPHY.
I FINALLY FIGURED OUT WHAT IT WAS THANKS TO MY DAUGHTER!
Wait, Mom...
Don't you know?
Michiru
WHAT IS IT?
KOKORO HAS TWO SISTERS! THEY'RE TWINS.
WE MUST HAVE SEEN TWO DIFFERENT GIRLS!
WHAT?!

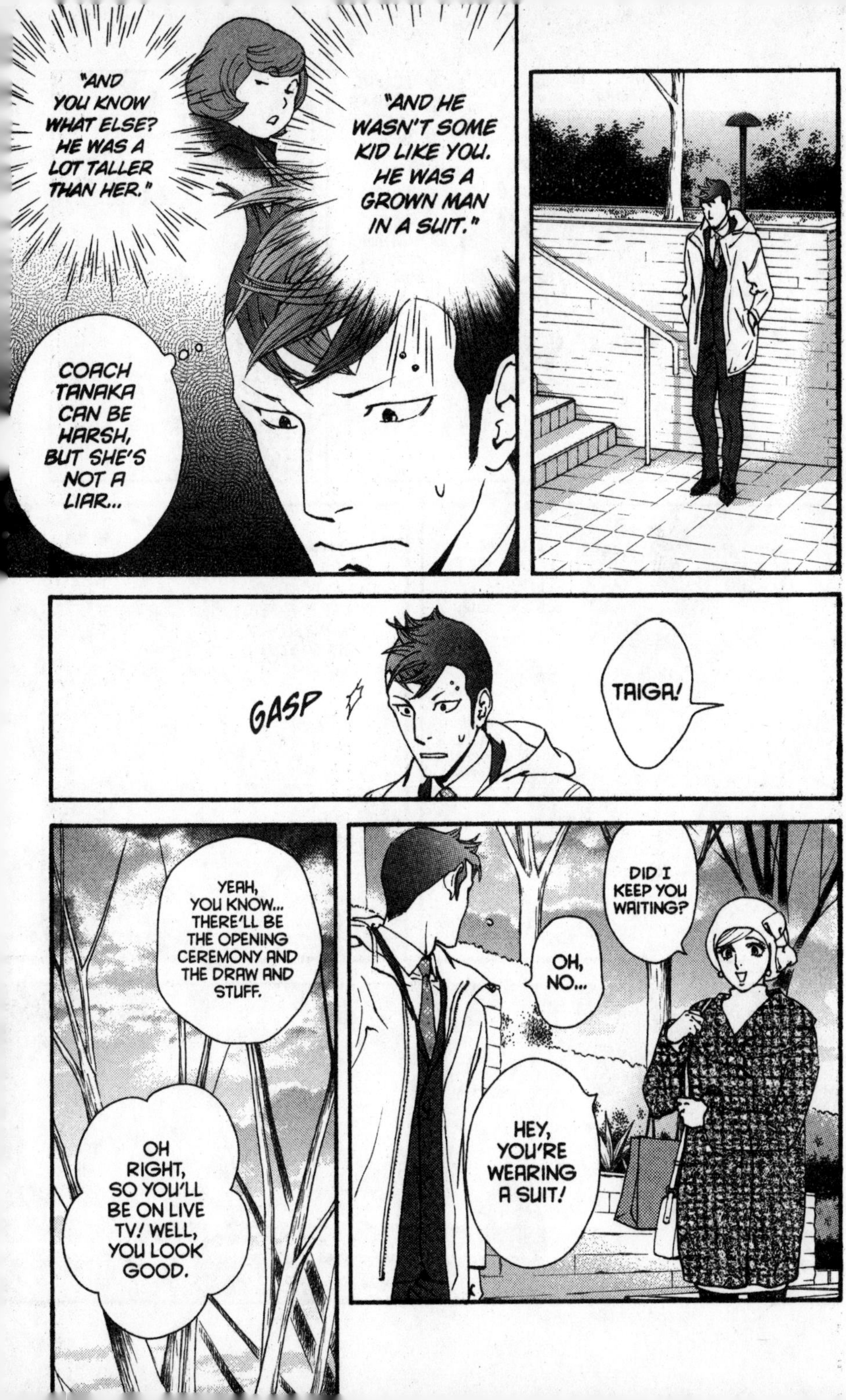
"AND HE WASN'T SOME KID LIKE YOU. HE WAS A GROWN MAN IN A SUIT."
"AND YOU KNOW WHAT ELSE? HE WAS A LOT TALLER THAN HER."
COACH TANAKA CAN BE HARSH, BUT SHE'S NOT A LIAR...
TAIGA!
GASP
DID I KEEP YOU WAITING?
OH, NO...
HEY, YOU'RE WEARING A SUIT!
YEAH, YOU KNOW... THERE'LL BE THE OPENING CEREMONY AND THE DRAW AND STUFF.
OH RIGHT, SO YOU'LL BE ON LIVE TV! WELL, YOU LOOK GOOD.

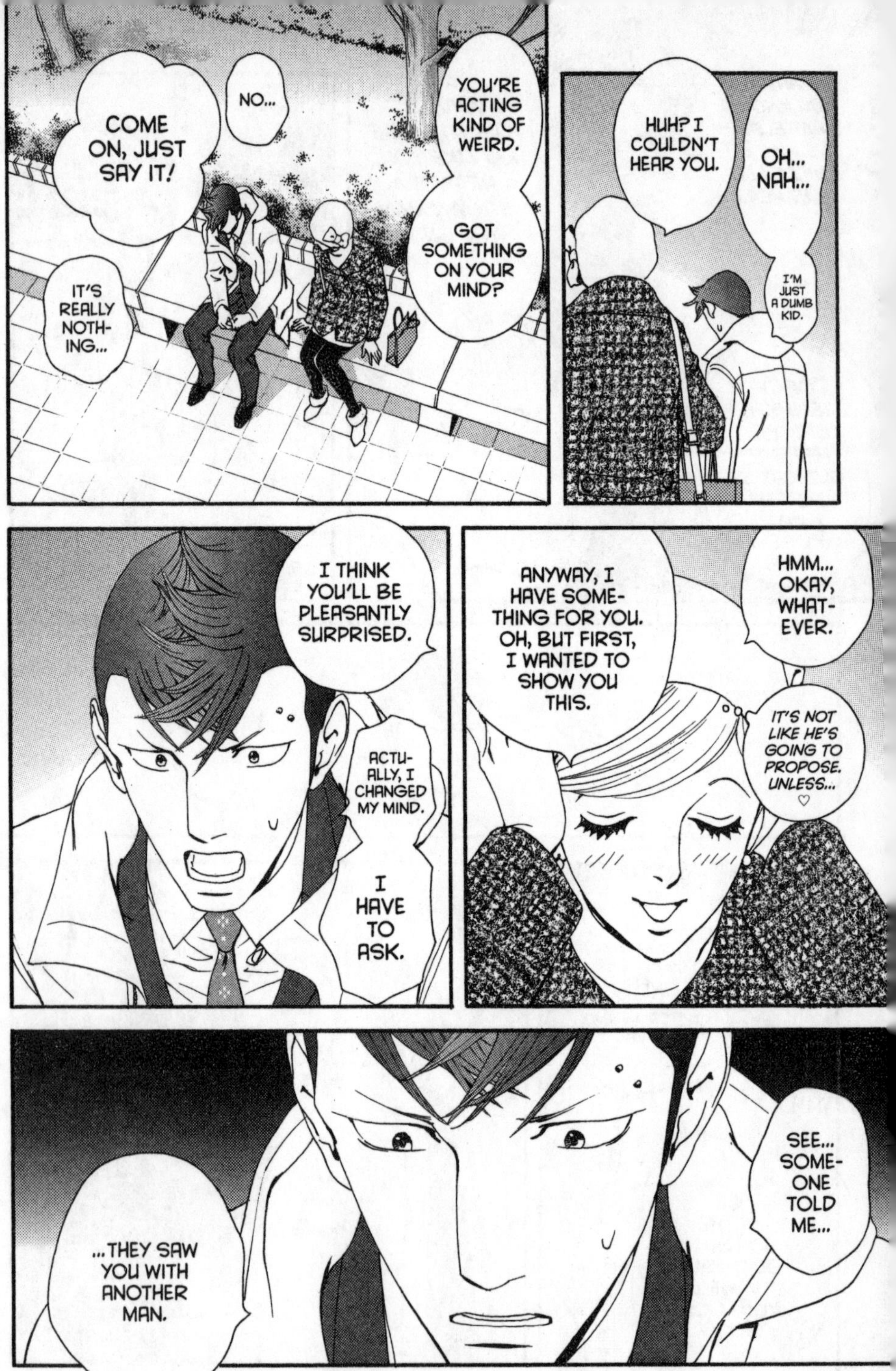
HUH? I COULDN'T HEAR YOU.
OH... NAH...
I'M JUST A DUMB KID.
YOU'RE ACTING KIND OF WEIRD.
GOT SOMETHING ON YOUR MIND?
NO...
COME ON, JUST SAY IT!
IT'S REALLY NOTHING...
HMM... OKAY, WHATEVER.
IT'S NOT LIKE HE'S GOING TO PROPOSE. UNLESS... ♡
ANYWAY, I HAVE SOMETHING FOR YOU. OH, BUT FIRST, I WANTED TO SHOW YOU THIS.
I THINK YOU'LL BE PLEASANTLY SURPRISED.
ACTUALLY, I CHANGED MY MIND.
I HAVE TO ASK.
SEE... SOMEONE TOLD ME...
...THEY SAW YOU WITH ANOTHER MAN.

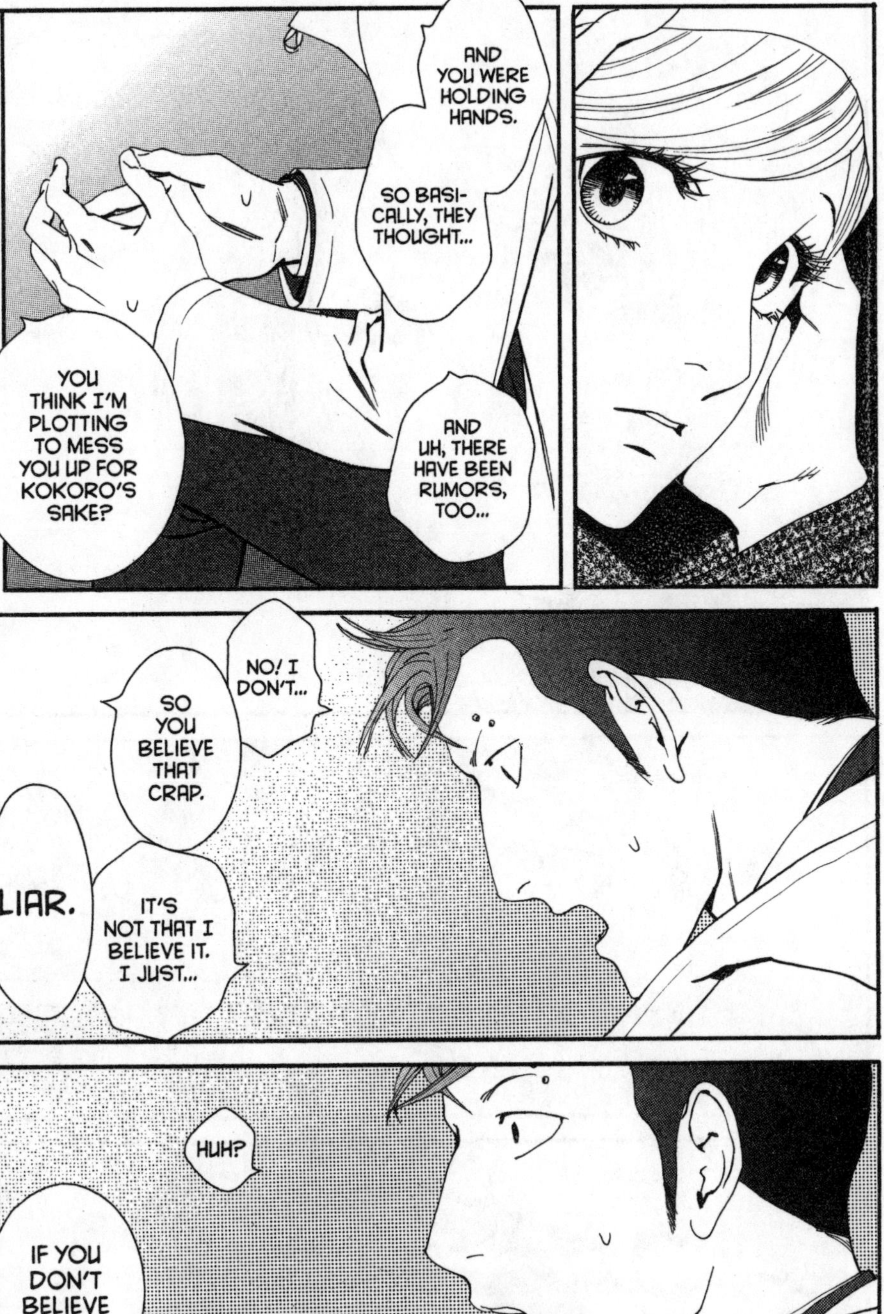
AND YOU WERE HOLDING HANDS.
SO BASI-CALLY, THEY THOUGHT...
AND UH, THERE HAVE BEEN RUMORS, TOO...
YOU THINK I'M PLOTTING TO MESS YOU UP FOR KOKORO'S SAKE?
NO! I DON'T...
SO YOU BELIEVE THAT CRAP.
IT'S NOT THAT I BELIEVE IT. I JUST...
LIAR.
HUH?
IF YOU DON'T BELIEVE IT...

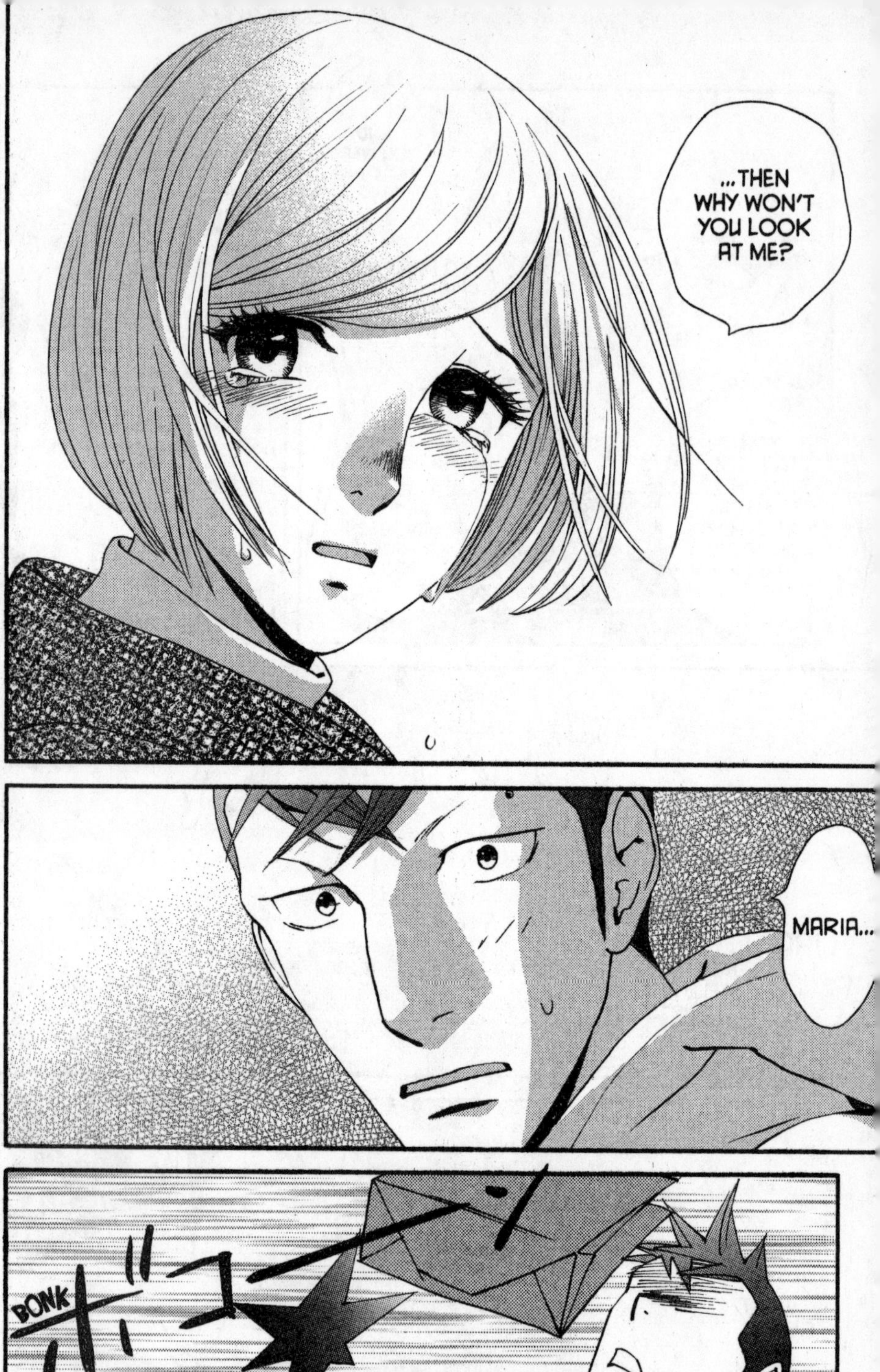
...THEN WHY WON'T YOU LOOK AT ME?
MARIA...
BONK

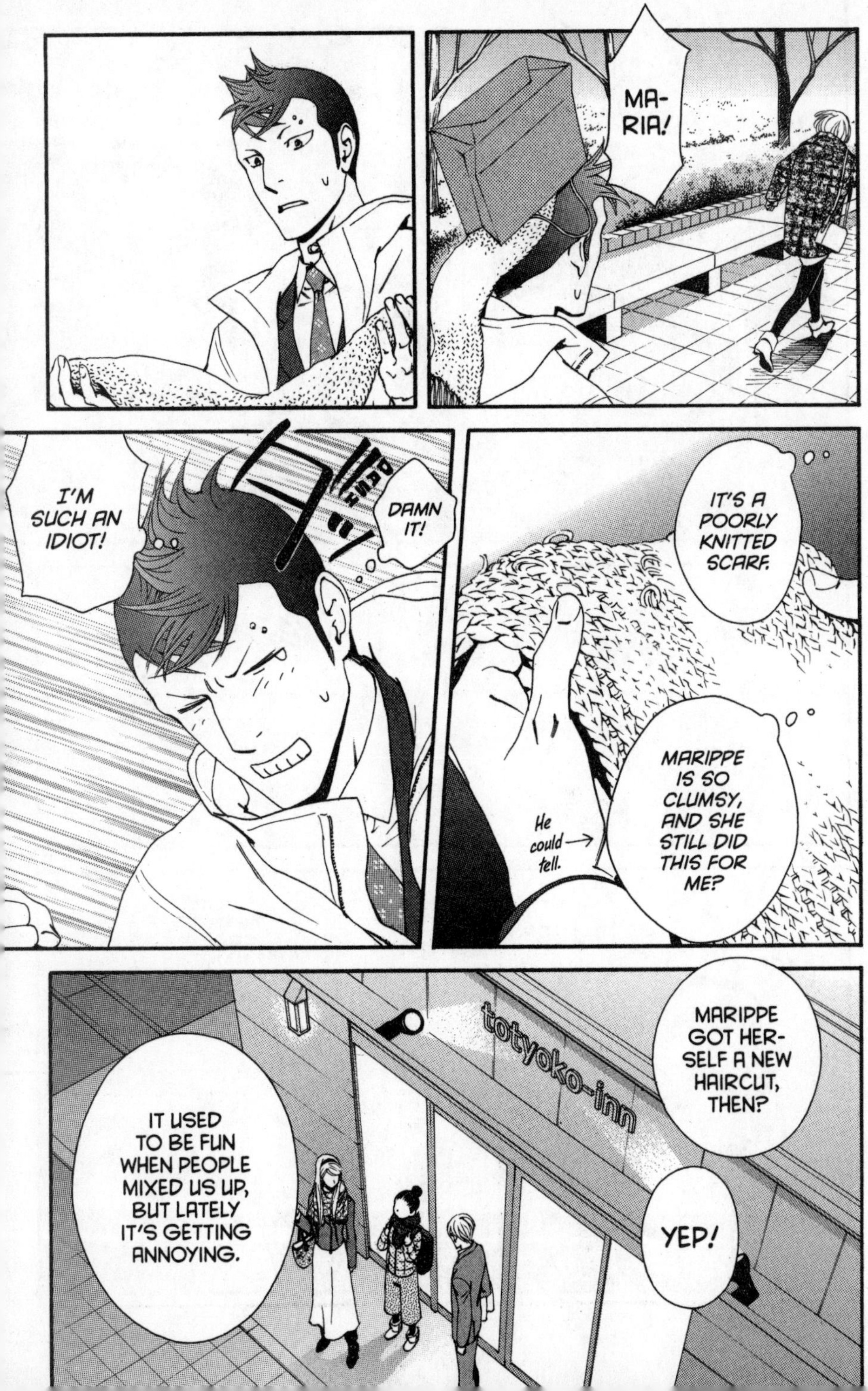
MA-RIA!
IT'S A POORLY KNITTED SCARF.
MARIPPE IS SO CLUMSY, AND SHE STILL DID THIS FOR ME?
He could tell.
DAMN IT!
DASH
I'M SUCH AN IDIOT!
MARIPPE GOT HER-SELF A NEW HAIRCUT, THEN?
totyoko-inn
YEP!
IT USED TO BE FUN WHEN PEOPLE MIXED US UP, BUT LATELY IT'S GETTING ANNOYING.

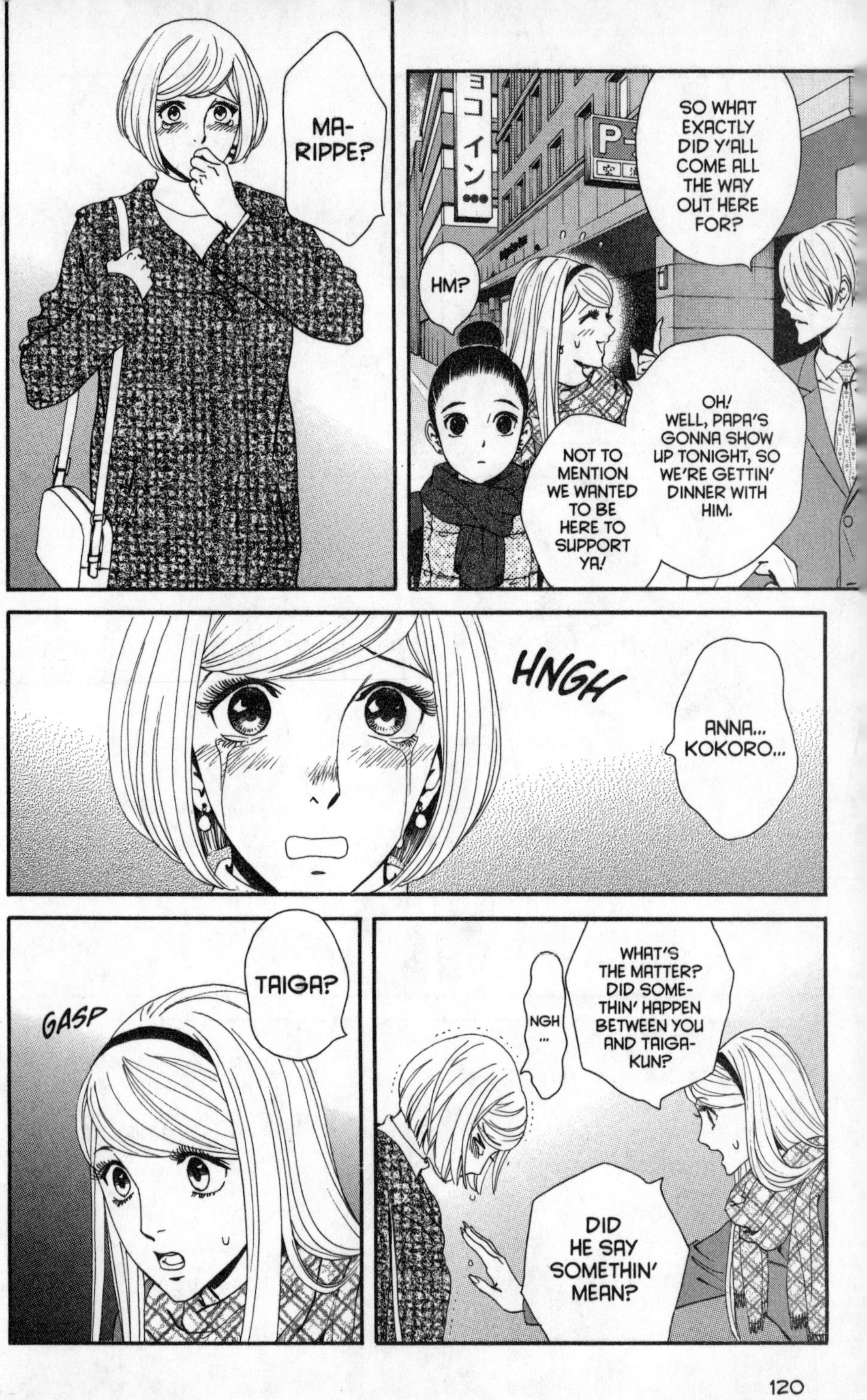
ヨコイン
SO WHAT EXACTLY DID Y'ALL COME ALL THE WAY OUT HERE FOR?
HM?
OH! WELL, PAPA'S GONNA SHOW UP TONIGHT, SO WE'RE GETTIN' DINNER WITH HIM.
NOT TO MENTION WE WANTED TO BE HERE TO SUPPORT YA!
MA-RIPPE?
HNGH
ANNA... KOKORO...
WHAT'S THE MATTER? DID SOME-THIN' HAPPEN BETWEEN YOU AND TAIGA-KUN?
NGH ...
DID HE SAY SOMETHIN' MEAN?
TAIGA?
GASP

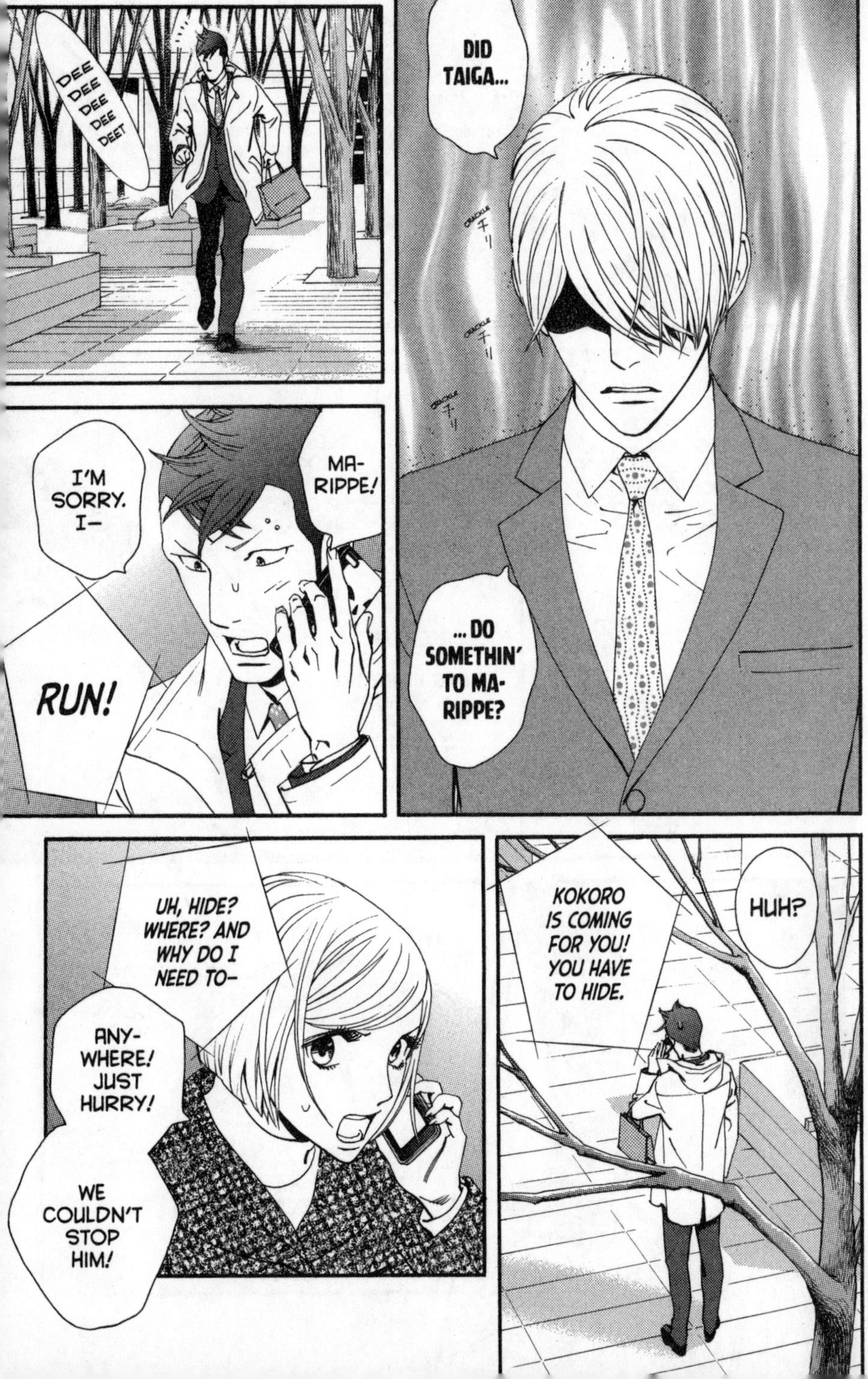
DID TAIGA...
CRACKLE
CRACKLE
CRACKLE
...DO SOMETHIN' TO MA-RIPPE?
DEE DEE DEE DEE DEET
MA-RIPPE!
I'M SORRY. I—
RUN!
HUH?
KOKORO IS COMING FOR YOU! YOU HAVE TO HIDE.
UH, HIDE? WHERE? AND WHY DO I NEED TO–
ANY-WHERE! JUST HURRY!
WE COULDN'T STOP HIM!

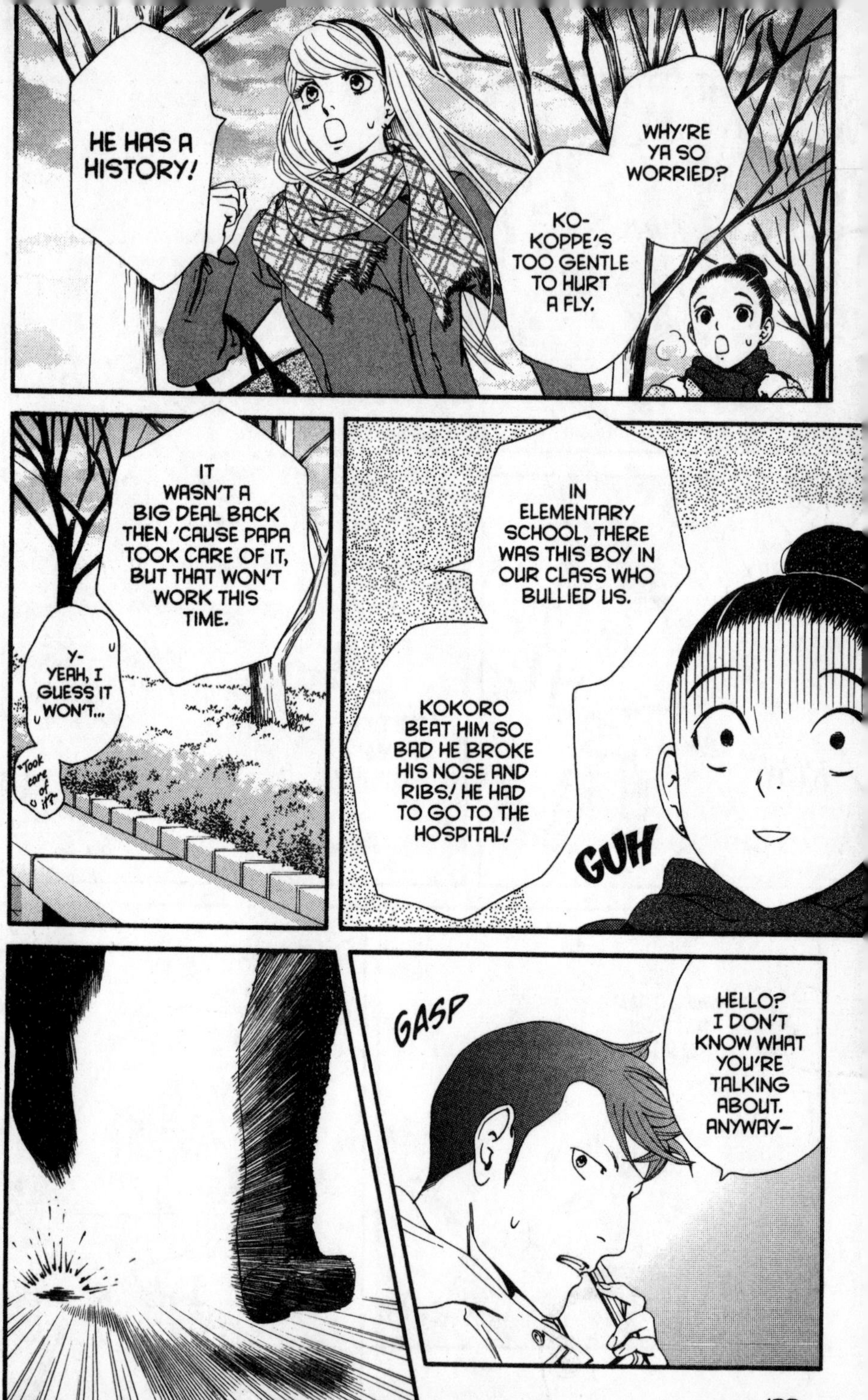
WHY'RE YA SO WORRIED?
KO-KOPPE'S TOO GENTLE TO HURT A FLY.
HE HAS A HISTORY!
IN ELEMENTARY SCHOOL, THERE WAS THIS BOY IN OUR CLASS WHO BULLIED US.
KOKORO BEAT HIM SO BAD HE BROKE HIS NOSE AND RIBS! HE HAD TO GO TO THE HOSPITAL!
GUH
IT WASN'T A BIG DEAL BACK THEN 'CAUSE PAPA TOOK CARE OF IT, BUT THAT WON'T WORK THIS TIME.
Y-YEAH, I GUESS IT WON'T...
"Took care of it?"
HELLO? I DON'T KNOW WHAT YOU'RE TALKING ABOUT. ANYWAY—
GASP

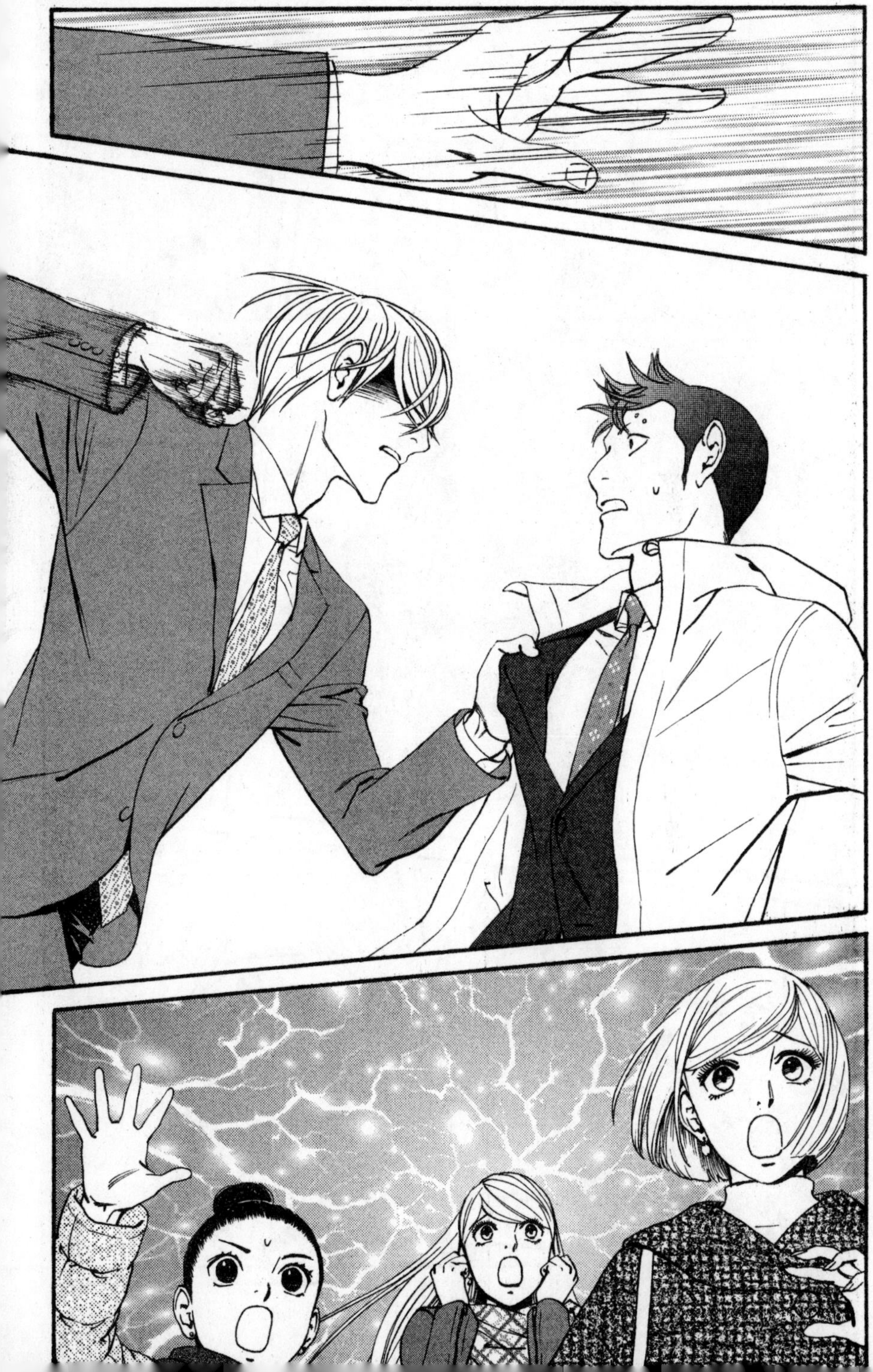

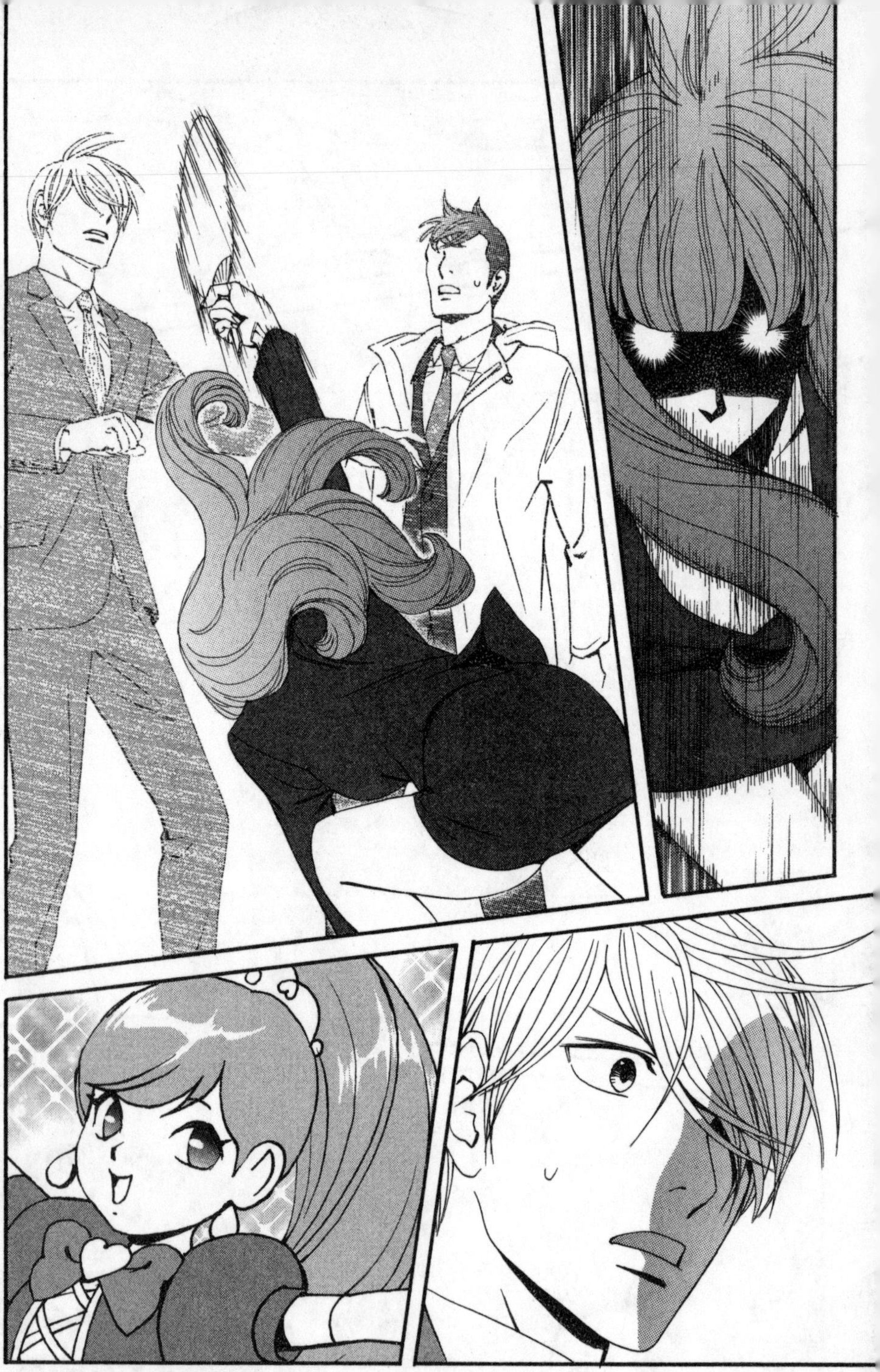

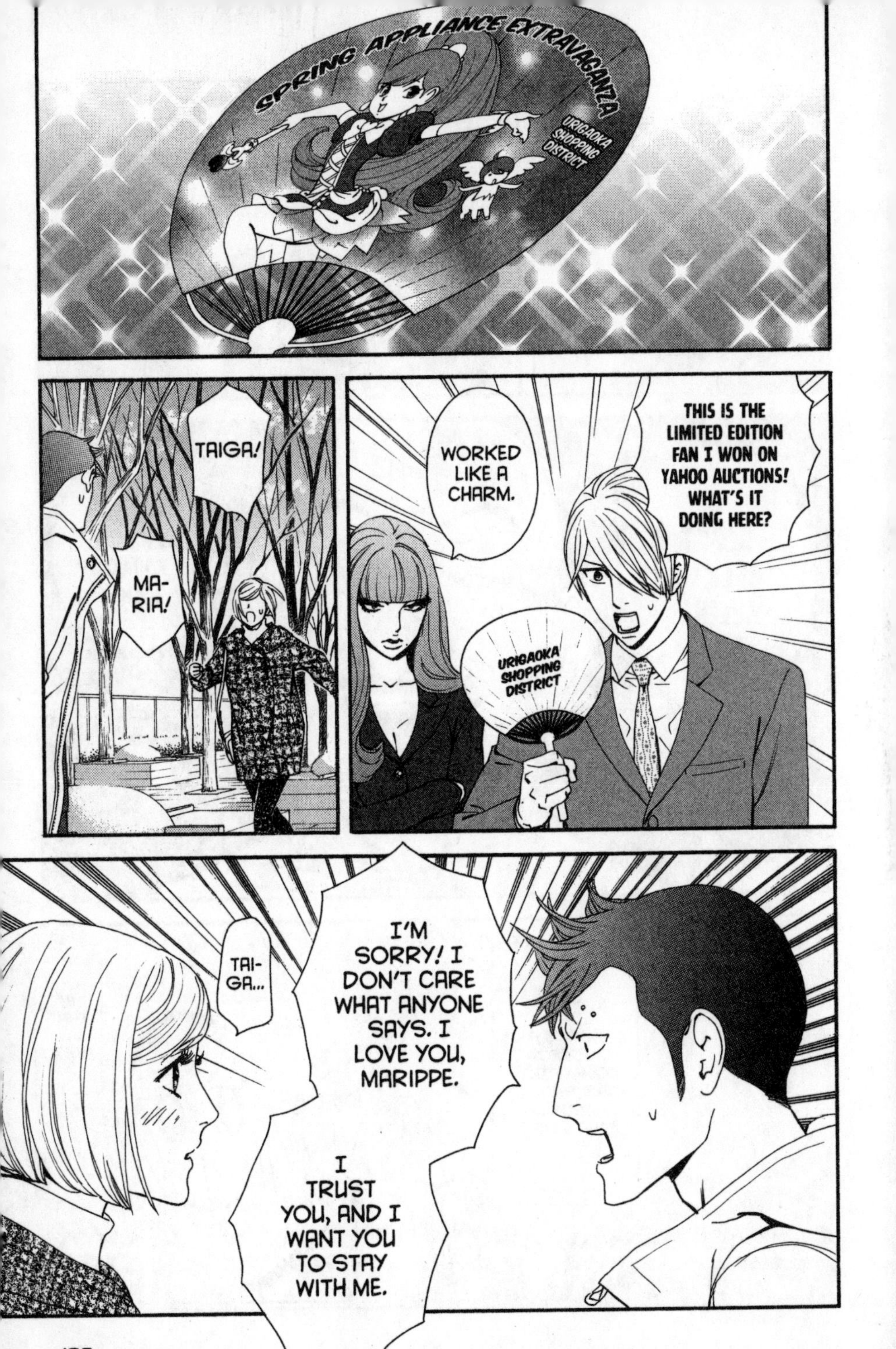
SPRING APPLIANCE EXTRAVAGANZA
URIGAOKA SHOPPING DISTRICT
THIS IS THE LIMITED EDITION FAN I WON ON YAHOO AUCTIONS! WHAT'S IT DOING HERE?
WORKED LIKE A CHARM.
URIGAOKA SHOPPING DISTRICT
TAIGA!
MA-RIA!
I'M SORRY! I DON'T CARE WHAT ANYONE SAYS. I LOVE YOU, MARIPPE.
I TRUST YOU, AND I WANT YOU TO STAY WITH ME.
TAI-GA...

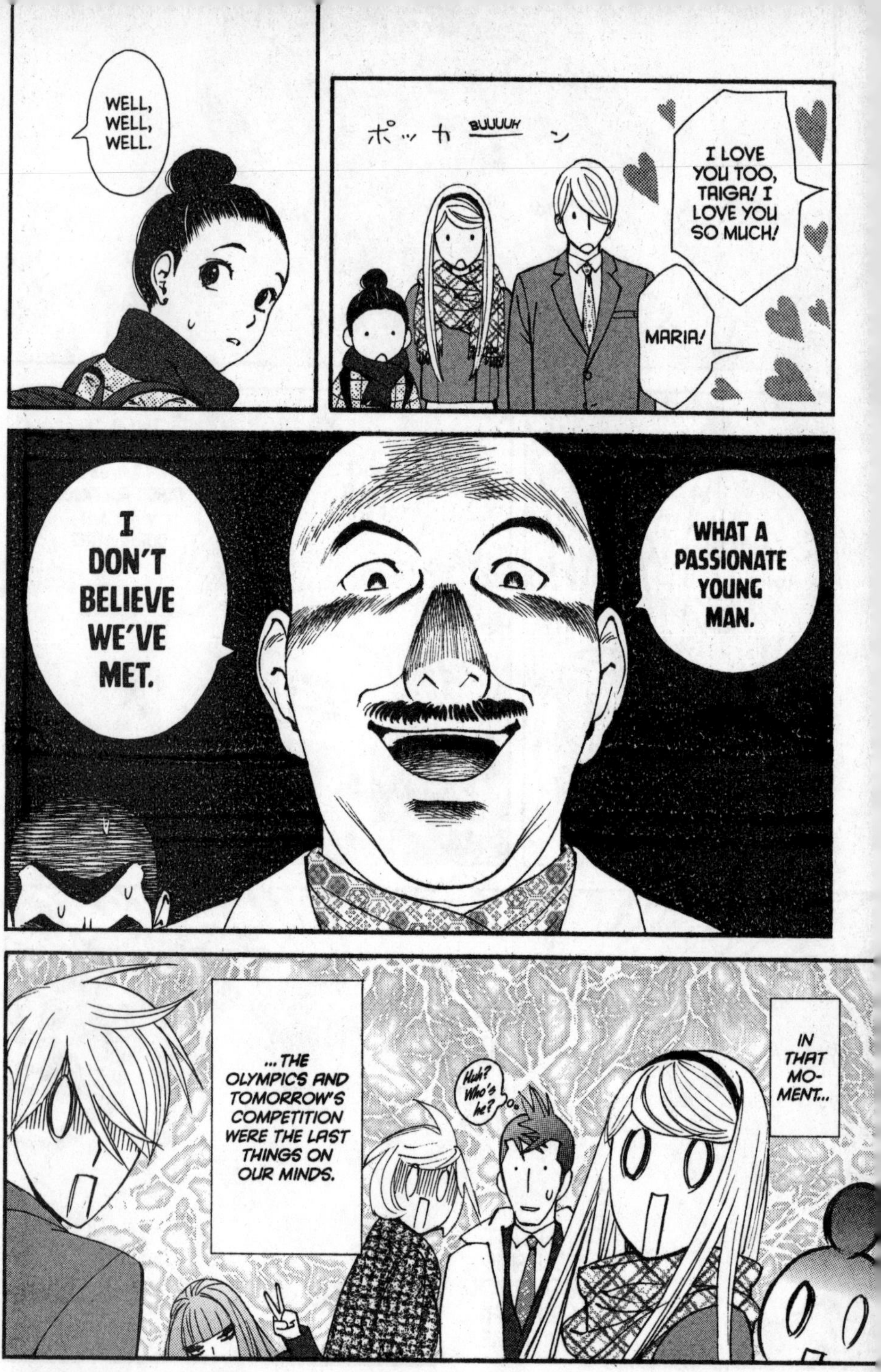
I LOVE YOU TOO, TAIGA! I LOVE YOU SO MUCH!
MARIA!
ポッカ BUUUUH ン
WELL, WELL, WELL.
WHAT A PASSIONATE YOUNG MAN.
I DON'T BELIEVE WE'VE MET.
IN THAT MO-MENT...
Huh? Who's he?
...THE OLYMPICS AND TOMORROW'S COMPETITION WERE THE LAST THINGS ON OUR MINDS.

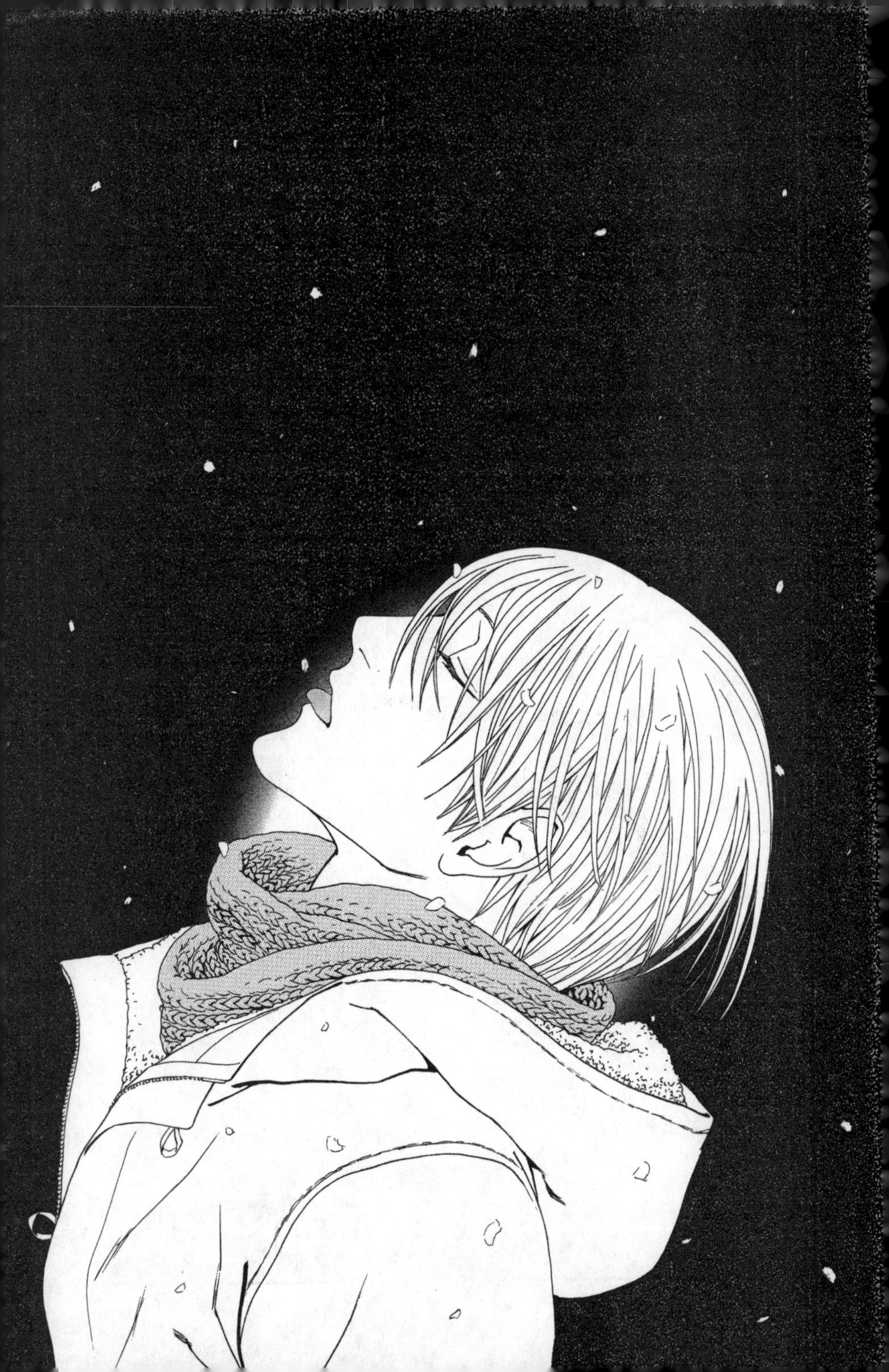

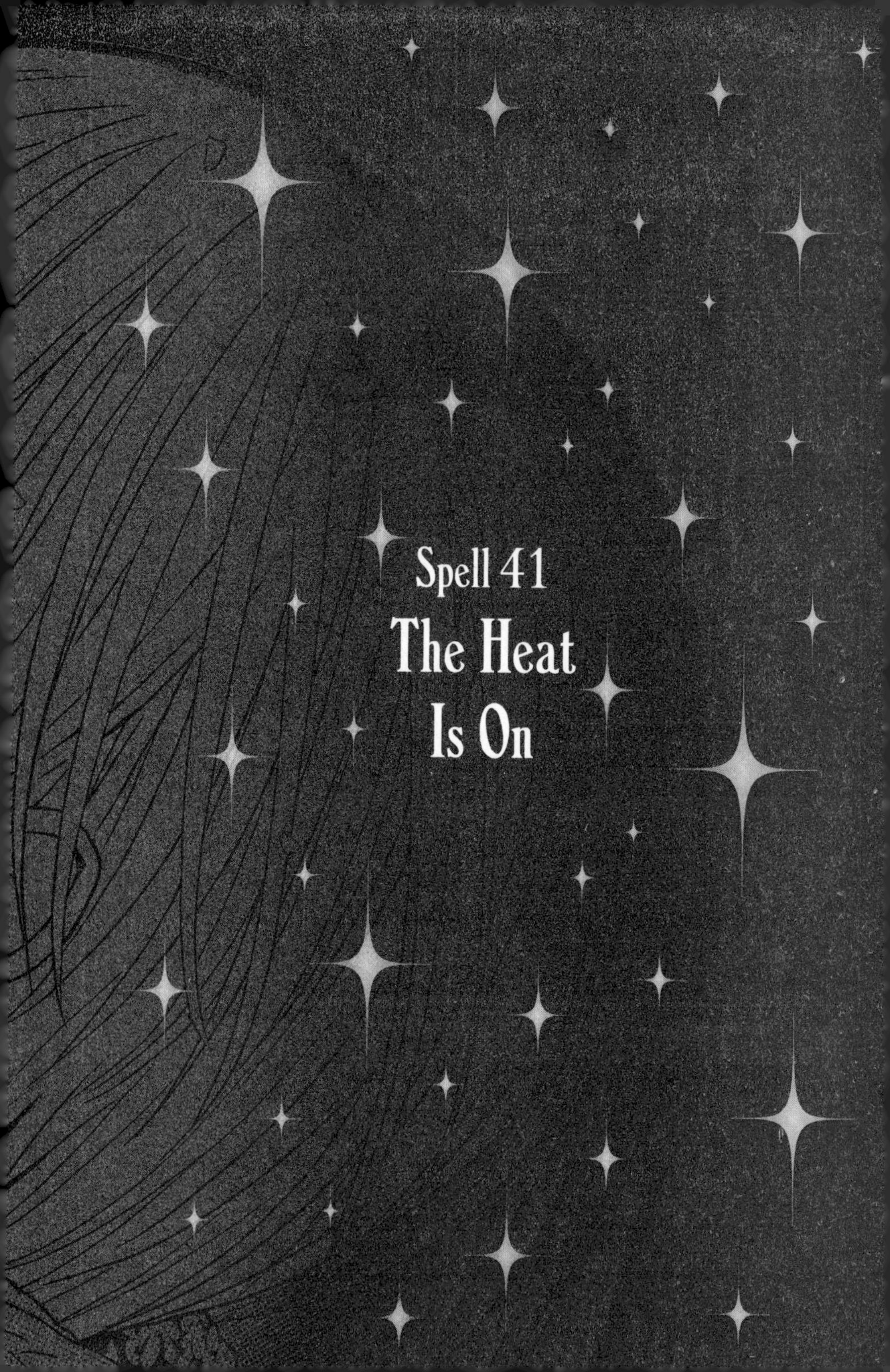
Spell 41
The Heat
Is On

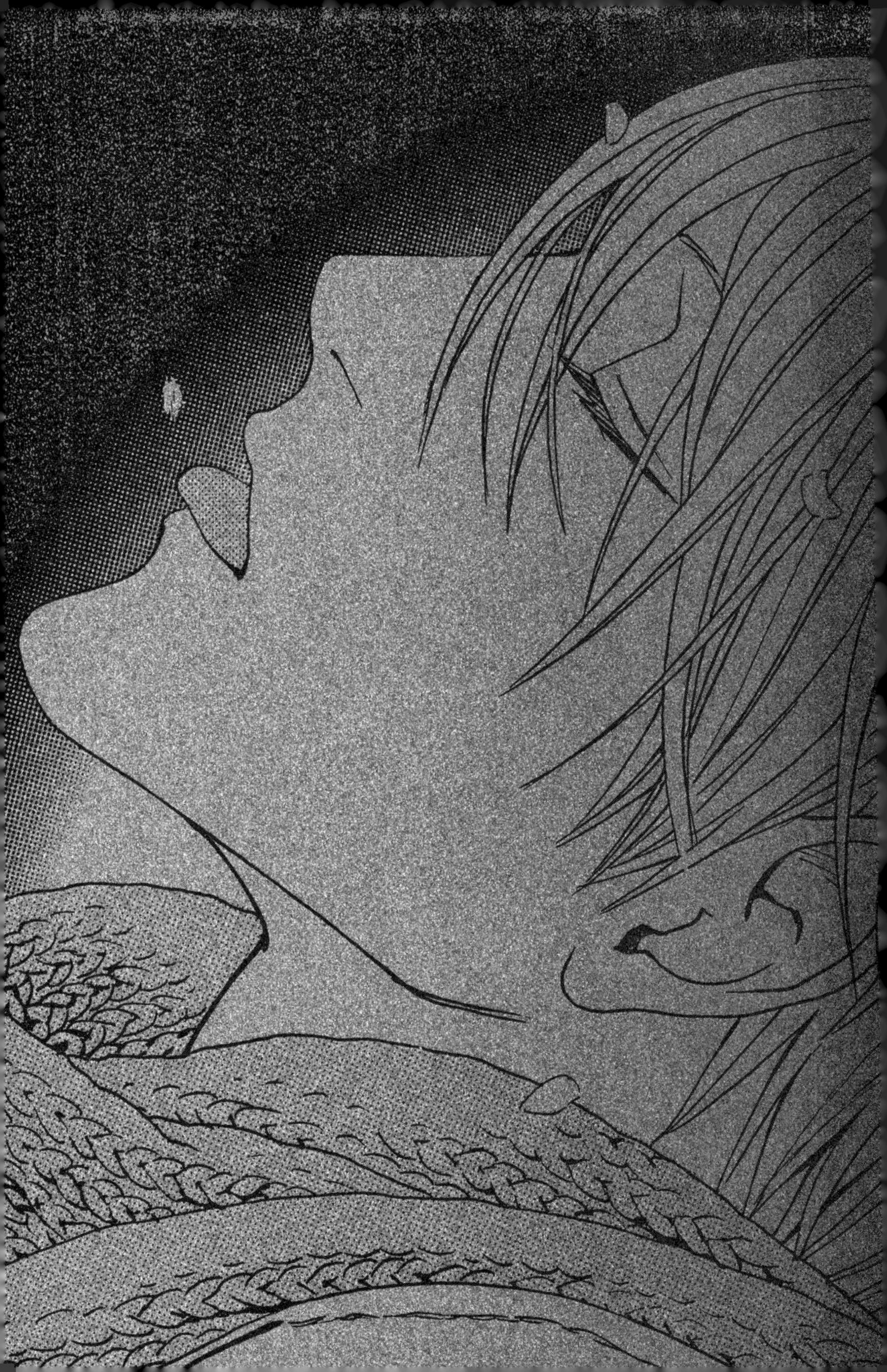

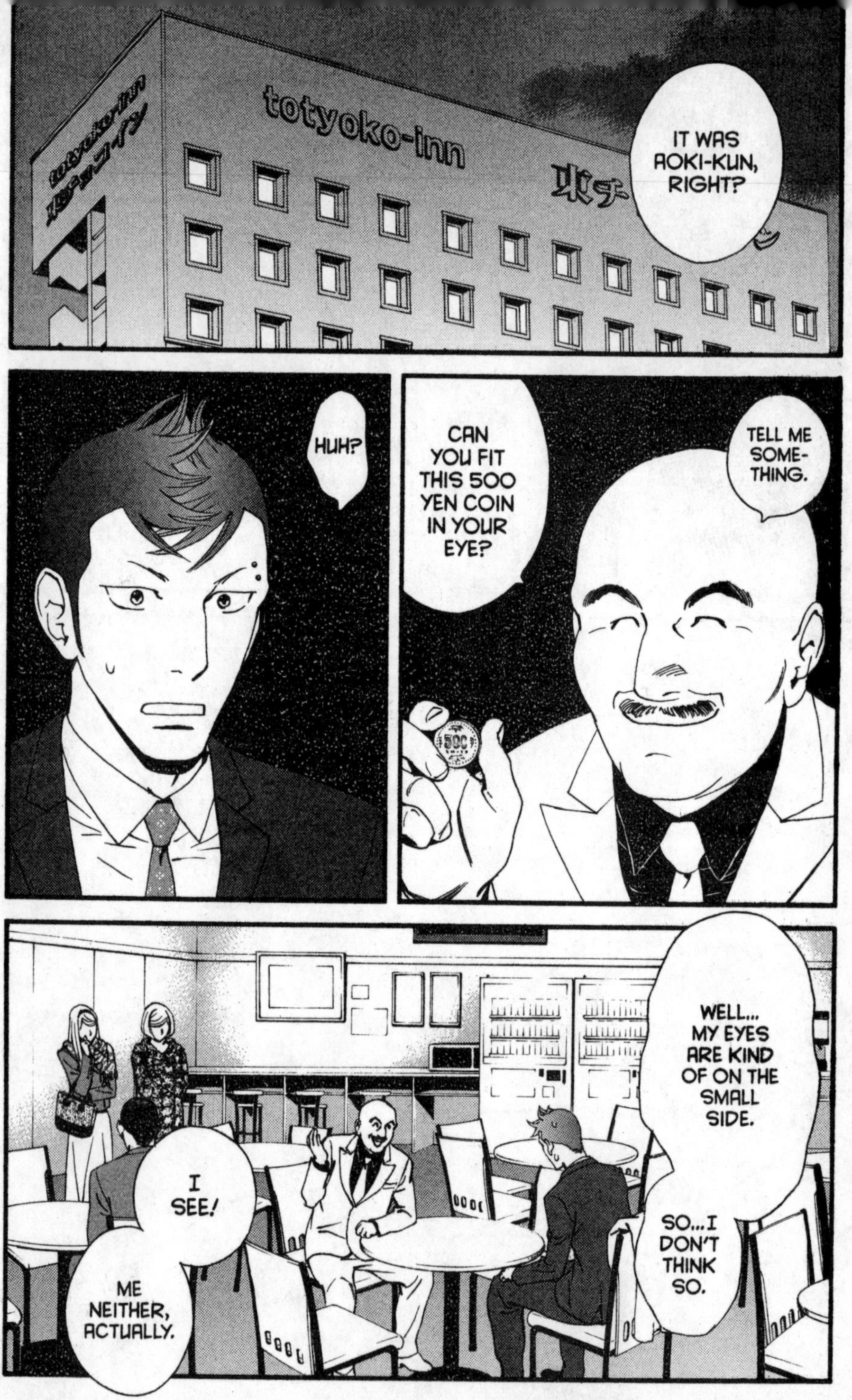
totyoko-inn
IT WAS AOKI-KUN, RIGHT?
TELL ME SOME-THING.
CAN YOU FIT THIS 500 YEN COIN IN YOUR EYE?
HUH?
WELL... MY EYES ARE KIND OF ON THE SMALL SIDE.
SO...I DON'T THINK SO.
I SEE!
ME NEITHER, ACTUALLY.

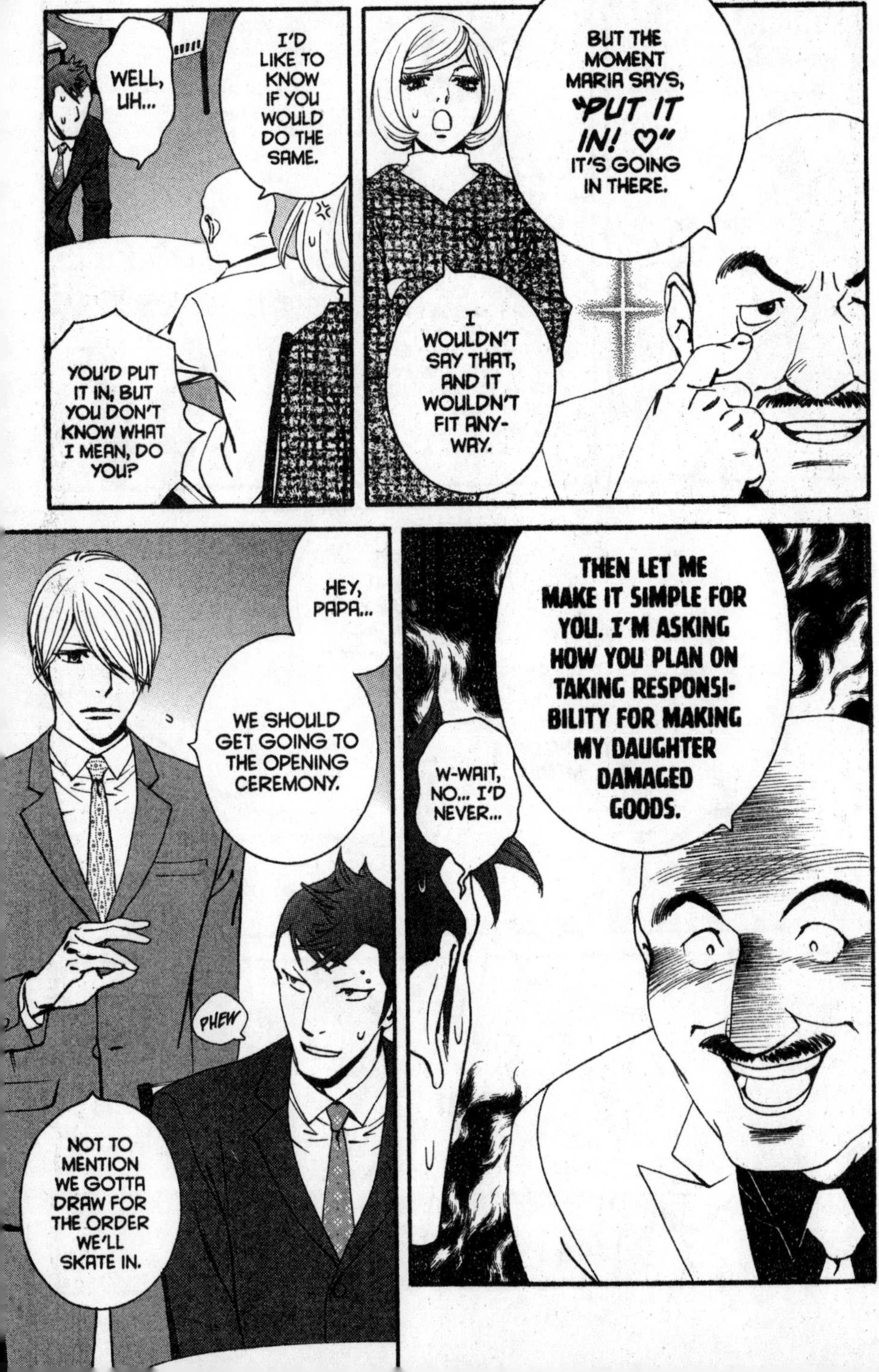
BUT THE MOMENT MARIA SAYS, "PUT IT IN! ♡" IT'S GOING IN THERE.
I WOULDN'T SAY THAT, AND IT WOULDN'T FIT ANY-WAY.
I'D LIKE TO KNOW IF YOU WOULD DO THE SAME.
WELL, UH...
YOU'D PUT IT IN, BUT YOU DON'T KNOW WHAT I MEAN, DO YOU?
THEN LET ME MAKE IT SIMPLE FOR YOU. I'M ASKING HOW YOU PLAN ON TAKING RESPONSI-BILITY FOR MAKING MY DAUGHTER DAMAGED GOODS.
W-WAIT, NO... I'D NEVER...
HEY, PAPA...
WE SHOULD GET GOING TO THE OPENING CEREMONY.
PHEW
NOT TO MENTION WE GOTTA DRAW FOR THE ORDER WE'LL SKATE IN.

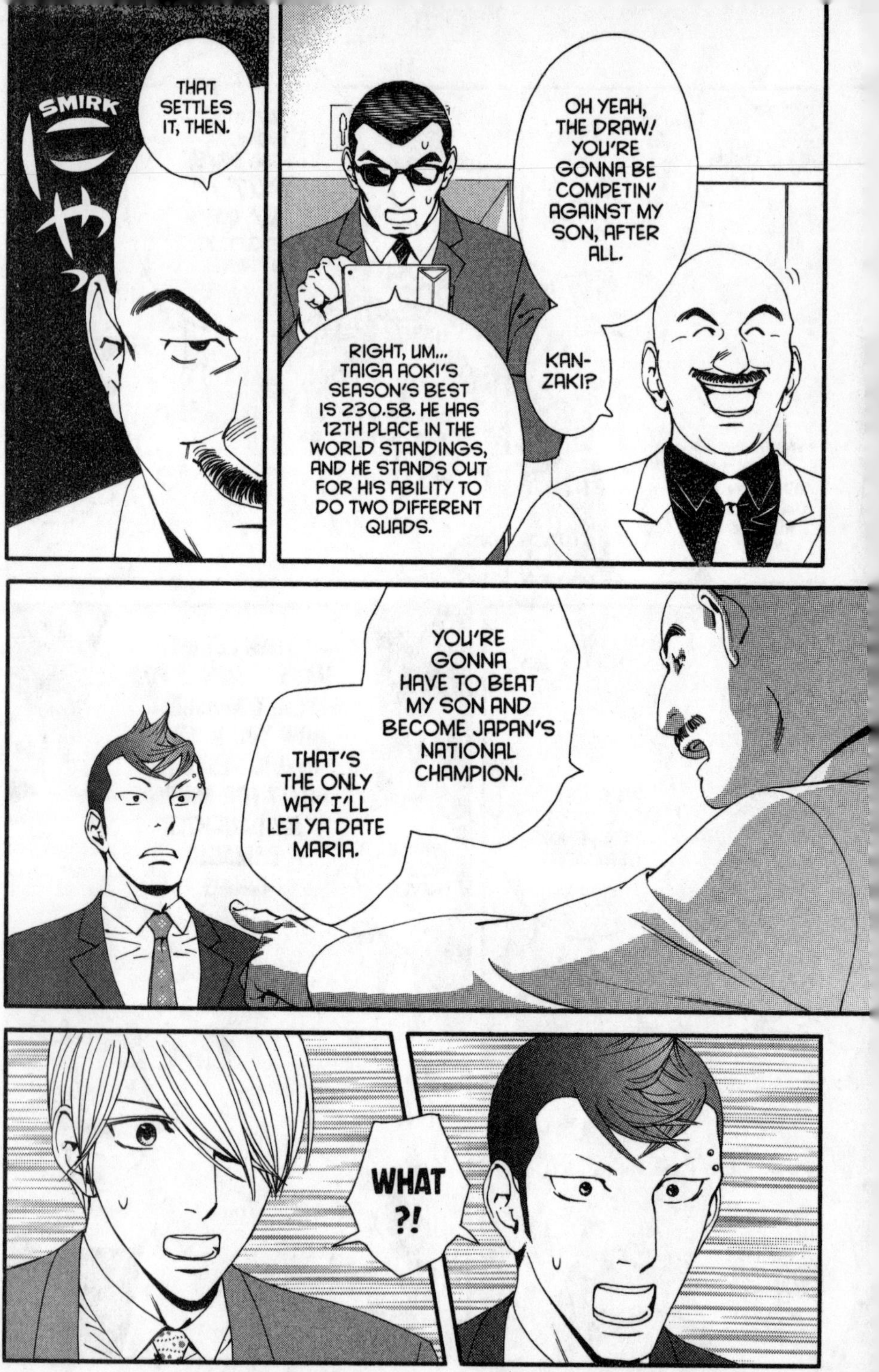
OH YEAH, THE DRAW! YOU'RE GONNA BE COMPETIN' AGAINST MY SON, AFTER ALL.
KAN-ZAKI?
RIGHT, UM... TAIGA AOKI'S SEASON'S BEST IS 230.58. HE HAS 12TH PLACE IN THE WORLD STANDINGS, AND HE STANDS OUT FOR HIS ABILITY TO DO TWO DIFFERENT QUADS.
SMIRK
THAT SETTLES IT, THEN.
YOU'RE GONNA HAVE TO BEAT MY SON AND BECOME JAPAN'S NATIONAL CHAMPION.
THAT'S THE ONLY WAY I'LL LET YA DATE MARIA.
WHAT?!

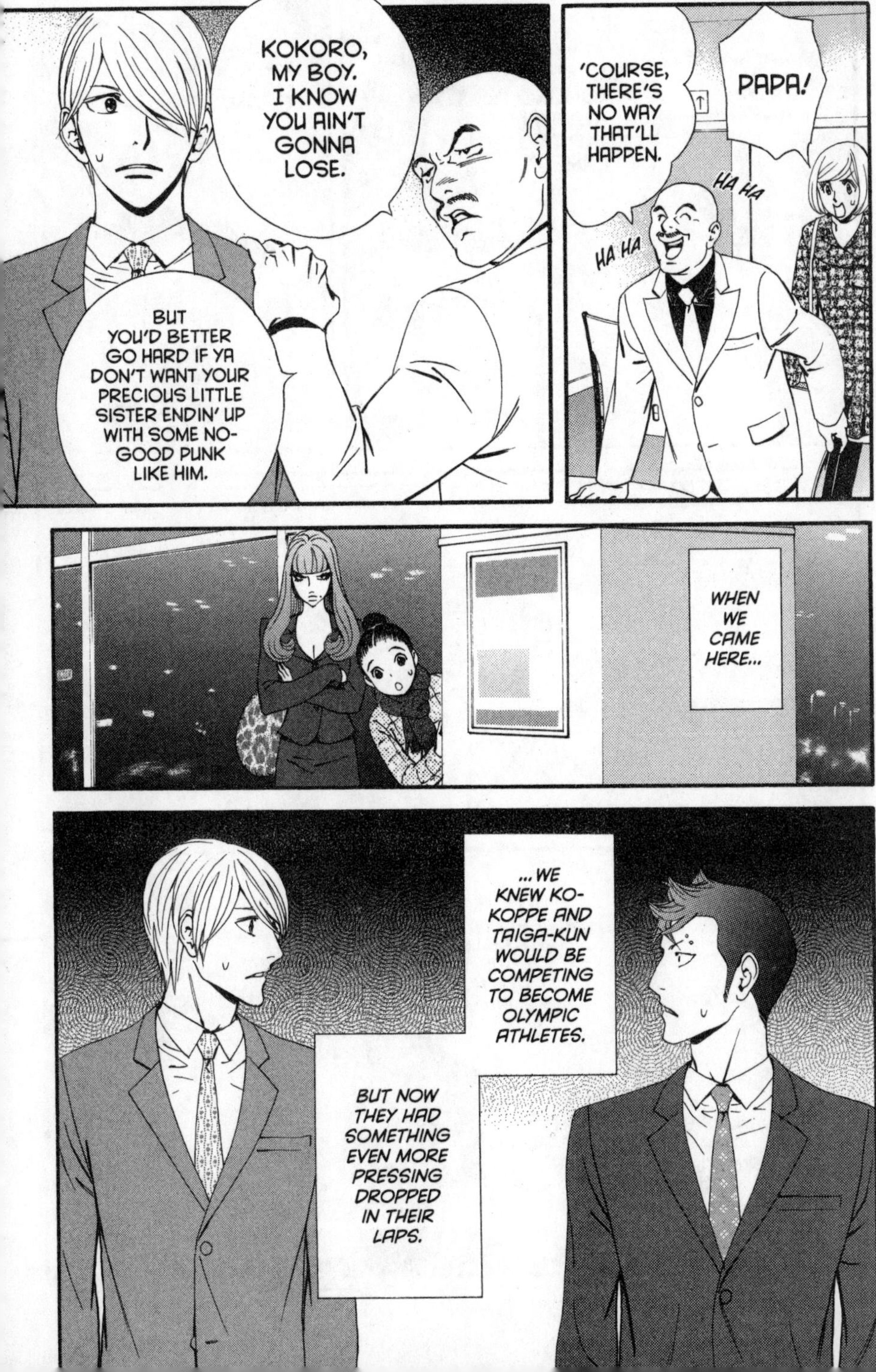
PAPA!
'COURSE, THERE'S NO WAY THAT'LL HAPPEN.
HA HA
HA HA
KOKORO, MY BOY. I KNOW YOU AIN'T GONNA LOSE.
BUT YOU'D BETTER GO HARD IF YA DON'T WANT YOUR PRECIOUS LITTLE SISTER ENDIN' UP WITH SOME NO-GOOD PUNK LIKE HIM.
WHEN WE CAME HERE...
...WE KNEW KO-KOPPE AND TAIGA-KUN WOULD BE COMPETING TO BECOME OLYMPIC ATHLETES.
BUT NOW THEY HAD SOMETHING EVEN MORE PRESSING DROPPED IN THEIR LAPS.

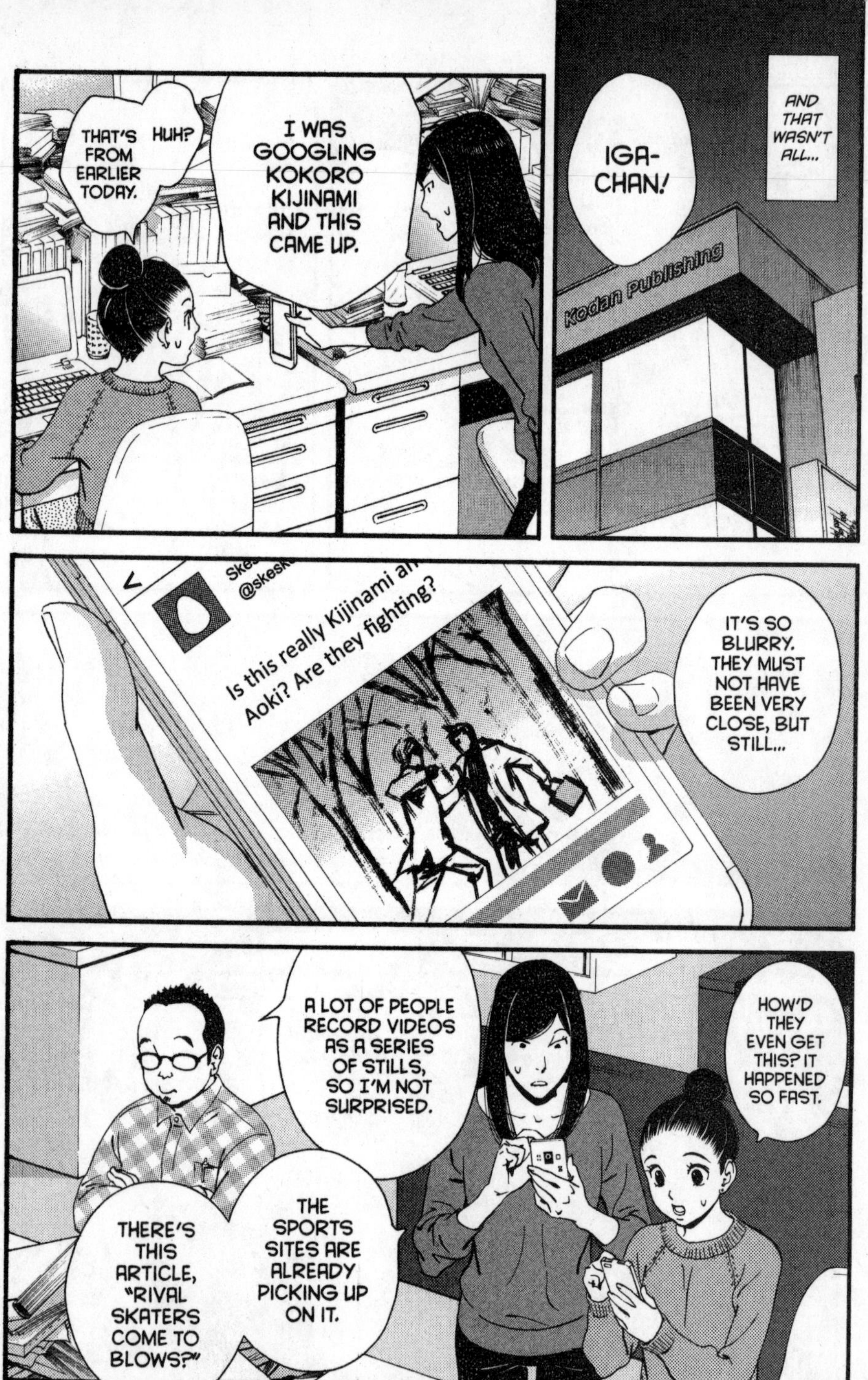
AND THAT WASN'T ALL...
IGA-CHAN!
Kodan Publishing
I WAS GOOGLING KOKORO KIJINAMI AND THIS CAME UP.
HUH?
THAT'S FROM EARLIER TODAY.
Is this really Kijinami an
Aoki? Are they fighting?
IT'S SO BLURRY. THEY MUST NOT HAVE BEEN VERY CLOSE, BUT STILL...
HOW'D THEY EVEN GET THIS? IT HAPPENED SO FAST.
A LOT OF PEOPLE RECORD VIDEOS AS A SERIES OF STILLS, SO I'M NOT SURPRISED.
THE SPORTS SITES ARE ALREADY PICKING UP ON IT.
THERE'S THIS ARTICLE, "RIVAL SKATERS COME TO BLOWS?"

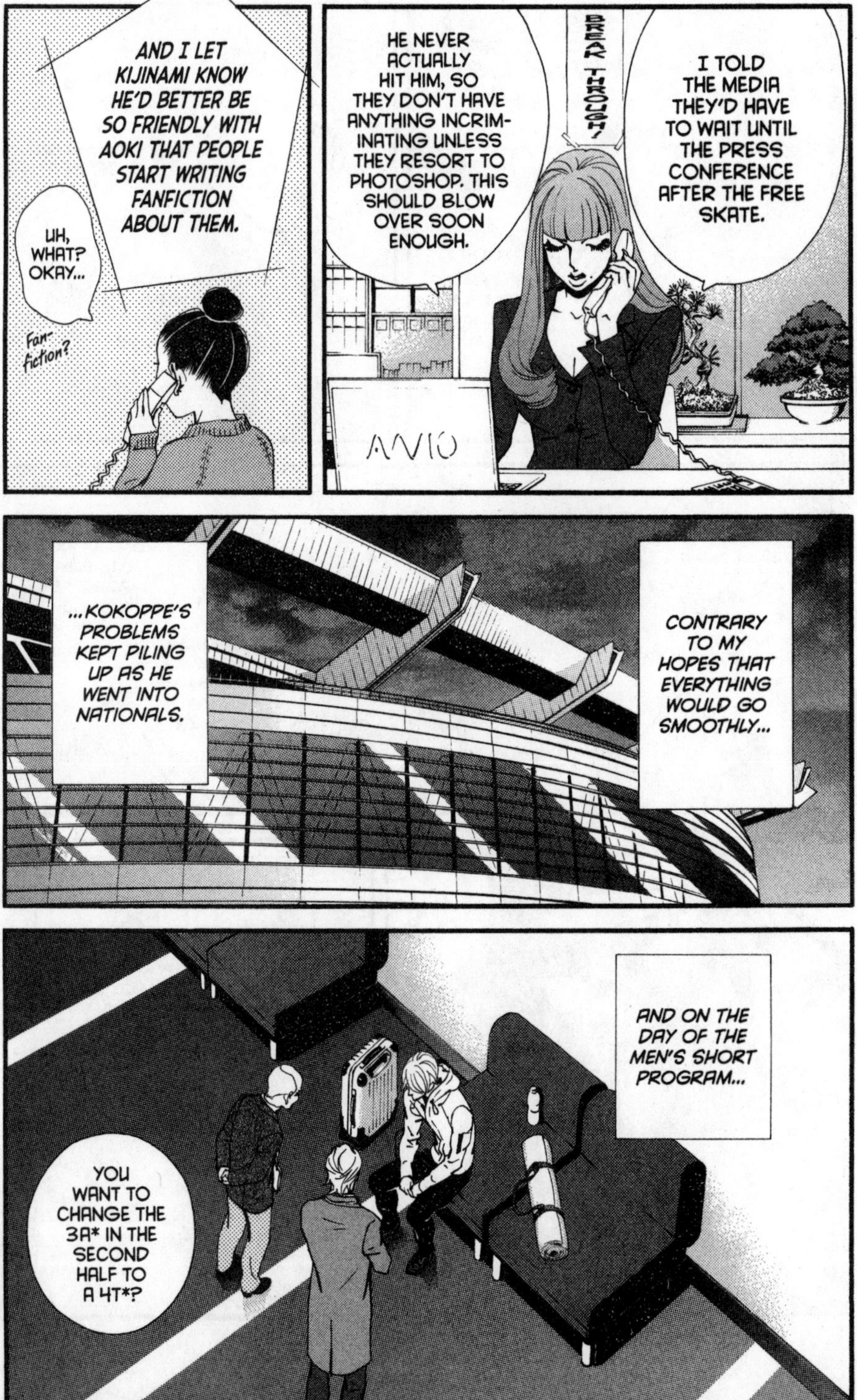
I TOLD THE MEDIA THEY'D HAVE TO WAIT UNTIL THE PRESS CONFERENCE AFTER THE FREE SKATE.
BREAK THROUGH!
HE NEVER ACTUALLY HIT HIM, SO THEY DON'T HAVE ANYTHING INCRIM-INATING UNLESS THEY RESORT TO PHOTOSHOP. THIS SHOULD BLOW OVER SOON ENOUGH.
AVIO
AND I LET KIJINAMI KNOW HE'D BETTER BE SO FRIENDLY WITH AOKI THAT PEOPLE START WRITING FANFICTION ABOUT THEM.
UH, WHAT? OKAY...
Fan-fiction?
CONTRARY TO MY HOPES THAT EVERYTHING WOULD GO SMOOTHLY...
...KOKOPPE'S PROBLEMS KEPT PILING UP AS HE WENT INTO NATIONALS.
AND ON THE DAY OF THE MEN'S SHORT PROGRAM...
YOU WANT TO CHANGE THE 3A* IN THE SECOND HALF TO A 4T*?

*3A: TRIPLE AXEL
*4T: QUADRUPLE TOE LOOP

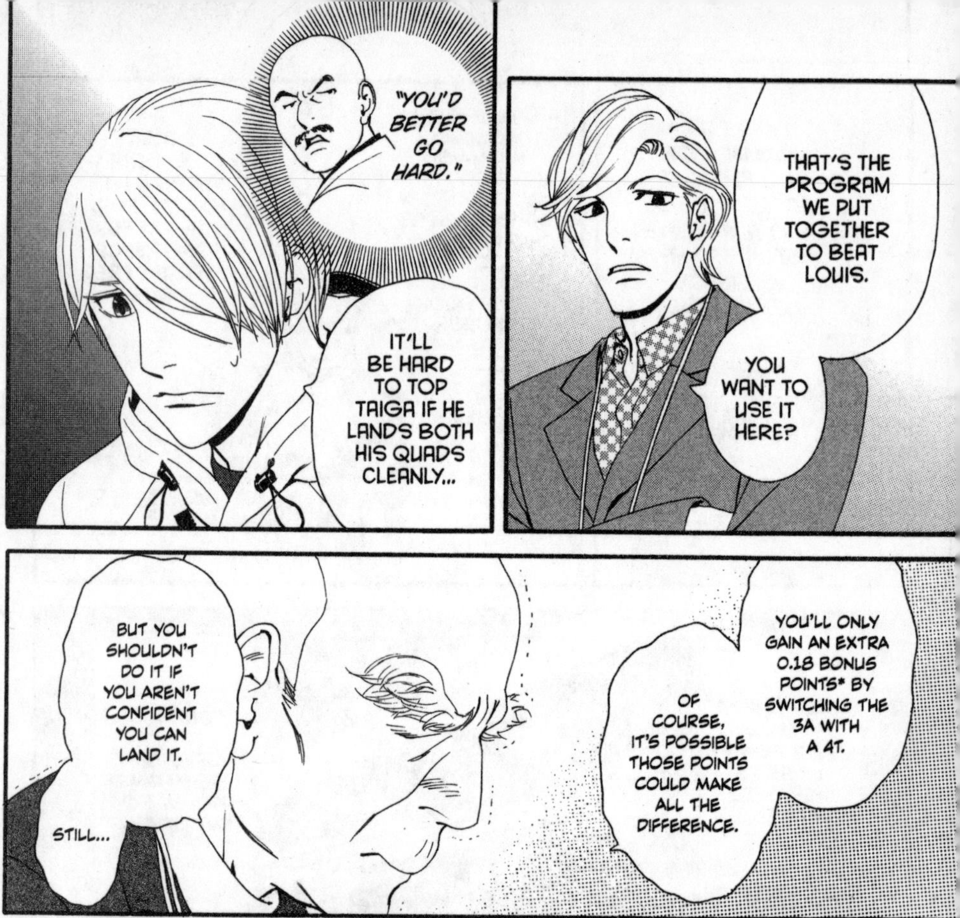
THAT'S THE PROGRAM WE PUT TOGETHER TO BEAT LOUIS.
YOU WANT TO USE IT HERE?
"YOU'D BETTER GO HARD."
IT'LL BE HARD TO TOP TAIGA IF HE LANDS BOTH HIS QUADS CLEANLY...
YOU'LL ONLY GAIN AN EXTRA 0.18 BONUS POINTS* BY SWITCHING THE 3A WITH A 4T.
OF COURSE, IT'S POSSIBLE THOSE POINTS COULD MAKE ALL THE DIFFERENCE.
BUT YOU SHOULDN'T DO IT IF YOU AREN'T CONFIDENT YOU CAN LAND IT.
STILL...

*JUMPS IN THE SECOND HALF OF A PROGRAM HAVE THEIR SCORE INCREASED BY A FACTOR OF 1.1.

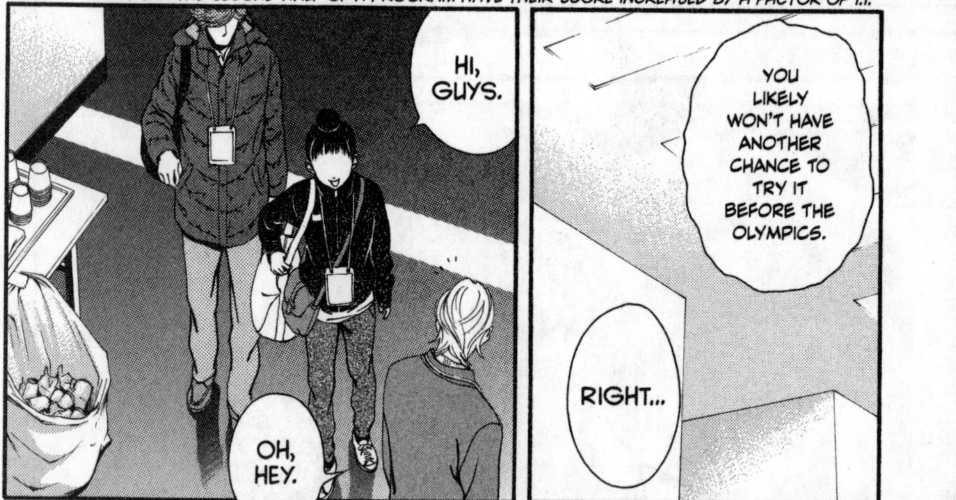
YOU LIKELY WON'T HAVE ANOTHER CHANCE TO TRY IT BEFORE THE OLYMPICS.
RIGHT...
HI, GUYS.
OH, HEY.

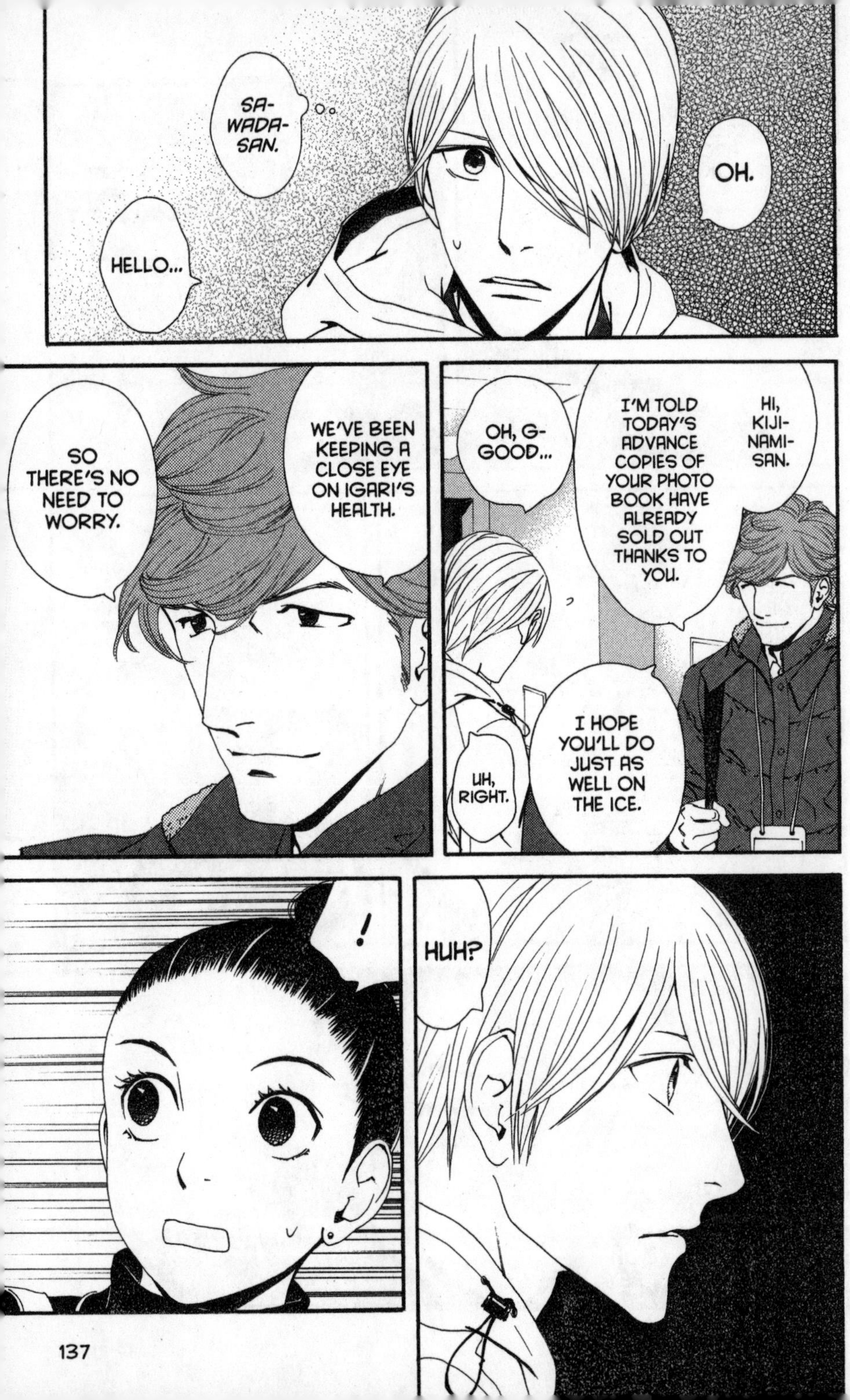
OH.
SA-WADA-SAN.
HELLO...
HI, KIJI-NAMI-SAN.
I'M TOLD TODAY'S ADVANCE COPIES OF YOUR PHOTO BOOK HAVE ALREADY SOLD OUT THANKS TO YOU.
OH, G-GOOD...
I HOPE YOU'LL DO JUST AS WELL ON THE ICE.
UH, RIGHT.
WE'VE BEEN KEEPING A CLOSE EYE ON IGARI'S HEALTH.
SO THERE'S NO NEED TO WORRY.
HUH?
!

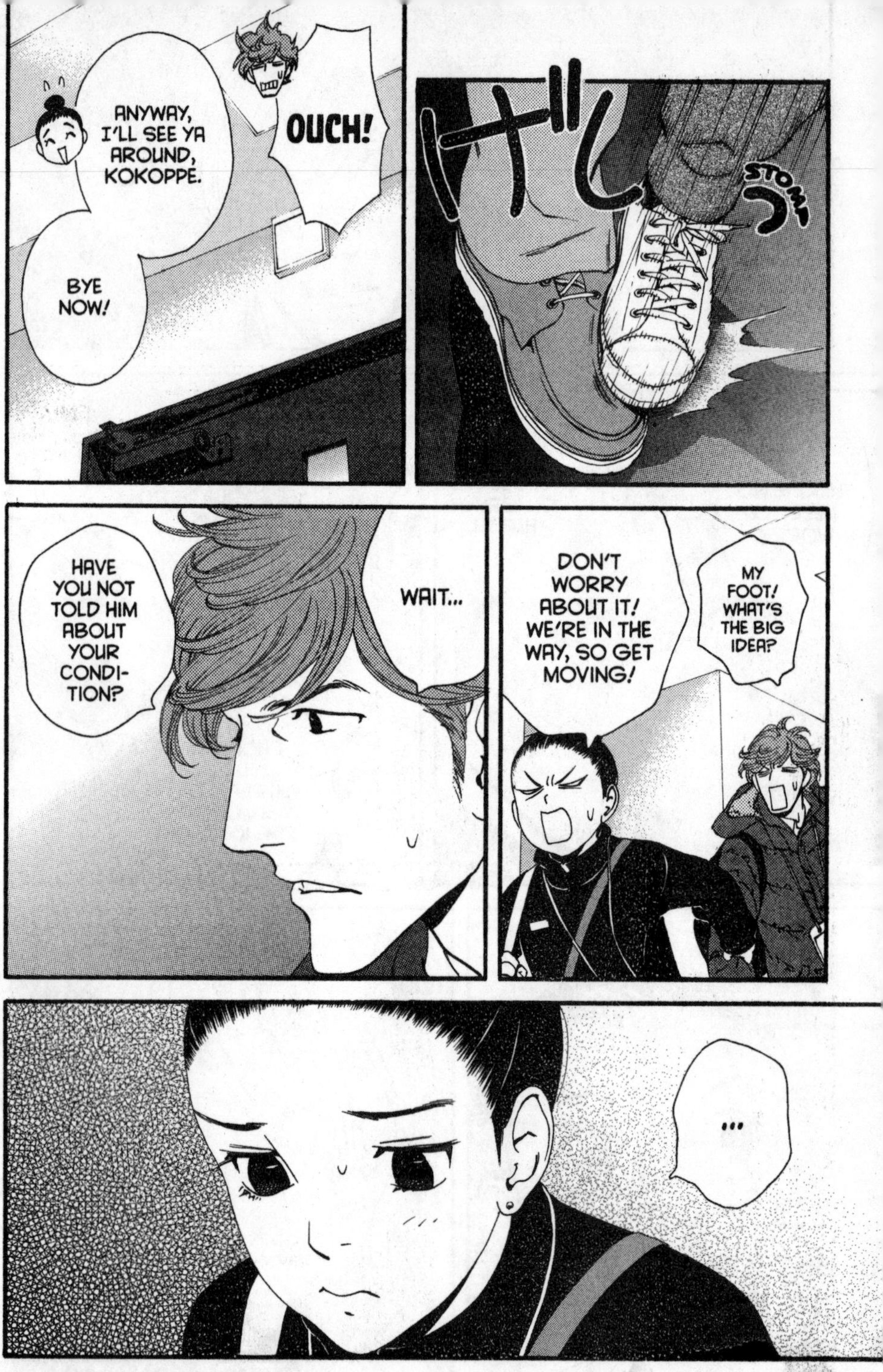
STOMP
ANYWAY, I'LL SEE YA AROUND, KOKOPPE.
OUCH!
BYE NOW!
MY FOOT! WHAT'S THE BIG IDEA?
DON'T WORRY ABOUT IT! WE'RE IN THE WAY, SO GET MOVING!
WAIT...
HAVE YOU NOT TOLD HIM ABOUT YOUR CONDI-TION?
...

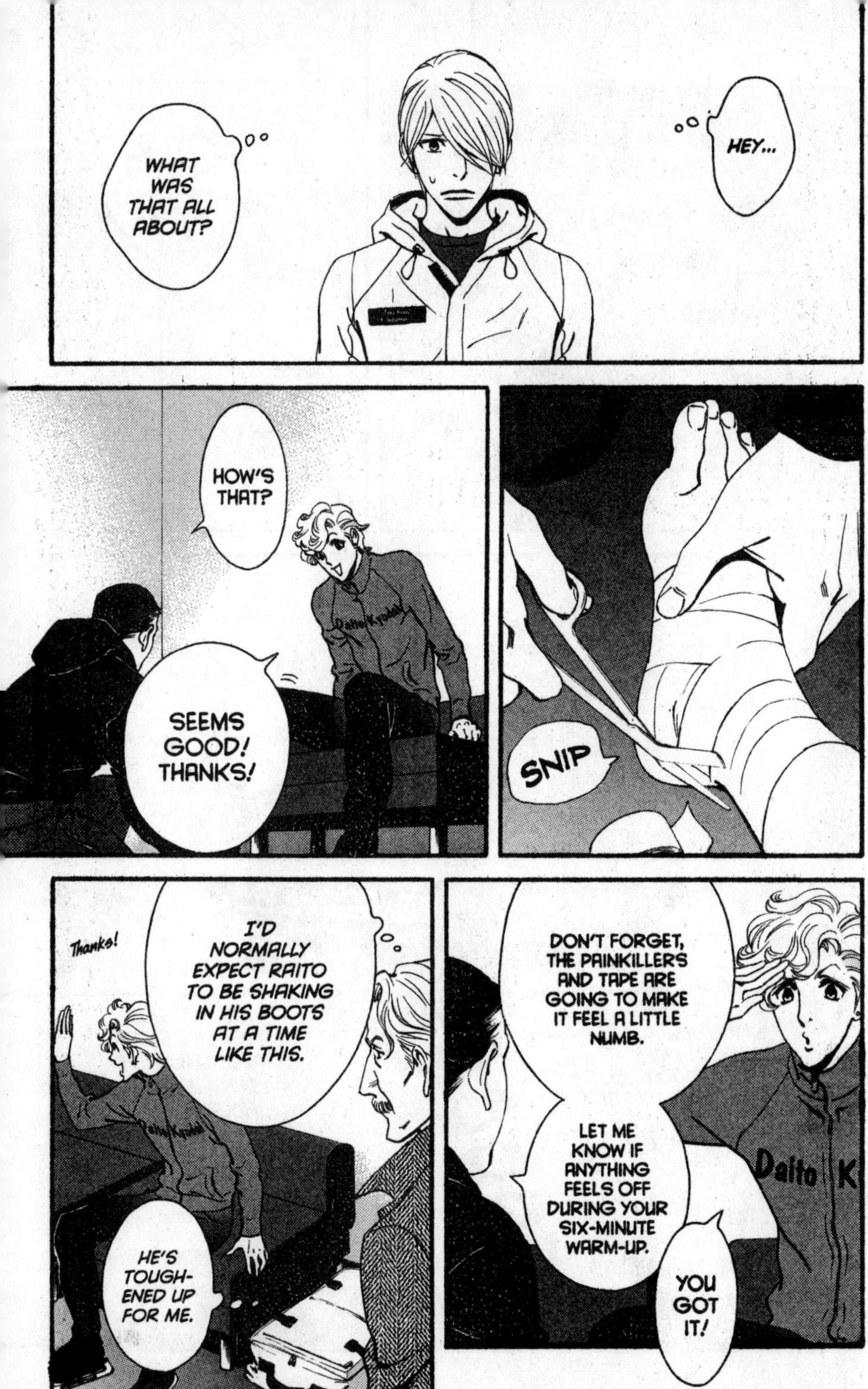
HEY...
WHAT WAS THAT ALL ABOUT?
SNIP
HOW'S THAT?
SEEMS GOOD! THANKS!
DON'T FORGET, THE PAINKILLERS AND TAPE ARE GOING TO MAKE IT FEEL A LITTLE NUMB.
LET ME KNOW IF ANYTHING FEELS OFF DURING YOUR SIX-MINUTE WARM-UP.
YOU GOT IT!
I'D NORMALLY EXPECT RAITO TO BE SHAKING IN HIS BOOTS AT A TIME LIKE THIS.
Thanks!
HE'S TOUGH-ENED UP FOR ME.

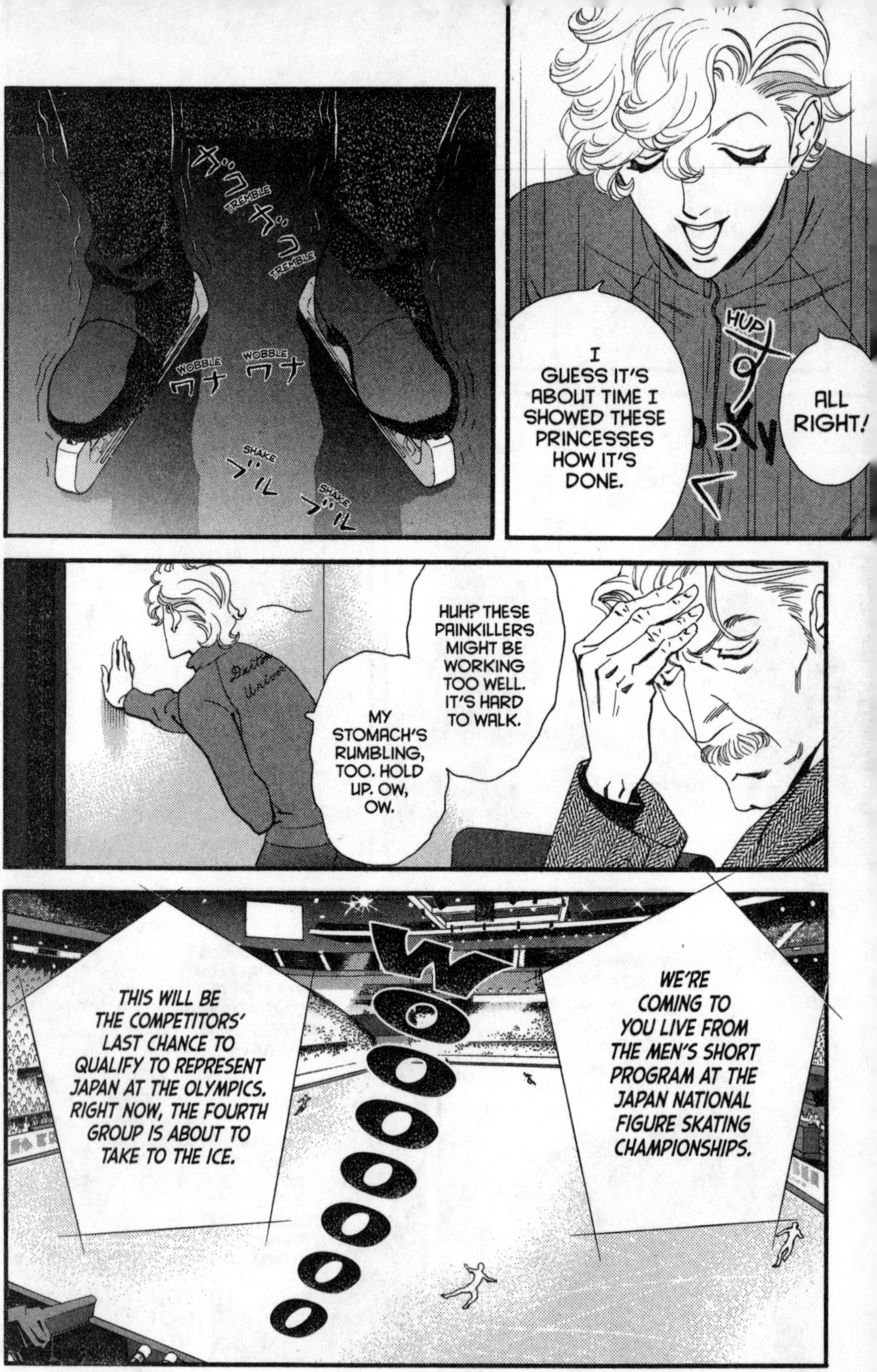
ALL RIGHT!
HUP
I GUESS IT'S ABOUT TIME I SHOWED THESE PRINCESSES HOW IT'S DONE.
TREMBLE
TREMBLE
WOBBLE
WOBBLE
SHAKE
SHAKE
HUH? THESE PAINKILLERS MIGHT BE WORKING TOO WELL. IT'S HARD TO WALK.
MY STOMACH'S RUMBLING, TOO. HOLD UP. OW, OW.
WE'RE COMING TO YOU LIVE FROM THE MEN'S SHORT PROGRAM AT THE JAPAN NATIONAL FIGURE SKATING CHAMPIONSHIPS.
THIS WILL BE THE COMPETITORS' LAST CHANCE TO QUALIFY TO REPRESENT JAPAN AT THE OLYMPICS. RIGHT NOW, THE FOURTH GROUP IS ABOUT TO TAKE TO THE ICE.

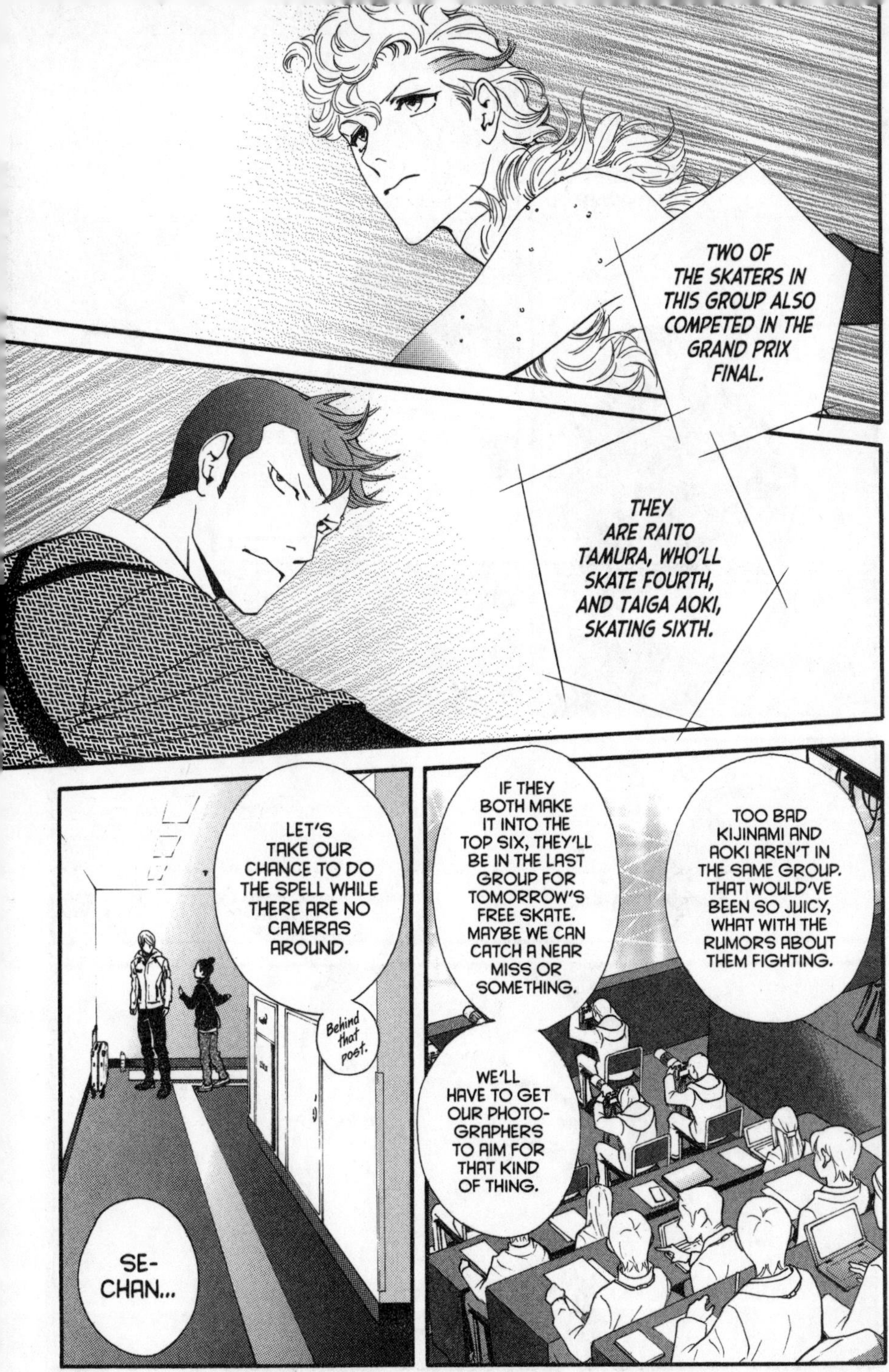
TWO OF THE SKATERS IN THIS GROUP ALSO COMPETED IN THE GRAND PRIX FINAL.
THEY ARE RAITO TAMURA, WHO'LL SKATE FOURTH, AND TAIGA AOKI, SKATING SIXTH.
TOO BAD KIJINAMI AND AOKI AREN'T IN THE SAME GROUP. THAT WOULD'VE BEEN SO JUICY, WHAT WITH THE RUMORS ABOUT THEM FIGHTING.
IF THEY BOTH MAKE IT INTO THE TOP SIX, THEY'LL BE IN THE LAST GROUP FOR TOMORROW'S FREE SKATE. MAYBE WE CAN CATCH A NEAR MISS OR SOMETHING.
WE'LL HAVE TO GET OUR PHOTOGRAPHERS TO AIM FOR THAT KIND OF THING.
LET'S TAKE OUR CHANCE TO DO THE SPELL WHILE THERE ARE NO CAMERAS AROUND.
Behind that post.
SE-CHAN...

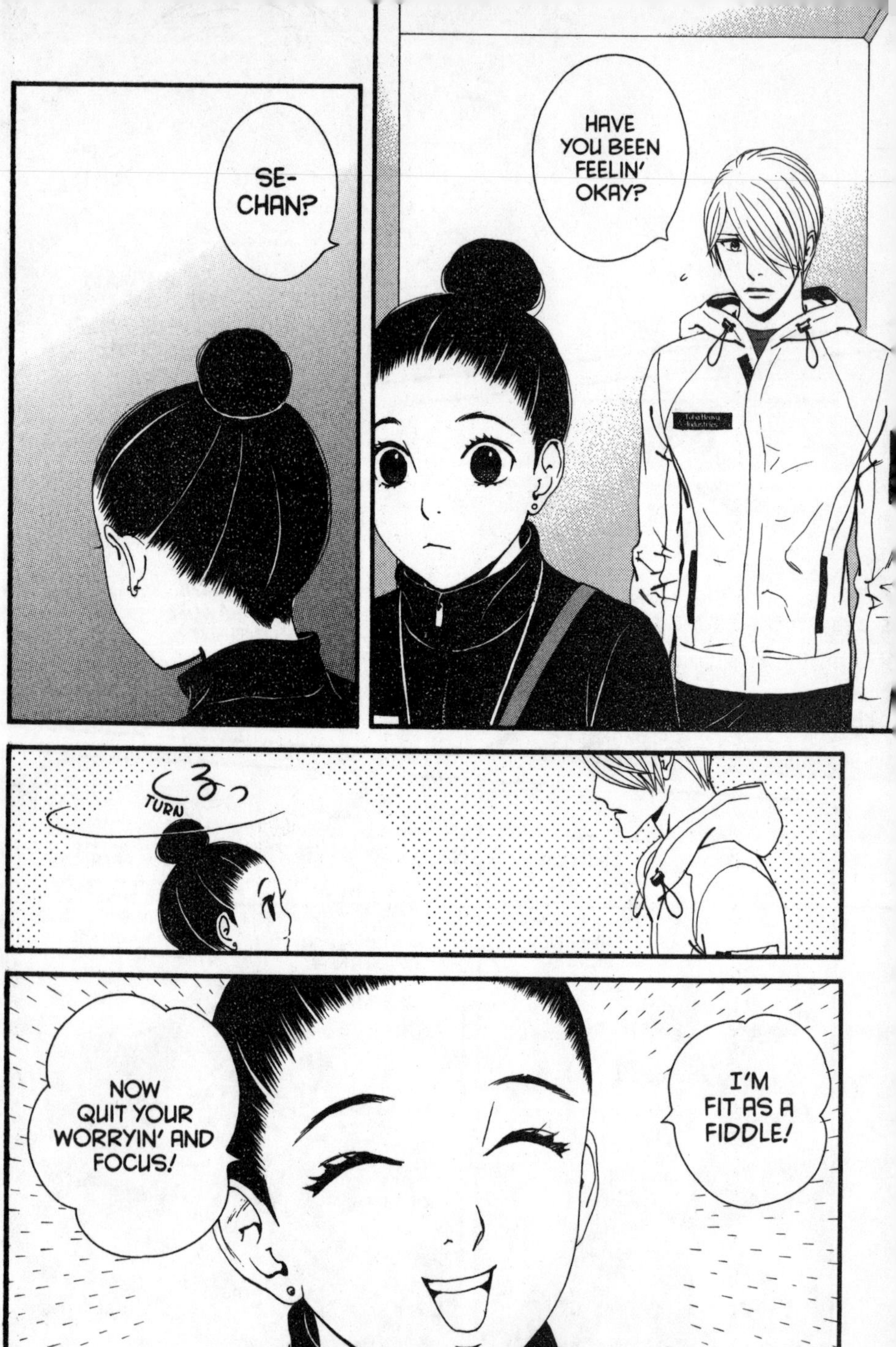
HAVE YOU BEEN FEELIN' OKAY?
SE-CHAN?
くるっ
TURN
I'M FIT AS A FIDDLE!
NOW QUIT YOUR WORRYIN' AND FOCUS!

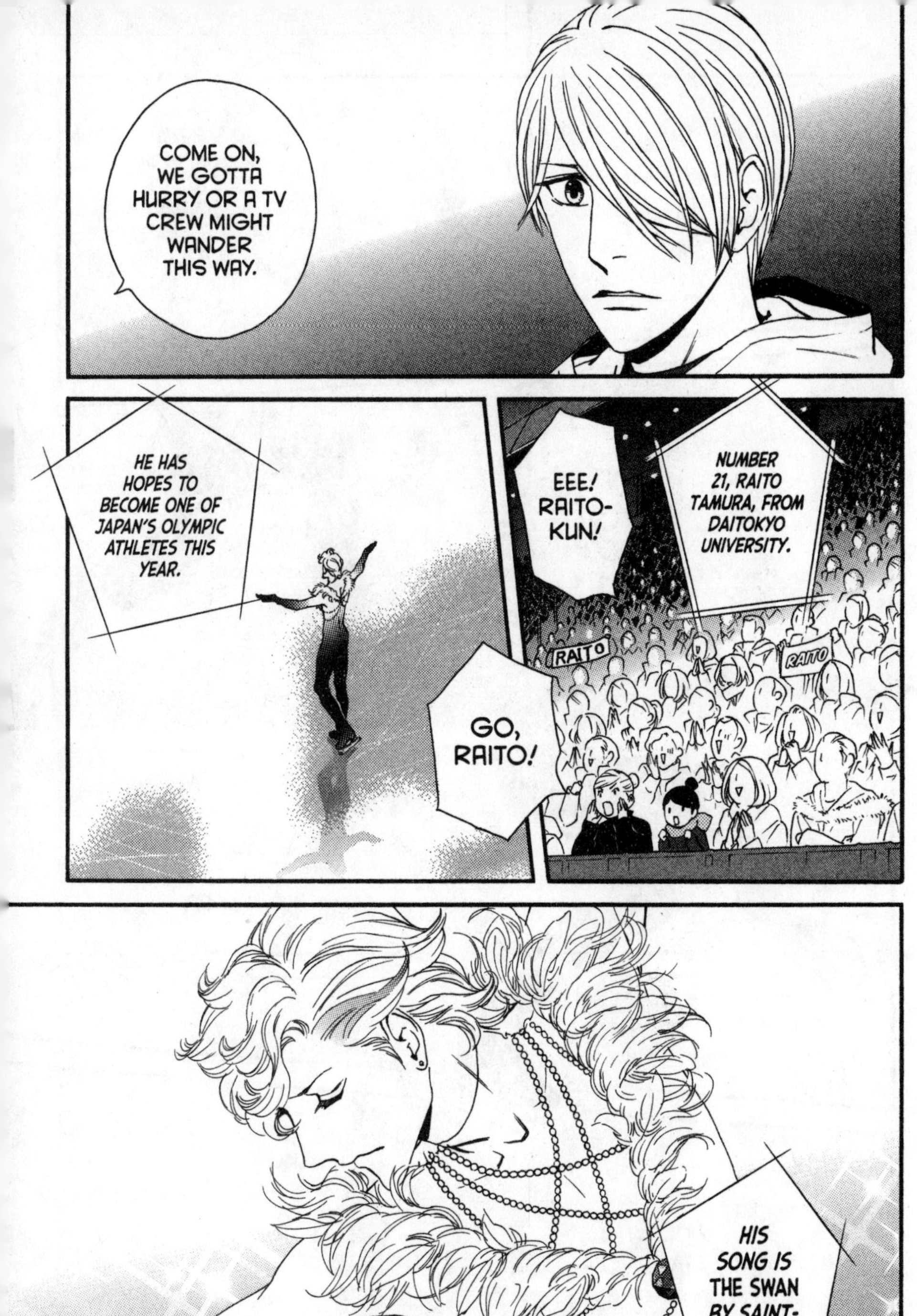
COME ON, WE GOTTA HURRY OR A TV CREW MIGHT WANDER THIS WAY.
NUMBER 21, RAITO TAMURA, FROM DAITOKYO UNIVERSITY.
EEE! RAITO-KUN!
RAITO
RAITO
GO, RAITO!
HE HAS HOPES TO BECOME ONE OF JAPAN'S OLYMPIC ATHLETES THIS YEAR.
HIS SONG IS THE SWAN BY SAINT-SAËNS.

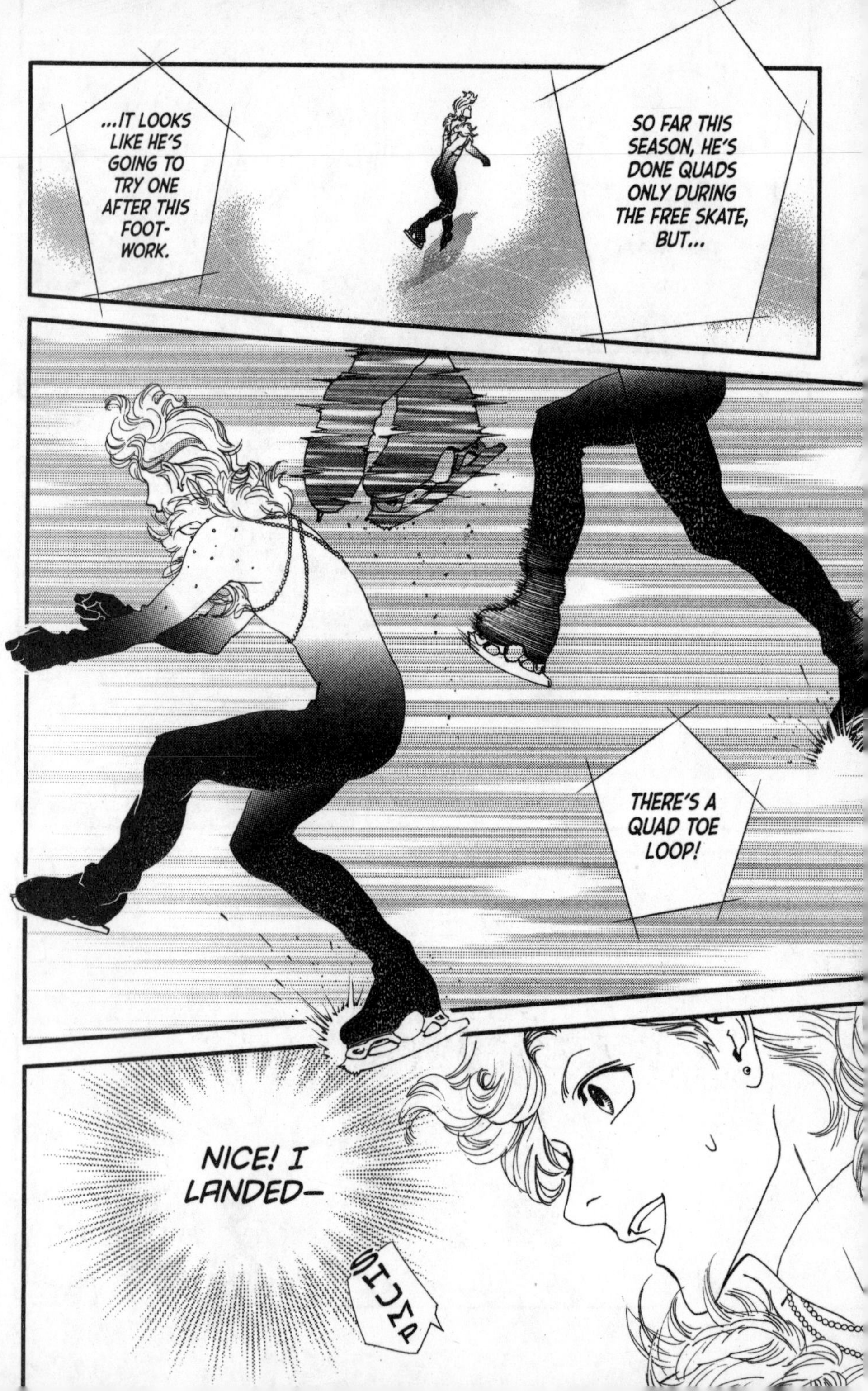
SO FAR THIS SEASON, HE'S DONE QUADS ONLY DURING THE FREE SKATE, BUT...
...IT LOOKS LIKE HE'S GOING TO TRY ONE AFTER THIS FOOT-WORK.
THERE'S A QUAD TOE LOOP!
NICE! I LANDED—

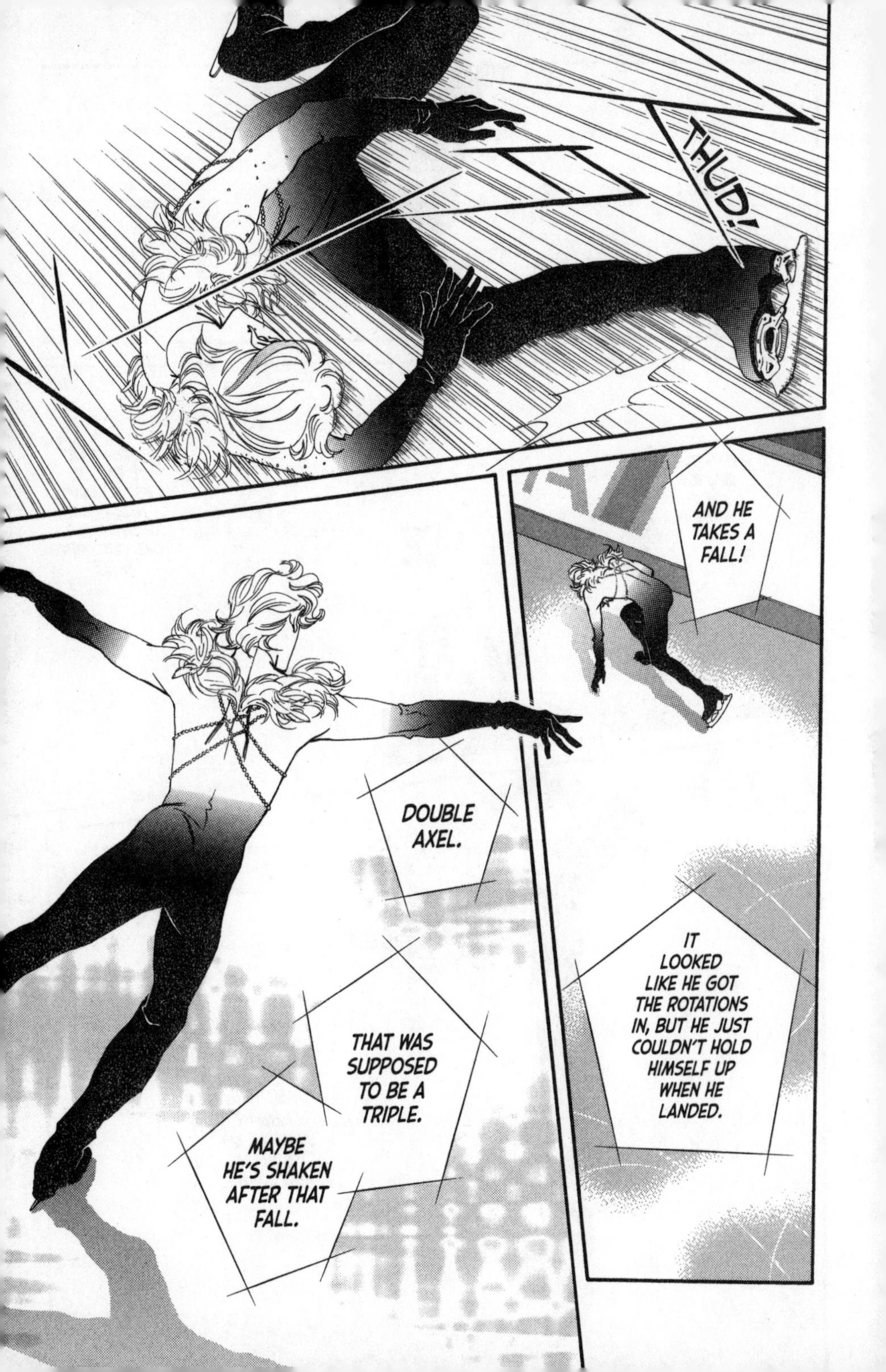
THUD!
AND HE TAKES A FALL!
IT LOOKED LIKE HE GOT THE ROTATIONS IN, BUT HE JUST COULDN'T HOLD HIMSELF UP WHEN HE LANDED.
DOUBLE AXEL.
THAT WAS SUPPOSED TO BE A TRIPLE.
MAYBE HE'S SHAKEN AFTER THAT FALL.

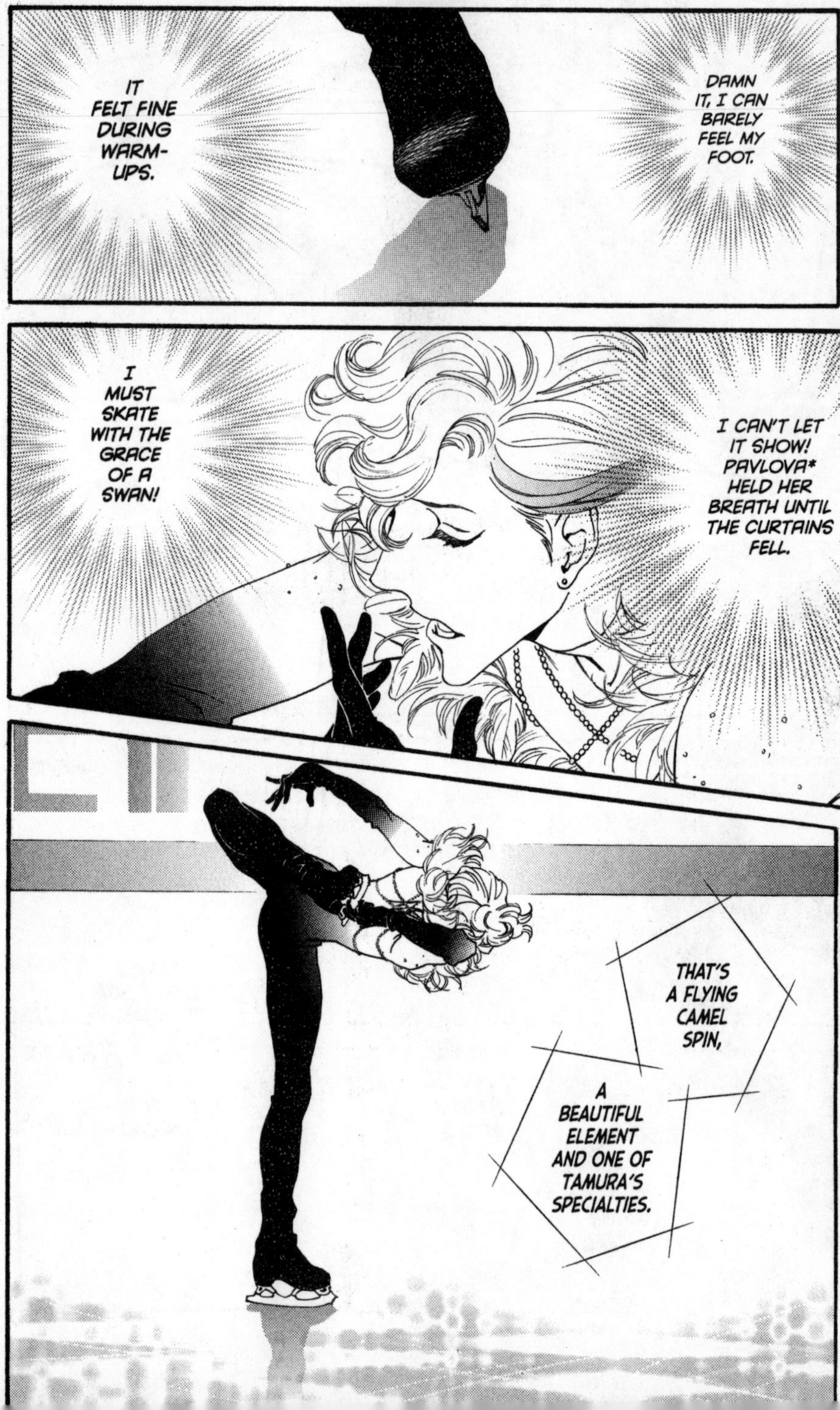
DAMN IT, I CAN BARELY FEEL MY FOOT.
IT FELT FINE DURING WARM-UPS.
I CAN'T LET IT SHOW! PAVLOVA* HELD HER BREATH UNTIL THE CURTAINS FELL.
I MUST SKATE WITH THE GRACE OF A SWAN!
THAT'S A FLYING CAMEL SPIN,
A BEAUTIFUL ELEMENT AND ONE OF TAMURA'S SPECIALTIES.

*ANNA PAVLOVA: A BALLET DANCER FAMOUS FOR HER PERFORMANCE IN THE DYING SWAN. LEGEND HAS IT THAT SHE HELD HER BREATH UNTIL THE CURTAINS FELL FOR THE SAKE OF HER ROLE AS A DEAD SWAN.

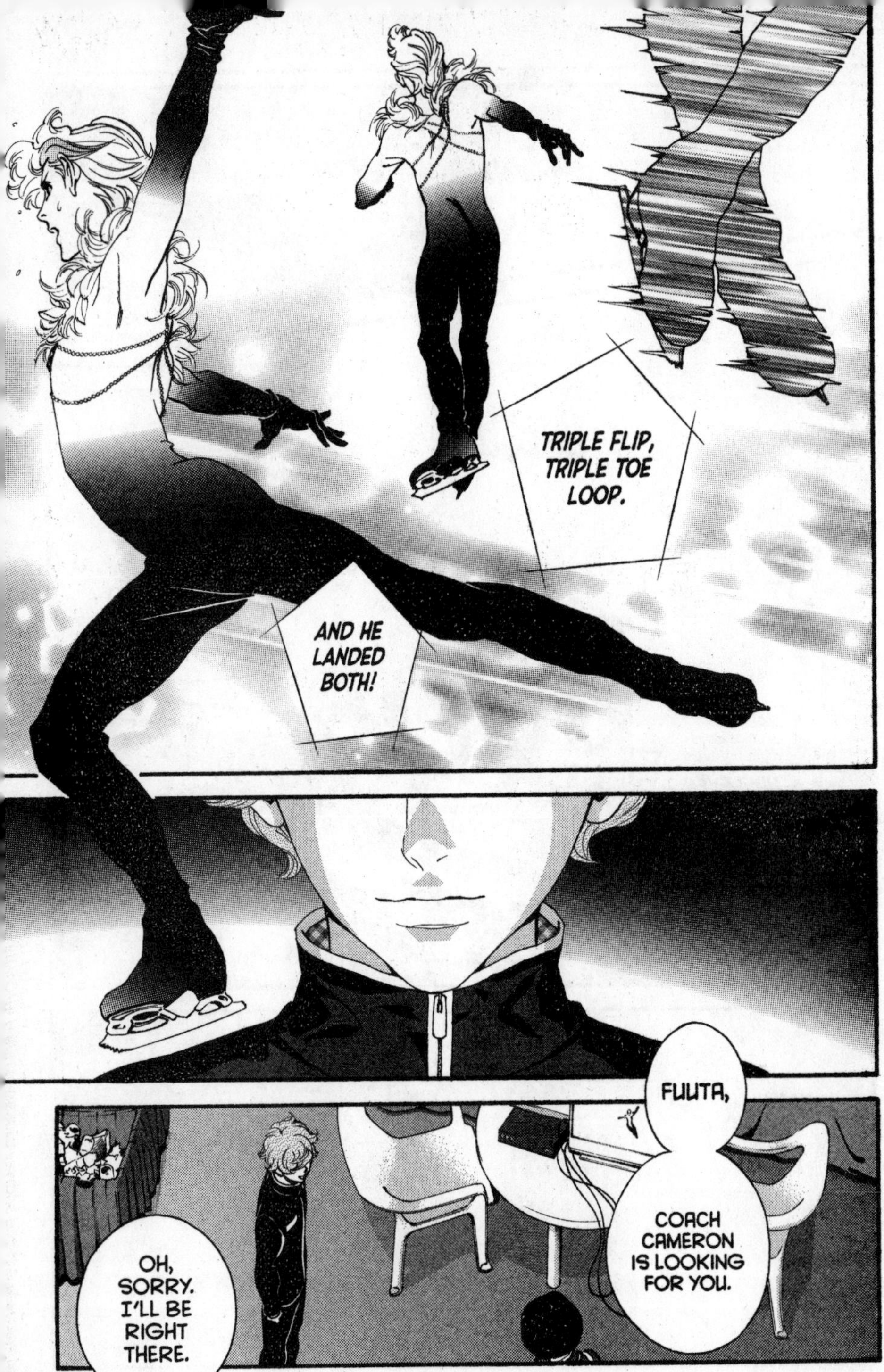
TRIPLE FLIP, TRIPLE TOE LOOP.
AND HE LANDED BOTH!
FUUTA,
COACH CAMERON IS LOOKING FOR YOU.
OH, SORRY. I'LL BE RIGHT THERE.

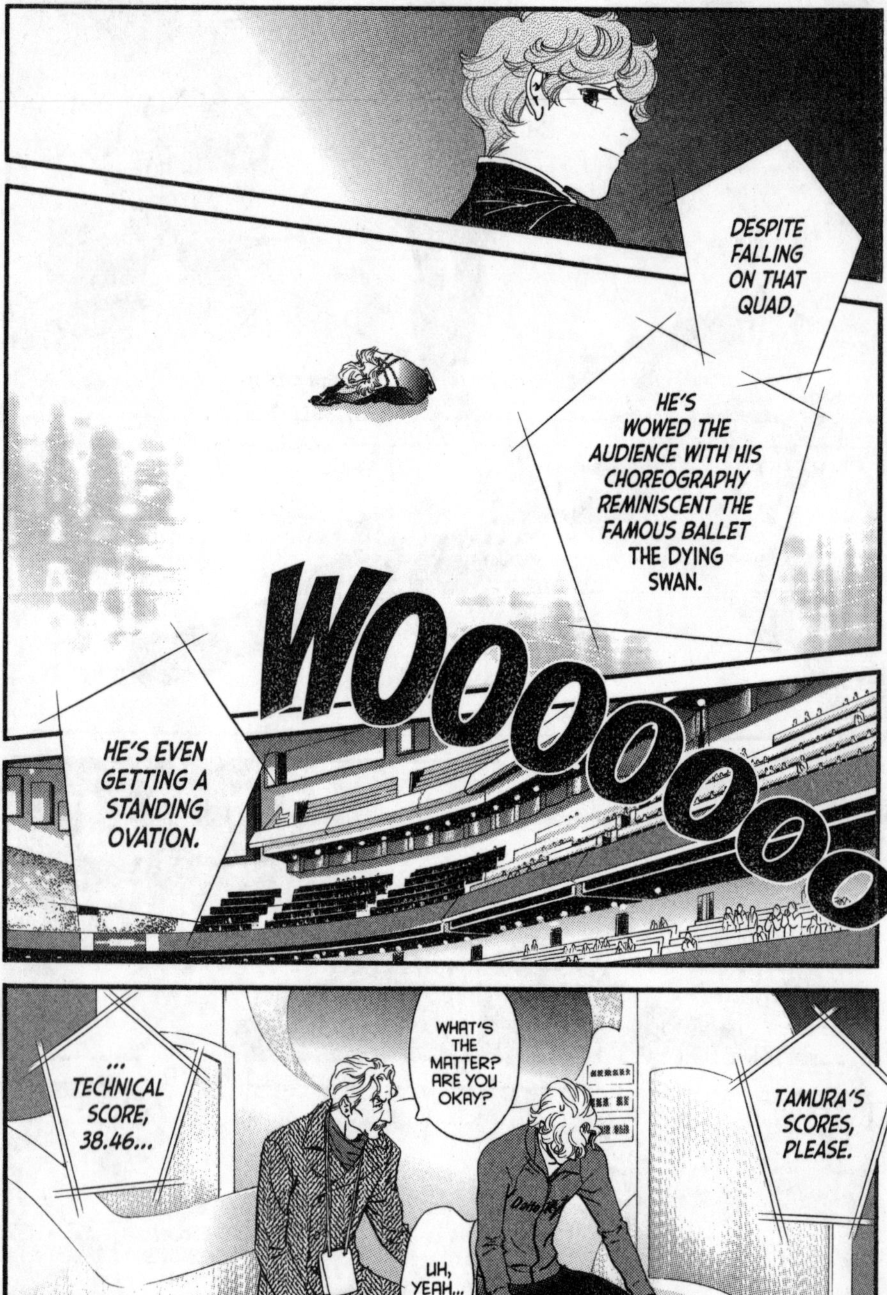
DESPITE FALLING ON THAT QUAD,
HE'S WOWED THE AUDIENCE WITH HIS CHOREOGRAPHY REMINISCENT THE FAMOUS BALLET THE DYING SWAN.
WOOOOOOOOO
HE'S EVEN GETTING A STANDING OVATION.
TAMURA'S SCORES, PLEASE.
WHAT'S THE MATTER? ARE YOU OKAY?
UH, YEAH...
... TECHNICAL SCORE, 38.46...

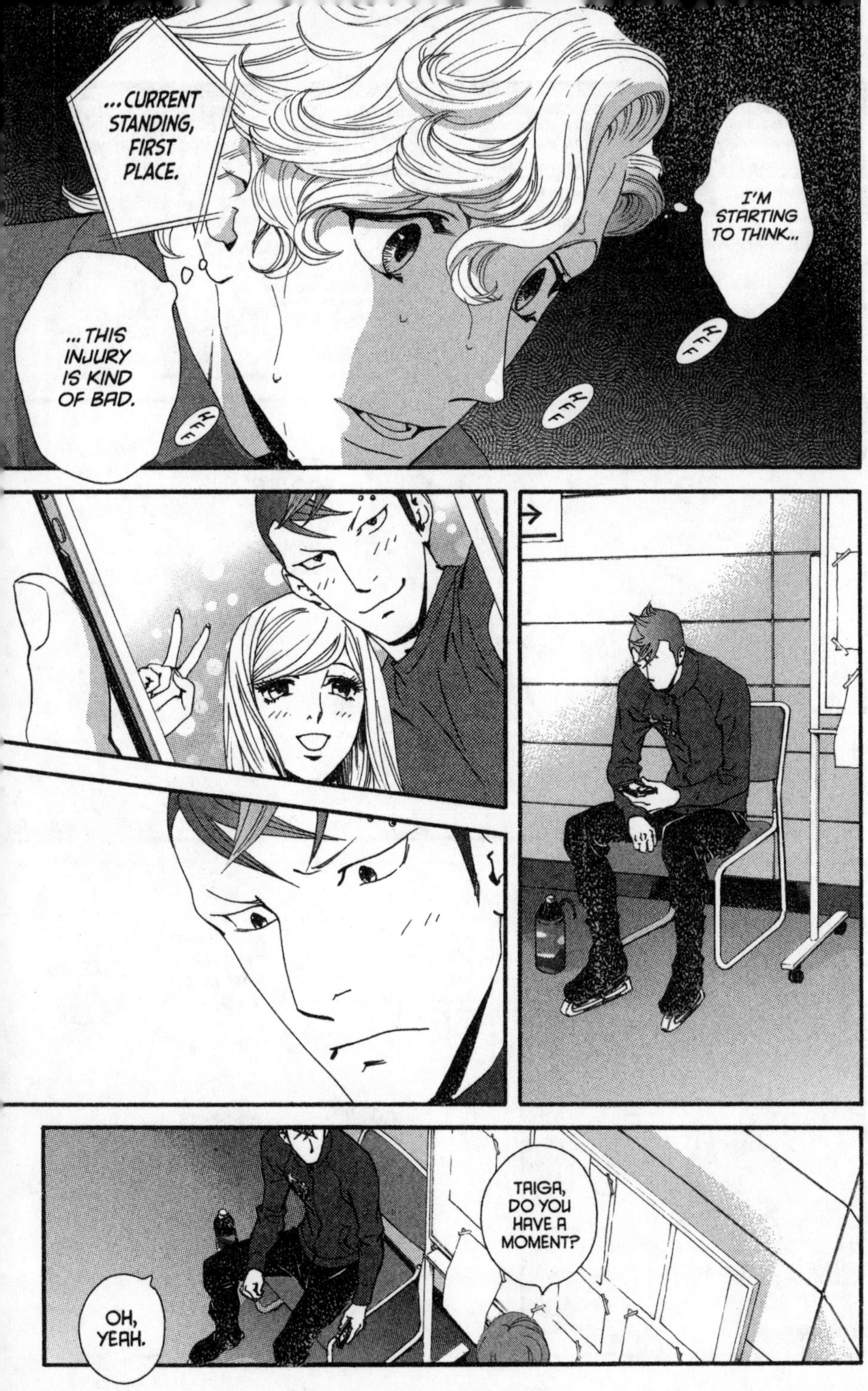
I'M STARTING TO THINK...
HEF
HEF
...CURRENT STANDING, FIRST PLACE.
...THIS INJURY IS KIND OF BAD.
HEF
TAIGA, DO YOU HAVE A MOMENT?
OH, YEAH.

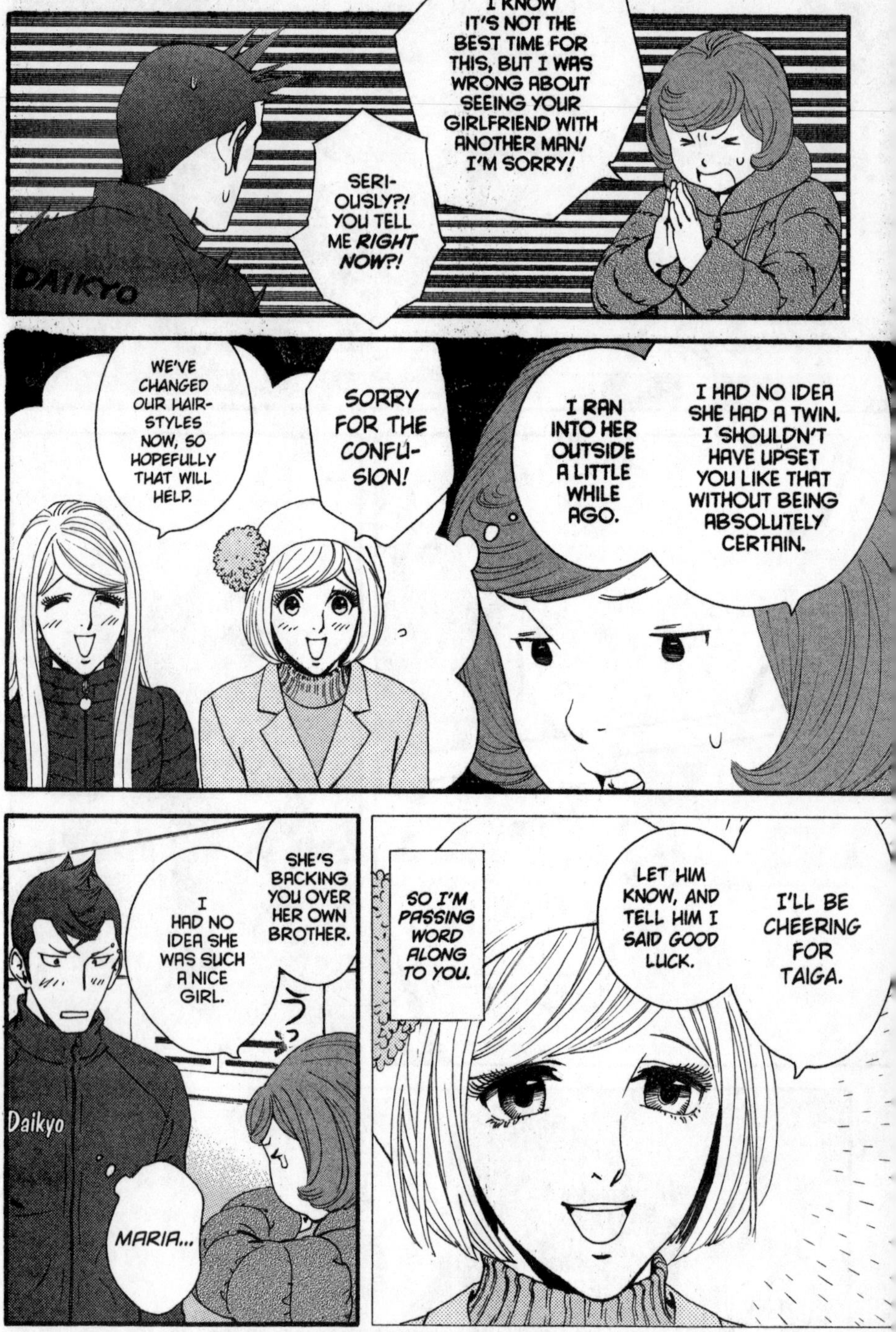

I KNOW IT'S NOT THE BEST TIME FOR THIS, BUT I WAS WRONG ABOUT SEEING YOUR GIRLFRIEND WITH ANOTHER MAN! I'M SORRY!
SERI-OUSLY?! YOU TELL ME *RIGHT NOW?!*
DAIKYO
I HAD NO IDEA SHE HAD A TWIN. I SHOULDN'T HAVE UPSET YOU LIKE THAT WITHOUT BEING ABSOLUTELY CERTAIN.
I RAN INTO HER OUTSIDE A LITTLE WHILE AGO.
SORRY FOR THE CONFU-SION!
WE'VE CHANGED OUR HAIR-STYLES NOW, SO HOPEFULLY THAT WILL HELP.
I'LL BE CHEERING FOR TAIGA.
LET HIM KNOW, AND TELL HIM I SAID GOOD LUCK.
SO I'M PASSING WORD ALONG TO YOU.
SHE'S BACKING YOU OVER HER OWN BROTHER.
I HAD NO IDEA SHE WAS SUCH A NICE GIRL.
うっ
Daikyo
MARIA...

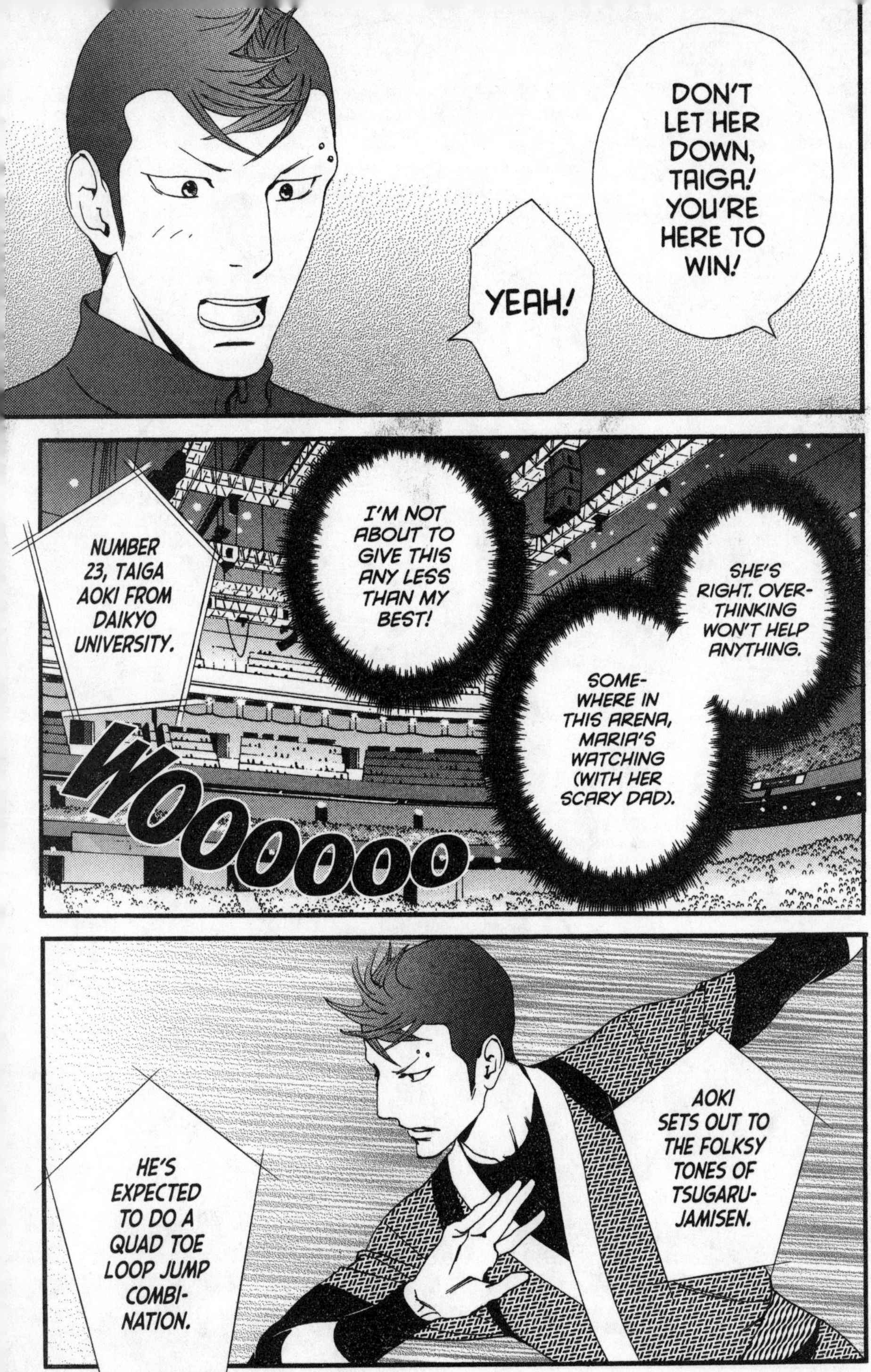
DON'T LET HER DOWN, TAIGA! YOU'RE HERE TO WIN!
YEAH!
SHE'S RIGHT. OVER-THINKING WON'T HELP ANYTHING.
I'M NOT ABOUT TO GIVE THIS ANY LESS THAN MY BEST!
SOME-WHERE IN THIS ARENA, MARIA'S WATCHING (WITH HER SCARY DAD).
NUMBER 23, TAIGA AOKI FROM DAIKYO UNIVERSITY.
WOOOOOO
AOKI SETS OUT TO THE FOLKSY TONES OF TSUGARU-JAMISEN.
HE'S EXPECTED TO DO A QUAD TOE LOOP JUMP COMBI-NATION.

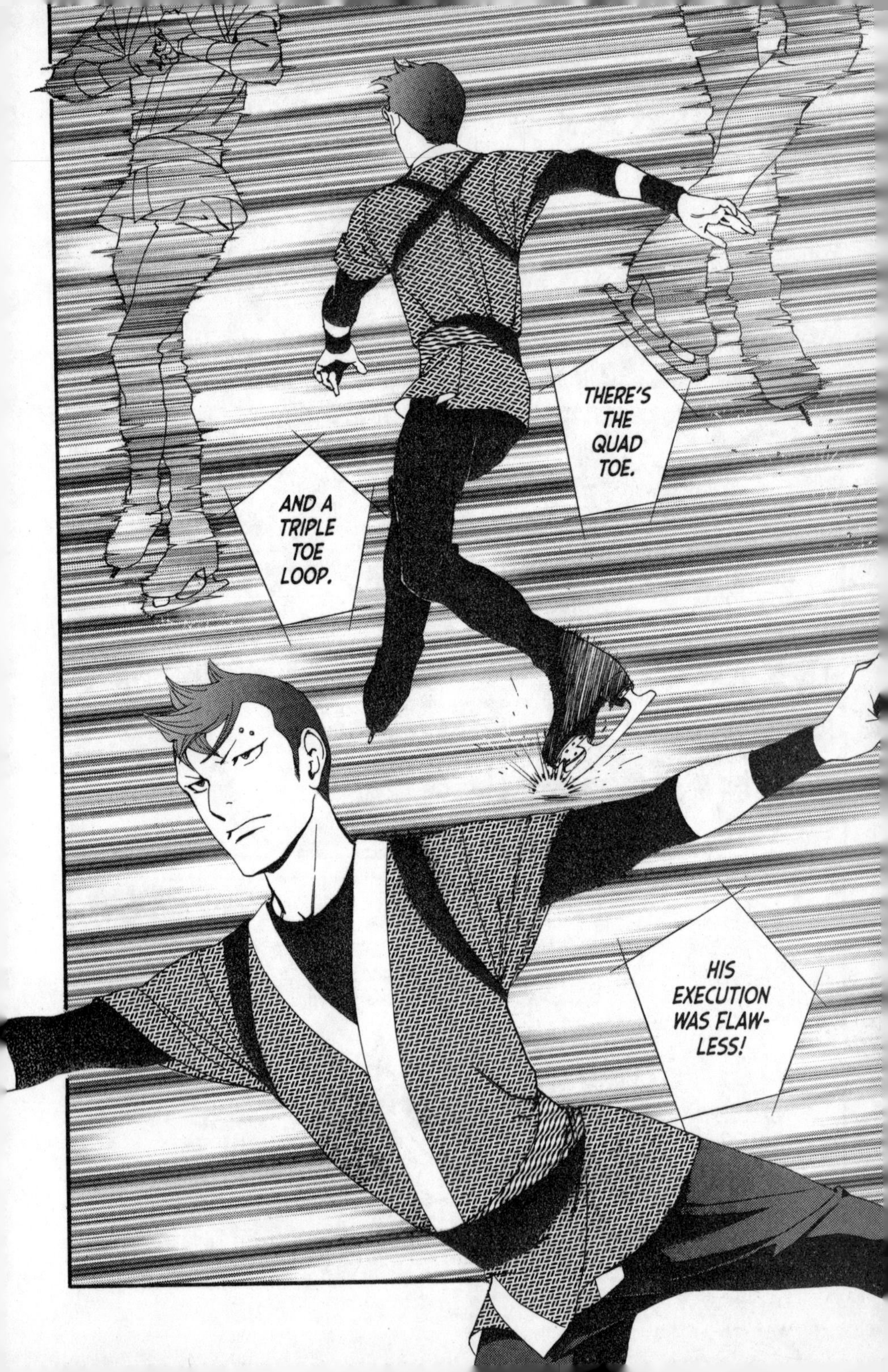
THERE'S THE QUAD TOE.
AND A TRIPLE TOE LOOP.
HIS EXECUTION WAS FLAW-LESS!

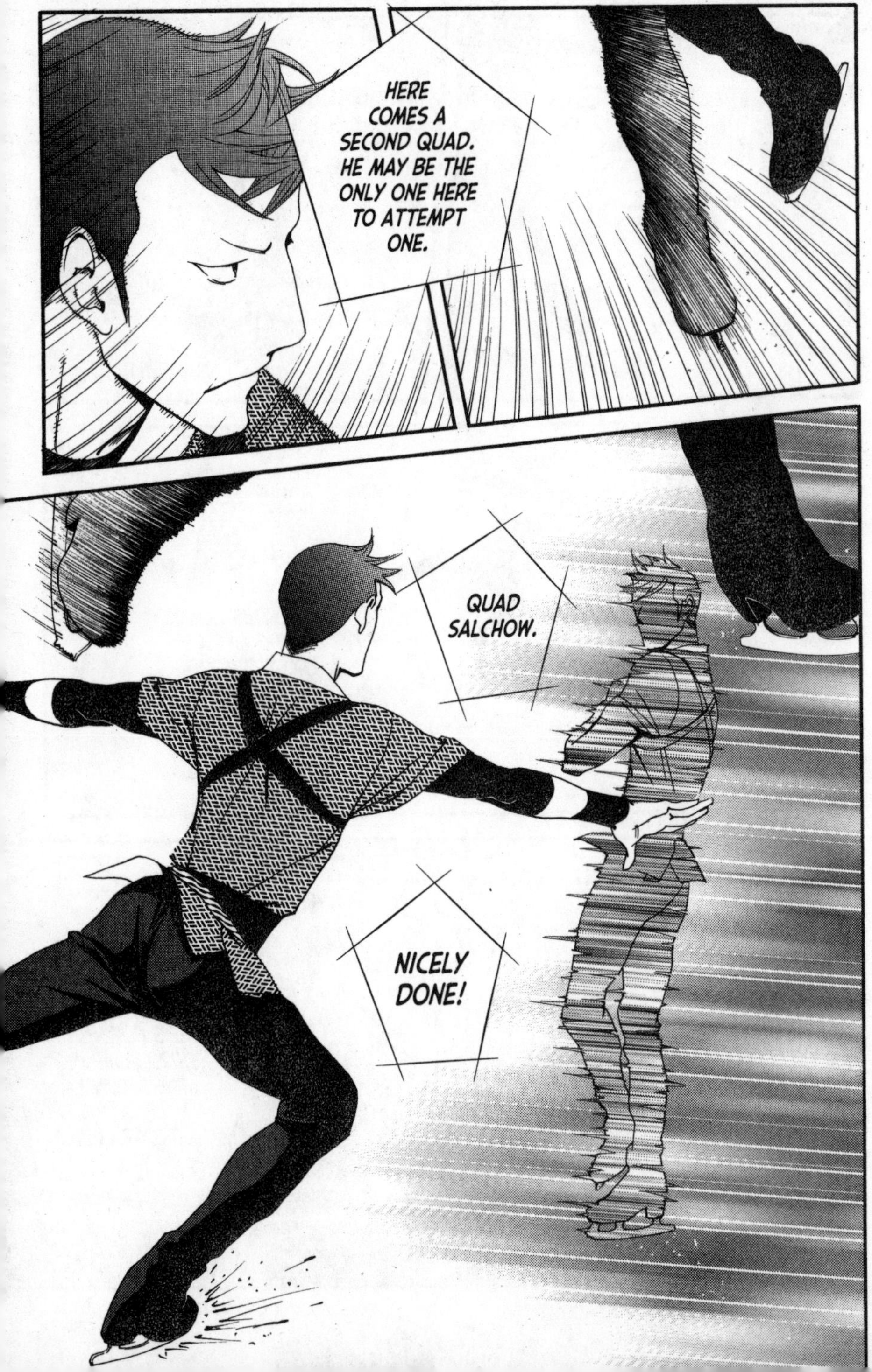
HERE COMES A SECOND QUAD. HE MAY BE THE ONLY ONE HERE TO ATTEMPT ONE.
QUAD SALCHOW.
NICELY DONE!

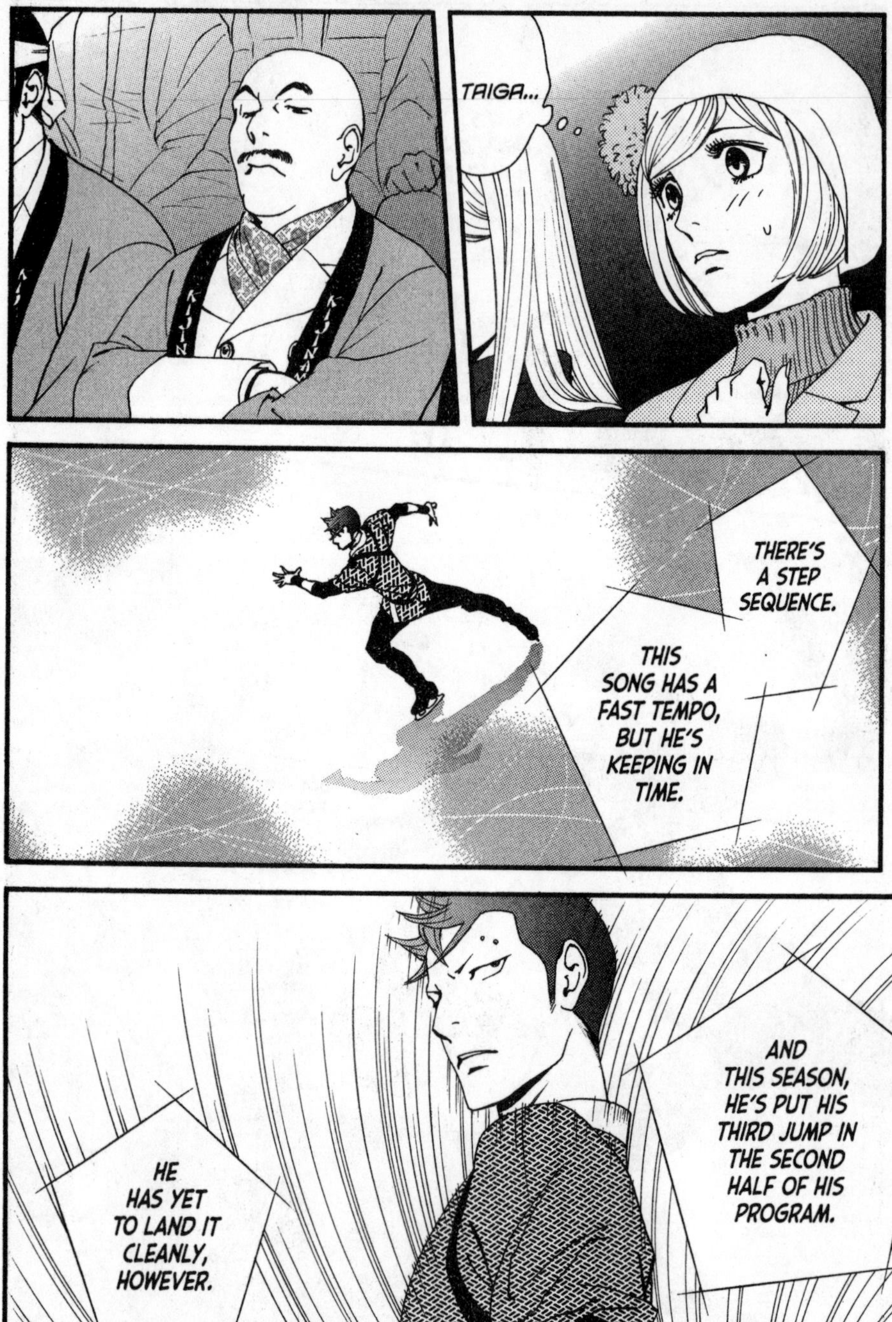
TAIGA...
KIJIN
THERE'S A STEP SEQUENCE.
THIS SONG HAS A FAST TEMPO, BUT HE'S KEEPING IN TIME.
AND THIS SEASON, HE'S PUT HIS THIRD JUMP IN THE SECOND HALF OF HIS PROGRAM.
HE HAS YET TO LAND IT CLEANLY, HOWEVER.

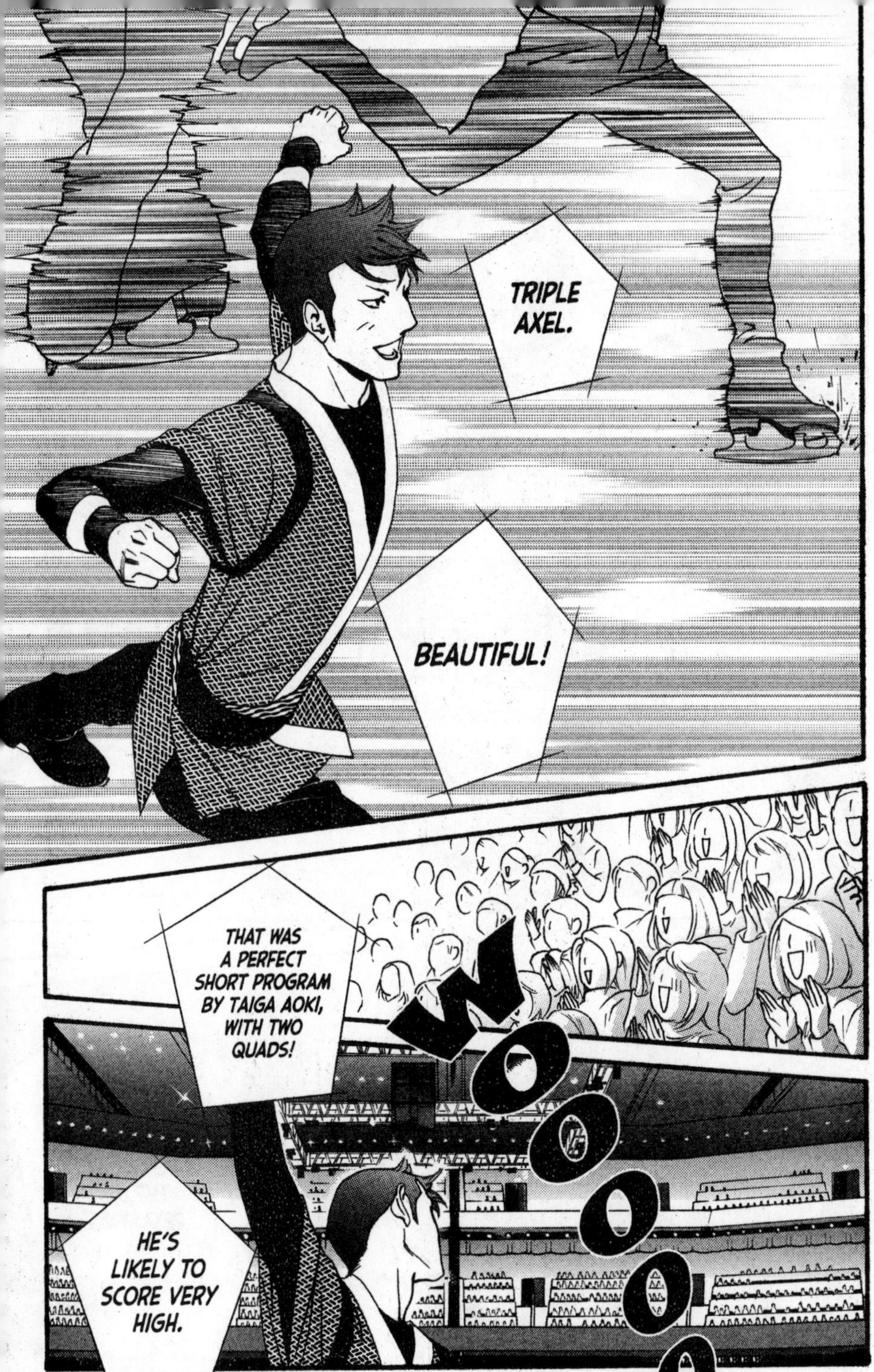
TRIPLE AXEL.
BEAUTIFUL!
THAT WAS A PERFECT SHORT PROGRAM BY TAIGA AOKI, WITH TWO QUADS!
WOOOOOOO
HE'S LIKELY TO SCORE VERY HIGH.

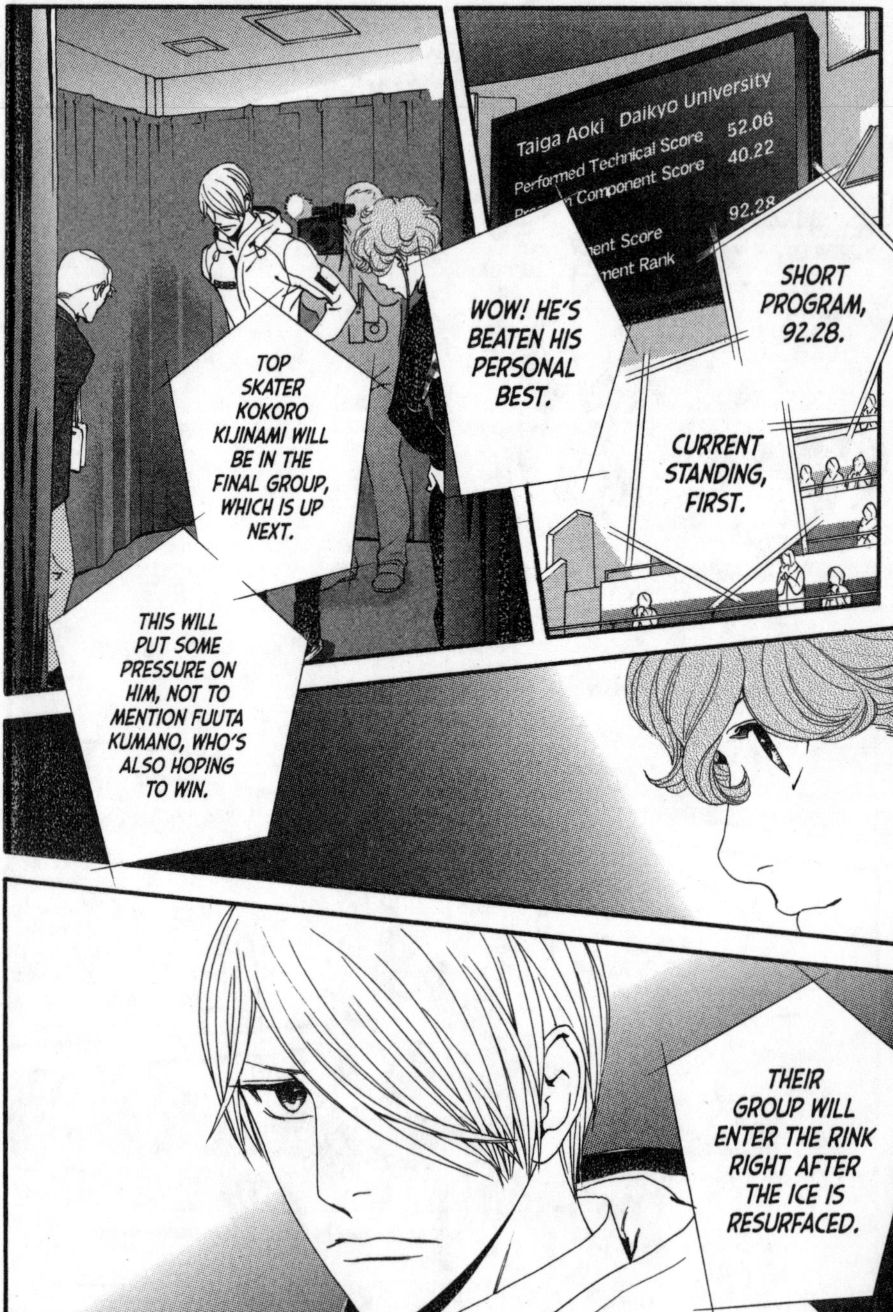
Taiga Aoki Daikyo University
Performed Technical Score 52.06
Component Score 40.22
92.28
SHORT PROGRAM, 92.28.
CURRENT STANDING, FIRST.
WOW! HE'S BEATEN HIS PERSONAL BEST.
TOP SKATER KOKORO KIJINAMI WILL BE IN THE FINAL GROUP, WHICH IS UP NEXT.
THIS WILL PUT SOME PRESSURE ON HIM, NOT TO MENTION FUUTA KUMANO, WHO'S ALSO HOPING TO WIN.
THEIR GROUP WILL ENTER THE RINK RIGHT AFTER THE ICE IS RESURFACED.

To be continued...

TRANSLATION NOTES

HEADBANDS, PAGE 8

It's worth noting that the name Kijinami is written with the Chinese characters for pheasant, child, and wave, and on these headbands, the character for child is the one inside the heart. Incidentally, Kokoro's name means heart.

HAPPI, PAGE 31

A happi is a wide-sleeved, open-fronted shirt often worn at Japanese festivals, especially in the summer. They typically have a crest of some kind on the back, and here, Kokoro's dad has had his crew and family show up wearing Kijinami happi.

MANJU, PAGE 41

Manju is a bun typically filled with red bean paste.

MAMADOR, PAGE 41

And a mamador is a cake typically filled with red bean paste. They're made in Kokoro's home prefecture of Fukushima, and if you refer to Kokoro's skater profile in volume 1, you'll see that they're his favorite food.

TSUGARU-JAMISEN, PAGE 151

This is a style of shamisen music that comes from the Tsugaru peninsula in north Japan. The shamisen is a three-stringed Japanese instrument similar to a guitar.

Glossary by Coach Akiyuki Kido

(based on January 2015 rules)

Grand Prix Final (page 8)
The six highest-ranking skaters in the ISU Grand Prix go on to compete for first in the Final. The ISU Grand Prix is a series of six competitions held between October and December, including Skate America, Skate Canada, the Cup of China, the Trophée Eric Bompard (France), the Rostelecom Cup (Russia), and the NHK Trophy (Japan). The order they're held in varies by year.

Free Skate (page 8)
In the free skating competition, skaters get to choose what elements and moves to use. Still, to ensure a well-rounded program, there are rules about what jumps, spins, and steps are required, as well as restrictions on the number of them allowed. In women's singles, this segment lasts four minutes, and in men's singles, it lasts four minutes and thirty seconds.

Short Program (page 9)
The short program is a segment in which the skaters have up to two minutes and fifty seconds to perform eight predetermined elements, such as jumps, spins, or steps.

Quad Lutz (4Lz) (page 10)
A Lutz with four rotations. The Lutz is considered the second hardest jump after the axel. It is named after the Austrian skater Alois Lutz, the first person to perform this jump. To perform this jump, a skater uses their right toe pick (the front of the skate's blade where it has teeth) to launch themself into the air from their left skate's back outside edge. Because of the difficulty of skating on this edge, many skaters make an edge error. Note that the roles of each foot are reversed for skaters who spin clockwise.

Quad Toe Loop (4T) (page 14)
A toe loop with four rotations. The toe loop is considered the easiest jump. The skater uses their left toe to launch themself into the air from their right skate's back outside edge. To date, no one has managed to execute this jump with more than four revolutions, and only a select few skaters can do even that.

Triple Loop (page 15)
A loop with three rotations. To do a loop, the skater both takes off from and lands on only their right foot. With their left leg crossed in front of their right, they jump from the right skate's back outside edge.

Footwork (page 15)
A skater's footwork is the way they weave together steps with elements such as turns. Moves such as the Mohawk, the chasse, the crossroll, and the Choctaw are steps, whereas the three turn, loop turn, rocker, counter, bracket, and twizzle are turns. A combination of steps and turns is called a step sequence.

Choreographic sequence (page 15)
For this step sequence, the skater is allowed a great deal of freedom in choosing their components and is scored on the sequence as a whole.

Technical score (page 18)
The technical score is determined by the technical elements included in the program and their quality. Jumps, spins, steps, and other elements each have a base value, which is modified by a grade of execution (GOE) to get the technical score. The GOE is the average of the modifiers assigned by the judges, excluding the highest and lowest. These modifiers have one of seven values between negative and positive three.

Program components score (PCS or presentation score) (page 18)
For this score, skaters are evaluated on the basis of five program components: skating skills, transitions, performance, composition, and interpretation. A skater's final score is the total of their program components score (PCS) and their technical score.

Salchow (page 20)
This jump is executed from the left foot's back inside edge by lifting the right foot forward and to the left. The way both feet face outward just before takeoff is a unique feature of the Salchow jump. It is typically considered an easy jump because its entrance from the back inside edge makes rotating less difficult. Still, although they are rare, there are some skaters who consider it to be their most difficult jump, often owing to personal difficulty skating on the back inside edge. It was named after the Swedish skater Ulrich Salchow.

Jump Combination (page 20)
A jump combination is when a skater performs a jump and then immediately performs another from the foot they land on. Since jumps are landed on the right skate's back outside edge (or the left skate's if you're spinning clockwise), all jumps after the first in a combination are limited to either the toe loop or the loop jump. If the skater weaves footwork between their jumps, it's called a jump sequence instead.

Triple axel (3A) (page 23)
There are six different jumps in figure skating. An Axel is the only one that begins with the skater facing directly forward (on the forward outside edge). It's the most difficult jump, and a triple Axel requires three and a half midair rotations. Midori Ito was the first woman in Japan to successfully execute this jump.

Level (page 23)
Elements such as lifts, steps, twizzles, and dance spins are categorized into levels on the basis of certain features. An element with a higher level has a higher base value in scoring, and the highest level is four. World-class skaters perform most elements at level four.

Open practice (page 56)
Open practice is typically held on the day before, or the day of, a competition. It's the skaters' last chance to polish their routines, and they're free to participate or not at their discretion. The technical panel—which consists of a technical specialist, an assistant technical specialist, and a technical controller—is required to watch and familiarize themselves with the skaters' programs.

Senior (page 57)
There are three age divisions in figure skating: novice, junior, and senior. The senior division includes skaters 15 or older, the junior division includes skaters ages 13 to 18, and the novice division is for skaters ages 10 to 13 (or sometimes 14). These ranges are based on their age on June 30th before the competition.

Flip (page 74)
To perform this jump, the skater rides the back inside edge of their left skate and uses their right toe to launch themself into the air. It is sometimes called the toe Salchow. Due to the relative difficulty of maintaining a vertical axis, this jump's base value is almost as high as that of the Lutz. Note that the roles of each foot are reversed for skaters who spin clockwise.

Spread eagle (page 77)
The spread eagle is a move in which the skater keeps both skates on the ice with the toes of each foot facing straight out to the sides.

Nationals (page 94)

The Japan Figure Skating Championships. They're held every year near the end of December to determine the best skater in Japan. The results of this competition largely determine who will represent Japan at the Olympics and World Championships.

Second half bonus (page 136)

Jumps in the second half of a program have their base value increased by a factor of 1.1.

Six-minute warm-ups (page 139)

At the beginning of a competition, each group gets six minutes on the ice to practice.

Flying camel spin (page 146)

To perform a flying camel spin, a skater leaps into a pose in which they hold their upper body and free leg a little higher than parallel with the ice to form a T shape while spinning.

Akiyuki Kido was born on August 28th, 1975. He represented Japan in ice dancing at the 2006 winter Olympics in Turin, Italy. He took fifteenth place, the highest Japan had ever placed in ice dancing at the time. Today, he works as a coach at the Shin-Yokohama Skate Center.

Knight of the Ice Skater Profile 8

8	Takejiro Honda

Height:

163 cm (when he was active)

Blood type:

B

Birthday:

January 3rd

Place of origin:

Hokkaido

Strongest element:

Spins

Strongest jump:

Salchow

Most difficult jump performed when active:

Triple Salchow

Strength:

His precise edgework

Weakness:

Expressiveness

Hobby:

Crossword puzzles

Talent:

Elvis Presley impersonation (although he hasn't shown anyone but his siblings and M-ko F-mori)

Family composition:

Bachelor, living with his sister's family

Favorite food:

Flan

Least favorite food:

None in particular

Notes:

He stops trembling the moment he starts skating

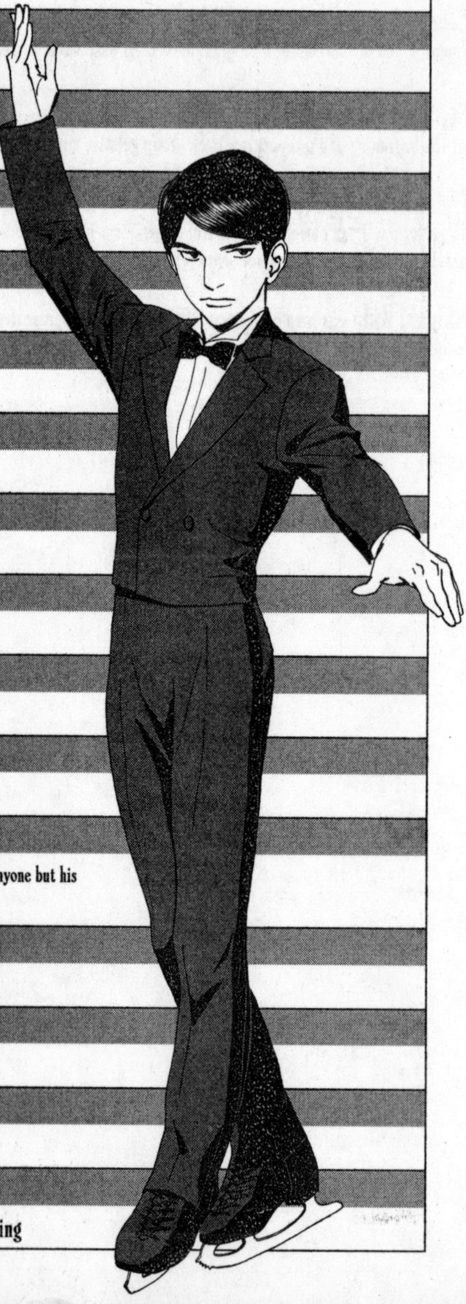

Divided Opinion

7

A Very Angry Sister

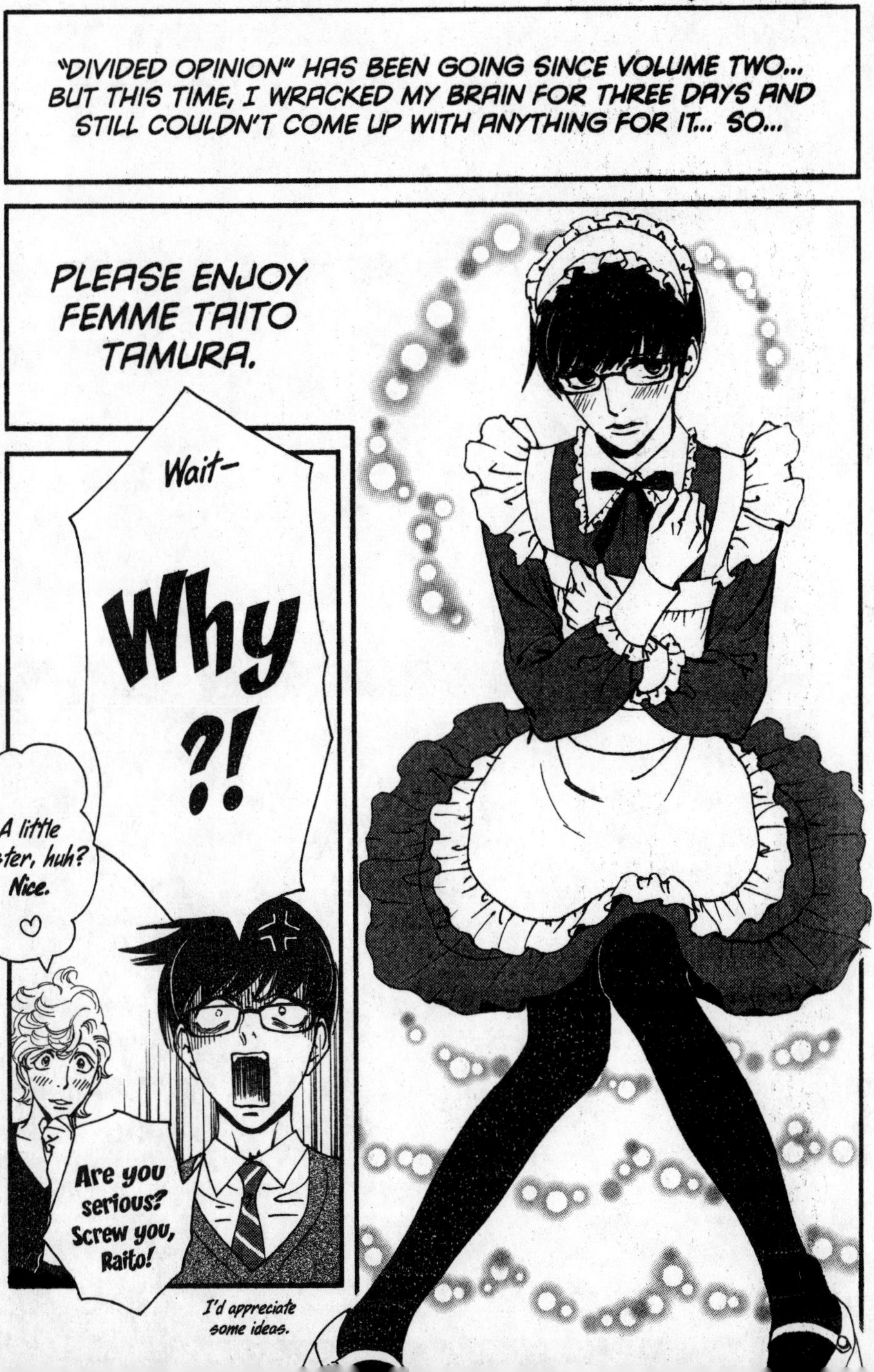
"DIVIDED OPINION" HAS BEEN GOING SINCE VOLUME TWO... BUT THIS TIME, I WRACKED MY BRAIN FOR THREE DAYS AND STILL COULDN'T COME UP WITH ANYTHING FOR IT... SO...
PLEASE ENJOY FEMME TAITO TAMURA.
Wait— Why?!
A little sister, huh? Nice. ♡
Are you serious? Screw you, Raito!
I'd appreciate some ideas.

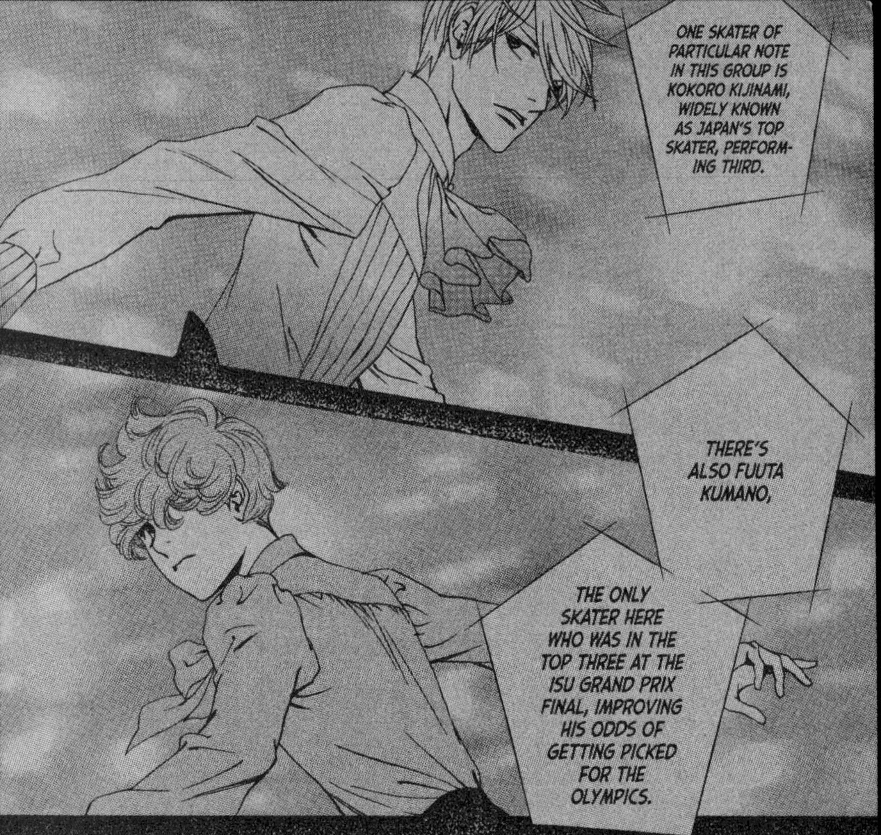
ONE SKATER OF PARTICULAR NOTE IN THIS GROUP IS KOKORO KIJINAMI, WIDELY KNOWN AS JAPAN'S TOP SKATER, PERFORMING THIRD.
THERE'S ALSO FUUTA KUMANO,
THE ONLY SKATER HERE WHO WAS IN THE TOP THREE AT THE ISU GRAND PRIX FINAL, IMPROVING HIS ODDS OF GETTING PICKED FOR THE OLYMPICS.

In the next volume...

Kokoro is increasingly unsure why he's even skating. Meanwhile, it seems nothing can wipe the serene smile off his rival Fuuta's face. How can Kokoro win the National Championship when he's up against such unflappable confidence? Not to mention, he may have figured out Chitose's secret...

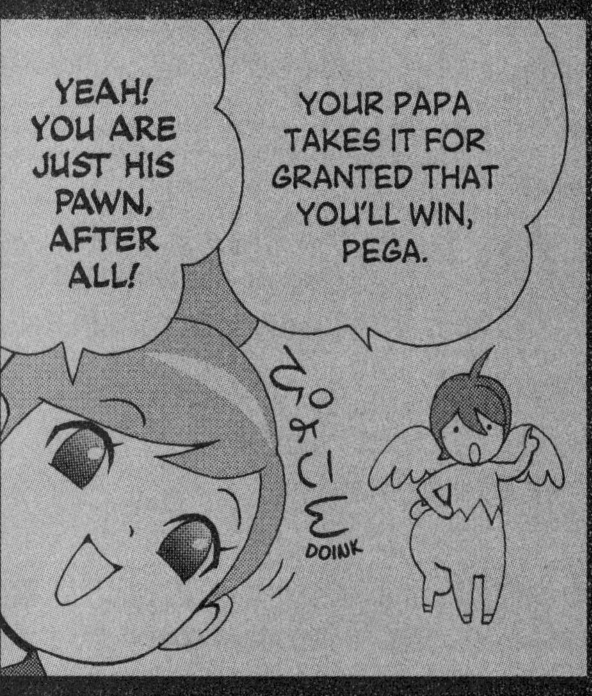
YOUR PAPA TAKES IT FOR GRANTED THAT YOU'LL WIN, PEGA.
YEAH! YOU ARE JUST HIS PAWN, AFTER ALL!
DOINK

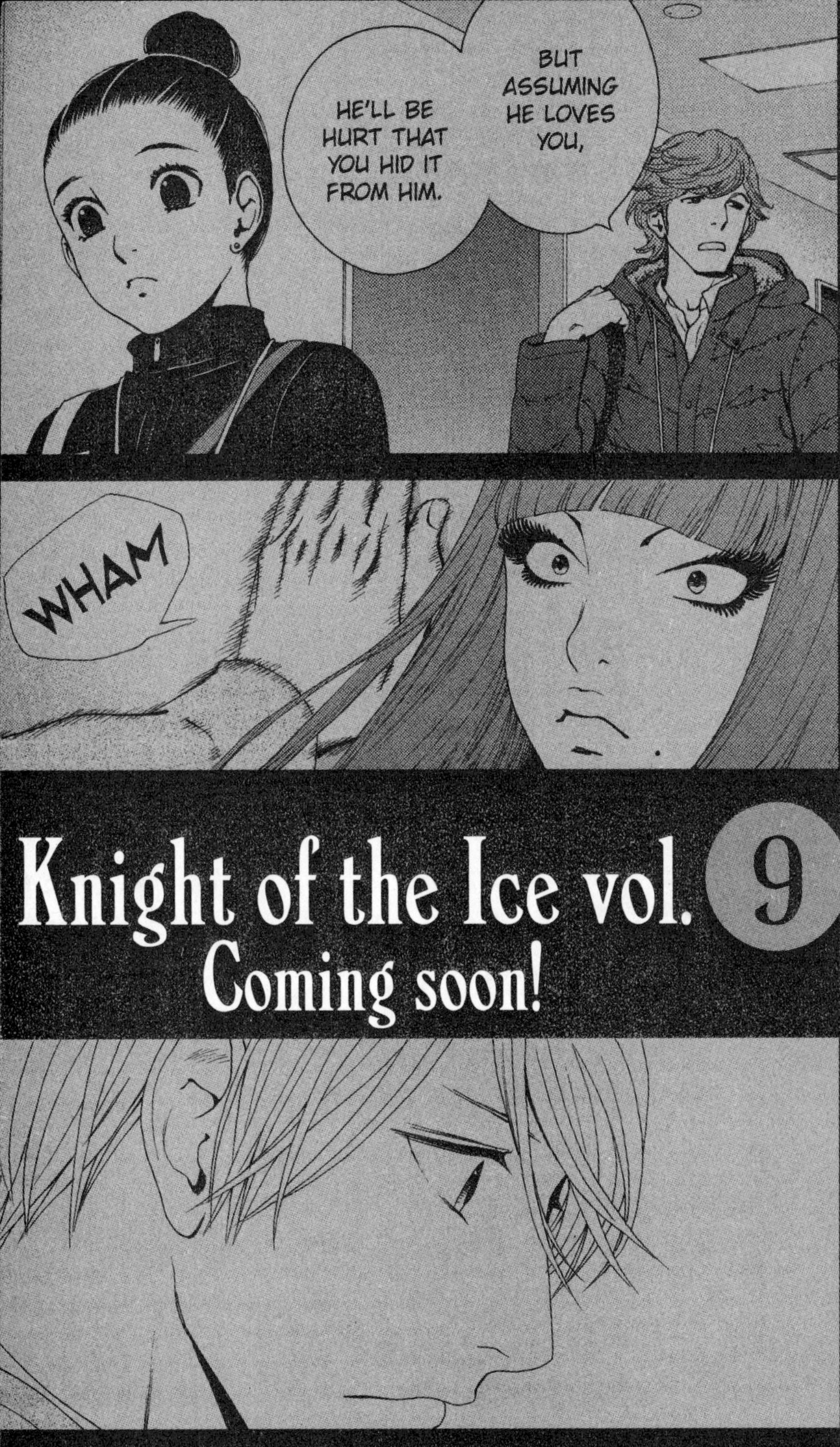
BUT ASSUMING HE LOVES YOU,
HE'LL BE HURT THAT YOU HID IT FROM HIM.
WHAM
Knight of the Ice vol. 9
Coming soon!

THE SWEET SCENT OF LOVE IS IN THE AIR! FOR FANS OF OFFBEAT ROMANCES LIKE *WOTAKOI*

Sweat and Soap © Kintetsu Yamada / Kodansha Ltd.

In an office romance, there's a fine line between sexy and awkward... and that line is where Asako — a woman who sweats copiously — meets Koutarou — a perfume developer who can't get enough of Asako's, er, scent. Don't miss a romcom manga like no other!

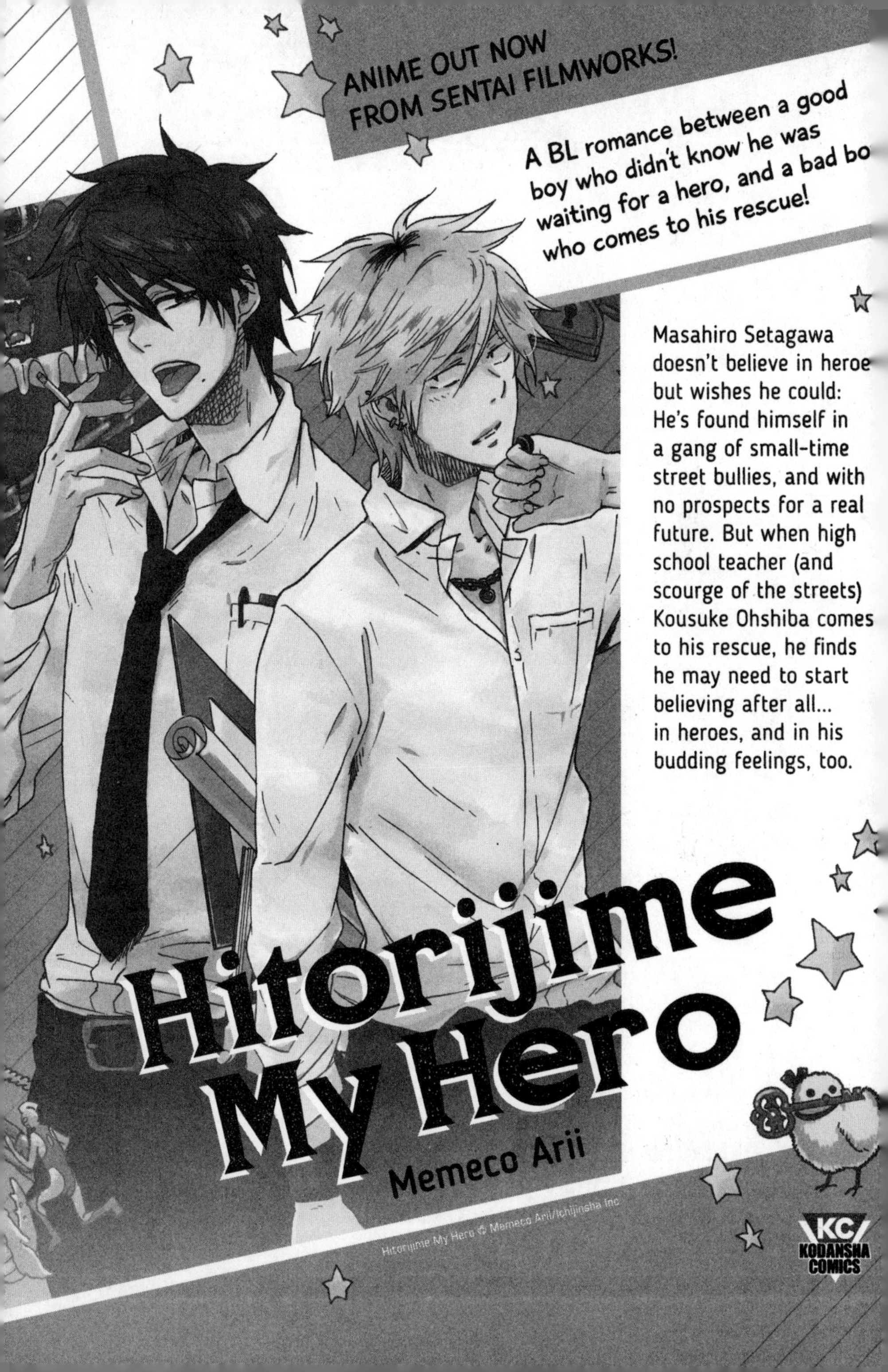
ANIME OUT NOW FROM SENTAI FILMWORKS!
A BL romance between a good boy who didn't know he was waiting for a hero, and a bad bo who comes to his rescue!
Masahiro Setagawa doesn't believe in heroe but wishes he could: He's found himself in a gang of small-time street bullies, and with no prospects for a real future. But when high school teacher (and scourge of the streets) Kousuke Ohshiba comes to his rescue, he finds he may need to start believing after all... in heroes, and in his budding feelings, too.
Hitorijime My Hero
Memeco Arii
Hitorijime My Hero © Memeco Arii/Ichijinsha Inc
KC KODANSHA COMICS

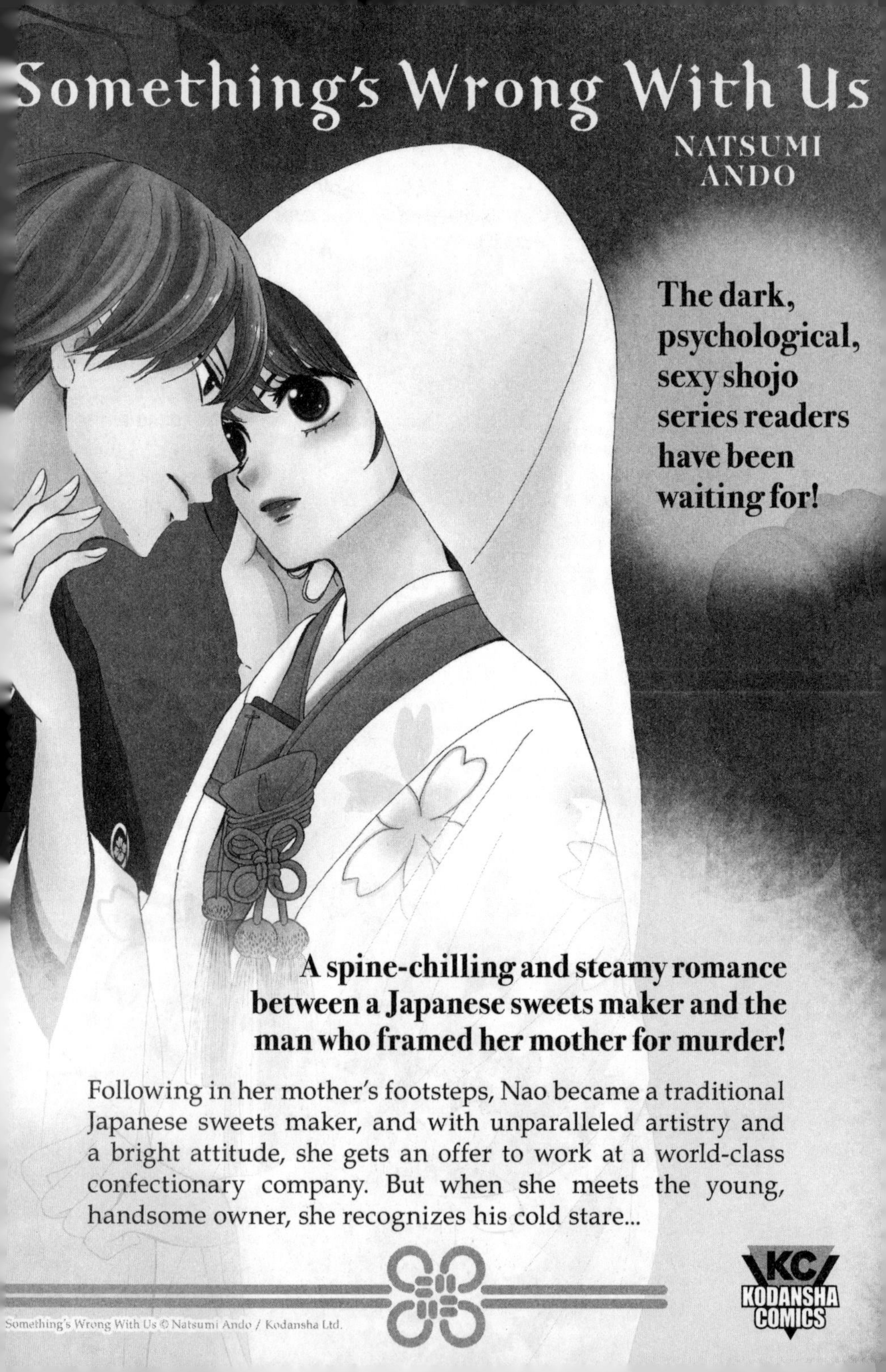
Something's Wrong With Us
NATSUMI ANDO
The dark, psychological, sexy shojo series readers have been waiting for!
A spine-chilling and steamy romance between a Japanese sweets maker and the man who framed her mother for murder!
Following in her mother's footsteps, Nao became a traditional Japanese sweets maker, and with unparalleled artistry and a bright attitude, she gets an offer to work at a world-class confectionary company. But when she meets the young, handsome owner, she recognizes his cold stare...
KC KODANSHA COMICS
Something's Wrong With Us © Natsumi Ando / Kodansha Ltd.

A SMART, NEW ROMANTIC COMEDY FOR FANS OF *SHORTCAKE CAKE* AND *TERRACE HOUSE*!

A romance manga starring high school girl Meeko, who learns to live on her own in a boarding house whose living room is home to the odd (but handsome) Matsunaga-san. She begins to adjust to her new life away from her parents, but Meeko soon learns that no matter how far away from home she is, she's still a young girl at heart — especially when she finds herself falling for Matsunaga-san.

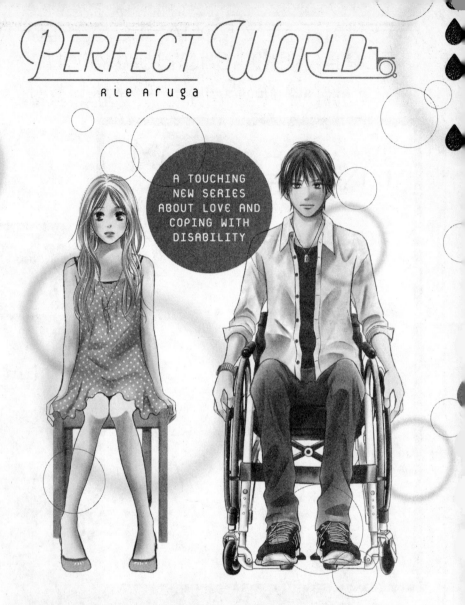

PERFECT WORLD

Rie Aruga

A TOUCHING NEW SERIES ABOUT LOVE AND COPING WITH DISABILITY

An office party reunites Tsugumi with her high school crush Itsuki. He's realized his dream of becoming an architect, but along the way, he experienced a spinal injury that put him in a wheelchair. Now Tsugumi's rekindled feelings will butt up against prejudices she never considered — and Itsuki will have to decide if he's ready to let someone into his heart...

"Depicts with great delicacy and courage the difficulties some with disabilities experience getting involved in romantic relationships... Rie Aruga refuses to romanticize, pushing her heroine to face the reality of disability. She invites her readers to the same tasks of empathy, knowledge and recognition."
—Slate.fr

"An important entry [in manga romance]... The emotional core of both plot and characters indicates thoughtfulness... [Aruga's] research is readily apparent in the text and artwork, making this feel like a real story."
—Anime News Network

Young characters and steampunk setting, like *Howl's Moving Castle* and *Battle Angel Alita*

Beyond the Clouds © 2018 Nicke / Ki-oon

A boy with a talent for machines and a mysterious girl whose wings he's fixed will take you beyond the clouds! In the tradition of the high-flying, resonant adventure stories of Studio Ghibli comes a gorgeous tale about the longing of young hearts for adventure and friendship!

The adorable new odd-couple cat comedy manga from the creator of the beloved *Chi's Sweet Home*, in full color!

Sue & Tai-chan

Konami Kanata

Sue is an aging housecat who's looking forward to living out her life in peace... but her plans change when the mischievous black tomcat Tai-chan enters the picture! Hey! Sue never signed up to be a catsitter! *Sue & Tai-chan* is the latest from the reigning meow-narch of cute kitty comics, Konami Kanata.

KC
KODANSHA
COMICS

The boys are back, in 400-page hardcovers that are as pretty and badass as they are!

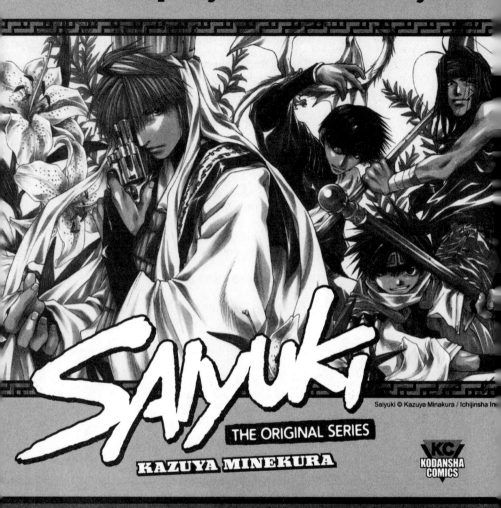

Saiyuki © Kazuya Minakura / Ichijinsha In

SAIYUKI
THE ORIGINAL SERIES
KAZUYA MINEKURA

"AN EDGY COMIC LOOK AT AN ANCIENT CHINESE TALE." —YALSA

Genjo Sanzo is a Buddhist priest in the city of Togenkyo, which is being ravaged by yokai spirits that have fallen out of balance with the natural order. His superiors send him on a journey far to the west to discover why this is happening and how to stop it. His companions are three yokai with human souls. But this is no day trip — the four will encounter many discoveries and horrors on the way.

FEATURES NEW TRANSLATION, COLOR PAGES, AND BEAUTIFUL WRAPAROUND COVER ART!

A Kodansha Comics Trade Paperback Original
Knight of the Ice 8 copyright © 2016 Yayoi Ogawa
English translation copyright © 2021 Yayoi Ogawa

Published in the United States by Kodansha Comics, an imprint of Kodansha USA Publishing, LLC, New York.

Publication rights for this English edition arranged through Kodansha Ltd., Tokyo.

First published in Japan in 2016 by Kodansha Ltd., Tokyo as *Ginban Kishi*, volume 8.

ISBN 978-1-64651-085-6

Printed in the United States of America.

www.kodansha.us

1st Printing
Translation: Rose Padgett
Lettering: Jennifer Skarupa
Editing: Tiff Joshua TJ Ferentini
Kodansha Comics edition cover design by Phil Balsman

Publishe⋯ ⋯ ⋯ugawara

Director of publishing services: Ben Applegate
Associate director of operations: Stephen Pakula
Publishing services managing editors: Alanna Ruse, Madison Salters
Production managers: Emi Lotto, Angela Zurlo